BERLIN IN THE TWENTI

Berlin has been the focal scene of some of the most dramatic and formative events of the twentieth century. Through periods of decadence, fascism, war, partition and reunification, it has seen both extraordinary constraint and creativity. Andrew Webber explores the cultural topography of Berlin and considers the city as key capital of the twentieth century, reflecting its history, its traumas and its achievements. He shows how Berlin's spaces and buildings participate in the drama by analysing how they are represented in literature and film. Taking his methodology from Walter Benjamin, Webber presents bold new readings of works synonymous with Berlin, with authors from Bertolt Brecht and Franz Kafka to Christa Wolf, and directors from Walther Ruttmann to Rainer Werner Fassbinder and Wim Wenders. Across this range of material, twentieth-century Berlin is seen to be as ambivalent as it is fascinating.

ANDREW J. WEBBER is Reader in Modern German and Comparative Literature at the University of Cambridge.

BERLIN IN THE TWENTIETH CENTURY

A Cultural Topography

ANDREW J. WEBBER

CAMBRIDGE
UNIVERSITY PRESS

CAMBRIDGE UNIVERSITY PRESS
Cambridge, New York, Melbourne, Madrid, Cape Town,
Singapore, São Paulo, Delhi, Tokyo, Mexico City

Cambridge University Press
The Edinburgh Building, Cambridge CB2 8RU, UK

Published in the United States of America by Cambridge University Press, New York

www.cambridge.org
Information on this title: www.cambridge.org/9780521188746

First published 2008
First paperback edition 2011

A catalogue record for this publication is available from the British Library

ISBN 978-0-521-89572-9 Hardback
ISBN 978-0-521-18874-6 Paperback

Contents

Illustrations

Acknowledgements

My principal thanks go to the Leverhulme Trust. The Major Research Fellowship they awarded me provided a privileged opportunity to conduct sustained research on this wide-ranging project. I am also grateful for the expert help of a number of archives and libraries, in particular: the Walter-Benjamin-Archiv, Bertolt-Brecht-Archiv, and Heiner-Müller-Archiv of the Akademie der Künste in Berlin; the Berlin Filmmuseum; and the Deutsches Literaturarchiv in Marbach. And I would like to thank the many friends, colleagues, and research students who have commented on aspects of the project or given other forms of support.

Versions of parts of the book have appeared in the following publications: 'Gender and the City: *Lola rennt*', *German as a Foreign Language* (1, 2003), 1–16 (www.gfl-journal.de/1-2003/webber.html); 'Falling Walls, Sliding Doors, Open Windows: Berlin on Film after the *Wende*', *German as a Foreign Language* (1, 2006), 5–23 (www.gfl-journal.de/1-2006/webber. html); 'Worst of all Possible Worlds? Ingeborg Bachmann's *Ein Ort für Zufälle*', *Austrian Studies* 15 (2007), 112–29; 'Döblin, *Berlin Alexanderplatz*', in *Landmarks in the German Novel (1)*, ed. Peter Hutchinson (Oxford: Lang, 2007), pp. 167–82; 'Symphony of a City: Motion Pictures and Still Lives in Weimar Berlin', in *Cities in Transition: The Modern Metropolis and the Moving Image*, ed. Andrew Webber and Emma Wilson (Wallflower, 2008), pp. 56–71; '"Unbewohnbar und doch unverlaßbar": Brecht in and through Berlin', in *Bertolt Brecht: A Reassessment of His Work and Legacy*, ed. Robert Gillett and Godela Weiss-Sussex (Amsterdam: Rodopi, 2008), pp. 153–67.

Abbreviations

References to key works are abbreviated as follows:

BA   Alfred Döblin, *Berlin Alexanderplatz: Die Geschichte vom Franz Biberkopf*, ed. Werner Stauffacher (Zurich: Walter, 1996)

BB   Bertolt Brecht, *Werke: Berliner und Frankfurter Ausgabe*, ed. Werner Hecht *et al.*, 30 vols. (Frankfurt am Main: Suhrkamp, 1988–2000)

HM   Heiner Müller, *Werke*, ed. Frank Hörnigk, 9 vols. (Frankfurt am Main: Suhrkamp, 1998–2005)

IB   Ingeborg Bachmann, *Werke*, ed. Christine Koschel *et al.*, 4 vols. (Munich: Piper, 1978)

SF   Sigmund Freud, *Gesammelte Werke*, ed. Anna Freud *et al.*, 18 vols. (Frankfurt am Main: Fischer, 1999)

TP   Ingeborg Bachmann, *"Todesarten"-Projekt: Kritische Ausgabe*, ed. Robert Pichl *et al.*, 4 vols. (Munich/Zurich: Piper, 1995), vol. I

UL   Christa Wolf, 'Unter den Linden', *Gesammelte Erzählungen* (Frankfurt am Main: Luchterhand, 1988), pp. 54–96

WB   Walter Benjamin, *Gesammelte Schriften*, ed. Rolf Tiedemann and Hermann Schweppenhäuser, 7 vols. (Frankfurt am Main: Suhrkamp, 1991)

ZA   Uwe Johnson, *Zwei Ansichten* (Frankfurt am Main: Suhrkamp, 1965)

Unless otherwise indicated, all translations are mine.

Berlin is worth a journey

I lower my head und find myself now on journeys from Berlin to Berlin.[1]

Aras Ören

This book takes its cue from the reconstruction and reinvention of Berlin as cosmopolitan capital of the 'new Germany' at the end of the twentieth century, which a recent cover title of *Der Spiegel* called the 'Comeback of a World City'.[2] The emergence out of the schismatic state of the post-war city and into a period of rebuilding and remapping has created possibilities for a critical awareness of topography unique amongst the metropolitan centres of the Western world. At the same time, that awareness is nowhere more challenged by complications. The remodelling of *Baustelle* or 'building-site' Berlin has served to reveal different types of historical maps, to privilege some and efface others. As the lines from Ören's pre-unification poem suggest, it is a city of plural identities and locations, a territory of transition, of departures and arrivals both internal and external. The bent head of the outsider journeying 'from Berlin to Berlin' indicates that the journey has to negotiate complex terrain, inclining the subject towards a melancholic posture. At the same time, the return to the city in the work of Ören and many others indicates that, as the popular slogan has it, 'Berlin is worth a journey', indeed demands one.

Berlin is a city with a telescopic archaeology, layered with the restored or demolished architectures of a dense and often traumatic century. As such, it is ripe for the sort of critical assessment of its cultural topography that is undertaken here in a sequence of journeys from Berlin to Berlin. These will be made looking down certainly, for it is thus that the traveller in Berlin might know where the Wall once ran or – through the *Stolpersteine*, the

---

[1] From Aras Ören, 'Berlin'den Berlin'e Yolculuklar' (Journeys from Berlin to Berlin), *Forum* 1 (1985), 130–1.
[2] 'Berlin: Comeback einer Weltstadt', *Der Spiegel* 12, 19 March 2007.

stumbling stones,[3] set into the pavement – come upon the places from which Berlin's Jews and other victims of National Socialism were deported. To invoke the title of a public sculpture by Karl Biedermann commemorating the pogrom of 1938, Berlin is a city occupied by 'abandoned space', the traces of which often have to be sought at ground level or underground (see Figure 1). To look down in this way also involves looking back, with an eye to other kinds of historical comeback. But, at the same time, there will be reason to look up, around, and forward.

Twentieth-century Berlin moves from its peripheral historical status, described by Scheffler in 1910 as a 'colonial' outpost on the border to the east,[4] to a centre, by turns integral and insular, of colonising ideologies. It provides the show-place for an unrivalled succession of occupying powers: an empire in the *ancien régime* style, a Socialist Republic, a fascist empire, the face-to-face showrooms and parade-grounds of high capitalism and Communism, and the unified centre of democracy in the New European style. The monuments of each of these regimes, often the same edifices or spaces re-appropriated, are of course landmarks in the historical map of Berlin. But each also served to organise the more general cultural life of the city, its mapping on a less monumental level. The many plans which trace and construct urban life in its political and technical aspects also relate to a different kind of mapping of consciousness, contributing to what has been called the 'Myth Berlin'.[5]

A key aim here is to track the relationships between the official or representative map of the city and the more shifting topographies that work on the level of imagination, both individual and communal, and are especially in evidence in the representations of Berlin life in textual, visual, and performance art. This version of metropolitan layout varies both diachronically, as culture changes through history, and synchronically, as it changes in cross-section, according to perspective, at given times. As the city mutates from colonial outpost into an imperial capital, is divided, colonised by other powers, and then 'reunified', so it produces a range of colonies both voluntary and involuntary in or around its precincts, from campsite colonies to ghetto sites and internment camps. This book aims to trace the colonisations and counter-colonisations of one of the world's most extraordinary cities in the 'long twentieth century' from the 1880s to the present.

[3] The *Stolpersteine*, brass cobbles installed by Gunter Hemnig, are inscribed with the names of the deported.
[4] Karl Scheffler, *Berlin – Ein Stadtschicksal* (Berlin: Fannei & Walz, 1989), p. 15.
[5] See Knut Hickethier *et al.* (eds.), *Mythos Berlin: Zur Wahrnehmungsgeschichte einer industriellen Metropole: Eine szenische Ausstellung auf dem Gelände des Anhalter Bahnhofs* (Berlin: Ästhetik und Kommunikation, 1987).

1 *Der verlassene Raum* (The Abandoned Room/Space), Karl Biedermann (1996), Koppenplatz.

On the one hand, then, I will follow the city history of the dominant ideological groupings, as focused in what Henri Lefebvre classifies as 'representations of space'. These are those representative structures of cultural space, 'tied to the relations of production and to the "order" that those relations impose'.[6] My study will consider the key sites, zones, and events of this official or 'frontal' history and examine the constructions and controls that they put upon the metropolis. The functioning of the city map will be considered through such generic controlling structures, places of passage, of inclusion and exclusion, as the station, the square, the bunker, the gate, the wall and the bridge. The specific key sites will include such 'lieux de mémoire' (after Pierre Nora) or memory sites as the Alexanderplatz, the Anhalter Bahnhof, Unter den Linden, the Kurfürstendamm, and the Potsdamer Platz. These are sites of memory never fully functioning as composite parts of a memorative environment, of what Nora would call a 'milieu de mémoire'.[7] They are characteristic both of the plenitude and vitality of metropolitan life and of the symptomatic vacant spaces that Andreas Huyssen has called 'the voids of Berlin'.[8]

My second line of enquiry will be concerned with Lefebvre's 'representational spaces', the sites of more localised or minority forms of culture, 'linked to the clandestine or underground side of social life, as also to art'.[9] The cultural hinterland of the Berlin *Kiez*, or neighbourhood, and the public-private space of the *Hof*, or courtyard, provide archetypal examples of this, amongst a range of other alternative and idiosyncratic urban places. My argument is that these alternative cultural sites sustain types of knowledge that act as a form of unconscious in relation to the urban designs of the successive versions of the dominant ideology. They represent a city map that has more or less hidden sites of special investment, of what psychoanalysis would call cathexis (*Besetzung*), and of resistance, or counter-cathexis. At the same time, such sites are, following Michel de Certeau, migratory; that is, the official, representative spaces of the city may be occupied, at least in passing, by the practices that belong in less evident spaces. For de Certeau, these unofficial practices of being in the city are

---

[6] Henri Lefebvre, *The Production of Space*, trans. Donald Nicholson-Smith (Oxford: Blackwell, 1991), p. 33.

[7] See Pierre Nora, 'Between Memory and History: Les Lieux de Mémoire', *Representations* 26 (1989), 7–25.

[8] Andreas Huyssen, *Present Pasts: Urban Palimpsests and the Politics of Memory* (Stanford: Stanford University Press, 2003), pp. 49–71.

[9] Lefebvre, *Production of Space*, p. 33. Art can of course also fashion 'representations of space', as in the monumental allegorical sculptures installed in key Berlin locations in the summer of 2006, representing it as capital of a 'Land of Ideas'.

aligned with the turns or tropes in the rhetoric of the unconscious, its displacements and condensations,[10] its overdetermined encounters and telling lapses.

What this book does, therefore, is take up a challenge that Lefebvre contemplates, and that de Certeau explores. While psychoanalysis can lead, says Lefebvre, to 'intolerable reductionism', he also sees it as open territory for research in the production of space, following the hypothesis that every city has 'an underground and repressed life, and hence an "unconscious"'.[11] This conjecture comes back to haunt his work at intervals.[12] While he recognises that psychoanalysis has a special affinity with the category of representational spaces, with the affect that inhabits them,[13] it is repeatedly invoked only to be charged with a mechanistic lack of dialectical finesse. This book aims to apply critical dialectics to the psychoanalytic method of understanding the production and representation of space.

What is proposed here is to construct and test an operable relationship between the city and the psyche, a metapsychology of city life. This will mean reading the texts, films, and other cultural artefacts that will be the main material focus of the book in a symptomatological fashion, looking for the structures of fantasy, dreams, trauma, melancholia, hysteria, and paranoia in the cultural cityscape. Roland Barthes suggests that psychoanalysis might deserve a place amongst the diverse requirements in the portfolio of the urban semiologist – geography, history, architecture, etc.[14] And he goes on to indicate that the 'language of the city' that interests him is to be understood semiotically, like the sign-system of the 'language of dreams' in Freud.[15] This urban semiotics combines the territory of psychoanalysis, in the erotics and traumatics of the city's encounters, with that of ideology: the enforcement of power.

The mapping of modern culture by Walter Benjamin exemplifies that which is proposed by Barthes and developed in the current study. Out of Benjamin's topographical analyses of nineteenth-century Paris and of Berlin *c.* 1900 as the city of his childhood, emerges a model of cultural understanding which sees the sites and passages of the city as subject to cathexis

---

[10] Michel de Certeau, 'Walking in the City', *The Practice of Everyday Life*, trans. Steven Rendall (Berkeley: University of California Press, 1988), pp. 91–110; p. 107.

[11] Lefebvre, *Production of Space*, p. 36.

[12] See Victor Burgin, 'The City in Pieces', *New Formations* 20 (Summer 1993), 33–45; p. 40.

[13] Lefebvre, *Production of Space*, p. 42.

[14] Roland Barthes, 'Semiology and Urbanism', *The Semiotic Challenge*, trans. Richard Howard (Oxford: Blackwell, 1988), pp. 191–201; p. 191.

[15] *Ibid.*, p. 195.

and counter-cathexis: occupied by ideological and psychical investments and disinvestments. These run parallel to the practical forms of occupation (*Besetzung*) and counter-occupation that operate on both a mass level, with occupying forces of various political colours, and on such local levels as the Berlin squat (*Hausbesetzung*). They are at work in the language and image systems of the city, in its rhetorical and iconographic representations of places. In particular, they inform the allegorical fashioning of its identity. Behind official representations in that form, managed by dominant ideologies, we will find more subversive kinds of allegory at work, representing alternative ways of speaking and seeing the city.

In the Introduction that follows, the ground will be prepared for this cultural topographical exploration of the city. Firstly, it provides a synoptic historical view of the city in its cultural and political aspects over the last century. This will involve scrutiny of ways in which the cultural topographical map of the city has been formed, through its key structures, figures, and elements. Secondly, it approaches the book's object from its historical boundaries, first by stepping back to the closing years of the nineteenth century and considering the ambiguous prospect that the twentieth-century city presents from there, and then by taking a retrospective view of it through an early twenty-first-century lens. Finally, and in conjunction with those boundary views, it sets out the principal theoretical assumptions of the study, as derived in particular from Benjamin and Freud. By way of scene-setting for the critical modality in which the book will work, there first follows a short sequence of excursions out of and into Berlin. That these travels explore the city from another place and encounter disorientation, makes them, paradoxically, especially suitable for the task of initial orientation. Like Ören, their protagonist moves to and from Berlin as a minority figure from without.

EXCURSION: KAFKA DREAMS OF BERLIN

This first excursion into the terrain of the city follows in the footsteps of Kafka in Berlin, or of his dream-self. This proxy takes him on psychical journeys through Berlin that enter both 'spaces of representation' and 'representational spaces'. Kafka, for whom Berlin was both a fantasy space (in his correspondence with Felice Bauer) and a real one (as visitor and, later, resident), sets out the experience of the city as a confusion of material reality and fantasy projection in a series of dreams recorded in his diary between 1912 and 1914. With characteristic ambivalence, Kafka embraced Berlin as a place of prospective freedom, whilst also experiencing it as a site of trial, specifically in the familial melodrama of the 'hotel tribunal',[16] leading to the breaking of his engagement to Felice. His Berlin visit of July 1914 on the occasion of that trial is characterised by a split sense of embodied psyche in the city. He is divided between the corporeal freedom of a minoritarian community, with Jews sporting in the open air at the bathing school on the Strahlauer Ufer,[17] and the experience of urban alienation, sitting alone on a seat on Unter den Linden, racked by pain and obsessed with the surveillant role of the ticket controller.[18] To use the terms applied to Kafka's writing by Deleuze and Guattari, he is at once deterritorialised in the foreign city, freed from old territorial claims, and reterritorialised, subject to new ones.[19]

The dream series is similarly divided between the freedom of the city and the experience of psychosomatic constraint. The first dream follows the oedipal logic so familiar from Kafka's writing.[20] He relates how he is riding through Berlin on a tram with his father. The city is represented only by a multitude of upright barriers that seems to take the place of urban buildings and crowds, open and yet experienced as an enclosing 'throng'. Father and son alight before a gate and step 'in through the gate'. While the logic of the journey might suggest that this would take them outside the city, the gate brings them back into it, but only in the shape of a wall that they have to climb. It is an experience of the city gates, in particular for Jews, which we will encounter again. The father dances effortlessly up the wall, while the infantilised son's own progress is impeded, not least by the excrement he finds on it. When he reaches the top, his father has already completed his visit to a certain Dr von Leyden (deceased),[21] and his son is relieved to find that he does not have to do the same. Behind them, in a room with glass walls, sits a man; not the lung specialist von Leyden it turns out, but his secretary. It was the secretary as 'bodily' representative of the doctor that the father had consulted, providing him with a justifiable basis for his 'judgement'. The dream, with its reference to the father–son contest, and questions of corporeal abjection, diagnosis, and judgement, plays out a classic Kafkan scenario in a dream version of the Berlin topography, represented by architectures and street furniture that impede and dislocate the progress of the protagonist. The scenario is reminiscent, in particular, of the story

---

[16] Franz Kafka, *Tagebücher*, ed. Hans-Gerd Koch *et al.* (Frankfurt am Main: Fischer, 1990), p. 658.
[17] *Ibid.*, p. 660.   [18] *Ibid.*, p. 659.
[19] Gilles Deleuze and Félix Guattari, *Kafka: Toward a Minor Literature*, trans. Dana Polan (Minneapolis: University of Minnesota Press, 1986).
[20] Kafka, *Tagebücher*, pp. 419–20.
[21] The funeral of the lung specialist von Leyden was reported during Kafka's visit to Berlin in 1910.

'Das Urteil' (The Judgement), which Kafka indeed saw as carrying encoded references to Berlin as a semantic field of memories and dreams through the name Brandenfeld.[22]

The second dream (which is, in fact, a pair of sequences) sees Kafka's dream-self walking through the streets of Berlin, ostensibly on his way to the house of a woman we might take to be Felice.[23] Despite his assured sense that he could reach it at any moment, the dream subjects him to displacement. He sees open streets, and a sign advertising an entertainment venue, the 'Prachtsäle des Nordens' (Stately Halls of the North). In the dream, the location of this attraction is displaced from Wedding in the north to Berlin west, and thus from working-class territory to that of the bourgeoisie. The displacement duly invokes a scene reminiscent of Kafka's gnomic narrative 'Gibs auf!' (Give it up!), as the disoriented subject asks a policeman in a servant's uniform for directions, but any prospect of orientation is waylaid by obscure directions that he cannot follow. He senses another figure at his side, but has no time to turn to identify it, only to feel haunted in his urban disorientation. It might be appropriate to understand this shadowy attendant as the 'bucklicht(e) Männlein' (hunchbacked manikin) as this figure is understood in Benjamin's reading of Kafka, embodying allegorically the principle of *Entstellung*: the distortions, displacements, and lapses in the psychical life of the misfit subject (WB II.ii 425–32). In Kafka's Berlin dreams, this figure, or 'disfigure', is a peculiar kind of urban attendant.

The second sequence sees the protagonist living in a hostel in Berlin, where apparently only young Polish Jews live. The scenario is here apparently shifted to the east. The protagonist spills a bottle of water, suggesting an incontinence to match the scatological character of the first dream. This is the sort of parapraxis that, following Benjamin's account of the 'bucklichte Männlein' in his *Berliner Kindheit um neunzehnhundert* (Berlin Childhood around 1900), gives evidence of his uncanny presence (WB VII.i 429–30). The dream-self keeps seeing what appears to be a street-plan in the hand of another resident, but finds that it is only an administrative list of Berlin schools or the like. The tantalising possibility of finding a map with which to negotiate the urban topography, and the psychical territory projected onto it, is never realised. Whether as a bachelor in search of his fiancée or an eastern Jew seeking orientation in the capital outside the ghetto, he is at a loss. The scene resonates with the (mis)guidance given to Kafka by the actor Löwy, as described in a letter to Felice of 1912, where he mimics his friend's

---

[22] Kafka, *Tagebücher*, p. 492.   [23] *Ibid.*, pp. 635–6.

Yiddish account of the route to take from the Alexanderplatz to the Immanuel-Kirchstraße, where Felice lives, only to arrive at the wrong address.[24]

The third dream takes the displaced protagonist into one of the city's most representative 'representations of space': 'Dream last night. With Kaiser Wilhelm. In the Castle. The lovely view. A room like in the "Tabakskollegium". Encounter with Matilde Serao. Unfortunately all forgotten.'[25] The dream of his imperial reception in Schloss Bellevue, in a room resembling the smoking rooms of the early Prussian courts, and in the company of the Italian writer and newspaper publisher Serao,[26] comes to nothing. The entry into the castle as seat of power and visual enjoyment is subject to the erasure of memory. The 'Schloss', in other words, becomes the sort of allegorical site of exclusion, of heteronomous authority, that features in Kafka's novel of the same name.

The dream texts combine uncertain modes of transport with the physical and psychical disorientation of the urban pedestrian and access only to elusive interiors. The protagonist encounters enigmatic texts, figures, and visual designs, but figuration here is recurrently displaced into forms of disfigurement. It thereby follows the principle of *Entstellung* that Freud establishes in his account of dream work, and to which Benjamin's use of the term is indebted. The dreams take a form that, in characteristic Kafkan style, suggests an allegorical principle of representation and elicits interpretation in that vein, but one that also eludes such interpretative mappings in the persistent otherness that it unfolds. As such, the texts are exemplary of the sort of complex experience between historical and geographical materiality and psychically determined fantasy that will recur here. The lures and the aporias of Kafka's dream-life encounters with Berlin establish a model that informs the method of this study: a cultural topography that maps the individual case onto the historical capital, from palace to ghetto.

In the spirit of this exploratory excursion, my book charts the territory between studies devoted to specific artists, movements, or genres and more general cultural historical accounts.[27] It will take a 'case historical' approach, illustrating general tendencies through the close reading of texts, films, architectures, and images. Lefebvre argues that the problem with considering

---

24 Franz Kafka, *Briefe an Felice und andere Korrespondenz aus der Verlobungszeit*, ed. Erich Heller and Jürgen Born (Frankfurt am Main: Fischer, 1967), p. 75.

25 Kafka, *Tagebücher*, p. 704.

26 Serao might represent the freedom of the city that Kafka imagined for himself as journalist in Berlin (*Tagebücher*, p. 508).

27 See, for example, Ronald Taylor, *Berlin and its Culture: A Historical Portrait* (New Haven/London: Yale University Press, 1997).

the production of space in literature is that it is to be found everywhere.[28] And this applies *a fortiori* both to the mobile medium of film, and to the largely still forms of architecture and of photographic and other images. In order to make sense of this ubiquity, however, the concern here will be with paradigmatic configurations of space, with topographical designs that are emblematic for the 'case history' of twentieth-century Berlin, such as those encountered in Kafka's dreams of the city. The particular combination of the psychical with the juridical and political, the clinic with the courts, that characterises the 'case' of Kafka's Berlin will be a recurrent theme throughout.

In its pursuit of the emblematic designs of such cases, the book's cultural historical mapping of Berlin works along two coordinated axes: it traverses the period from Fontane to Grass in a series of synchronic sections, while also staging thematically or generically based encounters between the cultural topographies of different parts of the century, measuring their diachronic links and breaks. It takes key examples from 'high' culture, but the readings show how these are embedded in popular cultural tendencies. It derives new perspectives on the city's culture by pursuing the vital interactions between different cultural media and considering the reciprocal impact of artistic production and the material conditions of the city, its social, architectural, transportation, and information systems. And it opens up new ways of understanding the historical map of the city by engaging both theories of cultural identity, place, and memory contemporary with the earlier material and more recent theoretical developments.

---

[28] Lefebvre, *Production of Space*, p. 15.

INTRODUCTION

Capital of the twentieth century?

The angelus novus berliensis looks back, but not into paradise.[1]

The title of this chapter, adapted from the cultural urbanologist who provides its primary methodological guidance, includes an element of speculation and of provocation. While Benjamin famously dubbed Paris the 'capital of the nineteenth century' (WB v.i 45–59), he could not yet make a binding claim for Paris or any other city as its successor in the twentieth, nor fully foresee the ways in which his home city would proceed to contest the title over the course of the century. Early twentieth-century Berlin certainly develops as the object of Benjamin's analytic attention, and the city in its Weimar period becomes – along with New York – the prime case for new urban discourses at large: a city coming late to modernity but embracing it with spectacular effect. It seems, therefore, that the city of Benjamin's childhood, as retrospectively recorded in *Berliner Chronik* (Berlin Chronicle) and *Berliner Kindheit* (Berlin Childhood), might indeed have begun to stake a claim to the somewhat hyperbolic heading here.

At the same time, another kind of historical claim was made at the point when Benjamin was forced to leave Berlin, and the city became the organising centre of capital crimes against humanity. The National Socialists converted the cosmopolitan model of the *Weltstadt*, the world city with the Friedrichstraße as what Siegfried Kracauer in a text of 1933 called 'the global axis',[2] stretching north–south and traversed by the east–west axis of the railway line, into a totalitarian topography of similar design and proportions. While Kracauer described the area around Friedrichstraße station as the 'centre of life', rather than a 'transit station',[3] his cosmopolitan

---

[1] Wolf Biermann, '"Ein Kuss in meiner Seele": Dankrede für Ehrenbürgerschaft', *Die Zeit*, 29 March 2007.
[2] Siegfried Kracauer, 'Lokomotive über der Friedrichstraße', *Schriften*, vol. v.iii, ed. Inka Mülder-Bach (Frankfurt am Main: Suhrkamp, 1990), pp. 194–5; p. 195.
[3] *Ibid.*

II

discourse of urban vitality was already in transition towards another, hegemonic model, with Berlin cast as central terminus for a global network of power and violence.

The plans developed for the National Socialist capital by architect *manqué* Hitler and his chief urban designer, Speer, aimed to dwarf the monumental cityscape of Paris, with super-scaled axes running from north to south and west to east. The obscene fantasy of Hitler's World Capital Germania, projected along those cardinal axes as capital city for a new global empire, had designs not only on the century but on the millennium: a topography of power on the model of the ancient empires. And it developed a topographics of terror to match. The ostentatious palaces, appropriated by or built for the National Socialist regime, and the squares, avenues, and stadia that provided its parade-grounds were also a façade for a more hidden network of bunkers and cells, excavated ruins of which now furnish the space for the documentation of Berlin's 'Topography of Terror'.[4] The railway stations were also façades and conduits for expanded topographies of terror, radiating from and reaching far beyond the capital. The view that Kracauer, as Jewish cultural commentator in 1933 Berlin, takes up towards the train on the railway bridge over the Friedrichstraße, and the view projected back onto that 'street of streets' by a passenger,[5] are both distracted by light and threatened by darkness. Two days after the appearance of Kracauer's allegorical account of an oblivious Berlin, the Nazis seized power in the capital, and the leisured critical mode of the *flâneur* was overtaken by the march of history.

The abjection that came of the political and topographical designs of power and terror, leaving both the fantasy and the fabric of the city in ruins, paradoxically also led to another version of the world capital idea. Cold War Berlin was the nominal capital of a small, frontline Communist state on one side of the divide, and an insular outpost of the West, capital *manqué* for one of its increasingly powerful economic engines, on the other. But it was also the place at which the competing world orders of the second half of the twentieth century were seen most trenchantly to confront one another. The capital, as Friedrich Kittler reminds us, derives from a symbolic conception of the body politic, as its head.[6] Cold-War Berlin saw a head-to-head contest of the two orders. Or, to formulate the image differently, it was a

---

[4] See also Aleida Assmann, *Erinnerungsräume: Formen und Wandlungen des kulturellen Gedächtnisses* (Munich: C. H. Beck, 1999), pp. 334–7.
[5] Kracauer, 'Lokomotive', p. 195.
[6] Friedrich Kittler, 'Die Stadt ist ein Medium', *Mythos Metropole*, ed. Gotthard Fuchs *et al.* (Frankfurt am Main: Suhrkamp, 1995), pp. 228–44.

city in the style of Janus, the Roman god of thresholds, sited upon a profoundly vexed geopolitical border, and looking both ways. Paradoxically enough, it is this split condition that perhaps most qualifies Berlin for the title of capital of the twentieth century, as exemplary of wider geopolitical divisions. Kracauer's Friedrichstraße station would become one of the most symbolically freighted topographical sites of the divided Berlin, a site of blockage and of strictly limited transit to the other side, complete with a *Tränenpalast*, a palace of tears, for the processing of passage.

If the President of the United States could famously pronounce his 'Ich bin ein Berliner' to assembled crowds before the Rathaus Schöneberg on 26 June 1963, this fantasy identity was borne by a sense of Berlin as indeed the head city of the Western alliance, the place at which citizenship was most acutely determined. Berlin was conceived in the rhetoric of Kennedy's speech as the counterpart to Rome as capital of the ancient world, his performative claim to citizenship in freedom a latter-day version of 'civis Romanus sum', here performed by the imperial head of the new world order. The identification has notoriously been seen to constitute something more grotesque (the President as self-appointed doughnut), and this failure to speak as a Berliner perhaps highlights the misidentification that haunted this new fantasy form of world capital, where the performative assertion of identity would always be subject to alterity, to splitting down territorial lines.

The unwitting associations released by Kennedy's pronouncement, as he styled himself as another kind of food-drop for the city, also nicely incorporate the principle of consumerism that sustained the identity of Berlin in its post-war restoration, principally on its Western side. He speaks as the consumable world leader of the new post-war consumer culture, and the embattled Berlin offers in return a unique stock of consumer capital, cultural and symbolic. JFK's flying visit, in the wake of the 'raisin bombers' that had superseded the allied bombing raids, is designed to seal the apotheosis of the city for capitalism, as *capital*. This is another case of the convergence of 'Kapitale' (capital city) with 'Kapital' that Benjamin saw in nineteenth-century Paris (WB v.i 52). Having been fed by air-bridge from the West, the hungering Western part of Berlin became once more a showroom of consumer culture, and what was pitted against it from the Eastern side was, not least, a counter-form of consumerism: the high-profile shopping mile of the Stalinallee or the Fernsehturm (TV Tower) as high-tech distributor of information and image. Kennedy's speech was one in a series of competing performances on either side of the Wall, with the performance conceived as an object of consumption.

The divided Berlin was a 'capital' both split and bound together by the competition between its two sides, as evidenced in the rival celebrations of the city's 750th anniversary in 1987. Whether the fall of the Wall, and the resolution of the two heads into the one capital of the Berlin Republic, has made the city ready to take on the mantle of capital of capitals in a more benign sense is another question. In October 1989, it certainly seemed that this was a fantasy that traversed the globe: Berlin as the capital of a new world order, notwithstanding Cassandra calls from both ends of the political spectrum. Since the *Wende*, the 'turn' of unification, the city has substantially rebuilt, reorganised, and re-imaged itself. Huyssen has described the palimpsest effect of the contemporary city's architectures and topographies, and the lack of centre that this implies. The new Potsdamer Platz is in this sense an engineered centre for the New Berlin – a Sony Center perhaps – that trades on the city as another marketplace for globalised capital in a transnational, telecommunicating, inter-city age, for which, according to Susan Buck-Morss, there can be no 'Capital City' in Benjamin's sense.[7]

The colonisation of post-unification Berlin under the signs of global capital is the latest inscription upon the palimpsest, but one that is subtended and disrupted by the evidence and after-effects of earlier colonial exploits and exploitations. The Walled city has become, in Huyssen's wry appropriation of a tour-guide slogan, an 'open city',[8] but this epithet must also carry the traumatic resonance of Rossellini's film *Rome, Open City* (1945) and of its Berlin counterpart, *Germany Year Zero* (1947). The city of 1945, at once stripped back to zero, opened up in its material, political, and ethical structures, and still fraught with closed spaces, repressions and denials, remains a part of what the open city has to seek to be open about. The rebuilding of present-day Berlin, inevitably echoing with its post-war reconstruction, carries the memories of past destruction in the urban spectacle that it creates, as promoted by the city authorities in the 1990s through the *Baustelle* as *Schaustelle*, or 'building-site-seeing', slogan.

The opening up of the ground of the city as building-site is also part of the logic of a focal building project designed to look like a monumental edifice that has never risen from, or has been reduced to, its foundation stones. The field of stelae that makes up Eisenman's memorial for the murdered Jews of Europe is indicative of the project for an open city: a

---

[7] Susan Buck-Morss, *The Dialectics of Seeing: Walter Benjamin and the Arcades Project* (Cambridge Mass.: MIT Press, 1989), p. 330.
[8] Huyssen, *Present Pasts*, p. 84.

conversion of the empty space inherited from the violence and division of the twentieth century into another kind of open space; a conspicuous space of unbuilt prime real estate, an expensive graveyard in the purview of Potsdamer Platz that cannot be reclaimed by venture capitalism; and an open space of remembrance which, however, encloses the visitor and provokes uncanny, psychosomatic memories of the city's past. Its exposure prompts a recall of agoraphobia (fears of the open) and the enclosure within a recall of claustrophobia (fears of hiding and imprisonment). It is the same sort of psychically fraught spatial memory that haunts the combination of open and closed spaces, arena and tunnel, in the refurbished stone structure of the Olympic Stadium. In 2006, seventy years after the Berlin Olympics, the 'open city' has redeployed the same arena to become the 'World Capital of Football',[9] thereby looking to find a redefined, focal place on the world stage and in the world market, opened up as 'Tor zur Welt' (Gate to the World) in a new century. It is imagined as both gate to the world (on the model of Berlin's most iconic structure, the Brandenburger Tor) and as goal ('Tor' in another sense), with Berlin playing for normalisation of its geo-political place.

While the sort of historical narrative sketched here in bare outline will certainly inform this study, it is primarily defined as a work of cultural topography, an extension of the kind of cultural analysis through space and place that is practised by such commentators as Benjamin or Kracauer. What this implies is already indicated in the schematic map that has begun to emerge through discussion of the open and closed city, the arena, the marketplace, and the gate to the world. On one level, this study investigates Berlin as a 'capital of culture' (as West Berlin indeed was in 1988): a place that produces and installs culture, both high and popular, in forms with representative reach. And it also considers key aspects of the city's cultural production through the optic of the organisation of space. Accompanying and enforcing the historical development of the city over the twentieth century is an unparalleled set of interventions in its topographical design, of which the ground plan for Germania and the Wall are only the most potent examples. This study is certainly concerned with such material aspects of the city's spatial organisation, but it focuses above all on their impact upon, and transmission by, the cultural imagination.

---

[9] As Mayor Wowereit in his 2006 New Year address for RBB (Rundfunk Berlin-Brandenburg) television called it.

One way of gauging the cultural history of Berlin since the late nineteenth century would be through a succession of what might be called epistemic *topoi*, spatial figures that also stand as models of how the city is thought or known. The topological or topographical knowledge of the city is cast between the actual shape of things on the ground and forms of figuration. Structures of knowledge are sustained by cultural topographical images. That is, the epistemological understanding of the city is always bound up with the Berlin imaginary, the way that the city appears in cultural imagination, from both within and without.

One of the key claims that this study makes is that inside and outside are peculiarly intermeshed in the case of Berlin. We might enter this conceptual territory through the next in a series of gateways, which will feature as framing structures here. The Berlin gate from Kafka's dream has introduced the experience of passing from a congested urban interior only to meet with enclosure, up against a wall. The next such structure is the market gate of Miletus, excavated by German archaeologists and reconstructed in Berlin's Pergamon Museum. For the protagonists of Peter Weiss's novel of resistance to National Socialism, *Die Ästhetik des Widerstands* (Aesthetics of Resistance (first published 1975–81)), the gate acts as a sort of allegorical image of passage from the topography of cultural history in the museum into the live territory of politics in the Berlin of 1937. In front of the gate, one of them remarks that the deployment of the displays creates the illusion of 'outer surfaces' being turned into 'inner walls'.[10] The ancient ruins of the gate of Miletus and the Pergamon altar are turned round, exterior walls grafted into the interior space of the modern city, as space and time become stretched and enfolded in a dizzying spatio-temporal structure.

This crossing of space and time evokes the relativity theory that Einstein developed in Berlin, and as the protagonists emerge from the interior– exterior, ancient–modern space of the museum and into a cityscape under the march of 'hobnailed boots', so this lesson in relativity theory transforms their 'orientation'.[11] The drastic turn from the interior, historical world of the artwork to the impact of present-day urban space is also marked by elements of continuity. The agonistic contortions of the sculptural figures in the extraordinary *ekphrasis* that introduces the novel stand allegorically for the contemporary struggles that will be its subject. And the museum is

[10] Peter Weiss, *Die Ästhetik des Widerstands*, 3 vols. (Frankfurt am Main: Suhrkamp, 1988), vol. I, p. 15.
[11] *Ibid.*

also the site for another kind of public display: the obscene emblem of the swastika on the arms of the crowding spectators. The allegorical entry to the novel also suggests a model for thinking about the relationship between art and politics, as programmed in the aesthetics and resistance of its title. By suggesting that the political arena of the city, the modern *agora*, can indeed be accessed through the aesthetic world of the museum – through the market gate and other art objects – the novel asserts a necessary, if fraught, connection between aesthetic and political culture.

The orientations of the art inside the public interior of the museum and the politics on the street and in the home are made relative to each other. And this 'theory of relativity' in the interaction between art and politics also informs the study here of the city of Berlin through its cultural representations. Following the principle of relativity, Weiss's museum scene might be aligned with a very different, contemporary artwork, an installation on the Berlin 'Museum für Kommunikation', publicising its contribution to the Einstein year in 2005. The continuous streaming in neon letters of EINSTEINEINSTEIN down one corner of the building relativises or deconstructs the name of the iconic scientist, making it readable as an elaborate play on questions of time and place, singular instance and repetition, memory and memorialisation, matter and light: 'EinStein' (one stone), 'InStein' (in stone), 'Einst ein Einstein' (once an Einstein), etc. The 'Nein' and 'NeinStein' (no stone) that are also subversively created by the unbroken stream of letters suggest that Einstein might refuse the memorial appropriation of him as native 'engineer of the Universe' by the city from which he was excluded. The mobile stream of letters in light, creating a kind of stumbling stone, might thus provide a more appropriate and ambivalent form of testimony to his historical place in the city. Whether by accident or design, the neon installation incorporates into what Lefebvre would call the representations of space the sort of protest voice that characterises the demonstration and graffiti work of the city's representational spaces, the spaces at the margin of the public sphere, or without.[12]

In its account of the relation between inside and out, as in many aspects, the present study follows the example of Benjamin, whose interest constantly modulates between interiors and exteriors, across the thresholds that at once unite and separate them. When, in his *Berliner Chronik*, Benjamin describes the scene in Potsdam or Babelsberg of the holiday homes of his Berlin childhood, he indicates that they were located 'outside' as seen from the city but inside 'as seen from the summer' (WB VI 512). The city is a place

---

[12] This is not to idealise the motives behind the generality of graffiti in the 'Graffiti Capital'.

of multiple interiors and exteriors, spatial and temporal, and one where the perspective upon inside and outside shifts according to time and place. From Benjamin's playgrounds to the battlegrounds of twentieth-century Berlin, the sorts of structures of inclusion and exclusion that determine all cities take on particularly acute forms here. A recurrent theme of this study is therefore the borderline between spatial dimensions: inside and out, above and below, here and there.

One of the effects that is produced by this liminal experience is uncanniness, caught between home space and the un-homely. If, as Anthony Vidler has argued, modern cities have uncanniness built into them, in their concrete forms and their imaginaries,[13] Berlin is the paradigm case for the uncanny city of modernity. We might figure this uncanny condition through two of the more internal topical figures from the Berlin imaginary, both of which, however, project outwards. Berlin is a city that also gives its name to a space of habitation: the 'Berliner Zimmer' or Berlin Room. This is a peculiar space within the archetypal Berlin apartment: a room that is also a hallway, only ever between rooms, a space of transition as much as of habitation, and one occupied by nostalgia. It has a special place in what might be called, following Bachelard, the poetics of space for inhabitants of the city.[14] Not for nothing is the corridor leading from the 'Berliner Zimmer' to the rear rooms of the apartment one of the haunted spaces of passage in Benjamin's *Berliner Kindheit* (WB IV.i 277). This is the *topos* as, in Bakhtin's terms, *chronotopos*, a site that is bound up with a certain time.[15] This is how it is represented in Jens Sparschuh's post-unification text in the feuilleton or reportage style, 'Transitraum Berliner Zimmer' (Transit Space Berlin Room), as reconstructed from the Pankow apartment of his early years in East Berlin. It is a space between room and passageway, an *Innenhof* or inner courtyard between inside and out,[16] light and dark, intimacy and exclusion, communication and isolation, accessible to memory only in the form of gaps and fragments.

The end of Sparschuh's elegiac piece, written in an elegiac genre with a particular Berlin pedigree, configures the 'Berliner Zimmer' with another iconic Berlin figure: the 'Koffer' or suitcase, which represents the narrator's

[13] Anthony Vidler, *The Architectural Uncanny: Essays in the Modern Uncanny* (Cambridge Mass.: MIT Press, 1992).
[14] Gaston Bachelard, *La Poétique de l'espace*, 4th edn (Paris: Presses universitaires de France, 1964).
[15] Pam Morris (ed.), *The Bakhtin Reader: Selected Writings of Bakhtin, Medvedev and Voloshinov* (London: Edward Arnold, 1994), p. 184.
[16] Jens Sparschuh, 'Transitraum Berliner Zimmer', *Ich dachte, sie finden uns nicht: Zerstreute Prosa* (Cologne: Kiepenheuer & Witsch, 1997), pp. 11–19; p. 13.

departure from this site of memory. This resonates with the suitcase of Siegel's song 'Ich hab noch einen Koffer in Berlin' (I still have a suitcase in Berlin), famously sung by Marlene Dietrich, Hildegard Knef, and others, and a staple object, a *common place* one might say, of the popular cultural discourse of the city. It is an object that has been used to represent longings of different kinds and qualities. It is available both for Berliners who have left the city, the one perhaps that Brecht left behind when fleeing to Denmark, and for visitors to the city, most flagrantly perhaps in the speech made by Ronald Reagan before the Brandenburg Gate two years before the fall of the Wall, another American President laying claim to Berlin as capital by proxy.

As the stake that those who have left the city retain there, this suitcase is caught between a sense of loss – most extremely as a figure of expropriation for elective emigrants like Brecht or Dietrich or those subject to more coercive forms of deportation – and a sense of potential return and recuperation. The suitcase is also an appropriate emblem of the uncanniness that stays with the city, a shadowy sense of expulsion, of being without, that goes with the experience of living in it. Dietrich's version of the song, that of the prodigal daughter of the city who only properly returned to it in her grave, comes from a different place from that of the daughter Knef, the 'woman like Berlin' who stayed.[17] Knef made her accommodations with the entertainment machinery of the Nazi regime, and then came to embody first the return of the traumatised survivor in Staudte's 1946 film *Die Mörder sind unter uns* (The Murderers are Among Us) and then the compromised double-agent figure in the Cold-War city of Carol Reed's *The Man Between* (1953). These 'sisters', as cast by Dietrich in a family drama of uncertain survival,[18] at once share in their experience of the suitcase in Berlin and are separated by it. And there is also always a third sister in the shadows, the real non-survivor, for whom the suitcase represents terminal deportation.

The *mise-en-abyme* of a 'Koffer in Berlin' pictured in a 'Berliner Zimmer', an image of interior space but fraught with transition and exclusion, can serve as an emblematic introduction to some of the key *topoi* of twentieth-century Berlin's cultural historical topography. It locates the interest of this study in the dimension of 'the between', of interstitial space. The understanding of the outward topography of the city can be properly addressed

---

[17] Knef was described thus at her funeral by Mayor Wowereit.
[18] In a verse to Knef from her final exile in Paris, Dietrich called her a survivor, holding her head above water in order to give life to her 'sister'. See Alex Rühle, 'Hildegard Knef: Eine Frau wie Berlin', www.sueddeutsche.de/kultur/artikel/83/67016/.

only by also considering both its more inward structures and its outside. Berlin's identity is partly constructed by identification or counteraction with other cities, ancient and modern: Babylon, Athens, Thebes, Sodom, Pompeii, Chicago, Vienna, and Istanbul. Especially in the context of exile, in the most exceptional times, the city is also defined through a series of other places: Paris, London, Moscow, New York, Los Angeles, Jerusalem, and – at limit – Theresienstadt or Auschwitz. Thus, the sober counterpart to the World Clock on the Alexanderplatz, casting Berlin into an internationalist community of cities in normal times (German calls a public clock *Normaluhr*), are the memorials on Wittenbergplatz or at Grunewald station, which indicate places in the network of deportation, from times of exception.

Exception operates here in the sense developed by Giorgio Agamben in his critical appropriation, or exceptional use, of Carl Schmitt's terms.[19] The state of exception that became the rule in Berlin from 1933 to 1945, characterised by the brutal *Ausnahme*, the removal or 'ex-ception' of Jews and other groups from the city and its legal terrain, means that this city is perhaps the paradigm case for the transformation that Agamben argues from the city to the camp as the topographical and biopolitical measure of modernity.[20] Theresienstadt and Auschwitz represent that transformation through enforced removal from Berlin to outposts of a new empire, but the state of exception also relates to the imposition of the camp regime onto the city. The death camps as territory of exception are constructed out of the incremental suspension of normal legal rights in respect of exceptional groups, which transformed the city space into proto-camp space for those groups from 1933 onwards. The memorial signs recording that process installed in the 1993 project *Orte des Erinnerns* (Places of Remembrance) by artists Stih & Schnock in one of the principal Jewish quarters of the city, the Bavarian Quarter, are thus appropriately designed as street-signs, topographical markers.[21] In their appeal to the images of the popular card game of 'Memory', a game that depends upon the player recalling locations and making matches, they employ a system of mnemonics in order to place the remembrance of lost civil ground.

[19] See Giorgio Agamben, *Homo Sacer: Sovereign Power and Bare Life*, trans. Daniel Heller-Roazen (Stanford: Stanford University Press, 1998).

[20] *Ibid.*, p. 181.

[21] See also Karen E. Till, *The New Berlin: Memory, Politics, Place* (Minneapolis: University of Minnesota Press, 2005), pp. 154–60.

One of the residents of that quarter in the early 1930s, inhabiting what he called a provisional address,[22] and made to play the memory game in earnest, was the topographical memorist or mnemotechnician Walter Benjamin.[23] It imposed upon him training in the techniques that would be demanded by the camp when he came to be interned in his French exile. The suitcase out of which he lived, and the case that he tried to carry over the Pyrenees in his final journey, are cases less *in* than *out of* Berlin, bearing the state of exception that transported him into that terminal exile. The camp as site of exclusion was, indeed, already included within the topography of the city before it came into being outside. The local camp at Sachsenhausen, a site at once outside and belonging to Berlin, figures the exception as always suspended between exclusion and inclusion.[24] The dialectical functioning of this *Ausnahme* is exposed in the construction of this camp back into the city through such inward outposts as the *Außenlager* (external camp) for slave labourers in the Sonnenallee. This is the paradoxical logic, or topologic, of the ban, which will be explored further in Chapter 1, and to which Berlin has a special relationship.

While the state of exception in the Nazi years is just that, it would be wrong to assume that other kinds of exception are not also the rule before and after the capitalisation of Berlin by the Nazis. Those exceptional times also relate to exception at other times in the twentieth century: the particular ways in which the city includes and excludes. The aftermath of the Nazi state of exception involves both imitative behaviours of neo-fascist exclusion and a level of cultural political inclusiveness that few cities manage. The special status of West Berlin as belonging *de facto* to the Federal Republic and yet *de iure* not fully sovereign territory, still regulated by occupying forces, represented another form of state of exception. The exemption from military service requirements is but one example of the exceptional conditions that operated in the post-war city and made it a place of immigration as well as emigration. And Berlin on the other side of the Wall was also under exception, as a sub-capital of a satellite state, by authority of Moscow.

---

[22] Walter Benjamin, *Gesammelte Briefe*, ed. Christian Gödde and Henri Lonitz, 6 vols. (Frankfurt am Main: Suhrkamp, 1997), vol. III, p. 538.

[23] Another Stih & Schnock work features a different kind of memory sign: a memo recording best wishes sent by Benjamin, posted to the doorbell plate of Madgeburger Platz 4, the address of his birth. The melancholic memo mimics iconic publicity for the furniture company Möbel-Hübner, giving a Benjaminian twist to questions of accommodation and removal.

[24] On Sachsenhausen as Berlin's 'home camp', see Wilfried F. Schoeller, *Nach Berlin!* (Frankfurt am Main: Schöffling & Co., 1999).

Topography is always bound up with history, yielding the second-order dimension of the chronotopical. We can see the experience of the city over the twentieth century as organised around a sequence of chronotopes that serve to define its disposition and orientation. As Karl Scheffler suggested, around 1900 Berlin could still be conceived as outpost. It was a city under extraordinary pressures of development, emerging as an arriviste: a 'Parvenupolis', as Rathenau called it in 1899, amongst the most powerful of modern metropolitan centres but still understood as an off-centre colony.[25] As capital of the Second Empire and a nation vying for a new version of its old dominance in Europe and beyond, it was always also preconceived as such a colonial outpost, arriving late and therefore too quickly.

In the Weimar period, Berlin is perhaps best understood, *pace* Janet Ward, through the idea of the surface.[26] It was the *locus classicus* of what Kracauer called the mass ornament, or the ornament of the masses, where identity was subsumed by the amassed designs of a capitalist economy of spectacle, sustained by mass entertainment, body culture, transportation, and mediatisation.[27] Weimar culture projected itself through a spectacular and specular construction of surface, but the glamour exemplified by the reflection of the city of light in the mirrors of its streets was a cover for more troubled developments and after-effects: the traumatic legacy of the First World War and the end of Empire, with the street as site of actual and potential revolt. The paradox of the imperial outpost is thus succeeded here by the paradox of the glamorous surface subtended, and ready to be disrupted, by foment.

Under the National Socialist regime, the reviled asphalt culture of surface was superseded by another kind of topographical fantasy, that of the city as centre of the totalitarian state, a state whose ideology seeks to make surface appearance true to organic identity, set in stone. Hitler's Germania, as elaborated by his court architect, Albert Speer, was designed to subject the city, and by extension the state, to the idea of a totalised disciplinary space on the model of the classical polis. Those parts of the scheme that were realised, such as the Olympic arena, certainly carry the imprint of such a totalisation, but here too the city is a site of paradox. While National

---

[25] Walther Rathenau, *Die schönste Stadt der Welt* (Berlin/Vienna: Philo, 2002), p. 17.
[26] See Janet Ward, *Weimar Surfaces: Urban Visual Culture in 1920s Germany* (Berkeley: University of California Press, 2001).
[27] See Kracauer, 'Das Ornament der Masse', *Schriften*, vol. v.ii, pp. 57–67.

Socialism did much to destroy the city's counter-spaces, it neither achieved a total clearance nor came to construct in full the capital of capitals.

In 1945, Berlin-Germania was reduced to ruins, and the dominant *topos* governing the city in the post-war period is another kind of paradox: the anti-topographical principle of the *tabula rasa*. It was the *Trümmerstadt*, or city of ruins, as no-longer capital, a city that appeared to afford no organisation of space, no cultural orientation. The *tabula rasa* is chronotopically bound up with the *Stunde Null*, a Zero Hour of cultural history displayed on an obliterated ground zero. The division of the occupied city into sectors put a new template upon it, but these policed boundaries served only to point up the status of the city as non-place: an outlaw site under competing jurisdictions. It was a place of retribution and fraternisation, of painful memory and oblivion. And the *tabula rasa* was also almost immediately a ground for reclamation and reconstruction out of its ruins, while always still haunted by them.

The building of the Wall in 1961 represented an ultimate form of topographical imposition. The figure of the city of ruins was superseded by that of the inwardly walled city, destruction by another form of colossal construction, a catastrophic resolution of space by its drastic division. It imposed a space of mortification through the city, a death strip above ground and the uncanny voids of the 'ghost-stations' between East and West underground. Like the structures of the fascist state before it, the Wall was an exercise in totalitarian architecture that was set to fail and fall. The Wall is as much recognised as a site of passage, licit and illicit, as one of separation: a structure bound into the tunnels that can run under it and the only ever virtually separable space of the skies over Berlin. It was an unnegotiable place of absolute opposition, but also one of threshold, of transactions and projections between its sides.

When the Wall did indeed come to fall or be felled, its place was taken by a more metaphorical form of topographical feature, in the form of the *Wende*. As Heiner Müller puts it in his text 'Berlin Twohearted City', the Wall was also a 'time-wall' between two speeds: acceleration in the West and retardation in the East. And unification broke that chronotopical structure, creating what Müller calls an explosive mixture, when the historical and topographical sectors were resolved into a 'zone of insecurity' (HM VIII 372). Berlin since 1989, reinstituted as capital of the united Germany, is in an ambivalent, post-*Wende* condition. The turn here is fantasised as a turn back to a whole condition, to the normality of a united capital for a united Republic, a normality that, however, had never been. The post-*Wende* period has shown that the turn is no more secure than the fall, witness the notorious 'Mauer im Kopf', the 'Wall in the head' that serves as a continuing blockage in the collective psyche to the idea of the achieved historical turn.

While the Wall has been more or less removed from the physical topography of the city, as we shall see, the *Wende* carries the echo of less tangible partitions, of *Wände* (walls) that still traverse the city at the end of its century as putative world capital. The Wall can be viewed as only the most extreme and long-lasting of a network of walling structures that runs through the city's modern history. This takes the form not least of the barricades, both state-sponsored and oppositional, that have been constructed on the city's streets at historical intervals: those of the Spartacist uprising in 1919; those of May 1929 recorded in Neukrantz's *Barrikaden am Wedding* (Barricades in Wedding (1931)); those of the GDR workers' revolt of 1953; those constructed as a prelude to the Wall; those erected by the radical Left on 1 May demonstrations in recent decades; and those constructed to block terrorist strikes around some of the capital's most sensitive 'objects of protection'. In the discussion of the Communard barricades of 1871 in his *Passagen-Werk* (Arcades Project), Benjamin notes an image of the barricade as urban ruin (WB v.i 199), and in its various more or less makeshift forms it can indeed be said to represent Berlin's irreconcilable differences and the spectre of ruination for the city as it stands.

The pattern that emerges from this schematic sequence is of forms of cover image that conceal, and are subverted by, contradictory currents. Or, to transfer this to the topographical realm, what we see here are mappings that fail to correspond to ambiguous movements on the ground. Berlin is grounded in sand, in the damp or shifting sands of the Mark Brandenburg (province of Brandenburg), and the proverbial condition of uncertain foundations, of being built upon sand, provides a constant refrain through its cultural history (as in the 'lovely illusions, built on sand' of Friedrich Holländer's 'Ruins of Berlin').[28] This is the *topos* as anti-*topos*, the commonplace as figure of displacement, with a profoundly ambiguous function for the grounding of topography. Sand is equivocal material for the construction of cities as well as a shifting and self-effacing material for recording signs or tracks and drawing lines. The city under reconstruction of the early twenty-first century shows its sandy foundations at every turn.

The sand upon which Berlin is built is also the pulverised remains of the sandstone from which so much of it has been constructed. If, following Hegemann's 1930 study of the city of *Mietkasernen* (tenements or 'rent

---

[28] As sung by Marlene Dietrich in Billy Wilder's *A Foreign Affair* (1948).

barracks'),[29] Berlin has carried the epithet of 'stone city', its sandstone element undermines the idea of a metropolis set in stone. Everywhere in the city are eroded surfaces and figures in this provisional material, as if allegorising its subjection to the sands of time. In the iconographic disposition of the Berlin *Stadtbild*, the cityscape or 'city image', the figure is thus always in the process of being reduced to ground. Sand seems to work as a material of both friability and frangibility, of potential disintegration, and also one of reconstitution, ready to be reshaped at a future time. It stands for what Kracauer calls 'the dubious relationship of Berlin to the earth'.[30]

If Berlin can indeed serve as a capital city for the twentieth century, a representative metropolis, it is not least because of the ways in which it shifts its shape to take the measure of internal and external forces. Perhaps more than any other modern city, Berlin has attracted and yet failed to secure definitions. 'Berlin bleibt Berlin' (Berlin remains Berlin) runs one popular saying, but its circularity promises little sense of what in fact remains in and of Berlin. Attempts to define it give the slip to the idea of defined character, as in the aphorism coined by Scheffler in 1910 that the topographically formless and historically indeterminate Berlin is condemned 'always to become and never to be'.[31] This condition of never finally coming to be certainly seems an attractive model for the fermentations that the city has undergone over the twentieth century.

As Huyssen remarks in the context of an advertising campaign of 1996 using the slogan 'BERLIN WIRD' (Berlin's becoming), Scheffler's formulation begs the question of what the city might be becoming.[32] It also corresponds to another famous formulation from the nineteenth century, when Heinrich Heine describes Berlin as 'no city at all': a site for the gathering of people, but without a settled identity of place.[33] The sometime Berlin resident Heine is a model case for a further well-known adage, Fontane's 'Der Berliner zweifelt immer'.[34] The Berliner as 'always doubting' is peculiarly apt to doubt that the city can ever come to be as such. The 2005 installation by artist Lars Ramberg of the word ZWEIFEL (doubt) in illuminated letters on top of the GDR Palace of the Republic, during its period of interim usage preceding demolition, was a nice reminder of

[29] Werner Hegemann, *Das steinerne Berlin: Geschichte der größten Mietkasernenstadt der Welt* (Berlin: Gustav Kiepenheuer, 1930).
[30] Kracauer, 'Berlin in Deutschland', *Schriften*, vol. v.iii, pp. 96–8; p. 96.
[31] Scheffler, *Berlin*, p. 219. [32] Huyssen, *Present Pasts*, p. 54.
[33] Heinrich Heine, *Reise von München nach Genua*, in *Historisch-kritische Gesamtausgabe der Werke*, ed. Manfred Windfuhr, 16 vols. (Hamburg: Hoffmann und Campe, 1973–97), vol. vii.i, p. 17.
[34] See Heinz Knobloch, *Der Berliner zweifelt immer: Feuilletons von damals* (Berlin: Der Morgen, 1977).

this abiding scepticism, written onto the doubtful fabric of the city at the start of a new century.

If such formulas have proved attractive over time, they must correspond in some sense to the unsettled feeling of the city's historical development. It might be argued that they are also applicable to all of the world's great cities, that the metropolis is constitutionally driven by the tension between settled identity and mobility. But Berlin has a particular claim here. If cities are indeed only ever conceivable as sites of being in transit, this city built on sand, with its extraordinary career of transitions between ideological extremes, between construction and destruction, seems ready to stand (and fall) as a paradigm case.

BERLIN IN ITS ELEMENTS

The building of a modern metropolis upon sand is a characteristic element of the Berlin imaginary. Gert and Gundel Mattenklott have described the city through its elements, suggesting that it develops, in particular, through constellations of air, water, and earth – as a 'castle-in-the-air', set upon water and sand – and that these constitute a city as station, between settled location and transition.[35] Similarly, Ulrich Giersch has argued that the role of sand in the 'Myth Berlin' is as a mediary substance *between* the elements.[36] The shifting sand of Berlin is, in this sense, a kind of meta-element, at once integral to the fabric of the city and subjecting it to breakdown into its elements. One of the images, under the heading 'Kaiserpanorama', in Benjamin's cultural-topographical study in urban transit, *Einbahnstraße* (One Way Street), describes the city as built upon an exclusion of the elements but constantly disrupted by their intrusion. The Kaiserpanorama, a device for image projection especially associated with imperial Berlin, is co-opted here to show what is conventionally hidden or effaced, and the irruption of 'elemental forces' is one such exposure (WB IV.i 100).

As the earth of Berlin is figured as sand, so water and air too are given special qualities. The three elements are configured in a poem of 1964 by Christa Reinig, tracking another excursion into the city:

---

[35] Gert Mattenklott and Gundel Mattenklott, *Berlin Transit: Eine Stadt als Station* (Reinbek: Rowohlt, 1987), p. 9.
[36] Ulrich Giersch, 'Berliner Sand ... Materie, Medium und Metapher einer Stadt', *Mythos Berlin*, ed. Hickethier *et al.*, pp. 71–8; p. 75.

Berlin

Die luft wie über wolken klar
und alles trübe hat der fluß getrunken
kanal den sein geländer lässig einfaßt
und oft einmal ein denkmal achselzuckend
und aus der welt
und brücken tragen schwer
durch eine stadt auf sand gebaut

die große stadt ist ganz auf sand gebaut
du läßt sie sinnlos durch die finger rinnen
und ungeduldig
denn klare sicht und wissenmüssen
daß alles fällt und aufgerichtet
wieder fällt
gibt den gedanken seltsame bewegung
und große worte spuckt man in den sand[37]

(The air clear as over clouds/and the river has drunk everything unclear/canal that's casually contained by its railing/and often there's a monument shrugging its shoulders/and out of the world/and bridges carry the weight/through a city built on sand

the big city is all built on sand/you let it run senselessly through your fingers/and impatiently/for clear sight and having-to-know/that everything falls and erected/ falls again/gives curious motion to thoughts/and you spit big words into the sand)

The poem posits the city between senseless flux (sand running like water) and recurrent collapse and confusion on the one hand, and urgent aerial clarity of vision and mobility of thought, on the other. It remains suitably uncertain whether the 'big words' spat into the sand are ultimately of the first or the second order. They most likely communicate between the two and therefore act as a suitable expression of the 'big city' built on and of that damp sand.

The city is built as much over water as it is on sand. Benjamin uses the sandy element of Berlin's foundations to imagine the threshold space of the Baltic dunes of his childhood holidays into the fringes of the city.[38] The beach is made fluid, transported by the metaphorical agency of the verb 'münden' (to issue/mouth), to achieve another version of the mingling of elements mouthed in the closing words of Reinig's poem (WB IV.i 246).

---

[37] Christa Reinig, 'Berlin', *Berlin am Meer: Eine Stadt in ihrem Element*, ed. Ulli Zelle (Berlin: Bostelmann & Siebenhaar, 2000), pp. 19–20.

[38] The 2006 relandscaping of the Nordbahnhof area where the Stettiner Bahnhof stood follows Benjamin's figuration in evoking the dunes and resorts of the Baltic coast.

Through its association with the shifting sands of the Baltic resorts, the colossal sandstone edifice of the Stettiner Bahnhof comes to merge with the street. Recurrently, cultural representations of the city displace it sea-wards in this way, as in the photomontages from the late 1920s by Benjamin's collaborator, Sasha Stone, *Wenn Berlin Biarritz wäre* (If Berlin were Biarritz), which sets the Zoo station on a beach, and *Wenn Berlin Venedig wäre* (If Berlin were Venice), which floods its streets. Berlin's lakes and waterways contribute a further sense of flux to the city's imaginary, and water and sand combine to swamp its foundations. There is a shiftiness and slipperiness of ground that recurs in representations of Berlin.

Berlin air is no less fluid a construction. Another of the city's putative distinctions is the proverbial 'Berliner Luft', the open air of the city of the plain, associated with the bracing character of its inhabitants. It is also construed as aura, following the etymology of that term: the special 'air' that surrounds it. The avowedly anti-auratic Bertolt Brecht, for one, however, was ambivalent about the Berlin air, taking draughts of it from his window in the Hotel Adlon when resident there amongst the ruins in 1948 but also declaring the city to be without air and uninhabitable in 1921.[39] And the words of the song that immortalised 'Berliner Luft', Paul Lincke's 1904 march of that name, which became the city's unofficial anthem, construct the ostensibly honest, open air in contradictory, self-ironic ways. 'Luft' may rhyme with 'Duft' or scent here, but also with 'verpufft pufft pufft' (goes up in a puff, puff, puff of smoke).

In the post-war years, the insularisation of West Berlin by GDR territory provoked the construction of an air-bridge, suggesting that the 'Berliner Luft' remains a resistant free element, like the airwaves propagating 'freedom' on the West Berlin RIAS and SFB networks. But the counter-suggestion in Christa Wolf's novel of German division, *Der geteilte Himmel* (The Divided Sky (1963)), is that this most intangible, groundless of spaces is the element that is subject to separation 'first of all'.[40] The 'Luftbrücke' or air-bridge that aimed to cross the division between East and West is a nicely impossible figure – an architectural span constructed in an element that cannot support it. The Mattenklotts' book includes an image of the sculpture commemorating the air-bridge in front of Tempelhof airport:[41]

---

[39] Diary entry of 12 December 1921 (BB XXVI 264). All references to Brecht's works (BB) are by volume and page number to: *Werke: Berliner und Frankfurter Ausgabe*, ed. Werner Hecht *et al.*, 30 vols. (Frankfurt am Main: Suhrkamp, 1988–2000).
[40] Christa Wolf, *Der geteilte Himmel* (Munich: dtv, 1973), p. 187.
[41] Mattenklott and Mattenklott, *Berlin Transit*, p. 288.

an incomplete bridge as stylised hand reaching up to the sky, representing the incommensurable relationship between ground and air.

The Mattenklotts' account excludes the fourth element, that of fire. And yet this too plays a key role in the cultural historical configuration of the city. Representations of Berlin in late nineteenth- and early twentieth-century writing recurrently figure its ambivalence as a place of at once powerful production and destructive threat through the element of fire. The construction of the city as industrial machine caused the sky over Berlin to glow with its fires, and the quarter around the Borsig works to be named 'Feuerland' (Tierra del Fuego or Land of Fire). Fire is both channelled into the electric creativity of the city and its construction as city of light, most spectacularly in the 'Berlin im Licht' (Berlin in Light) festival of 1928, and turned to more destructive purposes in the ritual and then routine burnings of the following years. One of the epigrams from Brecht's *Kriegsfibel* (War Primer), accompanying an aerial image of bomb damage, displays the logic of perversion that links light with fire and disperses the destruction it wreaks through the air in the form of smoke:

> Daß sie da waren, gab ein Rauch zu wissen:
> Des Feuers Söhne, aber nicht des Lichts.
> Und woher kamen sie? Aus Finsternissen.
> Und wohin gingen sie von hier? Ins Nichts.   (BB XII 170–1)

(That they were there, was made known by the smoke:/Sons of fire but not of light./And whence did they come? Out of darknesses./And whither did they go from here? Into Nothing.)

The fire that burns here is destined to be returned upon the city of darkness from which the German bombers have been dispatched, as the instructive image sequence of the *Kriegsfibel* serves to show.[42] The firestorm rains upon the ground from the air, and brings stone down with it, mixing the elements in monstrous hybrid forms, the 'stone rains' and 'incendiary air' of the scenes from Berlin in 1944 described in Peter Weiss's *Ästhetik des Widerstands*.[43] It is the catastrophic 'raging of the elements' that Döblin imagines when he returns to the burnt-out Berlin from exile in 1949.[44]

The firestorm is also a return from the air of previous fires in Berlin. The burning of the Reichstag and the burning of the books on the Bebelplatz are

---

[42] See Chapter 2, pp. 134–5.   [43] Weiss, *Ästhetik des Widerstands*, vol. III, pp. 177, 180.
[44] Alfred Döblin, *Die Schicksalsreise: Bericht und Bekenntnis*, ed. Anthony W. Riley (Solothurn: Walter, 1993) p. 340.

both inextinguishable elements in the Berlin imaginary. The contradictory character of fire for Berlin is aptly figured in the 'Brandmauern', the partition walls between buildings designed to protect them from fire. These firewalls are colossally exposed in the breached post-war city, always as much a reminder of the missing building that failed to be saved as a bulwark for what still stands. Christoph Boltanski's 1990 *Missing House* project on the Große Hamburger Straße, where the artist has placed the names of the predominantly Jewish inhabitants of a bombed and burnt-out house that no longer exists on the firewalls either side is an exemplary form of the ubiquitous lacunae (see Figure 2). The installation is a kind of evacuated form of one of the paradigms of memory space theorised by Aleida Assmann, the store or container.[45] Its companion piece is the archive of German parliamentarians installed by Boltanski in the cellar of the Reichstag, where nameplates are ranged on brick walls, as if in a filing cabinet, but where the tightly spaced walls also display the emptiness of the archive: a ghost space of memory stored and immured in the cellar of German democracy as its *memento mori*.

The painted walls in the Große Hamburger Straße, serving as exhibition walls for the labels without objects, memorialise the human violence done in a particular quarter of the city, but they also relate to forms of material damage that are in evidence in covered, stripped, or flaking firewalls throughout Berlin. As frames for missing houses, firewalls come to stand as monuments of the incendiary dangers they are supposed to block. As Hanns Zischler notes in his eulogy to this structure, there is a clue to its ambivalence in the name: it is called 'Brandmauer' rather than 'Brandschutzmauer' (fire-protection wall) for good reason.[46] The 'Brandmauer' as 'fire-wall' is a recurrent feature of representations of Berlin after the conflagration of war. It is thus hailed in the first poem in Günter Grass's *Gleisdreieck* (1960), where it stands between opening and closure, a canvas or page for acts of urban representation or a monumental block.[47] Later in the collection, in the poem 'Die große Trümmerfrau spricht' (The great Woman-of-the-Ruins speaks), with Berlin as the title figure, the poet imagines branding images of the city in that allegorical form into the 'Brandmauer'.[48] As the potential screen for such destructive representations, the *Brandmauer* provides a further kind of anti-figure, a

---

[45] See Assmann, *Erinnerungsräume*, pp. 375–7.

[46] Hanns Zischler, 'Brandmauern: Kleiner Nachruf auf eine grosse Sache', *Berlin: Metropole, Kursbuch* 137 (September 1999), 99–102; p. 99.

[47] Günter Grass, 'Brandmauern', *Die Gedichte: 1955–1986* (Darmstadt: Luchterhand, 1988), p. 59.

[48] *Ibid.*, p. 132.

2 *The Missing House*, Christian Boltanski (1990), Große Hamburger Straße.

self-consuming architectural *topos*. It is a screen which serves to represent the unrepresentable: the appalling burnings that went out from this city and were rained back upon it. Fire, fuelled by air, is what converts sand and water into the bricks that are the fundamental building-blocks of the city

(Grass's 'Trümmerfrau' consorts with a brick burner), but, in the form of the firestorm, it consumes and converts the other elements. At the same time, as an always latent presence, it renders the grounding of the post-war city volatile. When reconstruction is not hampered by subsidence or flooding, it is held up by the discovery of buried bombs.

If foundations of sand or water, the air-bridge, and the fire-wall, have been highlighted here, it is because they all indicate a concern with the insubstantiality and transience of the city, both material and imagined. This is Berlin as cast between Potemkin village, the imaginary outpost settlement, and Babylon, the model imperial city with global ambitions that overreaches itself and falls into ruination. The references to Berlin as Babylon are legion, not least in the Weimar era. Berlin as Potemkin features in the 'Grand Hotel Potemkin' (previously named after Bismarck and Göring) next to the ruins of the Anhalter Bahnhof in Billy Wilder's film *One, Two, Three* (1961). It is a wry reflection on the city's grand hotel film tradition from Murnau's *Der letzte Mann* (The Last Laugh (1924)), through Goulding's *Grand Hotel* (1932) after Vicki Baum's colportage novel *Menschen im Hotel* (People in the Hotel (1929)), to Baky's *Hotel Adlon* (1955), and the debasement and destruction behind the representative façade in each case. Under the sign of both Babylon and Potemkin, Berlin is a site at once of pioneering enterprise and potential and one of impossible, sometimes inhuman, fantasies, ready to succumb to disaster.

Writing at a pivotal point in the development of the city, Ernst Bloch in a *Frankfurter Zeitung* article of July 1932 explores the prospect of 'Berlin seen from the countryside',[49] gauging it dialectically through what lies around and below. Following the model of Fontane, he surveys the Mark Brandenburg, only in order to use this as a form of stage on which to display Berlin. The unreliable ground in which the city is constructed and which encroaches upon it is an agglomeration of swamp and sand. Much as in Benjamin's image of the elements irrupting into the city,[50] in Bloch's analysis, the sand of Berlin revisits it as 'symptom' of its lack of foundation. The para-urban ground provides a peculiar 'underground' for Berlin, as the city remains uncannily attached to the country it appears to have colonised, the 'unheimlich-heimliche' (uncanny-homely/secret) landscape of Brandenburg.

On this grounding, the city is characterised by the 'exchangeability of all elements', by a culture of speed ('Tempo') and a mercurial liability to turn in the wind. The city's virtual groundlessness accounts for both its

---

[49] Ernst Bloch, 'Berlin aus der Landschaft gesehen', *Frankfurter Zeitung*, 7 July 1932, pp. 1–2.
[50] Bloch's article is cited in Benjamin's notes for *Berliner Chronik* (WB VI 801).

distinctive potential and its political and cultural susceptibility to fluctuation. Just as its geographical grounding is uncannily shifting, so its location in history subjects it to extraordinary pressures. Set in the yielding elemental mix of sand and water, it is also 'the place of least possible resistance' not only for progressive cultural and political change, but also for more reactionary developments. Bloch's article finishes with a dialectically turned prognosis for this capital, a city ready to become a receptacle for change and yet primed in the uncanny form of a 'ghost of the future'.

The lack of resistance in the foundations of the city at once opens it up to the principle of hope and undermines the historical resistance of that hope. As potential ground for utopian constructions, it is indeed a no-place (*u-topos*). If the grounding of the city is so uncertain, there is perhaps some consolation in its longer term unsuitability as foundation for an empire built on an ideology of 'blood and soil' rather than water and sand. The sands of Berlin also incorporate other kinds of more resistant ground. In the Russian orthodox cemetery in Reinickendorf, the sand was replaced in 1894 by 4,000 tons of earth imported from Mother Russia, a symbolic implantation of immigrant Russian culture into the foundations of the city. And the Garden of Exile in Daniel Libeskind's Jewish Museum sets a column filled with sandy earth from Jersualem amongst those from Berlin. They provide the ground for ghosts of a potential better future.

TOWARDS THE TWENTIETH-CENTURY CITY

Following Bloch's gesture of assessing the city from askance, we step back at this point from the twentieth-century city in order to limn it out, approaching it from outside its temporal and spatial boundaries. This will be done first through an event that was mounted on the edge of the city and the threshold of the new century in celebration of its status as competitor for the title of world capital, the Gewerbe-Ausstellung (Trade Exhibition) of 1896, and then through a text written in the 1880s by a writer seen by Bloch as typifying the fluctuating cultural disposition of Berlin and set primarily in the space in flux around the margins of the city in that period: Fontane's *Irrungen, Wirrungen* (Confusions, Delusions (1887)).

The Gewerbe-Ausstellung, which drew seven million visitors, was mounted in the Treptower Park, on the south-eastern edge of the city, at the initiative of Berlin's entrepreneurial class. It was designed as a response to the great World Expositions of 1851 in London and 1889 in Paris, combining elements of global display with a monumental advertisement of the city's new industrial dominance. As Georg Simmel puts it, the

Gewerbe-Ausstellung answers the world exposition by showing how a single city extends over 'the totality of cultural achievements'.[51] In this display of global culture from within its own bounds, the city establishes itself as exemplary *Weltstadt*, a replica of the commercial forces of the civilised world at large.[52] At the same time, the exhibition displays not only what Simmel calls 'the shop-window quality of things',[53] but also the psycho-sociological principles that he identifies in the experience of urban modernity: an intense heterogeneity of impulse and impact, subjecting the spectator to both violent derangement and hypnotic entrancement.[54] This is mass distraction in the phantasmagorical form that Benjamin attributes to the exposition (WB v.i 50).

If Paris was indeed capital of the nineteenth century, by constructing this fantasy meta-city as a publicity image of itself, Berlin laid claim to the title of capital of the emerging century. One way in which the contest with Paris was played out was in the issue of precedence in the invention of the cinema. The Gewerbe-Ausstellung was one of the first events with global reach to be recorded in and to display the new medium of moving pictures, inaugurated in 1895 by the Skladanowsky brothers' *Bioskop*, as finale for a variety programme at Berlin's Wintergarten, and the Lumière brothers' *Cinématographe* in Paris. The Edison-Pavilion hosted demonstrations of the Cinématographe; the focal Industriehalle displayed new technologies of all kinds, such as Röntgen's new X-ray apparatus; and the site was illuminated by electric lighting provided by AEG, marking the dawn of the age of electricity. And alongside the exhibitions of industrial prowess were those of other worlds: a massive reconstruction of a pyramid in the Cairo section, an ethnographic section imitating 'primitive' life in Germany's African colonies, and views of space through the world's longest refractor telescope. A display of boats from the German fleet made it clear that the technological and colonial advertisements of the Gewerbe-Ausstellung were constructed under the sign of an ascendant imperialism.

The exposition established a kind of colony space for the city outside its limits, a site both for recreation and for the projection of expansionist ambitions. This market-city beside the city was designed to show Berlin at the centre of the worlds of knowledge and trade. As a spectacle of self-display for the city on the brink of the new century, it previewed key elements of what was to come. The extraordinary feat of electrification and

---

[51] Georg Simmel, 'Berliner Gewerbe-Ausstellung', *Soziologische Ästhetik*, ed. Klaus Lichtblau (Bodenheim: Philo, 1998), pp. 71–5; p. 73.
[52] *Ibid.*   [53] *Ibid.*, p. 74.   [54] *Ibid.*, pp. 71–2.

visual technologies looked forward to Berlin as city of light, but the machinery of fire also indicated dangers to come. A fire in the Edison-Pavilion in August 1896 introduced the threat attending the electrical apparatus of light. And the harnessing of the new technologies to the imperialist project would lead to the city's deployment and reaping of fire in the apparatus of war. The site of the exposition was chosen for its location by the Spree, providing an opportunity to display marine power in the capital. The telescope trained on the sky over Berlin and the giant viewing balloon floating overhead both looked towards an age of air-space competition and warfare: the age of the Zeppelin and other aircraft in the skies over Berlin and of surveillance from and of the air. The technical catastrophe that afflicted early cinema also marked the early days of manned flight, when, in the same month as the fire in the Edison-Pavillon, celebrated glider pioneer Otto Lilienthal died in Berlin following a crash. The Fliegerberg or flyer's hill he constructed in the Lichterfelde district would come to serve as the memorial for the fallen flyer. Berlin air, too, would prove to be a disturbed and dangerous element. And, on the ground, the pyramid was built on sand, as if an allegory of the condition of the city as whole. Designed at once to satisfy a curiosity for the exotic other, and to advertise the crypto-colonial exploits of Germany's pioneering archaeologists, it can also be understood as a *memento mori* for the imperial project: a grandiose edifice that represents the passing of a great empire, a superstructure for a tomb.

This reconstructed mausoleum as centrepiece might remind us of Benjamin's contention that the nineteenth-century expositions follow a dialectic between fashion and death (WB v.i 51). The fetishistic innovation that drives the spectacle is always ready to become obsolete. The simulation of the imperial tomb foresees the commemorative structures of twentieth-century Berlin. Indeed, the Treptower Park would feature another kind of heroic display in the second half of the twentieth century: the grandiose Soviet war memorial as monument to the dead but also exhibiting the supersession of one empire by another. Built out of the remains of Hitler's Chancellery, the memorial is testimony to the counter-colonisation of the city that had sought to be imperial capital of the twentieth century.

Fontane's *Irrungen, Wirrungen* provides another kind of approach to the twentieth-century city from its edges, as an 'Everyday Berlin Story'.[55] The novel is set in a borderline space, both topographically and historically. It is a narrative on the cusp of metropolitan modernity, split between anachronistic social structures and a new urban order. The text's title refers to the

---

[55] The novel was classified thus when published in the *Vossische Zeitung*.

confusions of the heart, but also to errancy or disorientation in and around the modern city. By setting the establishing section of the text in the suburban hinterland, the liminal space where the city is cast as village, Fontane establishes a distanced perspective on what has been called 'Fontanopolis'.[56] Berlin-Fontanopolis is constructed here under the topographical figure of the boundary, with past time and extra-urban space configured as a chronotopical alternative reality.

In its introduction to this chronotope, or time–space constellation, the opening section of the text functions as a highly theatrical *mise-en-scène*, of a piece with the frontier fantasy-city that was the Gewerbe-Ausstellung. The novel enters the modern city by way of a time-warp. Its object is not the new building projects or the burgeoning industrialisation of late nineteenth-century Berlin, but anachronistic scenery that has been displaced by those developments, its impermanence marked by the passing 'noch' (still) of the opening sentence.[57] This setting is only available to nostalgia. The opening sentence of the novel sets this out in its hypotactic clause structures, at once mapping a topographical location and marking it out with processes of retraction and transition. At this topographical crossing-point, with the great arteries of the imperial city (the Kurfürstendamm and the Kurfürstenstraße) still dispersing into open fields,[58] natural and cultural growth converging (in the zoo and the nursery), the narrative is established in a site both of temporal transience and spatial transition.

As prepared by its programmatic title, this is a scene-setting that works towards confusion, where the organisation of space seems designed to disorientate the reader-traveller. It appears to set a narrative scene, yet does so with an unsettling shift into the generic language of the theatre. It constructs a scene that mediates between the city and its surroundings, with a façade that might act as the face of the city to one approaching it, or its last outpost to one leaving it. But this façade is a cover that dissimulates. For the Berlin of 1870, never mind that of 1887 when the novel first appeared, was already a bustling imperial capital with around a million inhabitants. In 1875, where the 'still' of the opening line might be located, the Kurfürstendamm was transformed under Bismarck's orders from a

---

[56] See Charlotte Jolles, '"Berlin wird Weltstadt": Theodor Fontane und der Berliner Roman seiner Zeit', *Berlin: Literary Images of a City*, ed. Derek Glass *et al.* (Berlin: Erich Schmidt, 1989), pp. 50–69.

[57] Theodor Fontane, *Irrungen, Wirrungen, Werke, Schriften und Briefe*, ed. Walter Keitel and Helmuth Nürnberger, 20 vols. (Munich: Carl Hanser, 1962–97), part I, vol. II, pp. 319–475; p. 319.

[58] Gabriele Tergit evokes this scenery in her novel of the rise and fall of Weimar Berlin, *Käsebier erobert den Kurfürstendamm* (Käsebier Conquers the Kurfürstendamm (1931)), as Fontane's title wanders, as a literal form of 'Wanderschrift' (running letters), into a montage of city lights and sights. Gabriele Tergit, *Käsebier erobert den Kurfürstendamm* (Frankfurt am Main: Fischer, 1978), pp. 47–8.

sandy bridle path into a boulevard to compete with the Champs Elysées, the royal road of the capital of the nineteenth century. The scene memorialises the prehistory of a street that in its Weimar years would become, as Kracauer famously put it, a 'street without memory', subject to constant resurfacing and reconstruction.[59]

The novel's subsequent plot takes it both into and out of the city, its story of love lost charted through its negotiation of space, always with a sense of errancy and passage. While the *Irrungen* or errancies of the novel's title are principally traced in the borderline territory of the opening scene, the narrative also charts the movement of its protagonists into the city proper. Both Lene and Botho are made to feel their loss through encounters with the metropolitan topography. For Botho, this is in the form of a virtual traffic accident, when his carriage is held up on the way to the cemetery. The mass collision of the carriages ahead is felt by him with delay, in a stalled fashion that is characteristic of traumatic experience. He catches sight of a load of broken glass in the cart in front, and is made to feel the pain of his broken happiness.[60]

Lene suffers a street 'accident' of her own, when she almost bumps into Botho and his new bride on a busy thoroughfare.[61] The girl from the edge of town is first transfixed by the bustle of the market at the Magdeburger Platz,[62] only to be shaken out of this as a fire engine rushes by. The bells of the emergency vehicle are configured with the clock on the church tower, showing twelve o'clock, and marking the passage of time that works so relentlessly on the narrative after it has moved from the apparent time-lessness of the opening scene. She hurries on down the Lützowstraße, only to meet her own version of postponed accident: the shocking alarm of the fire bells has prepared the way for personal collision and injury. While Lene just manages to avoid Botho and Käthe by turning towards a shop-window, the missed encounter is rife with symptoms of traumatic impact. She finds herself standing on the cover for an opening into the cellar, which trembles under her feet as she grasps the brass bar in front of the window. She returns to the house on the edge of the city in a state between life and death, the leitmotif of the narrative.

That the two scenes described here should operate under the sign of the virtual accident is symptomatic for a narrative always out of joint in its

---

[59] Kracauer, 'Straße ohne Erinnerung', *Schriften*, v.iii, pp. 170–4; p. 173.
[60] Fontane, *Irrungen, Wirrungen*, p. 450.   [61] *Ibid.*, p. 415.
[62] 1888 saw the completion of the new Markthalle V on the Magdeburger Platz, which features as a chronotope for Benjamin's Berlin childhood (see Chapter 1).

spatio-temporal dimensions. The traumatic failure of love at the borderline of social arrangements is brought to bear in these chance events. The façade of the first page turns out to be a cover for the traumatic experience involved in passage from the enchanted boundary space into the time-bound space of the modern city. It can thereby also be viewed as an exemplary, ambivalent entrance into the Berlin which the present book sets out to describe: a city that so often conceals limit-experiences within its boundaries and behind its façades. Lefebvre conceives of the façade as a prime organising feature of the city, admitting 'certain acts to the realm of the visible', the 'scene', and consigning others to the realm of the 'ob-scene', the illicit space behind the façade.[63] This topographical disposition suggests a 'psychoanalysis of space',[64] where the opposition between 'conscious' and 'unconscious' is subject to slippage and switching. In the history of twentieth-century Berlin, the obscene also repeatedly irrupts into and changes places with the official scene before the façade.

The false start made by Fontane's novel is also true to what follows in the city of Berlin. The theatre walls in place of a city wall open up uncertain perspectives into the city one way, and 'into the fields' the other. In particular, they look forward to the summative mapping of the 'weites Feld' (wide open field) of Berlin in the long twentieth century that Grass will undertake in his millennial version of Fontanopolis. The programmatic errancies of Fontane's novel lead to the wandering topographical explorations of Grass's *Ein weites Feld* (Too Far Afield (1995)),[65] not least in the fields – no man's land, unofficial nature reserve, and killing field – that came to be incorporated into the city by the building out of place, at its centre, of another kind of false city wall, an obscene façade.

PSYCHO-TOPOGRAPHIES OF URBAN LIFE

The experiences of Fontane's protagonists in and out of Berlin in *Irrungen, Wirrungen* suggest the dimension of psycho-topography. The scenes highlighted above are constructed as accidents of human or vehicular traffic on the streets of the city, but their impact is felt on the level of psychosomatic distress. When Lene is caught before the shop-window, it seems that an underground space is ready to open up. The cellar with its trembling cover is a corollary of the Schloon channel as subterranean threat in the space between land and sea in *Effi Briest*. And for Effi the topography of Berlin,

---

[63] Lefebvre, *Production of Space*, p. 99.   [64] *Ibid.*
[65] Günter Grass, *Ein weites Feld* (Göttingen: Steidl, 1995).

built on sand, becomes a site of projection for the ghosts that haunted her outside the city. The view of the city from the apartment that Effi takes presents the life of the modern city, the transportation system and the Kreuzberg hill under reconstruction, but this against the backdrop of a churchyard, sustaining her morbid attachment to cemeteries.[66] Mortality and mobility are intermeshed here.

Key scenes from Fontane's novels also figure in the scenarios for some of the first motion pictures: Botho, as *flâneur* on Unter den Linden, is on the street that houses Berlin's first cinema in 1896 and is filmed by the Skladanowsky brothers in the same year. Another two of their films of 1896 feature sorties by the fire service, rehearsing Lene's alarm and arguably indicating something of the fire danger built into the new travelling image technology. And a further film, contributing to what fast becomes a genre-piece of early cinema, is of a train pulling into Schönholz station. Technologies of travel, and the image-streams that they present, at once prepare for and are in harness with the new technology of motion pictures. This film could be viewed in parallel with the arrival of Effi Briest at Friedrichstraße station in the novel published in the same year. The Skladanowsky film conjures up the panic at technology coming at the viewer that was famously provoked by the Lumières' 1895 film *Arrival of a Train at La Ciotat*, indicating a trauma inherent in the mythology of the birth of the new medium.

In *Effi Briest*, Fontane gives recurrent attention to technologies of travel and their departures and arrivals, scenes of embarkation and disembarkation. One example shows Effi in a sort of proto-cinematic state. Trams, too, soon become vehicles for film-making (in so-called phantom rides), and Effi is transported by one into a kind of film-scene, combining movement, a distracting spectacle, and the sort of mortal danger that participates in new technologies of both travel and image-making. When she has a chance encounter with her daughter on the latest mode of urban transport, the horse-drawn tram,[67] she has just been distracted by advertising images in a window. The street-scene of traffic and commerce, giving rise to a longed-for encounter, is here, as in *Irrungen, Wirrungen*, the vehicle for the sort of 'mortal fear' that Effi thought she had left behind her.[68] She disembarks

---

[66] Theodor Fontane, *Effi Briest*, *Werke, Schriften und Briefe*, part I, vol. IV, p. 259. The imprisoned view from Effi's window is recalled in Weiss's *Ästhetik des Widerstands* (vol. III, p. 211), now from an address in the topography of terror, the Gestapo prison in the Prinz Albrecht Straße.

[67] In the mid 1890s the horse-drawn tram was already obsolete; the first electric tram service worldwide was introduced in Berlin in 1891.

[68] Fontane, *Effi Briest*, p. 268.

from the front of the vehicle, without regard for safety regulations. It seems that there are ghosts in the urban machinery. The Berlin of the last decade of the nineteenth century is still that of E. T. A. Hoffmann and his uncanny 'deserted house' on Unter den Linden,[69] and already that of the different types of ghosts that will come to haunt it in the new century, those phantoms of history that Ladd describes in his *Ghosts of Berlin*,[70] and others besides.

The void beneath the feet of Fontane's Lene indicates the dubious grounding of life behind the façades of the city. It is the sort of opening up of a subterranean space that Benjamin documents as a source of uncanny fascination: the un-homely home-space of the 'bucklichte Männlein' in his *Berliner Kindheit* (WB VII.i 429). This finds its counterpart in a series of underground networks, the cellars, bunkers, and tunnels that run through Berlin's modern cultural history, functioning not least as a space for unacknowledged memories. While the psycho-topographical disorientations and divagations of the protagonists of *Irrungen, Wirrungen* are personally motivated, it is a principle of Fontane's texts that the love story, and the topography that it negotiates, is a cover for concealed threats of a more public nature, the political as 'hidden and dangerous'.[71] What overwhelms and injures the ex-lovers is not only their personal loss, but a more psychosocial sense of damage that arises out of the failures of a moribund order.

While many of the psycho-topographical experiences that figure in this volume arise out of personal narratives, they also contribute to a psychotopography that operates on a more general, socio-political level. The movements of individuals around the city intersect with those of groups, sometimes running in concert and sometimes at odds with them. Both invest Berlin with their desires and anxieties, and are in turn confronted by the disorientating or threatening effects of this. And the danger from her personal history encountered by Lene on and under the street in the Berlin of the 1870s can be associated with the sorts of concealed danger from collective history still felt in the topography of the city in the twenty-first century.

In the summer of 2005 the *Literaturhäuser* (Literature Houses) in Berlin and other cities mounted a reading campaign as a prelude to the 2006 soccer World Cup. One of the texts they used was a playful anti-poem by Elfriede

---

[69] See Chapter 1, pp. 94–5.
[70] Brian Ladd, *The Ghosts of Berlin: Confronting German History in the Urban Landscape* (Chicago/London: University of Chicago Press, 1997).
[71] In a letter of 2 July 1894 to Friedrich Stephany, in: Fontane, *Briefe: 1890–1898, Werke, Schriften und Briefe*, part IV, vol. IV, p. 370.

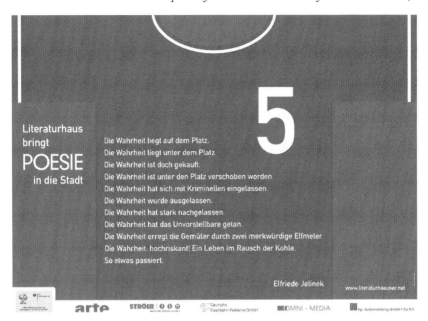

3 'Die Wahrheit liegt auf dem Platz' (The Truth is Lying on the Ground), Elfriede Jelinek (2005). (The truth is lying on the ground./The truth is lying under the ground./ The truth has simply been bought./ The truth has been displaced under the ground./ The truth has got involved with criminals./ The truth was left out./ The truth has left off markedly./The truth has done the unimaginable./ The truth makes emotions run high through two curious penalties./ The truth: very risky! Life on a cash high./It happens.)

Jelinek,[72] a notorious exposer of cultural-geographical duplicities and repressions (see Figure 3).

The poem consists of a series of variations on the football adage: 'Die Wahrheit liegt auf dem Platz' (meaning, 'the truth is there for all to see'), and the second line immediately turns this commonplace on its head, turning the 'Platz' (place or ground) over and revealing its false ground. The poster hung, for example, in the entrance to the Bundesplatz underground station, and might have provoked passers-by to consider the disposition of that square with the exemplary name, and of its underground. It is apt to question the toponymic regime of the city. If the place, square, or ground of this poem, number five in a formation of such texts, printed on a

---

[72] Jelinek described it to me as a simple series of variations on a sentence, but arguably also readable as a poem.

stylised red football jersey and set against a green ground, is to be understood as sports' ground, then perhaps we should think of the Berlin
Olympiastadion, elegantly refurbished for the World Cup, but with a
historically laden substructure that speaks of other kinds of dreams of
world championship. But Jelinek likes to see sport and its duplicities as a
paradigm for contemporary culture in general. In this light, it is no less clear
that the place in question could equally be the Heldenplatz of Jelinek's, or
indeed Thomas Bernhard's, Vienna. This is a 'Platz' that for both authors
gives grounds for what German calls *Platzangst*, or topophobia, the morbid
fear of space, of place, or of a place. This implies a revival of the psycho-
drama of Freud's topophobic Little Hans in early twentieth-century
Vienna, as symptomatic of that city's case history. Here, it is specifically
the fear of a place that the *Anschluss* turned into an extension of the parading
grounds of the new imperial Berlin.[73]

The place of the poem could also extend to a whole series of public spaces
in Berlin: the Potsdamer Platz as the symbolic place of the excavation,
covering over, and rebuilding of a walled and bunkered history, a place next
to a death-strip that architect Rienzo Piano described as a desert inhabited
by an unsettled ghost;[74] or the Bebelplatz, scene of the Nazi book-burning
and now housing Micha Ullman's *Bibliothek* (Library (1995)), an underground memorial to the burning of the books in the form of an empty
library sunk into the square. Like Boltanski's *Missing House*, the easily
missed void of Ullman's memorial to destruction acts as a counter-monument
in the sense developed by James Young, at once provoking acts of remembrance and representing the lacunary condition of 'memory lapse', a gap in
the city's narrative of itself.[75] It is thus performative of the elision and
repression that constitute the city's 'case history'. This sort of memorial in
negative space opens up the underground history of the city, projecting a
historical spectacle upon the 'Platz' into an inaccessible crypt beneath it, the
sort of subliminal spaces of which Berlin over the last century is full. In
other words, it projects the representative urban place, the *topos*, into the
unmappable ground of what J. Hillis Miller calls the atopical.[76]

The call to reading that is publicised in Jelinek's poster-poem is accordingly directed as much at the contradictory places and spaces of the city as at
literary texts. The variant that locates truth beneath the 'Platz' suggests the

[73] Bernhard staged the topophobia associated with the *Anschluss* in his play *Heldenplatz* (1988).
[74] Piano, interviewed for Gaby Imhof-Weber's film, *Architektur der Jahrtausendwende: Berlin* (2001).
[75] James Young, 'The Counter-Monument: Memory against itself in Germany Today', *Art and the Public
Sphere*, ed. W. J. T. Mitchell (Chicago/London: Chicago University Press, 1992), pp. 49–78; p. 69.
[76] J. Hillis Miller, *Topographies* (Stanford: Stanford University Press, 1995), p. 7.

place of the past, the site of 'Geschichte' (history) as 'Ge-schichte', a spatio-temporal 'layering' of past experience. The urban memory of a city like Berlin is at once in evidence in both intentional and accidental forms above ground and, as the poem has it, 'verschoben' or displaced under ground. This displacement below ground suggests a psychoanalytic reading of the stratified fabric of the city-text. For Freud, *Verschiebung* (displacement) is a constitutional function in the work of the unconscious, in its scenic and narrative logic as exemplified in dreams. It can be understood as a fundamental trope in the rhetorical operations of the unconscious, indicating one of the basic conditions of the psyche in Freud's definition as cast between the fixed system of topography and dynamic functions that traverse it. And this extends to the sort of understanding that psychoanalysis might have of the city through analogy with the psyche, as a place of both individual and more collective psycho-topographies. In Jelinek's formulation, 'verschoben' resonates at once with this kind of psychical displacement, with the idea of postponement, and with the sense of 'verschieben' as 'to traffic'. The game of football is subject to both of these other kinds of *Verschiebung*, and the city of Berlin, with its twentieth-century history of repression and of black-marketing is peculiarly suited to invoke the displaced meanings.

For Freud, psychical truth lies both underground, with the unconscious cast as the space below, and over-ground, but in forms that are necessarily dissembled, subject to both displacement and condensation. He thus attempts in the famous image from the beginning of *Civilisation and its Discontents* to engineer his understanding of the relations between personal and collective histories through the figure of the psyche as city. For this he chooses the 'eternal city' of Rome, where the archaeological layers of successive architectural and topographical orders are perhaps uniquely convergent. The elaborately constructed fantasy of the psycho-city fails because of the ultimate impossibility of representing the hypothesis of psychical simultaneity in spatial dimensions: the remainders of past eras can only be contiguous, not coextensive (SF XIV 428). Freud manages, however, to salvage a certain purchase from his broken model. This arises out of dialectical contradiction: the glimpse of what the psycho-city might indeed be is afforded, paradoxically, by the 'effect of contrast' that undermines the analogy (SF XIV 429).

The breakdown of Freud's model might also suggest that the archaeological principle that informs his project is in need of differentiation. The fracture between topical and temporal dimensions that Freud recognises in his modelling of the psyche is polemically reformulated by Deleuze in his 'anti-psychoanalytic' project. In Deleuze, the Freudian model, with its 'commemorative' preoccupation with historical origination, is challenged by a more geographical one, whereby experience is always principally inherent in its environment rather than in the subjective pre-histories of those who 'have' the experience. This is the basis of a 'dynamic cartography',[77] where new mappings are not understood through their relation to older ones as their site of origin, but as extending 'trajectories and becomings' through nomadic forms of displacement.[78] He adopts the key term of displacement from Freud's theory of the unconscious and repositions it, emphasising the principle of energetic movement away from teleological or genealogical lines into a more lateral field of enquiry.

Deleuze's correction of Freud indicates that a differentiated form of psycho-topographical work might be the most appropriate option to follow. This approach, modulating between history and geography, the narrative of origins and the mapping of displacements, can serve as a paradigm for the psycho-topographical treatment of cities. And this applies not least to the city of Berlin, which in the years of the Third Reich sought the status of a new eternal city, by analogy with Ancient Rome, and is still rife with the uncanny archaeologies of that brutal agenda for domination. While the city is so clearly dominated by its ghosts, it is salutary to consider Deleuze's injunction that the interpretive process should follow the tracks of 'beings in becoming' (*devenants*) rather than ghosts (*revenants*).[79] A suitable emblem for this might be one of the defining cultural moments of the post-*Wende* period: the wrapping of the Reichstag in 1995 by Christo and Jeanne-Claude, creating a spectacle of the city's past that operated, in every sense, as an *Aufhebung* or sublation. Wrapping the monument in a dust-sheet was an act at once of suspension and preservation, a figuring of it as cartoon ghost and potential *revenant*, and also a lifting and aesthetic sublimation of the historical form that had weighed upon the city. Even when most haunted by the Gothic narrative of its history, or case history, Berlin is also active with alternative mappings, and what is proposed in this volume is a negotiation between these two modalities.

The mapping of psyche onto city is a recurrent feature of Freud's work, be it in the Little Hans case history, the essay on Jensen's novella *Gradiva*, or the reading of E. T. A. Hoffmann's *Der Sandmann* (The Sandman) in *Das Unheimliche* (The Uncanny). Freud's psycho-topographical conjecture

---

[77] Gilles Deleuze, 'What Children Say', *Essays: Critical and Clinical*, trans. Daniel W. Smith and Michael A. Greco (London/New York: Verso, 1998), pp. 61–7; p. 62.
[78] *Ibid.*, p. 63.   [79] *Ibid.*, p. 66.

occurs in these works in terms of categories with a particular bearing on the case of Berlin: topophobia, archaeology, and uncanny returns. In Freud's analysis of Little Hans, the boy's fantasies and anxieties are transposed, or transported, onto the urban topography of Vienna and its transport systems. Hans's phobic condition is 'under the sign of traffic' (SF VII 319), whereby the fantasies of the exposure of parental intercourse, the sexual traffic associated with the primal scene, are relayed into the child's negotiation of urban space and traffic.[80] Topographical traffic is aligned here with linguistic and psychosexual motions and exchanges.[81] For Freud, Little Hans's psychical truth lies upon the 'Platz' in the form of his psycho-topographical anxieties, but also beneath the 'Platz', in terms of what motivates these. The child's *Platzangst*, the 'fear of place', its collapses and collisions, is graphically represented by the sketched street-plans.[82] The accidents that we witnessed in *Irrungen, Wirrungen* are evidence of this kind of urban *Platzangst* at work in Berlin.

In Freud's reading of *Gradiva*, the protagonist's dreamlike experience of a ruined city and its fissured topography arises out of catastrophe on a grand, historical scale: the eruption of Vesuvius. The ghosts of this traumatic catastrophe visit the city and at the same time become vehicles for the visitation upon the protagonist of repressed desires from the psychical household of his childhood. The post-catastrophic city is a stage for a drama of the return of the repressed: childhood and adult experience, Munich and Pompeii, are transposed into an uncanny psycho-topographical double-ground, as the archaeology of an undead love moves about the ruined city. While Little Hans's catastrophic fantasies are mobilised by the everyday life of the modern city, here the traumatic impact of mass destruction – and with it the 'psyche' in ruins of a once great city – is aligned with the disasters of the personal psyche, a case history of repressed desire that recalls that of Lene and Botho.

Hoffmann's *Sandmann* too is a sort of case history of personal trauma and lost love, albeit within a more Gothic framework. The uncanny here has its roots in private catastrophe, as located in the psychical household and landscape of the protagonist. The experiences of the home, and its *un-heimlich* secrets, are projected into the topographical space of the home town, as organised by the Sandman as uncanny visitant and guide to urban

---

[80] See also Deleuze's counter-reading in 'What Children Say', p. 61.
[81] Lacan draws this cross-trafficking out in his remapping of the case. Jacques Lacan, *Le Séminaire IV: La relation d'objet* (Paris: Seuil, 1994), pp. 303–35.
[82] See Anthony Vidler, *Warped Space: Art, Architecture, and Anxiety in Modern Culture* (Cambridge and London: MIT Press, 2000), pp. 41–3.

attractions. This text full of projective fantasies ends with a final projection of the pathological psyche into urban space: the townhall tower serves here as a kind of optical instrument, enabling the apparently recovered protagonist to take a view of his home town and the mountains in the distance, which are perceived in their turn as a 'giant city'.[83] And on the square, he perceives the repressed psychical truth as embodied by the return of the Sandman.

If the Sandman rises 'gigantic' above the assembled spectators,[84] he is identified at once with the mountains as 'giant city' and with the tower with its 'giant shadow',[85] a construction within a monstrously enlarged urban and para-urban architecture. The uncanny visitation of the subject by this gigantic topography is under the sign of *Entstellung*, the fundamental principle of dream- and other psychical work in Freud's account. The Sandman is perceived both as a monstrously overreaching building and, by virtue of his distinctive bushy grey eyebrows, as a mobile, grey bush. He returns, or re-turns,[86] upon the home town, casting its topography into uncanny motion, and projecting into it the sort of experience of urban circulation that Freud describes in his essay through his involuntary recursions to the red-light district of an Italian town (SF XII 249). And as a psycho-topographical figure, he is always also a dis-figure, an avatar of Benjamin's *bucklichte Männlein*. Following Freud's understanding of *Entstellung*, the Sandman's morphing and mobile shape embodies a principle of corporeal disfigurement (the sort of drastic change of shape that comes with catastrophe) and also one of removal: the propulsion of the subject into another scene. This psycho-topographical projection gives some sense of the sort of truth that Freud looks to find, less upon the 'Platz' than in the more reclusive ground of the 'anderer Schauplatz', the 'other scene' of the unconscious (SF II/III 51). The uncannily transformed topography of the square at the end of *Der Sandmann* seems to follow the design principles of just such an 'other scene': an allegorical site of spatial, psychical, and corporeal disfiguration.

Entstellung always follows this sort of model for Freud: at once a disturbing alteration, through internal condensations and displacements, of the psycho-corporeal figure, and an *Ent-stellung* as 'dis-location'. It is a process

---

[83] E. T. A. Hoffmann, *Der Sandmann, Sämtliche Werke*, ed. Wulf Segebrecht *et al.*, 6 vols. (Frankfurt am Main: Deutscher Klassiker Verlag, 1985), vol. III, p. 48. Peter Schneider transposes Hoffmann's small-town scenario to the divided Berlin in his *Paarungen* (Couplings) (Reinbek: Rowohlt, 1992), pp. 133–57.
[84] Hoffmann, *Sandmann*, p. 49.   [85] *Ibid.*, p. 48.
[86] See also Andrew J. Webber, *The Doppelgänger: Double Visions in German Literature* (Oxford: Clarendon, 1996), pp. 121–48.

that disguises psychical truth and embodies it in an encrypted form. Freud mobilises this double grounding in his study *Moses and Monotheism*. Here the exegetic, topographical, and ethnographical tracing back of the identity of Moses proceeds by means of what Freud calls 'Entstellungen' in the texts, disfiguring transpositions that evince the truth of the case as 'entstellt', or displaced (SF XVI 144). The analyst, working as criminologist, biographer, and cartographer is charged with putting that truth back into shape and place.

A correlation is made here between space and body as elements of the scene of the crime: the body as *corpus delictus*, whose disfigurements are also clues as to the violence done, is always also understood in its relationship to surrounding space. The bodily 'Entstellungen' that might follow from acts of violence can thus be projected into the topographical 'body' of the city. The eyebrows of the Sandman as metonymically embodied in a bush on the square, prefiguring the more drastic *Entstellung* of the protagonist as he lies smashed on that same place, provide an acute example of that disfigurement of body into city-body. It is a spectacle that we will encounter more than once in this volume. While the model of *Moses* suggests that the analyst is equipped to read that disfigurement back into a true sense of identity, Freud's acknowledgement that the act of recognition will not always be an easy thing serves a cautionary purpose. The scene of *anagnorisis*, the recognition of figure and ground, of the body and where it properly belongs, is always fraught with uncertainties and speculations. The psycho-topography of individuals, cities, or cultures, the way in which the psychical identity of each of these is inscribed into place, works on ambiguous ground, and this has implications in turn for their proper placement in memory, be it in the individual case history or collective history.

ARTS OF MEMORY

The *artes memoriae* or arts of memory famously originate in topography, leading scholars of urban history to return repeatedly to the originating scene, as described in the life of Simonides of Keos. This primal scene of memorative technique is also brought about through catastrophe: place as the carrier of clues for memory becomes so only under the impact of violent accident. And what here is enacted in a room that collapses is certainly extendable to urban topography under the impact of history.[87] In the story

---

[87] See discussion of the Mossehaus in Chapter 3, pp. 171–4.

of Simonides, as related by Cicero and Quintilian, the poet is called upon to provide a panegyric for the wrestler Scopas on the occasion of a banquet, but also provokes his anger by turning his praise to Castor and Pollux. The poet is called away from the table, and in his absence the banquet hall collapses and buries all present. The corpses are so terribly disfigured that they cannot be identified and therefore appropriately buried, but Simonides is able to identify them by remembering where each sat at the banquet table. He thus inaugurates the arts of memory by vesting mnemotechnics in spatial order. The mnemonic process is topographically conceived, as a writing or marking of place. Cicero, in his *De oratore*, compares the method to the act of writing, with the spatial disposition of the figures to be committed to memory modelled on the wax tablet.

With Cicero's wax tablet as memory frame, we return to Freud. For Simonides the truth is indeed located 'on the ground': the place of the disfigured body provides its true identity. But for Freud, as we have seen, psychical disfigurement also always implies spatial removal. He implicitly takes up the model of Simonides and develops it in a more psycho-topographical direction when he sets out his own art of memory in the introduction to his 'Note upon the "Mystic Writing-Pad", the 'Wunderblock'. He writes here of annotations on a writing tablet or paper that can be called upon in the aid of memory, thereby evading the sort of 'Entstellungen' to which they would otherwise be subject (SF XIV 3). But this process, too, relies upon remembering the location of the inscription. For Freud, Simonides' wax tablet, the topographical framework for memory, is not a dependable, or stable place. Memory for Freud is always subject to *Entstellung*, not only in its objects but also in its processes.

The psychoanalytic *artes memoriae* are inscribed in a different form of wax tablet: the 'Wunderblock' or mystic writing-pad. And this writing-place is – as in the analogy of the city of Rome – a site for the simultaneous crossing of the historically non-simultaneous. For Freud, the psyche as memory ground works in the fashion of a palimpsest, and each new topographical inscription is subject to *Entstellung*, transposition to another place, by those already inscribed or yet to be so. The 'Wunderblock' is a place of writing that is, as it were, always also beneath itself, under the 'Platz'. It is *geschichtet*, layered with its recording history. The memory machine of the 'Wunderblock' is thus also an analogy for psychical archaeology. When you write upon the block you leave passing traces on the place above, but also dig into the material below and leave lasting substructural imprints, inaccessible to the reader. The 'Wunderblock' is, in other words, a memory block in more senses than one.

This paradoxical model of mnemotechnical recording certainly applies to Berlin, the city that is, according to Andreas Huyssen, 'part palimpsest, part *Wunderblock*'.[88] If the city is to be understood in the way that Benjamin proposes, as an archaeological text or texture, the analysis of the layers that have gone underground as 'Ge-schichte' will always be complicated for the psycho-topographer by processes of *Entstellung*. This is the *Entstellung* that Benjamin, in his essay on Kafka, attributes to the failure of memory, as in the shape of Odradek, taking the disfigured form of things that are subject to forgetting (WB II.ii 431). Benjamin here sees Odradek as akin to the 'bucklichte Männlein', representing the psychosomatic disfigurement of acts of forgetting. More precisely, perhaps, it is the compromised form between remembering and forgetting that we saw at work in Kafka's dreams of Berlin, an intrinsic part of the city's cultural topographical fabric and the experience of deterritorialisation that inheres in it.

Another example of the principle of case-historical *Entstellung* might be cited here, in anticipation of fuller discussion in Chapter 5. Ingeborg Bachmann's *Ein Ort für Zufälle* (A Place of Coincidences (1964)) explores the Berlin of the early 1960s as a place at once of coincidence and of collapse, of 'zufallen' as 'falling to'. The text foresees the buildings of the restored city as being accelerated back in history, collapsing under the weight of what has 'happened' to happen here before, and reduced once more to the ruins of, and upon which they are uncannily constructed. For Bachmann, this glossy Berlin of the *Wirtschaftswunder* is, in more than one sense, 'geschichtet' (*TP* 215), heaped into the collapsed layering of its history. Berlin is thus a place designed to elicit the archaeological investigations of the urban psycho-topographer, and in the capital city of trauma, psycho-topography is always ready to collapse into psychopathography.

The 'Zufälle' of Bachmann's programmatic title are turned into a trope that can take on an exemplary character for the representability of Berlin as a representative city. The 'Ort für Zufälle' is in the first instance a *topos*, 'Ort' as a figure of location in space, and Bachmann's text teases away at the work of identifying a proper sense of place in the city. But the mobilisation of 'Zufall' involves a move from *topos* to *tropos*, the turning of a spatial location into a figure of movement. Topography is, in other words, turned here towards tropography. At the same time, 'zufallen' enacts a movement which is negative: it is an anti-trope. Rather than extending the terrain of the city into new dimensions, it suggests a collapsing of it back into the inescapable place of its foundations. Not for nothing has the German verb 'fallen' and

---

[88] Huyssen, *Present Pasts*, p. 52.

its cognates assumed such a key function for thinking the limits of representation, whether in Paul de Man's work on rhetoric or in its application to
trauma theory as developed by Cathy Caruth.[89] Berlin is, in these terms, a
fallen city, one that enacts in drastic form the sort of fall that is always the
accompanying trauma for the fantasy life of cities. It is, to invoke two cases
of twinning that are a recurrent feature of the city's imaginary, Berlin–
Babylon or Berlin–Sodom: the city of eros and entertainment under the
sign of ruin and disfigurement.

Like the *Entstellung* that went before it, this figure, or anti-figure, of
falling will be a recurrent feature of the account of Berlin in its cultural
topography given here. While the end of the Second World War is its most
drastic historical embodiment, the case of Fontane's *Irrungen, Wirrungen*
(the projected falling of the protagonist before buildings) has already shown
that it reverberates in other forms before as well as after that event. The
falling to the ground on the Potsdamer Platz building-site of the melancholic topographer in Cees Nooteboom's *Allerseelen* (All Souls (1999))
would be but one more recent example.[90] Both the collapsing of individuals
and the tumbling of buildings in response to ideological or other pressures
are constant features of twentieth-century Berlin; and falling becomes, of
course, the dominant trope of a later event of world historical import: the
dismantling of the Wall as 'fall', where the collapsing of a monumental,
totalitarian architecture is understood as creating new building-ground for a
reconstructed capital.

TOPOGRAPHICAL TURNS: ALLEGORICAL CITY

In its appeal to the categories of *Entstellung* and of the ruin, this study aligns
itself with the method of Walter Benjamin, as perhaps the most influential
figure in discourses of urban space and culture in the twentieth century. The
resurgence of interest in Benjamin in recent years has come with what has
been called the topographical turn.[91] And here, as much as with any of the
serial turns in critical thought and (inter-)disciplinary enquiry that have
been charted over the past decades, turn is an appropriate trope for what is at
stake. Trope, after all, means turn, and the key aspect of the topographical
turn is a turning towards tropography: the understanding of space as *figured*.

[89] See Cathy Caruth, *Unclaimed Experience: Trauma, Narrative, and History* (Baltimore/London: Johns
Hopkins University Press, 1996), p. 22.
[90] Cees Nooteboom, *Allerseelen* (Frankfurt am Main: Suhrkamp, 2000), p. 147.
[91] See Sigrid Weigel, 'Zum "topographical turn": Kartographie, Topographie und Raumkonzepte in
den Kulturwissenschaften', *Kulturpoetik* 2.2 (2002), 151–65.

Benjamin's influence here is, as much as anything, due to a principle of turning in his thought. At its limit, this is the distorted twisting of *Entstellung*, but it is always also at work in more subtle fashion, in the dialectical turning of his analysis and not least in his reading of spaces and places, topographies and architectures, as figures or configurations.

The massive exploratory undertaking of the *Passagen-Werk* is just such a turning, exploring a tropic territory where structures and materials are *turned* into other structures and materials. This is, in its broadest sense, the principle of allegory. Allegory is to be conceived here as following its etymology: as an other (*allos*) (market)place (*agora*) to speak (*euein*). The arcades are just such a marketplace for Paris as capital of the nineteenth century: the other place of the city in which things are made to speak otherwise, of other experiences in space and time. Benjamin's project, in the *Passagen-Werk* and elsewhere, is a mimographic recording and analysis of that speaking otherwise, its economy, its exchanges, its turns and returns. Benjamin's appropriation of allegory as master-trope for his cultural critical project relies on an understanding whereby the turning towards the other can indeed become a form of *Entstellung*, at once a removal to another place and a disfigurement or disfiguration. This is allegory functioning as what de Man designates as 'a figure that disfigures',[92] with decay or dissembly constructed into its figural logic. For Benjamin, allegory is always at base a melancholic process, attached to ruination (the ruin as paradigm for allegorical constructions) and mortification (the corpse as paradigm for allegorical bodies). And this model certainly inheres in the allegorical identities – topographical, architectural, and corporeal – of his home city.

We have already seen this allegorical principle at work in some scenes from Berlin-Fontanopolis, a Realist city on the brink of high modernity that is also by turns neo-Romantic and neo-baroque in its figuration. The *agora* that Fontane describes when his texts negotiate Berlin, a place for speaking otherwise of the city, is indeed a kind of marketplace, driven by forms of social commerce. When Lene and Effi are mortally struck in their movements around the city, this is mediated by the marketplace: Lene comes from a marketplace before her fateful encounter and finds her gaze traumatically fixed on banal commodities (mixed pickles) in a shop-window, while Effi's fateful encounter on the tram is introduced by a view of advertisement images in a window. In both cases, the protagonists exhibit the sort of double consciousness, split between violent impact and distraction, which

[92] Paul de Man, *Allegories of Reading: Figural Language in Rousseau, Nietzsche, Rilke, and Proust* (New Haven/London: Yale University Press, 1979), p. 198.

Simmel argues is constitutive of urban experience, and in particular shop-window commodities.[93] The late nineteenth-century market city of Fontanopolis is also represented in its shop-window: the marketed city of the Gewerbe-Ausstellung. And in both cases the marketplace speaks otherwise through the ambiguous effects of commodification. When Lefebvre, at the beginning of his *The Production of Space*, suggests that everyone knows 'what is meant when we speak of a … "marketplace"',[94] he sets up a truistic form of speech and understanding that cannot hold in the complex networks of the production of space. Indeed, the programme of Lefebvre's study is to dismantle such assumptions, as he gauges more contradictory and differential forms of space. The marketplace is always a site that is also otherwise, an example of what Lefebvre will call the 'counter-space within a particular space'.[95]

The moment of displacement that is built into this model form of urban place is nicely represented by the career of the allegorical figure of Berlin, the statue of Berolina that once stood on one of the city's principal historical marketplaces, the Alexanderplatz. It was first designed in plaster for the Potsdamer Bahnhof in 1889, then cast in copper for a new site on the Alexanderplatz in 1895, suffered damage in the November revolution of 1918, was removed to make way for construction work on the underground railway in 1927, re-sited on another part of the square in 1933, and finally dismantled in 1944. The statue was last sighted at the Neukölln freight station and is believed to have been melted down for the war effort. It is an allegory that is subject to historical events, removed from its proper place, disappearing from view and becoming an object of nostalgia or of mockery for the people of Berlin, a statuesque example of the *Puppen* (statues as 'dolls') that decorate its streets, bridges, and buildings. In particular, it appears to be ready to be taken for one of the city's most popular vernacular figures, the *Marktweib* (market wife), set as it was in 1895 on a historic marketplace and in front of the new form of urban market in the shape of the monumental Tietz department store. The displacement, ruin, and loss of the allegory seem all too appropriate for this city of displacement, ruin, and loss. As a banal allegorical artwork, the Berolina statue stands for the principle of commodification, the working and trading ethos of the city in its Wilhelminian heyday, and comes to speak otherwise through its subjection to history and the repeated transformation of the marketplace where it stands into other places: places of revolution, of urban transportation and

---

[93] Simmel, 'Berliner Gewerbe-Ausstellung', p. 74.
[94] Lefebvre, *Production of Space*, p. 16.   [95] *Ibid.*, p. 367.

commerce in their new forms, or of war. Like that other allegorical figure, the Roland of Berlin, the Berolina statue is a *Weichbild* in the ambiguous sense developed in Chapter 1 below, an iconic marker of urban order that is subject to transition.

In the Fontane texts, too, the language and imagery of the marketplace bear other meanings. The banal commodity image enters into the economy of artworks and other figures used to allegorise the condition of the protagonists: the everyday commercial material of the city is made to speak otherwise. The encounter on the streets, which is always waiting to happen in the urban topography, is in each case associated with a traumatic turn on the part of the protagonist. Turning to the shop-window or disembarking from the tram at an unscheduled stop represents the negotiation of topography as psycho-tropographic: figuring the traumatic turn. The surfaces of the urban marketplace become freighted with other meanings. The emblematic buildings that open *Irrungen, Wirrungen* (the 'castle' of market gardeners) prepare for the reading of a text that is laden with emblematic features, not least with serial variations of the *memento mori* figure. As a sort of gate to the city, a cryptically constructed entry-point to the confusions that provide the title of the work, and one which is under the sign of ruin, it corresponds to an exemplary version of the allegorical structure, and one that will recur throughout this study.

Fontane's 'gate' is thus related to the emblematic market gate of Miletus from the start of Weiss's *Ästhetik des Widerstands*. It is an isolated allegorical structure of entry, via which the *agora* and the arena of the modern city are negotiated. The mock 'castle' of *Irrungen, Wirrungen* also looks forward to the contemporary debates over the rebuilding of the Stadtschloss or City Castle on the site of the Palace of the Republic as a centre for dialogue between world cultures. Whether the *agora* or Humboldt-Forum that has been projected to replace the Palace, behind the façade of the old Stadtschloss, will serve as an allegorical forum for speaking otherwise in the city, for speaking of and with other cultures beyond the archaeological and ethnographic displays in its museums, remains to be seen. The gate to the projected *agora*, the portal from the Stadtschloss, is, at any rate, already installed elsewhere, as another kind of 'Gate to the World': the entrance to the global marketplace, in the shape of the European School of Management and Technology.

The view of Berlin offered in a perspective between proximity and distance on the opening page of *Irrungen, Wirrungen* is reminiscent of the objects that Benjamin assembles at the 'lost-and-found office' of his *Einbahnstraße* (WB IV.i 120). This is a particularly allegorical address in a text of cultural-topographical allegory, with the author as architect, construction engineer, and surveyor.[96] In the lost-and-found office, the prospect of the city, as viewed from the landscape, is caught in the sort of dialectic of near and far through which Benjamin characterises the auratic. This aura is the lost object that is produced by entry into the city, when, as he puts it, the landscape has disappeared like the façade of a house into which we have entered. The found object counterpart to this is the sort of 'blue distance' that will not cede to proximity, as displayed in the simulation of the stage-set: a land- or cityscape that always remains fixed at a distance.

Fontane's theatrical façade as allegorical entrance to his text and its city is cast in the dialectical interplay of the lost and the found, where loss is always only an effect of entry and proximity and retrieval an effect of fixture in estrangement. It is the story of his protagonists in *Irrungen, Wirrungen*, but also a determining experience of approach and entry into the city on a more general level. The experience of Lene, caught over a hole in the street, is also bound into Benjamin's *Einbahnstraße*, which he likens in its 'curious organisation or construction' to another stage-set. He describes the topographical design of the text as akin to Palladio's famous stage-design *The Street*, plunging the perspective into sheer depth (WB IV.ii 910). This *mise-en-abyme* function is duly redeployed in the photomontage by Sasha Stone for the cover of *Einbahnstraße*, where the superimposed road signs indicate a transversal direction across what is presumably a Berlin street-scene behind. The design suggests that each façade can also be penetrated as a kind of orthogonal side-street, and that these diversions off the one-way street are projected into a potentially infinite series, a deep and layered topographical field.[97] Accordingly, in the scene on the back cover, a bus and pedestrians are caught moving laterally across an open street, in the direction indicated by the signs on the front cover. The street-scene is ready for projection into the kind of archaeological space that Benjamin searches out through 'more secret, deep-set city-figures' (WB V.i 135), places encrypted under the more evident topographies of the city. Like Fontane before him, Benjamin construes the city street as a place of sudden arrest (an early title for *Einbahnstraße* was *Straße gesperrt!* (Street Blocked!)). And the street-sign title itself is subject to *mise-en-abyme*, with 'many others behind it' (WB IV.ii 909), indicating a projection into depths that are not (only) metaphorical.

---

[96] As Burgin suggests, the text's lay-out is topographical (Burgin, 'The City in Pieces', p. 33).

[97] Benjamin elsewhere describes the flight of courtyards in the particularly densely constructed tenement at Ackerstraße 132 as a tunnel. Such street-views cast the gaze 'into the deep' (WB VII.i 120–1).

If Benjamin is such a guiding presence in the varied enquiries that make up the topographical turn, this is explained not least by his own allegorical turn or return: his project to recuperate both the timeworn and discredited figure of allegory and, under the aegis of that figure, the obsolete arcades of Paris. This configuration also provides the frame for his work on Berlin. When Benjamin turns Berlin into another place, makes it speak and be read anew, it is not least as seen from the other places – the places of allegory – that he had already turned out of Paris. His speaking otherwise of his own capital will be the subject of Chapter 1. It will also set the framework for the subsequent chapters, as explorations of how Berlin has been turned in exemplary forms of cultural representation across the period since Benjamin's childhood.

Following Benjamin's example, the concern here will be as much with figurative turns in detail as with the bigger picture of Berlin's cultural topography. As exploration and inventory of the twists and turns of that topography over its twentieth-century history, the book will have something of the design of the *Passagen-Werk*, where different sites and their histories at once maintain a specific character and intersect with, turn or return upon, others. It is a spatio-temporal mapping exercise that, following the allegorical principle, seeks to figure the continuities of cultural developments and also to respect their discontinuities, their fragmentations. And this dialectic between continuity and discontinuity extends to the forms in which those developments are represented, their medial character.

In such texts as the *Passagen-Werk* or *Berliner Kindheit*, Benjamin establishes a particular kind of chronotopical model: the space–time constellation as evidenced in a collection of paradigmatic sites of memory. A key to the understanding of those sites, their cultural topographical placement, is the way in which they are mediated, and here a further structural aspect of the allegorical model comes into play. As a mode of speaking otherwise, allegory is at base an intermedial form, classically incorporating elements of text and image. Benjamin cites the view of Carl Horst that crossing categorical borders, specifically those between visual and 'speaking' arts, involves a wanton transgression (WB I.i 353). His own view of this crossing of boundaries is a more open and dialectically disposed one, and it is in this spirit that the present study also works. The discussion of Berlin's allegorical cityscape here recurrently negotiates combinations of text and image. It considers representations of the city in writing and in pictures, both still and moving, and in hybridisations of these media. And a further principle taken from Benjamin is that of performance: topography as a function of what is enacted in and through it, as in the sites of Benjamin's childhood play. Equally, the irruption of the other into those sites suggests that performance is also a matter of contestation. The performative construction of space and place is never simply a matter of free-play, but it can be a means of resisting more official mappings, of making the city be seen, read, or spoken in other ways, however locally or provisionally.

One of the most powerful recent interventions in the cultural cityscape serves as the final edifice in the emblematic series that has introduced this study. Libeskind's Jewish Museum can be understood as a constellation in the Benjaminian sense: it is a building that constructs itself into the history of its specific site and of the broader topography of the city. Its design maps the networks of German-Jewish life in Berlin, and not least the cultural topographical enterprise of Benjamin (after the street design of *Einbahnstraße*). It is determined to represent both cultural continuity and a sense of the radical discontinuities to which Jewish life in the city has been subject. The axis of continuity is thus crossed with the transverse axes of exile and Holocaust.

The museum performs upon the visitor as a place of recognition in estrangement. This most allegorical of buildings, figuring and enacting the experience of Jewish culture in Berlin, enclosed in itself and yet projecting to other places beyond its walls, is riven by the principle of *Entstellung*: by an uncanny sense of disfigurement and dislocation in its architectural and topographical contours. The building's recasting, whether in melancholic imitation or active appropriation, of two antithetical emblems, the lightning flash of the SS insignia and a dismantled version of the Star of David, is just one aspect of that *Entstellung*, as obscene. It embodies at once the scar which that part of Berlin's history leaves on the city, a scar that must inevitably hold the city in its traumatic and melancholic aftermath, and the generative potential for its remodelling or refunctioning. The insistence in this building upon the void as integral element is all the more important for a cityscape that is increasingly filling in its gaps. There are plans to reconstruct the Kaiser-Wilhelm-Gedächtniskirche, one of the most effective mnemotopes of the city's history of destruction, and thereby to fill in the gap that constitutes it as a memory-church of a more critical kind. The cavity in what is popularly known as the 'hollow tooth' stands to be prosthetically replaced and with it another of the symptomatic forms of *Entstellung* that befit the city's memory-scape. It is this principle of disfigurement that Libeskind's scar-building incorporates.

On the model of Libeskind's work of cultural (dis)continuity, this study seeks at once to map the continuities that subsist in the twentieth-century cultural history and topography of Berlin, and also to show that, in the dialectical manner that links the modernity of Benjamin's project with the postmodernity of Libeskind's, continuities are always mediated by forms of breach in experience over time and through space. Rather than relating a continuous chronological or chronotopical narrative, this study works both proleptically and analeptically, through techniques of flash-forward and flashback, and thereby shows that the city's history is always constructed as much through its future and its past as through the present moment. At the same time, this history is conceived as a kind of case history, the case history of a city that perhaps more than any other can be understood as fraught by psychopathologies in its everyday life, in its states of exception, and in the mapping of the one onto the other. The capital city of National Socialism and the Walled city of the Cold War may be understandable as sites of schizoid delusion, rife with the symptoms of paranoid schizophrenia,[98] and the times between and around these psychotic episodes as marked by neurotic after-effects and anticipations. Following a key feature of the case history as constructed by psychoanalysis, the history of the city is also configured by the principle of *Nachträglichkeit* or retroaction, which causes events to take effect in different ways after the fact. And this temporal dislocation is accompanied by a spatial one, following that other key psychoanalytic principle, *Entstellung*: an effect will often be found elsewhere, in another form and site. An account of the cultural history and topography of twentieth-century Berlin must seek to take the measure of these chronographical and topographical disfigurements and displacements.

This book cannot hope to provide a comprehensive cultural historical map or chronicle of the twentieth-century city. What it proposes is a contrapuntal account to be read alongside and against the sort of historical sweep established in Alexandra Richie's study *Faust's Metropolis*.[99] It works according to the belief that symptomatic effects of the general state of the city are to be traced in the most intimate details of its 'representational spaces', on the ground and in its figures, and in the cultural representations of that ground and those figures. It thus focuses on a select gallery of case studies and analyses their microstructures, after the fashion of Benjamin's cultural topographical work. Its intention is to project a more complete mapping and chronicling out of those examples by highlighting the exemplary ways in which they relate to one another, share a place, and in which they breach such relation, occupy another place. That is to say that it will trace both isotopical relations (following Lefebvre's glossing of isotopia as

---

[98] On urban paranoia, see Victor Burgin, 'Paranoiac Space', *New Formations* 12 (Winter 1990), 61–75.
[99] Alexandra Richie, *Faust's Metropolis: A History of Berlin* (New York: Carroll and Graf, 1998).

'analogous spaces') and heterotopical ones (with heterotopia as 'mutually repellent spaces'),[100] showing that the two models are codetermined in the cultural topography of Berlin.

The heterotopical here can also be understood in the way that Foucault proposes, as the kind of space, at once in and set apart from the real, that both reflects and inverts the normative regime.[101] The sorts of counter-cultural space he proposes for this can be aligned with Lefebvre's representational spaces, but the gloss that Lefebvre puts upon heterotopia suggests that these spaces other to the norm are also liable to be other to each other, incommensurable in their differences from the norm. And this in turn has implications for the psycho-topographics of the city, for the mapping of psychical investment and resistance, both individual and collective, through urban space. The mapping in question is perplexed by the difference it has to negotiate but also finds meaning in that difference. As in Freud's paradoxical mapping of the city of Rome as allegory for the psyche, the analogical construction is fraught with otherness, but thereby produces an illuminating effect of contrast even as it collapses.

To adopt the terms developed by Marc Augé, this psycho-topographical model of urban life modulates between place and non-place, spatial relation and a condition of unrelatedness, non-identity.[102] The failure of Freud's analogy is also one of cultural memory: a failure to make the memorative topography of the eternal city consonant with the historical condition of the modern psyche. And in the post- or supermodern city, the prime (dis)location of Augé's non-place, the gap in the analogy opens wider. If, following Huyssen, postmodern urban culture suffers from a kind of 'mnemonic fever',[103] a febrile proliferation of sites and objects of memory with no sense of proper placement or anamnesic effect, this mimics the condition of the contemporary psyche. According to this diagnosis, the postmodern city, like the hysteric in Freud's account, suffers from reminiscences, even as it pastiches and plays with them. It is a condition that already dwelt in the modern city of the early twentieth century and is virulent in the expanded non-places of its postmodern counterpart.

While much of the historical territory of twentieth-century Berlin is under the cultural historical sign of 'post' – post-war, post-Wall, postmodern,

[100] Lefebvre, *Production of Space*, p. 366.
[101] Michel Foucault, 'Of Other Spaces', *Diacritics* 16 (Spring 1986), 22–7.
[102] Marc Augé, *Non-Places: Introduction to an Anthropology of Supermodernity*, trans. John Howe (New York/London: Verso, 1995), p. 77.
[103] Andreas Huyssen, *Twilight Memories: Marking Time in a Culture of Amnesia* (New York/London: Routledge, 1995), p. 5.

posthistorical – this volume aims to resituate this condition of coming after. The modernity that energised Berlin in the early decades of the twentieth century and especially in the 'legendary' Weimar years was, notwithstanding its cultural dynamics, also marked by various forms of coming after: after the modernity of other great cities, after the first great catastrophe of modernity that was the First World War, after the convulsion of revolution and civil war. It is in these terms that Benjamin, a theorist associated so strongly with the Berlin of early twentieth-century modernity, can also provide a theoretical guideline for what comes after. Benjamin's theoretical history of modernity is always attentive to the 'coming after' that is inherent in the futural moment of all historical becoming: the impending supersession of historical periods and of their cultural edifices and maps. If the urban theorists of postmodernity, or a theoretically disposed practitioner of the postmodern like Libeskind, are so beholden to the model of Benjamin's city work, it is not least for this reason: it is work that is proto-postmodern in its logic, attentive to how modernity always comes after, is configured through, and set to become in its turn, cultural memory.

The kind of postmodernity proposed by Libeskind in his designs for Berlin is also bound to the memory of modernity, to the city of Benjamin and the Bauhaus, coming *after* it. From what he calls the 'Between the Lines' project for the Jewish Museum or the 'Out of Line' project for the Potsdamer Platz modelled after a broken avatar of Benjamin's angel of history, to the schemes for the Alexanderplatz, Unter den Linden, or the Sachsenhausen camp, his interventions in the postmodern mapping of Berlin are all attached to the traumatic matrices of a city which has made a particularly brutal break with the enlightenment project of modernity.[104] But his projections of boundary spaces, of sites that fall between or are out of line with established topographies – his 'Über den Linden' projected onto 'Unter den Linden', his 'archipelago' development giving new shape to the city limits, his 'City Edge' scheme cross-cutting Speer's axis, his programmatic transcription of Mourning as Morning in the Sachsenhausen project – these suggest more than just the 'mnemonic fever' of postmodernism. They rather make an effort to connect with the sort of *Zwischenräume*, the liminal 'between-spaces', that Benjamin opened up in his mnemotechnical mapping of the modern city. This is Libeskind's exemplary, anamnesic response to the painful and divided state of Berlin, as what Derrida,

---

[104] For accounts of the projects referenced here, see: Daniel Libeskind, *radix-matrix: Architecture and Writings* (Munich/New York: Prestel, 1997).

responding in turn to that response, calls the 'exemplary city' of a schismatic, non-identical century.[105]

The memory work to be done in this volume, elaborating relations between place and non-place, is the constitutionally incomplete, non-identical work of allegory, the signature structure of Benjamin's project as of Libeskind's. The principle of relations founded on difference, of similarity that is constructed in another place, is indeed that of allegory. The six chapters that follow are all structured according to this principle. They are each primarily sited in a particular cultural historical period – the first four in the 'pre-war' heyday of the modern city, the fifth in the 'post-war',[106] Walled city, and the sixth in the postmodern, post-Wall city. The *prima facie* weighting towards Weimar Berlin is redressed, as the chapters both reach forward and look back from their primary historical site. Each chapter has an emblematic double spatial structure attached to it in the subtitle, encompassing the contradictory allegorical shaping of the city over time. The allegorical principle, in its Benjaminian logic, is representative at once of cultural historical and cultural topographical meaning and of the limitations upon such meaning. As Freud's allegory of Rome is only imperfectly able to give shape to the psyche, so Berlin cannot fully work as an allegorical representation of the psycho-political condition of twentieth-century humanity, as its representative 'capital'. What the series of case studies that follows sets outs to show is an allegorical understanding of this most complex and fascinating, unsettled and unsettling of cities: the city speaking and spoken otherwise.

---

[105] *Ibid.*, p. 111.
[106] The terms 'pre-' and 'post-war' are in themselves indicative elisions (of the First World War by the Second) in the master narrative of European modernity.

CHAPTER I

Berlin chronicle: thresholds and boundaries

> and tomorrow I was indeed in Berlin.[1]
>
> Walter Benjamin

Following the charting of some of the outline features of the cultural historical map of Berlin in the Introduction, this chapter aims to map in detail some of the key allegorical constructions that Benjamin puts upon the spaces of the city. These topographical figures are elaborations of some of those already encountered, focused upon sites of boundary and transition, and not least the transition between time and place: the fluid conjunction of history and topography. Early twentieth-century Berlin is understood here, according to the allegorical principle, as a place, or a network of places, for speaking otherwise: speaking of time through place, of the public through the private, of the interior of the city through exclusion, of life through death (each of these also vice versa). The chapter focuses on a number of generic topographical and tropographical sites in Benjamin's mapping of Berlin, understood as examples of what he calls the *Schauplatz*, the scene or 'show-place' for structures and relationships both evident and subliminal. The principle sites in the urban *Schauplatz* are the *Hof* (court or court-yard), the *Weichbild* (city limits), the *Marktplatz* (marketplace), and the *Bannraum* (space of exclusion). These will be seen as exemplary instances of Benjamin's allegorical work on Berlin, his project for speaking otherwise of the city, illuminating its historical-topographical conditions from alternative perspectives.

TIME-DREAM-SPACE

By investing Paris with the title of 'capital of the nineteenth century', Benjamin engages in his favoured critical pursuit: allegoresis. The capital

---

[1] A future-past structure from 'Von der Sommerreise 1911' (On the Summer Trip of 1911 (WB VI 251)).

city of France is transformed allegorically into the capital of an historical age, deemed to be the city that paradigmatically displays the conditions of that age. The *genius loci* is at the same time a *genius saeculi*. It embodies the city of the century as 'Zeitraum' (space of time) but also as 'Zeit-traum' or 'time-dream' (WB v.i 491), an oneiric form of time-space that requires subjection to analytic anamnesis and dialectical awakening.[2] And the analytic work that goes into interpreting the chronotopical dream and assessing its paradigmatic function is, above all, the work of allegoresis: the reading of topographies both broad and particular as figuring historical conditions in allegorical fashion. The etymology already established for allegory – as the (market)place for speaking otherwise – is especially borne out in Benjamin's work on the arcades. The *Passage* is the characteristic marketplace of nineteenth-century Paris, and a topographical site that is inherently also chronographical: charting historical processes. The *Passage* is so preoccupying for Benjamin's project of exploration of the capital of the nineteenth century because it is an exemplary spatio-temporal site or chronotope. It represents the 'ambiguity of space' (WB v.ii 1050), a site between inside and out, full of mirrors and other simulated spaces. It resonates at once with the idea of a textual passage (the *Passagen-Werk* as a network of such passages) and of a marine passage (the *Passagen-Werk* as a work of navigation),[3] thus mapping the negotiation of textual space onto that of space at large. And it combines this transitional spatial character with a constitutional ambiguity of time. It is a topical structure that especially belongs to the history of the nineteenth century, connecting up its moments in a topographical assemblage, but is always also passing from it. The *Passage* communicates between the streets of the city, but also communicates the condition of passage in time: it is a (market)place for speaking otherwise of the historical process in its topographical effects.

   One aspect of Benjamin's other form of speaking (of) Berlin is the incorporation of the Parisian model into it: behind the street-scenes, the marketplaces, the exteriors and the interiors of Benjamin's early twentieth-century Berlin, lies the allegorical mapping of the 'capital of the nineteenth century'. Adorno thus calls *Berliner Kindheit* the 'subjective counterweight' to the masses of material assembled for the *Passagen-Werk*.[4] Benjamin

---

[2] For Benjamin, the dialectical image is cast between the effects of dream and the 'break-in points' of awaking. See his letter of 16 August 1935 to Gretel Karplus and Adorno, *Gesammelte Briefe*, vol. v, p. 145.

[3] The latter resonance is at work in a sketch with the title 'Rousseau-Insel', mapping the 'Passage' that is the grandmother's apartment onto the waters around the Rousseau island in the Tiergarten (Walter-Benjamin-Archiv (Akademie der Künste, Berlin), ref. 886).

[4] See Adorno's afterword to Walter Benjamin, *Berliner Kindheit um neunzehnhundert* (Frankfurt am Main: Suhrkamp, 1950), pp. 176–7.

describes his life in the mid 1920s as tracking elliptically between Paris and Berlin,[5] and a similar orbit between capitals informs his work. The streets of Paris lead to those of Berlin. The 'capital of the world' Paris (WB IV.i 356), as 'mirror-city' (WB IV.i 358), is reflected in the specular surfaces of its late-comer rival Berlin, the established 'ville lumière' projected into the spectacle of the *arriviste* 'Stadt des Lichtes' (City of Light). In this way, the Passage de l'Opéra as model arcade is mapped onto the 'Kranzlerecke' on Unter den Linden as a special *Schauplatz* of less public aspects of the city's cultural economy (WB V.i 88). But the mapping of Paris onto Berlin also involves an adjustment for 'the differently turned (round)' ('anders umgewandte') style of the Berlin streets (WB VII.ii 707) and thus to other modes of navigation. An emblematic site would thus be the Krumme Straße (Bent Street), the ambiguous inner and outer topographies of which are mapped in *Berliner Kindheit* (WB VII.i 415–16). Berlin is at once comparable to Paris and differently turned, or troped, displaying its own distinctive topographical and tropographical features. Its streets are turned round towards the off-street space of the arcades, but also especially towards that of the *Hof* or courtyard.

The notes to the *Passagen-Werk* record the need also to consider the various 'Passagen' of Berlin, not least the arcade and colonnades at the Hallesches Tor (WB V.ii 1022). This is a suitable frame or gate through which to enter Benjamin's Berlin and to explore the mnemotechnics of his memoir project on the city. Perceiving his home town via the optic of the foreign capital, Benjamin sees the Hallesches Tor through a tourist image in the shape of a postcard from his childhood collection, one that also appears as an image of Berlin both in *Berliner Chronik* and in the 'Winterabend' (Winter's Evening) scene of *Berliner Kindheit*. This urban image, brought to life by interior lamplight, and resonating in its name less with the city of Halle than with an encounter between two sites of passage – 'Gate and Hall' (WB VII.i 414) – represents the city as cast between its interiors and exteriors, between manipulated image and urban reality, between memory and presence. And memory here introduces the further category of dream. If the 'Hallesches Tor' is no longer a Gate (WB VII.ii 705), it functions nonetheless as a psycho-topographical gateway.

In the version of the card recalled in *Berliner Chronik*, and taken as a model for an experience of the city as seen in another light, the narrator concedes that it may be the memory of a dream version of the city that has taken the place occupied by the card as 'place-holder for reality' (WB VI 507).

---

[5] In a letter to Gershom Scholem of 18 September 1926, *Gesammelte Briefe*, vol. III, p. 195.

The postcard thus serves as a relay between 'Zeitraum' and 'Zeittraum', time-space and time-dream. As object of display, and memento of one of the representative spaces of *fin-de-siècle* Berlin, the card can be understood as a version of the exhibition hall, like the arcade or the railway station (both also part of the Hallesches Tor topography), one of the key transitory architectures of the nineteenth century and repositories for what Benjamin calls the 'vestiges of a dream world' (WB v.i 59). Benjamin's work on Berlin, too, is a kind of 'passage-work' and work of passage, not least working the passage between the dream-space remnants of the nineteenth century and the historical conditions of a new 'Zeitraum'. The 'Passage' and the 'Schwelle' (threshold), the determining topographical figures of the Parisian *Passagen-Werk*, are also at work in the representation of Berlin as a metropolis on the threshold, in passage, into the twentieth century.

As the arcade is understood as a form of passage that is a threshold in extension, a place of movement into another space but also one of hold-up, so Benjamin comes back again and again to the scenes from his early life at the threshold to the twentieth century, recording and revising the sites and rites of passage of a childhood in allegorical form. This 'Jahrhundertschwelle', or threshold of the century, is the temporal site or chronotope from which the 'bucklichte Männlein', the emblematic attendant who records his childhood experiences in the manner of a camera, calls (WB vii.i 430). What this differently turned figure – or disfigure – embodies, visualises, and invokes, is the placing of *Entstellung*, of psychocultural disfigurement and displacement into the sites and rites of urban passage. Part of the contortion involved here arises from looking both ways, so that the *bucklichte Männlein* as camera-man works in both past and future modes.[6] Benjamin's threshold memoir is Janus-faced, looking back from the 1930s to *c.* 1900, surveying the nineteenth century that lies behind it, and foreseeing what is to come of that outlived world in the catastrophe of the First World War and the social upheavals that follow. It is an account of origins, his own and those of the twentieth-century city, that – like the arcades in Benjamin's account – creates a hothouse of libidinal energies and attachments, but where the blocking of any possibility of traffic into spaces beyond also has pathological effects (WB v.i 93).

---

[6] In the 'Stefan Exemplar' version of *Berliner Kindheit* (Walter-Benjamin-Archiv) the role of the 'bucklichte Männlein' as camera-man is figured in a manner that combines the archaic technologies on one side of the threshold (the proto-cinematic flip-book) with the twentieth-century innovation of 'Momentaufnahmen' or snapshots.

In his preface to the final manuscript version of *Berliner Kindheit*, Benjamin describes the programmatic intent of the text as 'vaccine' (WB VII.i 385), giving controlled homeopathic doses of homesickness against that which might otherwise overwhelm him in exile. And in a letter to Bryher of 1937, the metaphor is repeated in a scene of unconscious reckoning that in its figurative logic already sets the author over the threshold into exclusion. He describes how he administered the vaccine against home-sickness when exile from the city of his childhood 'stood at the door' in 1932.[7] The account of the child's fever is only one form that this exposure to home-sickness takes, and inoculation is an appropriate, protective figure from childhood to apply to it. But this *pharmakon*, controlled above all through the practice of allegory, is also symptomatic of a chronically recrudescent melancholia, personal, cultural historical, and cultural topographical.[8]

Benjamin's analysis of allegory is established in *Ursprung des deutschen Trauerspiels* (Origin of the German Mourning-Play), where it is seen as the constitutive structural principle of the German baroque 'mourning-play'. The *Trauerspiel* exemplifies the work of the allegorist as alterist, manipulating things in order to speak of other things: 'In his hand the thing becomes something else ("etwas anderem"), he speaks through it of something else' (WB I.i 359). The very term *Trauerspiel* becomes such an altered thing here. The thesis works under an at once playful and mournful title, modulating between play and loss, the *Spiel* and the *Trauer* of the *Trauerspiel* genre. It is not properly speaking an analysis of the origins of that genre, for its concern is with speaking otherwise, away from origin. *Ursprung* is conceived here not as the moment, the particular temporal site, of the genre's coming-into-being, but as a complex spatio-temporal construct. The prefix of temporal originality, *Ur*, is projected into a figure of spatial mobility – *Sprung* as leap;[9] and what is derived from this speaking otherwise of *Ursprung* is a particular kind of chronotopical understanding. Origination is understood as a process over time and space: 'Origin ('Ursprung') does not mean the coming into being of what has arisen ('Entsprungenen'), but the coming and passing of what is arising ('Entspringendes')' (WB I.i 226)). It is turned towards historical contiguities, which Benjamin calls the 'pre- and post-history' (WB I.i 226) of the moment in question. It is inhabited by a different kind of direction, the dialectically turned lines of thinking

---

[7] Letter to Bryher of 19 December 1937, in Benjamin, *Gesammelte Briefe*, vol. V, p. 629.
[8] In his afterword to *Berliner Kindheit* (p. 177), Adorno describes it as capturing the irrecoverable in allegorical form.
[9] See also Samuel Weber, 'Genealogy of Modernity: History, Myth and Allegory in Benjamin's *Origin of the German Mourning Play*', *Modern Language Notes* 106.3 (April 1991), 465–500; pp. 469–71.

that project singularity, the spatio-temporal moment, into the historical-topographical fabric of repetition (WB I.i 226).

Origin implies at once repetition in time and redirection in space. Indeed, in Benjamin's thinking, the one dimension cannot be thought except through the other. The 'temporal process of movement' already mobilises time into being spoken otherwise, in terms of spatial procession, and it is in the form of a 'space-image' ('Raumbild') that it is captured and made amenable to analysis (WB I.i 271). The transposition of the historical process into topographical reckoning is the fundamental principle of the Benjaminian project in its various forms. Thus, his biographical project in *Berliner Chronik* is displaced from the sort of diachronic narrative that might be expected of the chronicle genre into speaking of space and of the temporally discontinuous (WB VI 488). The speaking of life here is also a speaking of death, and Berlin is distinguished as a city rife with places and moments 'when/where ('da') it bears witness to the dead' (WB VI 489). Under the sign of death, place and time become strangely enmeshed in another kind of *Zeitraum*, as witnessed by the 'da' that is used here in double apposition, incorporating the dimensions of time and space.

The speaking otherwise of origin applies as much to Berlin around 1900, Benjamin's personal *Zeitraum* of origin, as to the origins of the baroque mourning-play. Berlin at the start of a new century is also bound into what precedes and what succeeds it: it will give account of what has been, of what will come to be, and of what will come to have been. And its temporal dialectics are repeated and complicated by spatial dialectics: the topography of origin is displaced both inwards and outwards: to covert spaces in the interior and to other urban or extra-urban places. The preposition 'um' thus marks a chronotope or chronotrope, turned in order to mean around and about in both temporal and spatial terms.

Paris as 'capital of the nineteenth century', the city with which Berlin most directly competes as capital of capitals, is a key part of that dialectical rethinking of the chronotopical site of 'Berlin um 1900'. And the city of passages establishes a model that is comparable in many respects to that of the mourning-play: caught between the dynamic economy of play and the work of mourning what is past or becoming past. The allegorical disposition of the mourning-play is thus transferred, *mutatis mutandis*, through the passages of nineteenth-century Paris into the chronotopography of early twentieth-century Berlin. The corpse that is the 'key figure' for the early allegory of the baroque is converted through its passage into late modernity into the form of 'Andenken', the memento (WB I.ii 689): the cult of the souvenir as the commercial object that embodies the conversion of present experience into the recollection of what is lost in the past. Behind the memento lies the *memento mori*; not for nothing does a death's-head find its place among the street-scenes of *Einbahnstraße*, at an address advertising 'fancy goods' (WB IV.i 112). Indeed, the corpse that has supposedly been superseded is still built into the allegory of the modern city, emerging here in the form of the 'cadaver', which is dreamt up in the 'basement' of the allegorical 'house of our life' (WB IV.i 86).

The one-way street of this text is, in part, to be understood as a two-way conduit from Paris to Berlin, set in the former but also incorporating mementoes of the latter.[10] The inhabitant of the modern city thus assumes the role of the tourist, recollecting the experience of it after the event and at a distance. Benjamin puts 'Andenken' in quotation marks as if to register the way in which it speaks otherwise: a noun that retains a curious attachment to the verbal form from which it derives, so that the object becomes deployed into the temporality of the memorative process. Nineteenth-century allegory is, indeed, itself a kind of memento of the earlier baroque form, which acts as its displaced origin. For Benjamin, the *Passagen-Werk* too is a work of 'Ursprungsergründung' (establishing of the ground of origin (WB V.i 577)), where the origin is grounded precisely in the dialectical time-space of *passage*, deployed over the prehistory, the history, and the post-history of the arcades. This is the ambivalent disposition of the mnemotechnical enterprise. And Benjamin's work on the origins of twentieth-century Berlin is no less ambivalently cast between the mobility of development and the melancholy of time and space lost.

PALACES AND OTHER SHOW-PLACES

The Berlin of 1900 was, in many of its representative structures, a baroque city. The architectural and topographical image of the baroque court was spread through its centre in a series of palaces and their landscapes, and the baroque style returned in the exteriors and interiors of much of the new construction that occurred in the decades around 1900. It seems plausible, therefore, to understand this key element of the city's architectural and topographical heritage as an appropriate stage-set for the mourning-play of the city's twentieth-century history, its *Schauplatz*: scene, stage, and show-place. Two examples of the grafting of modern structures onto baroque

---

[10] Thus, at the address 'Vergrößerungen' (Enlargements), we find passages borrowed from the territory of *Berliner Kindheit* in the shape of the child's memento collection, described as a sort of crypto-city of spectacle, where drawers become 'arsenal and zoo, crime museum and crypt' (WB IV.i 115).

architectures may illustrate this: Erich Mendelsohn's 1923 reconstruction of the Mossehaus with its neo-baroque interior, as discussed in Chapter 3, and Daniel Libeskind's building of the Jewish Museum onto the baroque palace that housed the Berlin Museum. In either case, the reworking of the baroque style is understandable as a performing of traumatic historical experience and of the mourning that follows upon it. The tension between continuity and discontinuity, the traumatic ruptures of history, is programmatic for Libeskind's building, and the grafting of his irregular postmodern block onto the side of the baroque museum, represents the first-order form of that principle. It exemplifies Freud's dictum that historical succession is only representable in the form of spatial contiguity, all the more so when the axis of historical continuity has been traumatically breached. The baroque edifice, notwithstanding its symmetry of form and surface, is peculiarly ready to supply the visual frame for such an experience of historical trauma and the melancholic *vanitas* that is attached to it.

In Benjamin's account, the baroque court is at once the place and the non-place of the mourning-play. The court becomes the appropriate interior framework and décor of display, the 'innermost scene' ('innerste Schauplatz') for the fixing of historical experience in the dimension of space (WB I.i 271). And yet, this scene or stage for displaying history is also mobile, subject to topographical shifts. It is no real site, but, bound to the itinerant court, a 'wandering stage' (WB I.i 298). The *Schauplatz* for the baroque dramas of passage is in itself a thing of passage: a '*non-lieu*', as Samuel Weber calls it, where mobility of location, suspension of place, also implies a limit to jurisdiction.[11] The mobile *Hof* thus also slips into and mobilises the *Gerichtshof* or tribunal, as a place of judgement.[12] And this is certainly the case with the baroque styling of the stage for the historical drama of twentieth-century Berlin. The courts and courtrooms of the twentieth century move around the city, from palace to palace, and with them move the scenes of the juridical and political drama. The baroque palaces of the Wilhelminian era are appropriated for new regimes to hold court. The Prinz-Albrecht-Palais was first an imperial residence, then quarters for guests of the Weimar Republic, then the headquarters of the SS Security Service. And the Stadtschloss provided the setting for Karl Liebknecht's declaration of the establishment of the Räterrepublik from the balcony of the Eosander-portal on 9 November 1918, then came to make

---

[11] Weber, 'Genealogy of Modernity', p. 490.
[12] See also Kafka's Berlin 'tribunal', where the 'Askanischer Hof' hotel came to function as *Gerichtshof*, a place of judgement in passage.

way for the GDR Palace of the Republic, and is now ready to make way in its turn for a return to the baroque. As Christa Wolf writes in *Leibhaftig* (In Person (2002)), the Palace of the Republic is 'built to go under',[13] always already a ruin and so emblematic for what she sees as a city in demise.

In the period since the *Wende*, the Palace of the Republic has been in an extended process of what might be called, following the 1996 work by Sophie Calle that features the building, *Entfernung* or detachment.[14] This melancholic process of dismantling and displacement is nicely captured in time-based form by Tacita Dean's film piece, *Palast* (Palace (2004)). The work seems to be in dialogue with Calle's piece, as indicated by its featuring of graffiti reading 'AWAY' on one of the panels of the palace. The place of the detached GDR emblem, which is the focus of Calle's work is not seen in Dean's film, which remains fixed on the more general texture of the building. The film records the passage of time, but is also melancholically fixed in its focus, with barely any movement of image, so that the framework of the panels seems to suggest a fixing of the medium itself in freeze frames. The melancholic effect is heightened by the reduction of the palace to its parts, its shrinkage into a projected image the size of a TV or home movie screen, and the distressing of the surface of the image with lines running down it as if the substance of the building were bleeding or weeping out of it: the sands of time, or metal and glass in molten flow. By mimicking the material vulnerability of old film, Dean's piece sees the palace itself as a kind of old film, with images of the city reflected in more or distorted forms in its framework. It performs the paradox of the melancholic condition: holding temporal and spatial passage in a frozen state.

Arnolt Bronnen's reading of the allegorical figures on top of the Stadt-schloss in a feuilleton piece from 1929 seems to foresee the building's melancholy history: nine withered men, one of them holding up his hand in warning. When he looks through the Eosander-portal, also known as the Liebknecht-portal, with its 'strange, grey stone',[15] it is with a view rendered melancholic by what has gone before. In Benjamin's account, stone is the particular material of melancholic *acedia* or torpor. The Eosander-portal was subsequently fixed to the Staatsratsgebäude (National Council Building), another of the GDR palaces of the people (or their representatives), and now taken over by the European School of Management and Technology, which recognises the commodity fetish value of the

[13] Christa Wolf, *Leibhaftig* (Munich: Luchterhand, 2002), p. 146.
[14] See also Charity Scribner, *Requiem for Communism* (Cambridge Mass.: MIT Press, 2003), pp. 24–43.
[15] Arnolt Bronnen, 'Unter den Linden', in Knobloch, *Der Berliner zweifelt immer*, pp. 455–6; p. 456.

refurbished GDR interiors. As a remnant of the baroque ruin was appropriated into the building as memento of, and *memento mori* for, the *ancien régime*, so the Socialist Realist allegories are now appropriated in similar style and strategy by high capitalism, mementoes made to speak otherwise in the international marketplace.

In the light of the characteristic, motley careers of these palatial buildings, it is perhaps appropriate that the German Historical Museum is now located in one of the representative baroque palaces of the city, Andreas Schlüter's Zeughaus or arsenal building on Unter den Linden, but with a postmodern glass extension by Pei built onto it. The double structure at once drastically marks historical difference, the new start of millennial Berlin, and constructs a transparent viewing frame upon the past, serving the spectacle of the baroque palace and its emblematic insignia. Glass looks upon stone. Benjamin reports the view that the baroque palace tends to be allegorically inhabited by 'sad Melancholy' (WB i.i 322), and much of what the Historical Museum has to show is indeed melancholic. It bears witness to the melancholy histories of the city's other palaces and the courts that inhabited them. The inner courtyard of the Zeughaus building is lined with a sequence of decapitated heads in atrophy or agony, larding the composed architectural lines of the baroque style with the physiognomy of death. And while most of the figures on the outside of the building are headless and bodiless collections of armour, an exception is the head of the Medusa, an apotropaic figure that both embodies and wards off the threat of decapitation and death. The arsenal building at once celebrates the martial project and exhibits its dreadful consequences. It is the representative depot of a militarism that fuelled two world wars and a Cold War, and like the processing hall attached to Friedrichstraße station for crossings between East and West, is a palace of tears.

The ruin-in-the-making of the Palace of the Republic presents the most recent version of the scene and spectacle, the *Schauplatz*, of Berlin's historical melancholy. The twentieth-century version of the melancholic condition has moved from the preserve of court culture to a people's palace, where a new regime, already defunct, held court. At its most sleek and glamorous, this was a palace that sat uncomfortably with the ruins that the East German state maintained, and now, as the ruinous surfaces of so much of the Eastern part of the city have been restored, so the parade building is itself made into a spectacle, a *Schauplatz*, of ruin.

Benjamin's account of the allegorical disposition in *Ursprung* is constantly organised around the *topos* of the *Schauplatz*, projected through the relay of the stage, the palace and the wandering court. As an allegorical construct, this scene is inherently of the other, a space of alterity. Its archetypal form is thus the ruin in the landscape, representing the transfer of history into the 'Schauplatz' (WB I.i 353). As it incorporates history (WB I.i 355), the 'Schauplatz' becomes less the show-place for other spectacles than the spectacle in itself. The ruin, and with it the 'Schauplatz' that has incorporated it, is the corollary of the mortified physiognomy, the *facies hippocratica*, which allegorical thinking recognises and figures in things. What is untimely, painful, and failing in history is thus represented less by a face than by the baroque emblem of the death's-head (WB I.i 343), or the agonised physiognomies of the Zeughaus heads.

Beneath the extravagance of baroque architectures and cultural representations lies the recognition of 'lack of freedom, incompletion, and brokenness' (WB I.i 352), and the allegorist textures representation to incorporate those melancholy insights. Ostentation is also inherently ruination, as in the elaborate facture of Calderon's works, like a wall exposed when it has lost its rendering (WB I.i 355). The example from Calderon instantiates the principle of the *Schriftbild*, the 'image' of the writing on the page, which provides the intermedial model for allegory. Its constitution is dialectically divided between excess and lack, overloading and amorphous fragmentation (WB I.i 351–2). The architectural façade under the sign of ruin, the face as Hippocratic landscape, and the inscription of history in its plenitude and emptiness form a constellation that is at once figure and ground, show and place. It is a site of preservation and passage, spectacle and void.

Benjamin's melancholic *Schauplatz* of history can also be understood in a more psycho-historical way: as the show-place for psycho-topographical condensations and displacements. In other words, this scene, which is defined by its speaking otherwise of historical experience, can be aligned with the allegorical other *Schauplatz* that defines the place of the unconscious for Freud. The allegorical mode speaks, through its emblematic transcription of one thing into another, of other, covert or cryptic places; and the unconscious might well be understood as a privileged form of such a 'domain of hidden knowledge' (WB I.i 359). In both the allegorical mode and the figurations of the unconscious, the principle of showing hidden knowledge that is at work is a form of *Entstellung*, following de Man's gloss of allegory as the 'figure which disfigures'. The paradigms for allegorical representation – the Hippocratic physiognomy or the skull, the corpse, the ruin, and the fraught text-image – can all also be understood as mapping out the otherness at work in psychical (dis)figuration, its other scene.

Benjamin works to show that allegory, in the exemplary form of the baroque *Trauerspiel*, incorporates both a melancholic moment of fixation and a form of irregular mobility that is inherent in the principle of speaking otherwise of things. It is characterised by an 'intermittent rhythmics of constant arrest, sporadic flipping over, and renewed paralysis' (WB I.i. 373). This is the distinctive rhythm of Benjamin's signature structure of thought, speech, and image, 'Dialektik im Stillstand' (dialectics at a standstill). It is an imagistic holding in place that also turns out of place, and hence is an incorporation of *Entstellung*. The rhythm that Benjamin describes here seems appropriate as a model for the ways in which history takes disfigured form in the *Zeitraum* of twentieth-century Berlin, and for the inevitable twists, turns, and fixtures that must figure in, and disfigure, the accounting of it.

Following Freud's account in *Moses and Monotheism*, *Entstellung* also embodies a form of irregular removal: the estranging form of displacement that is implicit in the notion of the scene of the unconscious *qua* other. Freud's case here is the scene of a crime, both actual and textual, and it lends itself to thinking about the evidence of historical violence, which – subject to repression – returns elsewhere, in other forms. The tracing of these returns, which make up the dispersed but interconnected structure of the 'other scene', is the work of the psycho-topographer. For Benjamin, as for Freud, psycho-topographers both, *Entstellung* is a performative term, representing the principle of disfigurement in its own structure, demanding to be read in itself as a condensed and displaced configuration of meanings. This is the implication of Benjamin's hyphenation of the term when he makes a parallel between the 'eccentric' psycho-physicality of the clown and of 'primitive peoples', suggesting that both involve a 'dislocation of shame', understandable as 'Ent-stellung' (WB VI 132). Benjamin's hyphen incorporates the same opening up of the register of *Entstellung* as in Freud, acting at once upon the figure and its ground, body and place.

A similar principle of 'Ent-stellung', of dis-figurement and dis-location, applies to the workings of memory, both individual and collective, in Benjamin's account. Mneme, the muse of memory, is to be found in physical bodies and in space, bearing the *memento mori* (WB I.i 392) and so marked out as a martyr to memory. She is an emblematic figure for the 'speaking otherwise', the disfigured and displaced speech, of allegory, and thus inhabits both the individual body, under the disfiguring sign of decay, and the ruin. The particular kind of memory that is subject to the disfiguring and displacing of repression has to be teased out of urban topography; and the psycho-topographer in search of a Mneme disfigured and displaced by the history of the city where she resides cannot always guarantee to realise Freud's criminological model and recognise the disfigured truth of the 'other scene'.

In the course of her discussion of the relationship between Freud and Benjamin, Sigrid Weigel notes a slip in Benjamin's notation of a passage from *Jenseits des Lustprinzips* (Beyond the Pleasure Principle): Freud asserts that consciousness arises 'an Stelle der Erinnerungsspur' (in place of the memory trace (SF XIII 25)), while Benjamin records this as 'an der Stelle ...' (in the place of ... (WB I.ii 612)). Weigel takes this discrepancy as evidence that Benjamin was working from memory here, aided by notes. We might say that he was working from the *aide mémoire*, which, following our discussion of the 'Wunderblock', takes the place of memory through a process of 'Ent-stellung'. Weigel calls the quotation distorted, 'entstellt',[16] and it seems tempting to see it as an example of what we saw Freud call 'Textentstellung'. The altered quotation is, precisely, an 'Ent-stellung' – a dislocation of the 'Stelle' construction, introducing slippage into what Benjamin calls Freud's 'fundamental sentence' (WB I.ii 612). The dialectical constitution of the relationship between consciousness and memory trace, the fact that the former arises in place of but also in *the* place of the latter, is given emphasis by Benjamin's slip. This is the allegorical site of the allegorical figure Mneme, her *Schauplatz* we might say, her other scene.

That the truth of the 'other scene' must be a melancholy one, marked by memorative dislocation, is undeniable. But the melancholic in Benjamin's analysis does not have to remain fixed in negation, as it appears to be constructed in the Manichean model of Freud's *Mourning and Melancholia* (*Trauer und Melancholie*). In that essay, melancholy is the psychopathological fixation upon, incorporation of, the lost object, while mourning undertakes work with the loss. Freud himself came to reassess this model in a more dialectical fashion, and this is certainly more in keeping with Benjamin's thinking on the modality of melancholy. For, while Benjamin recognises the Hippocratic face of history as melancholic, he also sees the potential for work and play in, and in spite of, the melancholic condition. While the prefix 'Trauer-', as derived from the 'Trauerbühne' as stage and catafalque, has what Benjamin describes as a vampiric, fixing effect upon that to which it attaches itself (WB I.i 299), when attached to 'Spiel' it is inevitably subject in its turn to more vital and dynamic forces. The 'Trauerspiel' becomes something more dialectical, therefore, a version perhaps of the game of loss and recuperation that is played by Freud's grandson as the prelude to *Beyond the Pleasure Principle* and seen in that essay as a model for how adult dramas and narratives work. The 'fort-da' game, projecting into the territory beyond

---

[16] Sigrid Weigel, *Body- and Image-Space: Re-reading Walter Benjamin*, trans. Georgina Paul *et al.* (London and New York: Routledge, 1996), p. 117.

the principle of pleasure ('Lust'), beyond for instance the stage-space of the 'Lustspiel' (comedy), is fundamentally driven by the death drive, but never simply located on the side of that drive.

Notwithstanding its melancholic predisposition, Benjamin's account finds creative energy in the model of the 'Trauerspiel' and its allegorical workings. As in the proto-baroque iconographics of Dürer's allegory of *Melencolia I* (1514), a more dialectical functioning emerges, whereby the saturnine figure is attached to both destruction and creativity. Benjamin cites the contention from the classic reading of the image by Erwin Panofsky and Fritz Saxl that it is this dichotomy that makes melancholy at once 'so enviable and uncanny' for later times (WB I.i 327). Certainly, the winged Melancholy has that uncanny attraction in his own work. And the attraction of the Berlin of Benjamin's time, like that of our own, is often the uncanny, not to say perverse, one of the *Schauplatz* of historical melancholy. What the more dialectical understanding of the figure of melancholy suggests, however, is that, rather than being irremediably fixed in negative space, it can also sustain creative work of critical representation and analysis. Dürer's angel is preoccupied with work of measurement, and behind the figure stands a block of stone, either abandoned against, or ready to be hoisted up, a ladder. The relative position of the two objects and their framework is curiously uncertain: the ladder seems to twist out of one plane into another as the eye follows it up and is leaning on a wall that is at once inside and outside, as the figure is disfigured in its relationship to its ground. This icon of melancholy thus establishes a special relation between that condition and architectural construction and framing, under the sign of *Entstellung*. The polyhedral block becomes a special iconographic emblem for the disposition of melancholy. It stands for work, but also resists a workable function, suggesting an irregular hole in the building that is impossible to fit.

The building block is uncannily close to representing the ruinous failure of building work. Thus Cranach's reworking of the melancholic angel in his *Melancholie* (1532) transforms the irregular block into a void in the curiously distorted shape of a window frame, and takes out the back wall of the building as if for another monstrously outsized window. Inside and outside are uncannily open to each other, displaced over irregular thresholds, in these renderings of the *Schauplatz* of melancholy. The preponderance of German works – from Dürer and Cranach to Immendorff and Kiefer – in the *Melancholie* exhibition mounted in the New National Gallery in Berlin in 2006, led to renewed debates over whether melancholy is a 'German feeling'. There certainly seems to have been a special affinity between the concerns of the exhibition and the disposition of the German capital hosting it in early 2006. The regular glass box of Mies van der Rohe's gallery served as an apposite mediating frame between the exhibition, with its recurrent iconography of irregular stone blocks, and the 'stony city' caught in the melancholic humour of an extended (post-unification) winter without.

If the Berlin of early 2006 seemed cast under the sign of melancholy, this should perhaps be seen in conjunction with the watchword of unification in 1989: euphoria. This would diagnose twentieth-century Berlin as schizoid in disposition. Thus, Jürgen Böttcher's documentary film *Die Mauer* (The Wall (1990)) records the euphoria of the mass events around the dismantling of the Wall, but also its more melancholic aspects. A female performance artist in a tulle dress and clutching a rose is shown pressing herself into the partially dismantled structure, as if in an impossible melancholic-hysterical attachment to it. Just as the euphoria of 1989 was accompanied by more melancholic counter-reactions, so the melancholy of early 2006 ran alongside the anticipated euphoria of hosting the World Cup: *Trauer* conjoined with *Spiel*. Thus, the representative space of the Platz der Republik around the Reichstag was prepared by Adidas for a mock-up of the Olympic Stadium, a simulacrum of Berlin-Germania at the heart of the city.

This was also the scene of another spectacle in the summer of 2005, when an amateur pilot crashed his plane in front of the parliament building, a desperate suicide raising fears of a copycat Berlin 9/11.[17] The burnt-out ground where the wreckage had lain was the photo-shoot of the moment: a melancholic scene of personal misery but also the shadow-site of another German autumn, provoking debate over no-fly zones over the centre of the capital in the age of high-tech, international terrorism. The patch of burnt grass can be understood as a trace of the absence both of the actual act and of the fantasised, terrorist version of it – of a Berlin ground zero. In this, it follows the pattern set out by Benjamin in his account of 'Accidents and Crimes' in *Berliner Kindheit*. The perverse predicament of the *flâneur* as voyeur is never to be 'there on the spot' (WB IV.i 291), always to arrive after the event at scenes of urban catastrophe, accidental or criminal. The scene of the accident or the crime thus takes on a melancholic cast, the *Schauplatz* as object of fixation in loss.[18] Even in open space, the catastrophic element follows the elusive logic of the destructive flame, concealed 'deep in the

---

[17] The spectacle recalls that described by Kracauer after the burning of the Reichstag in 1933, the smouldering ruin as an image of the historical abyss with an aeroplane circling above as if anticipating future modes of destruction. See Kracauer, 'Rund um den Reichstag', *Schriften* V.iii, pp. 211–12.

[18] The same form of melancholic late arrival afflicts Kracauer in his recording of Nazi vandalism against Jewish businesses. See Kracauer, 'Zertrümmerte Fensterscheiben', *Schriften* V.ii, pp. 236–7.

interior of the courtyard' (WB VII.i 424). It is a threat to the protective structures of the city's architectures, not least in the most distinctive of Berlin's vernacular spaces, the courtyard or *Hof*.

COURTS AND COURTYARDS

> And how hopeless it would be
> In the name of the city of Berlin
> Only to wish first to speak of its streets
> Which have least within them and not
> Of its courtyards which hold the most   (WB VII.ii 708)

In its exemplary, baroque form, allegory is a thing at once of play and of uncanny mortality, enacted in the court as show-place. Allegory is attended here by a *Hof*, the 'figural centre' surrounded by a constellation of emblematic attendants (WB I.i 364). The *Hof* is the court both as spatial frame and as assembly of figures. Whether in the baroque or in Romantic reworkings of it, the court acts as a site of confusion for the performance of contradictory principles. *Der verwirrte 'Hof'* (The confused 'court') accordingly serves as an exemplary title for Benjamin, whereby the principle of 'Sammlung' – the gathering of courtly persons and objects – is confused with that of 'Zerstreuung', both 'distraction' and 'scattering'; the law of the court combines the two (WB I.i 364). While Benjamin cites Carl Schmitt's model of exceptional sovereignty in his discussion of the baroque monarch (WB I.i 245), he casts the autonomy of this model and its power of assembly into a more confused state here. This is to say that the court as space and assembly is ruled by a law of exception, where, to use Schmitt's terms, as borrowed or excepted by Giorgio Agamben for more ambiguous purposes, an *Ordnung* (order) incorporating a principle of dispersal maps onto an *Ortung* (placement) without coherent boundaries.[19] Collection or assembly mixed with distraction or dispersal must result in a dislocated order. The court is cast between *nomos*, the order entrenched in its spatial regime, and the legal and topographical disorder of *anomos*.

   In this spirit, the *Hof* as show-place of Benjamin's account of the baroque *Trauerspiel* also looks forward to the other kind of court(yard) that is the figural centre of the chronicle of the city of his childhood. Here, too, the centre is a contradictory, off-centre site – a space for speaking otherwise,

---

[19] For Agamben, Schmitt fails to see the 'zone of indistinction or exception' that dislocates his model. Agamben, *Homo Sacer*, pp. 19–20. He elaborates this 'non-place' in his *State of Exception*, trans. Kevin Attell (Chicago/London: University of Chicago Press, 2005).

askance from the official, frontal narrative. It is neither inside nor out, a space between the domestic domain and the topographical territories without. Like the classic urban *Zwischenraum* (between-space) of the arcade as intermediary between 'street and interior' (WB I.ii 539), the *Hof* is an interstitial and a liminal site. On the one hand, it is a particular and private space, the narrator's 'court' as both viewing and listening space, following the model of the baroque court as innermost 'Schauplatz' (WB I.i 271). On the other, it is a generic space, a systemic feature of the city structure, projecting the exterior interior across the city and into other urban spaces. The intimate space of the 'court', as adopted and adapted from the courtly model by the bourgeoisie, is shadowed by the abject forms it takes in the deprived areas of the city. These other courts – *Hinterhöfe* (rear-courtyards) we might call them – are the abject counterpart to the *Hof* proper and an example of how the latter carries a constellation of others with it. The pattern of the central figure surrounded by a scattered assembly is reproduced in the relation of the child's own *Hof* to a court of other, attendant courtyards. The most immediate and concentric of these are such as the 'Blumeshof' where his grandmother lives, and the most remote those seen behind tenement façades elsewhere in the city. Then there is the wider genus represented by institutional sites of assembly, each of them interstitial spaces between inside and out: the *Bahnhof* (station), the *Schulhof* (schoolyard), and the *Friedhof* (graveyard).

The function of the *Hof* as figural centre for the autobiographical text is established in the scene that Benjamin sets as a programmatic 'self-portrait' at the start of the final version of *Berliner Kindheit*, 'Loggien' (Loggias).[20] While the 'Mummerehlen' scene had provided a more direct, photographic kind of emblematic signature at the start of the earlier version, 'Loggien' displaces the establishing focus onto the spatial framework of the *Schauplatz*. The loggia serves here as an intermediary space, a zone of transit, between domestic interior and *Hof*, as the child's experience is projected outwards into a wider visual frame and echo chamber. As the oriel is a niche of the house projected into the street and vice versa (WB V.i 512), so the loggia projects the apartment into the *Hof* and vice versa. It serves as a kind of camera and listening device, a prosthetic apparatus for the infant and the developing child, helping to register the sights and activities of the courtyard *in camera*.

The child's cradle is guarded by the caryatids from the neighbouring loggia, setting him programmatically under the architectural sign of

---

[20] See Benjamin's letter of 12 August 1933 to Gretel Karplus, *Gesammelte Briefe*, vol. IV, p. 275.

allegory. At the same time, these figures more commonly found supporting portals are here removed from the façade to the 'Rückfront' (literally, 'rear front'), indicating the 'differently turned (round) style of the Berlin streets'. Under the aegis of these allegorical figures, the child adopts the *habitus* of the allegorist, with the dark patch of earth behind bars around a tree in the courtyard the special site of his melancholic interest. From here, the 'gloomy musings' are relayed to the similar holes in the surface of the city to be found at the 'carriage stops' ('Droschkenhaltestellen') and so at once projected into the mobility of the transportation network and yet melancholically held up at the point of projection. These sites of arrested observation thus become colonised for the court or courtyard as extensions of its proximal regime: 'more remote provinces of my court' (WB VII.i 387).

The regime of this first *Hof* is a melancholy one, setting the biographical origin under that disposition, after the fashion of the baroque *Trauerspiel*. Thus, the loggia is also a melancholic 'show-place', an uninhabitable room, a ruin, and a tomb. It is a place of second-order exile for the palm-tree, all the more homeless for having been evicted from its first place of exile, the neighbouring salon. It is marked by Pompeian red, as if in anticipation of its own ruin. Anthony Vidler sees Pompeii as the uncanny city of the past that haunts the modern metropolis with the prospect of being buried alive,[21] and the un-homeliness of the home city is encoded here into home space. In the *Passagen-Werk*, Benjamin draws a parallel between the effect of stepping over the threshold into an early nineteenth-century panorama and the discovery of the buried civilisations of Pompeii and Herculaneum on the one hand, and the aftershock of the French Revolution on the other (WB V.i 511). The Pompeian decoration of the loggia as threshold space of the early twentieth-century Berlin bourgeoisie might be seen to carry the threat of revolutionary ruin or of incendiary catastrophe for this class.

While the loggia is coloured with the prospect of ruination, this is also recuperated, to a degree at least, through the idea of the ruin as memorial. The viewing and listening box is also a sort of memory box. In *Berliner Chronik*, Benjamin figures the faculty of memory – *Gedächtnis* – as the medium and 'Schauplatz' of recall, like the earth in an archaeological dig (WB VI 486). Here, the Pompeian structure of the loggia is configured with the earth that the child views from it as a medium and framing site as well as an object of memory, and hence a model entry point for his text of personal and collective cultural archaeology. The 'spot' ('Stelle') in the dark ground that fascinates him is the equivalent of that invoked in the archaeological

---

[21] Vidler, *Architectural Uncanny*, p. 47.

allegory of memory work in *Berliner Chronik*, in the form of 'this dark happiness of the place ('Ort und Stelle') of finding' (WB VI 486). Placement here is not merely a mnemotechnical instrument; it forms part of the very substance or medium of memory. Indeed, in the textual archaeology of *Berliner Chronik*, the site itself has a special material status, given that 'von Ort und Stelle' (literally 'of the place and spot') is one of the very few additions made to the manuscript.[22] It is a place, it seems, recalled and recorded after the fact. It at once indicates the vital importance of place in the mediation of memory and its mobility and contingency in that role. If we follow Davide Giuriato's micrographical analysis of the childhood memoir texts, which sees the manuscript and typescript versions of *Berliner Chronik* and *Berliner Kindheit* as constructing through their layout on the page a topographical 'Schauplatz' for the memory text,[23] we can understand 'Ort und Stelle' as a kind of found object, exposed in the manuscript only to be concealed in the textual medium in its final form.

If the happiness of the site of the find is, like the 'dark earth' of memory, a sombre one, it indicates something of the infection of the archaeological work of memory with the condition of the 'dead cities' (WB VI 486) that are its object. The archaeological allegory of *Berliner Chronik* also establishes the ground for the investigations of *Berliner Kindheit*, where the logic of the 'Stelle' as memory site is projected into that of *Entstellung*: removal to another place. The obscure 'Stelle' of the patch of earth in the courtyard thus projects the child's investigation onto the 'Halte-Stellen' or stopping-points as other places of arrested attention. With its bars running over underground space, it can also be understood as foreseeing the fascination of the child for that inhabitant of the urban underground, uncanny home visitor and embodiment of *Entstellung*, the 'bucklichte Männlein', also fantasised as seen through a grate in his other place (WB VII.i 429). For both *Berliner Chronik* and *Berliner Kindheit*, the city is a network of other places in this sense, at once a site of creative reconstruction and revival and a dead city with only disfigured and displaced survivals. What we can call, following Freud, the 'Textentstellung' of the insertion of the 'Ort und Stelle' phrase – a felicitous find for the textual archaeologist and topographer – can be understood as evidence of that alteration of place, even as it serves to establish the primacy of the act of location. And the tautology of the formulation, its excessive placement, serves only to emphasise the sort of

---

[22] The addition is marked by a cross on p. 23 of the manuscript held in the Walter-Benjamin-Archiv.

[23] Davide Giuriato, *Mikrographien: Zu einer Poetologie des Schreibens in Walter Benjamins Kindheitserinnerungen (1932–1939)* (Munich: Fink, 2006), p. 124.

relaying and altering of place and space that is at work in an archaeological site like the loggia, with uncanny echoes of Jensen's *Gradiva*.

The loggia remains cast between the vital work of recall and morbidity. When the child's reading group gathers to read *Romeo and Juliet*, another drama that might go under the heading of the 'confused court', so the call-and-response from the balcony is refigured into a scene of *prosopopoeia*, with Romeo's last sigh seeking an echo from beyond the grave in the *Hof* as tomb. The group reads by gaslight, which for Benjamin is the ambiguous lighting effect inherited from the nineteenth century, and in particular from its original 'Schauplatz' (WB v.i 45), the arcades, suggesting that the loggia is the domestic equivalent of that display structure between interior and exterior. Gaslight is a recurrent feature of the *mise-en-scène* of these texts and always suggests forms of ambivalence, a projection of outer spaces into interiors (WB I.ii 552) and vice versa. It characteristically falls on surfaces that are 'doppelbödig', implying false or double ground: on asphalt or tiles that suggest another surface below, whether outside or in. Thus Benjamin's review of Hessel's *Spazieren in Berlin* (Walking in Berlin (1929)) describes gaslight as casting an 'ambiguous light' over the 'double ground' of the cobbles, challenging the mnemotechnical skills of the *flâneur* (WB III 194). And the 'Gasstrumpf' (gas-mantle), in particular, associates this form of lighting with the conundrum of the rolled-up socks ('Strümpfe'), which are described as an innermost core of the domestic world of *Berliner Kindheit* (WB VII.i 416), where inside and outside, container and content are, however, collapsed. The centre of this at once epicentric and excentric figure is only another surface.

The loggia is the architectural equivalent of this emblematic figure: the focal point that is also at the edge, an other scene between inside and out. While the loggia marks the boundary between domestic space and the domain of the 'city god' Berlin, the liminal place at which the urban deity is deemed to be perfectly self-present, it is also, by virtue of this, uninhabitable. The allegorical constellation of the caryatids is replaced here by that of Berlin, with Place and Time at its feet, a 'Zeitraum' or time-space configuration in which the child is also enclosed as if in his dedicated mausoleum (WB VII.i 388). The place of origin is always already a place of death, or of burial alive, at the boundary, the viewing- and hearing-post between home and the city.

From this first *Hof*, the autobiographical texts unfold a sequence of others. Their constellation – the form of the 'meta-*Hof*', the court of courts as assembly described above – is variable, playing with the multiple resonances of the word *Hof*. It modulates between the image of the aureole or corona disposed around a central figure (such as those that surround the child's memories of the theatre when they emerge out of the fog of his childhood with their 'Höfen' (WB VI 505)) and that of the flight or tunnel (WB VII.i 120), whereby one *Hof* leads to another in a structure of *mise-en-abyme*. The first of these is established in the home-from-home of the 'Blumeshof', residence of the child's maternal grandmother, where the child is more at home than in the parental apartment, as though displacing this from its position of origin.

The 'Blumeshof' is allegorically constructed as a centred figure: the grandmother as regent in her court and centre of its flower. As a traveller, she provides the model of the mobile court, creating 'colonies of the Blumeshof' (WB VII.i 411). And from her loggia, too, the child has access to views and sounds of strange 'Höfe' and their assemblies (WB VII.i 412). Yet this centric, imperial model is also subject to pressures of dislocation. The exclusion of misery from this 'court', and in particular the experience of death, also makes it an uncanny place, the 'Schauplatz' of bad dreams (WB VII.i 412). It becomes an other scene for the return of the repressed, its stairway and threshold in the thrall of an 'Alp' or nightmare figure. This is the counter figure to that of the 'Blume-zof' (WB VII.i 411), the corruption of the 'Blumeshof' that constructs it as a configuration of flower ('Blume') and maid ('Zofe'). The servant figures that are the benevolent guardians of the thresholds in the bourgeois homes of Benjamin's childhood, retainers at its court, here meet their mythological match in the allegorical figure, or disfigure, of the malevolent *genius loci*, associate of that other threshold disfigure, the *bucklichte Männlein*.

The 'Blumeshof' is thus projected from the centric constellation of the flower with its astral corona towards the figure of flight under the aspect of *Entstellung*, of disfigurement and displacement. It is telling that when, in *Einbahnstraße*, Benjamin uses 'Hof' in the sense of corona or aura,[24] it is in conjunction with the anticipation of loss: when he lost a beloved object he had the sense that it had had a 'Hof' of mockery or mourning about it (WB IV.i 142). This is taken from a section under the address of clairvoyant Madame Ariane, 'second court on the left' (WB IV.i 141), and it suggests that there is always such a second 'Hof' shadowing the first with its anticipation of loss, mockery, or mourning. The court of courts leads from the home court/yard, via the 'Blumeshof' as ostensible home-from-home and the more

---

[24] See also Samuel Weber, *Mass Mediauras: Form, Technics, Media* (Stanford: Stanford University Press, 1996), pp. 93–4.

abject or illicit likes of Madame Ariane's 'second court', to more institutional or public versions of the *Hof*.

The network between the home 'Hof', the abject other courtyards, and the 'Hof' as institutional space is given in *Berliner Chronik*, in a sequence of moves from private to public and back again. The focus of one section of the text starts in the inner sanctum of the child's bed and introduces 'the city' into it in the form of a ray of light under the door (WB VI 503). By being described as 'inside', the social gathering that embodies the entry of the city also implicitly turns the bedroom out of its innermost position into an outpost (WB VI 503). This expulsion or release from interiority then leads, via the echo chamber of the 'Hof' outside, to the stations of the city at large, so connecting it with the world beyond. Under the sign of the 'Bahnhof', the child is transmitted across the constellated spaces, moving in and out. The 'Höfe' that took the child in or released it are duly associated with 'Bahnhöfe', the stations as places of panoramic viewing at the moment of departure (WB VI 503). On the one hand, the station as show-place opens up the vista of travel beyond the city, albeit in the form of the frame of a 'fata morgana', with the rails merging in the fog. On the other, on the way back into the city, arrival in the station opens up other closed-off spaces, closer to home. The traveller is made to look awry, adopt a transversal perspective upon his city, in the sidelined shape of the abject courtyards seen from the tracks. The light that came under the door at the start of the section, embodying the city for the child's gaze, now returns in the form of the light from windows in those courtyards, transmuted into his eyes as 'courtyard windows' set in damaged walls (WB VI 503).

In the revision of this section for the early version of *Berliner Kindheit*, in the scene 'Abreise und Rückkehr' (Departure and Return), the shaft of light under the door is appropriated as a sign of preparations for departure, and compared to the expectations raised by the light under a theatre curtain. The scene of departure is duly played out under the sign of dream-theatre. When he awakes from his dream, the child feels as if he already has the journey behind him. And when the journey starts, he is beset by a sense of sadness that the 'dreary company' still continues ('noch anhielt' (WB IV.i 245–6)). This persistence of the domestic status quo even in the act of travel asks to be double-read as a form of dream-language that has entered waking discourse. For, if the Anhalter Bahnhof is given special status as mother of all stations on account of the play that is made on its name, as the place where the trains 'had to stop' ('anhalten mußten' (WB IV.i 246)), the earlier use of the verb 'anhalten' in 'noch anhielt' suggests a different kind of being at home: a state of melancholic arrest.

The Anhalter Bahnhof as 'maternal cave', an over-ground space in the urban topography opened up to its underground, is figured at once as a primal site of origin and emergence and as a place of arrested development. The 'fata morgana' of the view from the station thus blocks the perspective from the station, the running together of the lines in the fog suggesting a premature end to the journey. While the proximity of the home now recedes, it is only for it to be expropriated, as the child imagines burglars breaking into it (WB IV.i 246). Accordingly, he returns in a state of home-lessness, and the lights from the abject 'Höfe' become an object of envy and then of melancholic asylum, projecting him into abjection. As the train is held up in its entry into the station, so the child's eyes take on the melancholy light of the courtyard windows. The child is exiled towards these abject courtyards, facially and optically identified with their temporarily exposed façades, their damaged walls and dim lights, and yet unable to be at home in them.

It is small wonder that, when he casts his expropriated eyes upon another site of his childhood, the 'Schulhof' or schoolyard, it too is caught in the light of redoubled loss. A space that had always been estranged for the child during his schooldays is also already, in retrospect and at a distance, a place of estrangement. It is a particular kind of chronotopical site, a *topos* of missed appointment. It is a place at which the child always arrives too soon (when the door is still locked) or too late, so that the time of this place is out of joint, subject to damage on his account (WB VII.i 395). And the damage is incorporated into the schoolyard as site of memory. The 'Schulhof' enters into the network of *Höfe* by virtue of this open part of the school being seen from another of these, the Bahnhof Savignyplatz (WB VI 509). Yet this exposed view of the 'Schulhof' is also at once too late and too soon, coming after the event of school-life and yet already too routine to yield any meaning for archaeological memory-work. While the narrator can garner individual finds, allegorical objects that might stand in metonymically for the whole, the framing image – the *Hof* – to which these might relate has lost all individual character and become a site only of dispossession. The 'Schulhof' is a debased form of mock-imperial court, as indicated by the forlorn plaster cast of Kaiser Friedrich set against a 'Brandmauer' in its remotest corner (WB VI 473). It is an other scene, under a heteronomous regime, like the other *Höfe* of Berlin, caught in an ironic tension with the sovereign, representative claims of the royal court.

The final site in the chain of *Höfe* is the 'Friedhof' or graveyard, under-stood, on the model of the Parisian Père Lachaise cemetery (WB V.i 522), as a necropolis within the city walls, a para-city that, as much as the city proper, requires a map for its negotiation. In the notes for the *Passagen-Werk*, Death is described as 'the dialectical central station' (WB v.ii 997) at the hub of the city's networks and so of the *Passagen-Werk* project, but it is part of its dialectical working to be represented not in the central terminus but obliquely or at the edge. It is to be discovered by the topographer in unforeseen places, such as in the two examples recorded in the notes for *Berliner Chronik*: the discovery of the morgue in the Hannoversche Straße (WB vi 801) and, more figuratively, the 'dead street' recently discovered in Schöneberg off the Potsdamer Straße (WB vi 800). If Death is an allegorical central station, it operates under the principle of transition that is proper to the 'Bahnhof', as to the other passage-sites of the city: buildings that serve 'transitory purposes' (WB v.i 46). Benjamin describes the work of the *Passagen-Werk* as a layering of networks of such topographical construc-tions, and puts examples of the *Höfe* into the sequence of sites of passage to be elaborated: 'its arcades and its gates, its graveyards ('Friedhöfen') and brothels, its stations ('Bahnhöfen') and its ...' (WB v.i 134–5). The inter-rupted sequence might be completed by 'Höfen', certainly when the topo-graphical project is transferred to Berlin, where the Parisian *Passagen-Werk* has its counterpart in what we might call a *Höfe-Werk*. The graveyard is embedded into the sequence as if to elide its terminal status, but also perhaps to indicate that the terminal moment is already anticipated in the *Höfe* that have preceded it.

CITY LIMITS

The image of the working-class *Höfe* that appear to the bourgeois child as he nears the station and remain with him as a transformation of his vision can be understood as an exemplar of the *Weichbild*, a recurrent term in Benjamin's urban topographies and the site of special interest for his topo-graphical work. The term *Weichbild*,[25] designating municipal territory and its boundaries, derives from the pole standing on the marketplace in medieval settlements and bearing the insignia of the authority under whose protection it operated (the king's arms, the image of a local saint etc.). The emblematic image is thus projected into the territory of juris-diction that it occupies, into the marketplace and, by extension, the boundary of the settlement.

The *Weichbild*, as allegorical image, combines territory with law, *Ortung* with *Ordnung* in the Schmittian sense, but in Benjamin's usage the space of

---

[25] 'Weich' here is derived from the 'vyeche', the folk-mote.

jurisdiction is subject to shifting. Here, the *Weichbild* is also an emblematic figure for the speaking otherwise of the marketplace and for the urban space for which it stands. The *Weichbild* is the fringe of the city, the boundary line, but also the soft ('weich') edge areas of the *Stadtbild* or cityscape that lead to its boundary, carrying the secondary meaning of yielding ('Weichen'). As Benjamin reminds us, stations, like cities, have their 'Weichbilder' (WB VI 472), so that the *Weichbild* can be seen as an accompanying counter-image for the *Hof*, standing for the principle of the shift of attention from the 'Bahnhof' to the urban texture of courtyards and streets that surrounds it. It seems that the 'Weichen' (railway points) that might indeed be associated with the station exercise a subliminal influence here, serving to deflect attention along alternative lines. The railway points, in turn, are relayed in the direction of 'Weichen' in a further sense, the flanks or loins of the urban body, also suggesting the groin area.[26] If the station appeared in the same topographical sequence as the brothel in the inventory of Parisian sites of passage, this is because one of its special functions is a site of prostitution in passage. The prostitutes, who inhabit the rear courtyards of the station's *Weichbild*, ply their trade on such sites of transition and traffic as the railway platform. The station thus becomes an exemplary threshold space. In *Berliner Chronik*, Benjamin adopts the threshold, social and topographical, to the space of prostitution as a key rite and site of passage (WB VI 471–2). And the social and spatial thresholds are also psychical and temporal, involving the passage out of childhood, and the characteristic scene of walking the streets with his mother, and into an other space of fantasy, a topography of street-walking of another kind, extending to such liminal sites as the doorways of tenements and the muted asphalt of station platforms (WB VI 472).

Stations and their associated territories are particularly suited to this sort of multiple threshold experience. The short text 'Traum' (Dream) locates Sodom in the 'Weichbild' of a station (WB IV.i 430). In this urban underbelly, the representative metropolis is mapped onto other kinds of city, dream versions of itself. And like the Pompeii that is marked into the loggia, Sodom here also stands for the city visited by destruction. As part of his series of texts on urban and other catastrophes, Benjamin records how the second is inscribed into the first in the form of an uncanny piece of

---

[26] While 'Weichen' are the flanks of the body, 'Weichengegend' is a euphemism for the groin, suggesting an anatomical yielding in that direction.

graffiti, as '"Sodom und Gomorrah" is the last uncanny inscription in the walls of Pompeii' (WB VII.i 220). The 'Weichbild' would seem, in these terms, to be a marginal site, where the city shows uncanny knowledge of its demise, its subjection to passage. And when the figure is transferred from the 'Stadtbild' onto the body-image, the same sort of threat operates, with the fingers that are the playthings of the feverish child described as dubious figures at work in the 'Weichbild' of a city after a conflagration (WB VII.i 405).

The eccentric principle of street-walking, which Benjamin adopts from the nineteenth-century *flâneur*, involves an inflection of attention from the established point of interest to the marginal, to that which is in passage. The urban explorer is, in these terms, following the same orientation as the unconventional marine navigator in Benjamin's account, intentionally (mis)guided by the magnetic North Pole and its 'Abweichungen' (deflections) from the 'true' course (WB V.i 570). He goes on to indicate that he seeks to construct his project upon the 'differentials of time' that are conventionally seen as distractions to be avoided. The 'data' that Benjamin follows here according to his cultural topographical compass are chronotopical, coordinated in spatial and temporal dimensions. According to this at once chronographic and topographic compass, the 'um' of *Berliner Kindheit um neunzehnhundert* is, as already suggested, also readable as a spatial preposition, proposing an exploration of the temporal territory or time zone around this datum. This follows the principle of one of the model 'data' of Berlin's topography: the 'Siegessäule', a datum as point of reference for both spatial navigation and the city's historical self-image. If the victory column stands on its open square like the red 'Datum' on a tear-off calendar (WB VII.i 389), however, this only serves to suggest that the datum should have been torn down or off long ago. The obsolete monument is thus subject to displacement in Benjamin's account. When it appears as a motto to the different versions of *Berliner Kindheit*, it is strategically dislocated from its historical site into the fantasy space and time of the nursery, as a gingerbread column cast in sugar 'from the days of childhood' (WB VII.i 385).

This misappropriation is the prelude to a displacement of topographical attention from this datum into the more ambiguous territory that surrounds it, which notes for *Berliner Chronik* call the 'underworld realm' (WB VII.ii 709) beyond the Siegesallee and the 'magical topography' (WB VII.ii 713) of the Tiergarten and its allegorical street-names. The allegorical fantasies elicited by this topography are in fact frustrated. They speak otherwise in a different sense, a form of 'Versprechen' in its second sense, 'promise' turned into 'failed speech', as in the disappointed courtly suggestions of the Hofjägerallee or Courthunter Avenue (WB VII.i 394).[27] The column as representative topographical and historical pointer, marking the red-letter day of the anniversary of the battle of Sedan, is also misleading, as it is subjected to differential forms of temporal and spatial calculation. The child's attention is successively displaced: from the column to its base, from here to other monuments in the Tiergarten, from those monuments to their bases, and thence into the surrounding terrain, with the labyrinth as the emblematic site. The budding cultural topographer's 'Abweichungen' or deflections from the established data of the imperial city thus lead the courthunter into the *Weichbild*.

The scene from his childhood in which Benjamin explores the nearby Zoologischer Garten, in order to ascertain the character of its inhabitants through the physiognomy of their habitations, is accordingly devoted to its *Weichbild*: the otter's enclosure on the edge of the zoo approached by the least frequented gate. The point of access to the carceral domain of the 'internees' of the 'Weichbild' (WB VII.i 407), is the Lichtensteinbrücke. And it is possible to read between the lines of the description of this *Weichbild*, hard by the Landwehrkanal and described in the language of death, a memorial for another body in the water: Rosa Luxemburg, who was killed there. Her long-buried body continues to haunt the topographical scene of her death, still described as swimming in the canal as a martyr to resistance in the war-torn Berlin of 1944 in Peter Weiss's *Ästhetik des Widerstands*.[28] It is a corpse that we will encounter many times in this study as allegorical embodiment of the city's melancholic ruin.

The *Weichbild* is described here by Benjamin as a threshold place where topographies meet and die, but which also thereby has the power to foresee deaths of other spaces. The account of the scene in the *Berliner Chronik* sees the threshold zone of the *Weichbild* as projecting 'an image of what is to come', specifically foreseeing the decline in the 1920s of the spa resorts that it resembles and of the ball culture that flourished nearby. It is one of those places that seems to project the future into the past (WB VII.i 407), thus putting the bourgeois city chronicle into the melancholy tense of the future perfect, of what will have been. It is the same form of chronotopical dialectics that Kracauer identifies in his account of the affinity between the Tiergarten, understood as a space between inside and out, present and

---

[27] Reinhard Jirgl exploits the same pun regarding the 'failed speech' of the 'great capital promise' ('Große Hauptstadt-Versprechen') of contemporary Berlin in his word-playful *Abtrünnig: Roman aus der nervösen Zeit* (Munich/Vienna: Carl Hanser, 2005), p. 296.

[28] Weiss, *Die Ästhetik des Widerstands*, vol. III, p. 181.

past, and photography, with both caught on what he calls the 'threshold of yesterday'.[29] But Benjamin's account of the fringes of the Tiergarten as threshold space might also be understood as providing a premonitory image of his own particular, representative form of Berlin life, born into the bourgeoisie but fighting for the demise of that class, a life that will have been lost from this place by the time he writes his memoir texts. If, according to the preface to the final manuscript version of *Berliner Kindheit*, the images of the author's city childhood are perhaps able to 'prefigure' later historical experience (WB VII.i 385), the unlikely conjunction of the otter enclosure and Luxemburg's death might be such a form of historical adumbration.[30]

The deflection or *Abweichung* into the *Weichbild* follows a paradigmatic logic of *Entstellung*, or, more precisely, of Benjamin's hyphenated 'Ent-stellung'. The softening, yielding, and shifting of position that resonate in the term *Weichbild* give it a particular attachment to disfigurement and displacement. This dual logic of *Entstellung* is at work, for instance, in the scene 'Die Mummerehlen' from *Berliner Kindheit*, where the child inhabits the nineteenth-century 'like a mollusc ('Weichtier') in a shell' (WB VII.i 417), only to be evacuated from it at the turn of the century, left to hold the empty shell to his ear. This 'Weichtier' (literally, 'soft animal') is a protean figure of *Entstellung* through imitation of its surroundings, prefiguring the subject's disfigured state as 'entstellt' in his similarity to his environment (WB VII.i 417). As the earlier version of the text has it, it is a displacement or disfigurement of the child into image: 'ins Bild entstellt' (WB IV.i 263). As such, it is a counterpart to, or imitation of, the mumming figure of the title, the 'Mummerehlen', a figure that through disfigurement comes to contain its environment. The verse from which the title is taken is disfigured ('entstellt') and thereby becomes a place for the no less disfigured or displaced world of childhood to inhabit (WB VII.i 417). The principle of *Entstellung* can thus afford a repository for what has been lost, a *Weichbild* that is soft enough to incorporate the disfigured character of experience within its contours; but the 'Weichtier' of 'Die Mummerehlen' is also an animal that is found to be gone, leaving only the echoing repository of the carapace that surrounded the *Weichbild* it presented. It is akin to the socks in 'Der Strumpf', a figure promising plenitude of experience for the child in possession of its soft ('weichen') woollen mass (WB VII.i 416), but also emptied out, withdrawn in the act of its enjoyment. *Weich*, in other words,

---

[29] Kracauer, 'Photographiertes Berlin', *Schriften*, V.iii, pp. 168–70; p. 170.
[30] We thus might reassess Benjamin's complaint that he always arrived too late to witness the spectacle of drowning in the Landwehrkanal (WB VII.i 422).

carries a secondary meaning, aligned with *Abweichung*, which leads to its retraction. *Entstellung* here also implies the removal of the (dis)figure.

The *Weichbild* is an allegorical image, one that incorporates the allegorist principle of speaking otherwise and does so through visual disfigurement and displacement. We therefore find it amongst the more explicit games that Benjamin plays with language, following the model of dream-work. Here, the *Weichbild* functions as a kind of rebus, a dialectically charged riddle of a word-image, such as Freud identifies at work in dreams. Benjamin's riddle dismantles *Weichbild*, drawing as it were on the recessive or repellent energy of *weichen* in order to map the routine urban category into a phantasmagorical image. The riddle reads:

> Der heilige Antonius schreit
> Die Worte in die Einsamkeit.
> Die Grenzen einer großen Stadt
> Man nachmals so bezeichnet hat.   (WB VII.i 302)

(St Anthony cries / The words into solitude / The borders of a great city / Were then so named.)

St Anthony cries 'Weich' Bild!' (Retreat image!) to the grotesque images that torment him and, according to Benjamin's playful word-history, thereby provides an *après coup* model for the naming of the fringes of the city. St Anthony, the archetypal melancholist in the desert, thereby foresees, out of his displacement, the *Entstellung* that is the phantasmagorical shape of the great city. Another of the word-pairs in the riddle sequence is 'Ruine'/ 'Rune', whereby the mysterious linguistic fragment merges with the ruin under the sign of allegory: the rune is the ruin spoken otherwise. And it seems that this convergence of language and ruination is also at work in the 'Weichbild' example. The contours of the city are haunted by the melancholy after-image of ruin.

If the visions of St Anthony provide a nightmarish version of the dislocated logic of the 'Weich-bild', the Kaiserpanorama, the classic piece of urban visual machinery, inherited from the passages of the nineteenth century, provides another. The Kaiserpanorama, with its sequence of images always ready to be saturated with the pain of departure, serves as a *mise-en-abyme* for *Berliner Kindheit*, as a respository of images of the lost city. The stereoscopic images are at once given a memorial quiddity by the medium of the panorama apparatus and yet marked by the passage of time. While St Anthony's visions suggest an apocalyptic dream-image of the modern metropolis, the Kaiserpanorama presents a more wistful kind of image, where 'weichen' is the recessive agency of the image itself, always ready to be lost, rather than the desperate imperative of the viewer, who might rather call for it to stay in place.

The panorama apparatus is aligned with the threshold experiences of the city, its rites and sites of passage, hence its function in the short text 'Das zweite Ich' (The Second Self), where the protagonist sees his own past threshold experiences as *Doppelgänger* images in a melancholy panorama (WB VII.i 296–8). The passageways of the city are dream-spaces without an 'outer surface' (WB V.i 513), their contours receding before the topographer, who passes through them on a ghost-track, as the walls 'yield' ('weichen' (WB V.i 516)). This form of passing through is always in ghostly attendance at new movements across the thresholds of the city. While the doorbell that rings as a prelude to the crossing of threshold exercises 'despotic terror', potentiated by the 'magic of the threshold', it also evokes its shadow version: the antiphonal ringing of the ghost-bell that might mark departure (WB V.i 141). These are part, as it were, of a carillon, an assemblage of bells, both actual and metaphorical, which sound over the thresholds of the text. The tectonic and ritual space of the 'Schwelle' makes itself present through the resonance it carries of 'schwellen' (swelling), and it thus spreads into a zone rather than a boundary line. At the same time, the swelling in question is loaded for Benjamin with implications of transition, both spatial and historical, and with the more threatening potential of flooding (WB V.i 618). The 'Glocke' is the appropriate receptacle shape for the threshold bell to adopt,[31] striking the melancholic tone associated both with the departure that shadows arrival and with the aftermath of catastrophe, as in the phantom bells that the child might have heard when the apparatus of the Kaiserpanorama fails and the discoloured landscape is displayed under an ashen sky (WB VII.i 389).

It is in the character of the liminal zone and the ringing that accompanies it to shrink as well as to swell, so that the reverse movement across the threshold is set under the sign of 'weichen'. The ringing that announces departure has the tone of the bell that marks the loss of one image and the imminent arrival of another in the Kaiserpanorama, ushered in by the trembling of the yielding image ('des weichenden Bildes' (WB V.i 141). The Kaiserpanorama, as site of passage, an apparatus that sets the viewer in a sequence of thresholds, is set under the allegorical sign of the *Weichbild* as

---

[31] Apart from the bells that are literally heard at such liminal moments in the text, there are more figurative sound effects. When the child lies in bed, the 'bell' of the lamplight approaches him over the threshold (WB VII.i 405). This 'bell' echoes in the ringing sound of the 'Lampenglocke' (lampshade) later in the text (WB VII.i 417).

yielding image, announcing new images but only in the melancholy fore-
knowledge of their readiness to retreat.

MARKETPLACES

If the *Weichbild* is an exemplary figure for Benjamin's allegorical work on
the cultural topography of Berlin, this is partly because of the potential of
the internal dialectics of this image-word. The *Weichbild* is a paradigm case
for the principle of 'dialectics at a standstill': a mapped boundary that is
nonetheless mobile in its chronotopic fixture, in place and yet receding, a
hard contour and yet also softened into alternative shapes. It is thus an
adequate vehicle for the transformative speaking otherwise of the city. And,
as such, it corresponds to another of the exemplary scenes from Benjamin's
chronicle of his Berlin childhood: the 'Markthalle' (market hall). This is
another space of passage between inside and out, and accordingly rich with
allegorical presences. The site of passage is an extended 'Schwelle', as
encoded in the swelling bosoms of the colossal, hieratic 'market wives'
and of their own corporeal thresholds, demarcating the passage to fruitful,
swelling terrain (WB VII.i 402). The threshold is invested here with the sort
of erotic 'Schwellensymbolik' or threshold symbolism that features in
Freud's *Interpretation of Dreams* (SF II/III 508–9), taking a form that is at
once blatant and encoded, following the disfiguring principles of dream-
work. Freud's discussion of this threshold symbolism focuses on how it
might represent what he calls 'Schwankungen' at 'Stellen' – oscillations at
points – between dream and awakening. It is as if this movement over the
boundary between consciousness and the other scene of the unconscious
reverberates in the transformation of 'Stelle', via the (perhaps also phonetic)
interference of 'Schwankungen der Schlaftiefe' (fluctuations in the depth of
sleep),[32] into the place of passage that is the 'Schwelle'. That is, 'Stelle' is
displaced by effects of 'Entstellung' into the psycho-topographical ambiguity of 'Schwelle'. This suggests in turn that for Benjamin the particular
form of threshold between dream and reality (WB VII.i 423), is always built
into this determining psycho-tectonic feature.

The dream-worked encoding of the allegorical threshold figures of the
market is in keeping with that of the place as a whole, which operates
according to the *Weichbild* principle, through an *Entstellung* of word and
image out of their original form. Habits of speech cause the 'Markt-Halle' to

---

[32] This chimes with Benjamin's alliterative collocation 'schwankend über die Schwelle' (swaying over
the threshold (WB VII.i 405)).

be pronounced in distorted form as 'Mark-Thalle', and this other speech provides a model for all the images that the boy encounters in the market-hall (WB VII.i 402). This is the market as special site of allegory, of speaking otherwise, as formulated in the curious misuse of the verb 'sprechen' in the formulation 'man sprach' – one spoke – '"Mark-Thalle"', as though this were itself the other language being spoken. Bernd Witte may well be right in suggesting that 'Thalle' here resonates with the Greek *thalassa*, confusing the urban ground of the Magdeburger Platz market-hall with the fluctuation of the sea.[33] The vernacular corruption of the site accordingly figures the city in its primal state as a swamp, cast between the elements of earth and water. As in the case of 'Blume-zof', this speaking otherwise resolves the generic site – 'Halle' or 'Hof' – into a place of *Entstellung*, merging them across the threshold with their epithets and leaving both elements 'effaced'.[34] As so often in the other scenes of this text, *Entstellung* is symptomatic of a twisting of embodied life towards death. As the 'Blume-zof' is under the thrall of an uncanny, mortifying *genius loci*, so the 'Mark-Thalle' sequence finishes in a kind of living death for the protagonist as a *flâneur* out of his element, an exhausted, sinking swimmer.

The allegorical *Entstellung* of the market-hall works in a tradition of the marketplace as the site of other forms of language and image. For the purposes of his topographic work on Berlin, Benjamin adopts this above all from E. T. A. Hoffmann, a guide in his native city, like Baudelaire in Paris. Hoffmann belongs for Benjamin to the category of the *flâneur* as 'observer of the market' (WB V.i 537), but it is telling that the text that he cites as a particular model for his urban *flânerie* is one fixed in interior space above a market scene: *Des Vetters Eckfenster* (My Cousin's Corner Window). In these terms, the 'Markthalle' as threshold space, serves as a dialectical incorporation of the street-scene into an interior viewing space. In both cases, the marketplace stands allegorically for city life, a place at once everyday and other, and the perspective cast between inside and out is intrinsic to the work of the allegorist in figuring that other place.

Benjamin introduces Hoffmann in another set of texts concerned with Berlin childhood: the *Rundfunkgeschichten für Kinder* (Radio Tales for Children). The introduction is given in 'Straßenhandel und Markt in Alt- und Neuberlin' (Street Trading and Market in Old and New Berlin), not

---

[33] Bernd Witte, *Walter Benjamin: An Intellectual Biography*, trans. James Rolleston (Detroit: Wayne State University Press, 1991), p. 146.

[34] Another example is the Stieglitzer Straße, a speaking otherwise of the Steglitzer Straße, incorporating the mimicry of the 'Stieglitz' or goldfinch (WB VII.i 399).

through *Des Vetters Eckfenster*, but through Hoffmann's allegorical fairy tale of everyday life, *Der goldene Topf* (The Golden Pot). The beginning of the text in question, set in Dresden rather than Berlin, is itself highly allegorical. The student Anselmus, rushing into the city, collides with the wares of the strange old 'apple woman', who then becomes a figure for the *Entstellung* of the narrative, a threshold figure first encountered at the gate to the city and coming back to haunt the portals of the protagonist's stumbling, allegorical journey between the topographies of reality and fantasy. She is the counterpart to the *bucklichte Männlein* of *Berliner Kindheit*, a 'disfigure' that comes unbidden to supervise the damage done by the inept protagonist. The disfigured market-woman at the threshold is also disfigured in her speech; she speaks otherwise, in the language of allegory.

This is the appropriate threshold figure for Benjamin to co-opt for the entry into his own text, to be followed by a reference to another text of fairy-tale *Entstellung*, Hauff's *Zwerg Nase* (Dwarf Nose), a more everyday reference to the listening Berlin children accompanying their mothers to market (in the style of the 'Markthalle' scene from *Berliner Kindheit*), and then to a recent film of the market on the Wittenbergplatz (Basse's *Markt am Wittenbergplatz* (Market on the Wittenbergplatz (1928)), which is described as more exciting than many a detective film (WB VII.i 74). What the film omits, however, and what the 'Markthalle' scene sublimates into the text, is the 'Marktgespräch', the conversation or discourse of the market, which Benjamin sees as the necessary counterpart to the visual impact of the marketplace, and of which the 'apple woman' provides an uncanny example. He goes on to supply a sequence of more everyday examples, such as another 'fruit woman', this time sitting by the Brandenburg Gate and asked by a visitor to the city about the identity of the Viktoria figure on the Gate. The old woman gives evidence of Benjamin's claim that the 'Berliner Schnauze' (Berlin snout or gob) has the monumental dimensions to incorporate the Gate (WB VII.i 68), with the facetious historical account she gives, speaking otherwise, in Berlin dialect (WB VII.i 76).

The 'Schnauze' is a particular faculty of the marketeer, as exemplified for Benjamin in the radio tale on Berlin dialect by the street-trading of Döblin's Franz Biberkopf, whose 'Schnauze' extends to the dimensions of a department store (WB VII.i 72), such as Warenhaus Tietz on the Alexanderplatz.[35] Market-speech becomes marketplace here: the quintessential location of Berlin speech. 'Market and street trading' are 'one of the places in which

---

[35] This is echoed in the broadcasting of 'Schnauze' as both word and faculty over the marketplace by Franz Biberkopf as street-trader in Jutzi's 1931 film of *Berlin Alexanderplatz*.

Berlinese can be best heard in its development and mobility' (WB VII.i 75). Benjamin's market-woman at the Brandenburg Gate, like Hoffmann's, inhabits the streets and guards the gates of the city as marketplace, an allegorical figure of speaking otherwise in Berlin, here speaking otherwise of one its prized allegorical figures. The 'Markthalle' is still a place, Benjamin tells his auditors, that he will occasionally visit to find it unchanged from the childhood scene, and in the market-speech of the city he finds a repository for old Berlin.

Benjamin pursues the Hoffmann connection in another of the radio tales, 'Das dämonische Berlin' (Demonic Berlin). The 'Gespenster-Hoffmann' or 'Ghost-Hoffmann' who was the forbidden reading of his childhood, shut away in the parental bookcase (WB IV.i 284), is presented here as a model for the physiognomic reading of the city and its inhabitants. If Hoffmann was only to be read in the home in 'heimlich' fashion, this also in its turn makes the home uncanny,[36] releasing domestic demons (WB VII.i 88). A text like *Das öde Haus* (The Deserted House), turning on the obsession of a *flâneur* narrator with a mysterious house on Unter den Linden, its façade a show-case for strange visions and imitating in its desolation the *Entstellung* it conceals, is exemplary for Hoffmann's teasing of the demonic out of the everyday topography of the city. Here, too, the opening up of other ways of seeing and speaking is prompted by dealings with a street-vendor, who sells the protagonist a magic mirror. But for Benjamin, the uncanny house on Unter den Linden stands for a more general principle of the exposure of what is hidden in the physiognomy of the city, its habitations and inhab-itants. Benjamin records the framing conversation staged between two of Hoffmann's figures, when the listener tells the narrator that he did well to transpose the scene to Berlin and name the streets and squares, as the physiognomic 'Schauplatz' of Berlin's topography brings his uncanny story to life (WB VII.i 90). It is an apt other *Schauplatz*, the appropriate scene for the display of the urban unconscious.

The young Benjamin described as transfixed by the forbidden Hoffmann text corresponds to the protagonist of *Das öde Haus*, fixed upon the house in question, as well as to the other kind of fixation that is described in *Des Vetters Eckfenster*, the deathbed text discussed at the end of 'Das dämonische

---

[36] Hoffmann's rendering of underground activities in *Die Bergwerke zu Falun* (The Mines of Falun) seems to represent a particular uncanniness (WB VI 800). Carol Jacobs accordingly reads the mine in Aunt Lehmann's apartment as a *mise-en-abyme* of the domestic milieu, casting it into an uncanny, subterranean topography. See Carol Jacobs, 'Walter Benjamin: Topographically Speaking', *Walter Benjamin: Theoretical Questions*, ed. David. S. Ferris (Stanford: Stanford University Press, 1996), pp. 94–117; pp. 108–14.

Berlin'. This is a text divided between the vital pulse of the city, as exemplified by the commerce of the marketplace seen by the cousins as the allegorical stage for life at large, and pathologically marked fixation. If this more documentary text belongs with the others under the heading of 'Demonic Berlin', it is by virtue of the demons of melancholia that haunt its framework. The paralysed cousin, an erstwhile *flâneur* now incapacitated, is in a chronic anatomical and psychical condition of melancholic homesickness, confined to his room and excluded from the home-ground of his writerly inspiration. This condition is broken only for the interlude of his participation in the observational, or voyeuristic, dialogue with the narrator on the comings and goings of the Gendarmenmarkt, which the latter apparently comes to write up as amanuensis. It is a condition that the Benjamin of *Berliner Kindheit*, also a one-time *flâneur* in the streets and marketplaces of Berlin, imitates in his homesick exile. If Benjamin treats that text as an inoculation, it is in part in response to Hoffmann, whose uncanny narratives were once infectious for the young reader (WB VII.i 88), and for whom the 'blackest melancholia' of the cousin,[37] still full of stories of the Berlin streets but unable to write them, is no less of a contagious threat. The texts of Hoffmann, and the Berlin as 'other scene' that they invoke, are at once one of the nostalgic objects of his Berlin childhood and a melancholy reminder of the sorts of latter-day demons that can revisit the reality of the lost city and its marketplaces.

BANNING SPACES

The paradoxical condition of being at once fixed within and excluded from the city, or spaces within its topography, is circumscribed by another key *topos* in Benjamin's writing: the *Bannraum* or *Bannkreis* (space or circle of exclusion). Like *Weichbild*, *Bannraum* is a term that follows from his preoccupation with boundaries and with liminal states. *Bannen* and its cognates apply variously, and often in ambivalent combination, to the topographically disposed fears and desires of the Berlin childhood: to the haunted staircase of the 'Blumeshof' (WB VII.i 412), to the mortified name and associated topography of Luise von Landau (WB VII.i 401), or to the erotica section in the twilit rear of the shop in the Krumme Straße (WB VII.i 416). It is a dialectically bound term, suggesting at once banishment or banning from a space and spellbound fixture on the spot.

---

[37] Hoffmann, *Des Vetters Eckfenster*, *Sämtliche Werke*, vol. VI, p. 469.

The threshold or boundary is the interstitial space or zone where the dialectic of *bannen* can take place, where the subject can be fixed into a space and yet in a state of exclusion from it. *Bannen* is also a temporal term: it may be enforced in permanence or for a specified time. In the part of *Berliner Chronik* that records the anxiety-ridden memory of the child's walk to school on the Savignyplatz, it is given as a form of *Zeitraum* on the face of the clock, which always reads 'too late' in the 'Bannraum' between the ten and the twelve (WB VI 494). He is always excluded from the space of the appointed time of arrival. And just as *Zeitraum* is transmitted by Benjamin into its oneiric other scene, the *Zeittraum*, so *Bannraum* also slips into the alternative psychical space of the *Banntraum*. This arises in the fear of the approach to another threshold, that of the sanctuary of the 'Blumeshof', where the stairs are the 'Schauplatz' of such a 'Banntraum' (WB VI 501), and so are transmitted into an other psycho-topographical scene under the thrall of a ghost. Space comes under the control of the other, even in its most intimate transmission through the dream-life of the subject.

This sort of other scene, understandable as the site of the unconscious of the city, at once transfixes the subject who comes under its sway and yet, as constitutionally other, also exercises exclusion. The *Bann(t)raum* is a heteronomous time-space, under the jurisdiction of alterity; where it seems to belong to the subject, it in fact belongs to the other that operates upon and within the subject. This is the logic of the hiding-place, as developed in the 'Verstecke' (Hiding-places) scene from *Berliner Kindheit*, where the hiding child becomes hidden at the point when he is discovered by and subject to the other, under a banning (the verb is 'bannen') that may be a life sentence (WB VII.i 418) or decree an afterlife as ghost. It is the same principle as fixes space in the photographic image, leaving it 'gebannt' on the plate (WB VI 516). The subject, too, is banned into the image by the snapshot, and, while apparently going about everyday experience, is subjected to the shock of the sudden exposure to the other, felt in a psychic place that is other ('an anderer Stelle' (WB VI 516)). While the space that is thus 'banned' into the image might appear to be that of the subject, it carries with it this other place of traumatic experience, and accompanying this the principle of *Entstellung*, as in the photographs of 'Die Mummerehlen'. In Benjamin's analysis, the medium of photography has a special relationship to death, and, at limit, the 'Platte' or plate upon which the photographic image is fixed or banned, is also understandable as *Grabplatte* (grave-slab).

Like the *Hof*, the *Bannraum* is a space of sovereignty, and like the *Weichbild* one of legislative control, but it carries the same ambivalence of disposition as its corollaries. In appearance, the mother's sewing table is invested with the authority of a fairy-tale court, as it exerts its 'Bannkreis' (WB VII.i 425). Yet the fairy-tale example also implies that the 'banning circle' may be turned back upon the monarch. This is the work of spells in fairy tales, but also of the transfers of power that are wrought by history. In the historical process, the sovereign may also become subject to banning or banishment. The statues in the Tiergarten of King Friedrich Wilhelm and Queen Luise are therefore described as 'wie gebannt', as if spellbound or banished, by the magical curves of the water flowing before them (WB VII.i 394). It is also the child's condition to be caught between the two senses of *bannen*, as in the scenes from his school-life described in *Berliner Chronik*, when he resists allowing his teachers into the 'Bannkreis' of his private existence, but is himself subject to the 'Bann' of their primitive methods of discipline (WB VI 508).

The same pattern can be followed when the 'Bannkreis' of the mother's sewing table is superseded by Benjamin's reading table in the Berlin Staatsbibliothek or State Library: the glazed space before his seat in the library is described as a 'Bannkreis' (WB V.i 571) and so as virgin territory for the figures that he conjures up. Here, the autonomous territory can become a heteronomous space, excluding the reading subject except in fantasy, subject to the law of the other and as such delimiting the ambit of personal space. The glazed 'Bannkreis' is reminiscent of the space under or behind glass ruled by Aunt Lehmann, as described in *Berliner Kindheit* and *Berliner Chronik*, and emblematised in the model mineworks under a glass cover, a terrain that is never properly accessible. Like the name of Luise von Landau, which draws the child into its 'Bann' (WB VII.i 401), the 'good North German name' Lehmann gives licence for power over place (WB VII.i 399). As Carol Jacobs has pointed out, however, while this aunt is given the status of a governor, 'Statthalterin' (literally, 'place-holder' (WB VI 472)), over the Steglitzer Straße, her name resonates subversively with the condition of feudal bondage ('Lehmann' as vassal).[38] The 'Statthalterin' stands in place or instead of another authority, not specified in this case. And here the homophony of 'Stadt' (city) and 'statt' (instead) carries further subversive potential.[39] A 'Statthalterin' might appropriately govern a city, as 'Stadthalterin', but this one governs a street instead, and is figured both as removed from the street she governs and in exile from her home territory in the country.[40] That Lehmann is also a good Jewish name only accentuates

[38] Jacobs, 'Topographically Speaking', p. 111.

[39] A similar placing of 'Stadt' in stead of 'Statt' occurs in Jirgl's *Abtrünnig*, with Berlin as a city full of places where it fails to take place (or 'take city') and be found ('STADT nicht Stadt-findet' (p. 478)).

[40] This territory is represented in another set of *Höfe*, seen by the subject from a passing train (WB VII.i 399).

the provisional character of the territorial power that she might appear to exercise. The institutional boundaries of the library or the domestic ones of Aunt Lehmann's territory are as ambivalent as those surrounding the psychical space of the subject when under the influence of the 'Bannkreis' of dream (WB IV.i 85) and unable properly to take control of that space of enthralment except, heteronomously, from the other scene, subject to other laws, of waking consciousness. As in the case of the strange 'Höfe', which the child might seem to have under colonial control as provincial outposts of his own, but which in fact hold him strangely, uncannily in their thrall, sovereignty in the public-private spaces of Benjamin's world remains vexed.

The *Bannraum* of the benevolent sovereign on the model of the mother as fairy-tale queen can also take more tyrannical, coercive forms. This is the principle of *bannen* as it might apply to particular parts of the urban population in states of exception. When Giorgio Agamben develops his theory of the *Ausnahmezustand* or state of exception, after Schmitt and under the mediating influence of Benjamin, it is bound up with the *Bannraum* as sovereign space. The state of exception is a condition neither inside nor outside the order of things, but set into its threshold. The principle of the *Ausnahme* functions as the power to exclude, to take out by exception, but also the power to except what conventionally lies outside sovereignty *into* the purview of its regime. In this light, Agamben posits the ban as a 'limit form of relation',[41] a dialectical space where certain relations are maintained across categorical boundaries even where the state of exception seems absolute, a 'zone of indistinction between outside and inside, exclusion and inclusion'.[42] *Bannen* embodies at once the sort of exceptional powers arrogated by the National Socialists, the powers that banished Benjamin and others from Berlin, and at the same time the potential, however limited, of the subject to except him or herself from such banning.

At the *Einbahnstraße* address marked 'Normaluhr' (Public clock), a state or space of exception is proposed that works against the normal regime of history in the person of the genius who embraces the caesuras and vicissitudes of the historical process and works to circumscribe them as fragments shored against historical ruin in the form of a 'Bannkreis' (WB IV.i 88). This is the sort of 'Bannkreis' that might counter the terrorising 'Bannraum' of the clock in the 'Schulhof' by incorporating it into the fragmentary album of Berlin images. The historical caesura that breaks the normal time and space regimes of Berlin in the early 1930s is, though, of another order of terror, one that brooks no resistance. If the bourgeois enclave of the Berlin

---

[41] Agamben, *Homo Sacer*, p. 29.   [42] *Ibid.*, p. 181.

West End could be experienced as a ghetto by the young Benjamin (WB IV.i 287), the ghetto now becomes the enforced *Bannraum*, the place and condition of exception in the city, and maintaining a relation to those who are banished from it, whether through emigration or deportation.

In the preface to the final manuscript version of *Berliner Kindheit*, Benjamin styles it as a text of departure, where 'Abschied' is spoken otherwise, converted from the moment of leaving into a protracted absence as leave-taking, perhaps for the duration (WB VII.i 385). The commemorative text is thus cast into a 'Zeitraum' of departure, an extended threshold experience, as exile stands at the door. Like Pausanias's topography of Greece, written only when many of its monuments were already in decay (WB V.i 133), the project is always already in departure from, and homesick for, the *Zeitraum* that it maps. In *Berliner Chronik*, the autobiographical project is fantasised as a mapping exercise, transmitting 'the space of life' – *bios* – into a graphic form (WB VI 466). It is a fantasy, however, that itself remains fixed on the threshold. While the fantasy map for the autobiography, or auto-topography, had at first taken the form of a Pharus map, Benjamin is now more inclined to think of a 'Generalstabskarte' or ordinance map, transferred into the terrain of the city. It is a type of map yet to exist, in ignorance of future scenes of war – 'Kriegsschauplätze' (WB VI 466). These 'Schauplätze' are in fact arguably already indicated at the time that Benjamin is writing, as mapped out by Goebbels in his memoir *Kampf um Berlin* (Struggle for Berlin (1934)) and then catastrophically finalised in his orchestration of the 'Schlacht um Berlin' (Battle for Berlin).[43] Indeed, Gabriele Tergit records the implementation of an ordinance map for Berlin in the satirical account of the conquering parade of the Stahlhelmführer down Unter den Linden in her *Käsebier erobert den Kurfürstendamm*.[44] Even if Kurt Tucholsky, in a *feuilleton* essay on the Stahlhelm Day procession of 1927, could describe it as a parade of waxworks and compare it to the Kaiserpassage off Unter den Linden as an anachronistic diversion,[45] it was a rehearsal for, or passage to, the conversion of the city into a 'Kriegsschauplatz' proper. The parade- and battle-grounds of the Second World War and its aftermath would indeed come to redraw the map of the city, ravaging the topography and the mappability of Benjamin's Berlin and its other scenes.

[43] The 'Kampf um Berlin' slogan was coined by Goebbels in an incendiary account of the battles following the showing of *All Quiet on the Western Front* at the Mozartsaal cinema on Nollendorfplatz on 8 December 1930, describing the march of the brown-shirts through the streets of the 'Jewised West' of the city. Josef Goebbels, 'Kampf um Berlin', *Der Angriff*, 9 December 1930.

[44] Tergit, *Käsebier*, p. 227.

[45] Kurt Tucholsky, writing as Ignaz Wrobel, 'Stahlhelm oder Filzhut?', *Die Weltbühne*, 17 May 1927.

The portrait and topographical images in Benjamin's album from his Berlin childhood are, like the photograph in *Berliner Chronik*, under the ambivalent rule of *Bannraum*. They isolate images of the city that are, like the photographic medium itself, anachronistic, incapable of grasping the modern city in the way that the film medium or the 'cinematic' urban writing of Döblin might. These are images both fixed and in passage, in the style of the Kaiserpanorama. In his discussion of the *flâneur*, Benjamin invokes the idea of a film derived from the map of Paris, condensing the topographical motions of a century into the 'Zeitraum' of half an hour (WB v.i 135). And, while the railway station as point of arrival for the nineteenth-century city is of a piece with still photography (as evidenced in the stopping moment of the Anhalter Bahnhof), he argues that the appropriate medium for entry into the motorised city of the twentieth century, rolling out from its 'Weichbild' (WB vi 470), is film. However, the 'Weichbild' here perhaps carries the resonance of the 'weichendes Bild' in the Kaiserpanorama, with film as a medium that accelerates the process of loss and gain of image. Certainly, the filmic versions of Berlin considered in this volume still carry the melancholic traces of the loss of urban life as well as its energetic capture.

The isolated scenes of *Berliner Kindheit* also stand at the threshold to and, in accordance with Benjamin's intention, 'prefigure' the historical experience of, the twentieth-century capital. These 'stills' embody the principle of 'dialectics at a standstill', images that are held up in time and space but also incorporate, through their strategies of speaking otherwise, dialectical potential that exceeds the time and place in which they are held. They are at once allegorical enchantments of the subject in the historical spaces of the city and repeated enactments of disenchantment, of injury and exclusion, both private and public. In his compulsive, photographic returns to these scenes, Benjamin is, as it were, in the condition of the hysteric, suffering from reminiscences, as Freud and Breuer put it (SF i 86), and compiling an iconography of their after-effects of psycho-somatic *Entstellung*. The distorted shape of the companion figure and camera-man, the 'bucklichte Männlein', representing the repeated physical lapses and contortions of the subject, the 'Fehlleistungen' or paraxes as one of Benjamin's sketches has it,[46] could be said to embody this hysterical principle for the autobiographical project. Benjamin diagnosed his contemporary, the itinerant cabaret artiste Else Lasker-Schüler, as hysterical in her extravagant literary and social performances both in the café that was her home-from-home and

---

[46] Walter-Benjamin-Archiv, ref. 906.

at large in the city,[47] and here that condition is found in his own compulsive return to the theatre of childhood scenes and portraits in Berlin. The two Jewish writers in and of Berlin, the performance artist and the cultural critic and allegorist, come together in their exile from the city.

In its attachment to pathology and to the medium of photography, the *Bannraum* is always also a space of death. It is constitutive of what Gerhard Richter calls the 'thanatographical scene' of Benjamin's writing, whereby his autobiographical texts function through *prosopopoeia*, 'coming from beyond the grave – even before death',[48] as we saw in the evocation of the loggia. As Adorno puts it in his afterword to *Berliner Kindheit*, the text is a collection of scenes of awakening into mortification, 'Schauplätze' surrounded by lethal air.[49] In his account, this deathliness in Benjamin's version of 'Berliner Luft' derives from the future 'shadow of Hitler's Reich' that falls upon his images of the city.[50] Adorno's vision appears to conflate the scenes of *Berliner Kindheit* with Benjamin's essay on 'Die Waffen von Morgen' (The Weapons of Tomorrow), which foresees the sort of gas-war that would create a ghostly front, penetrating both over-ground and underground topographies of the city and leaving the vaunted Berlin air 'suffocating' (WB IV.i 474).

While shadow and air are both operative in Benjamin's construction of aura, and the constellation of proximity and distance that it involves,[51] this long historical shadow, projected backwards upon the spaces of his child-hood memoirs, is complicit in the undoing of their aura that Adorno describes.[52] The shadow that falls on these scenes is less in the mode of aura than in that described by Freud in his account of melancholy: the shadow of the lost object that falls upon the bereft ego (SF X 435). It at once projects personal and collective loss from the past onto the self and its recollected territories and foreshadows a repetition of loss on a catastrophic scale in the future. In their repetition of childhood experience in turn-of-the-century Berlin at (and as) the threshold to the twentieth century, repeated again in the successive versions of the autobiographical or auto-topographical project, these scenes carry something of the uncanny effect

---

[47] For a reading of the spatial praxis of Lasker-Schüler's Berlin cabaret, see Andrew Webber, 'Inside Out: Acts of Displacement in Else Lasker-Schüler', *The Germanic Review*, 81.2 (Spring 2006), 143–62.

[48] Gerhard Richter, 'Acts of Self-Portraiture: Benjamin's Confessional and Literary Writings', *The Cambridge Companion to Walter Benjamin*, ed. David S. Ferris (Cambridge: Cambridge University Press, 2004), pp. 221–37; p. 230.

[49] Benjamin, *Berliner Kindheit*, p. 178.   [50] *Ibid.*, p. 177.

[51] In the famous formulation from the *Kunstwerk* essay, aura is described in the aerial terms of a shadow cast upon and inhaled by the resting viewer (WB I.ii 479).

[52] Benjamin, *Berliner Kindheit*, p. 177.

of *déjà vu*, as Benjamin describes it. They are accordingly returns from the past that have the exceptional power to 'ban us into the cool tomb of what was' (WB VI 518), casting their spell over present and future. The various auto-topographical spaces that Benjamin depicts are all also enclosed, encrypted by the shadow-site of this *Bannraum*.

This encryption extends to the domestic space of the hallway that Benjamin, in the notes for *Berliner Kindheit*, fantasises as the scene for the display of his biographical project on a map of his home city. This is a scene of passage from inside to out, with the encoded map as mediating image. The map incorporates the external sites of life and death into the interior, as a sort of para-city, so making ready for further sorties. It represents the fantasy of the city as personal *Bann(t)raum*, a space of sovereign autonomy for the subject, a ground for the figuration of his intimate topographies. It is located in a domestic scene that we might also take to be in Berlin, but that is, in the historical event, banned from the city, along with all it represents, for the writer who dies prematurely and in exile. The Pharus plan of the city is mapped onto unpunctuated discourse in loose verse form, with the sort of non-standard grammar that suits its allegorical purpose of speaking the city otherwise:

> Wenn ich alt bin so soll im Flur bei mir
> Ein Pharusplan von Berlin hängen
> Mit einer Zeichenerklärung drunter
> Blaue Punkte die Straßen in denen ich wohnte
> Gelbe die Stellen wo meine Freundinnen wohnten
> Braune Dreiecke die die Gräber bezeichnen
> Wie auf den Berliner Friedhöfen die liegen die mir nah waren
> Und schwarze Linien die die Wege
> Im Zoo nachzeichnen oder im Tiergarten
> Welche ich in Gesprächen mit Mädchen machte   (WB VII.ii 714)

(When I'm old then in my hallway / A Pharus map of Berlin shall hang / With an explanation of signs beneath / Blue dots mark the streets in which I lived / Yellow ones the places where my girlfriends lived / Brown triangles the graves / As those who were close to me lie in the cemeteries of Berlin / And black lines that trace the paths / In the Zoo or in the Tiergarten / That I walked in conversation with girls)

It is a map at once of urban erotics and mortality, charting the subject's agency in the spaces of the city and the loss marked within it, whether of old habitations or old friends. There is a feature missing from the map, one that could stand as a monument to the exclusionary principle that is built into the history of the city and re-emerges with a vengeance in the 1930s: the Rosenthaler Tor, the gate through which Jews had to enter the city until well into the nineteenth century,[53] marking their entrances and returns as under exception. Gillian Rose thinks of it as the point of entry into Berlin for three Jewish women, Rahel Varnhagen, Rosa Luxemburg, and Hannah Arendt, outsider citizens representing a 'third city' between Athens as the bounded city of law and the utopia of Jerusalem.[54] This would also be Benjamin's city, but as he writes of it his Berlin map has already passed with him in banishment out of the gates of the city.

The unrealised scene of the map in the hallway follows the sort of model of urban mapping that Benjamin describes in a letter to Gershom Scholem of 1924.[55] There, in connection with a visit to Assisi, he sets out his strategy for approaching great works of architecture, where the exploration of the topographical territory around places, their *Weichbild* we might say, is a necessary prelude to a proper viewing. But this topographical work excludes time for the equally important task of reading about the place, never mind the actual act of viewing. What he achieves in this mapping exercise, at once optic and haptic ('feeling the way through the city'), is an outstanding topographical image, preparing him for a 'sovereign' experience of the city upon his return. A stay in such a place based on anything but the strictest preparation cannot 'avoid a sense of the subaltern'. Benjamin's textual-topographical work on Berlin can be understood, in these terms, as preparation for a return in sovereign mode to a city that he has made his own, as *Hof*, as *Weichbild*, as (market)place for speaking otherwise, and as *Bannraum*. But the repeated return to the scenes of the city is also in the uncanny character of Freud's compulsive return to the same spot in a town not his own. The act of mapping, and the proper form of return that it might enable, is also beyond the sovereign control of the subject, when the ordinance map is in the hands of historical *force majeure*. The reverse-side of the *Bannraum*, not its enchantment but its attachment to heteronomy, also leaves him caught on the threshold to that return, in a subaltern position, a state and place of exception. As exceptional allegorist of his city, Benjamin prefigures much of what will be encountered in the chapters that follow, introducing a series of cultural practitioners whose works show the cultural map of Berlin from other angles, through other scenes.

[53] See Heinz Knobloch, *Herr Moses in Berlin: Auf den Spuren eines Menschenfreundes* (Berlin: Der Morgen, 1979), pp. 38–42.

[54] Gillian Rose, *Mourning Becomes the Law: Philosophy and Representation* (Cambridge: Cambridge University Press, 1996), p. 39.

[55] Benjamin, *Gesammelte Briefe*, vol. II, p. 502.

CHAPTER 2

Berlin ensemble: inhabitations and accommodations

Gap, something in between, then:
You too, many-citied Berlin
Busy under and over the asphalt.[1]

BRECHT AND COMPANY

This chapter borrows its title from one of Berlin's trademark institutions: the ensemble founded by Brecht. Its principal subject will be Brecht's own relationship to Berlin, but it will also give consideration to those of his collaborators (the 'and company' that Fuegi facetiously attached to him)[2] and to his most significant successor, Heiner Müller. The Berliner Ensemble, resident in the Theater am Schiffbauerdamm, has been, from its earliest days, an institution of collective effort, but also of personal celebration for the most influential figure in twentieth-century theatre. It is always in danger of becoming a theatre museum, a site of Brechtian memory industry, or – as Müller has it – a tomb (HM IX 178), complete with Cremer's memorial sculpture on its forecourt. It is perhaps only appropriate to one side of Brecht (the self-fashioning cultural icon of the Weimar Republic and elder statesman of the early GDR) that he should be memorialised in this way, but the official memorials set in stone and bronze here and elsewhere in Berlin should be seen alongside more transitional forms of remembrance, which accord with another side of the man and his work. The model here might be the post-*Wende* graffiti inscribed on a cemetery wall in Kreuzberg, citing Brecht's verse 'Auf einen chinesischen Theewurzellöwen'

---

[1] From Brecht's poem 'Über Deutschland' (On Germany), as incompletely recalled in *Flüchtlingsgespräche* (Emigrant Conversations) (BB XVIII 258).
[2] John Fuegi, *Brecht & Co.* (New York: Grove, 1994).

(On a Chinese Tearoot Lion) with the tag 'B. Brecht'.[3] The relationship between Brecht and Berlin is represented both in his incorporation as cultural trademark for the city and in more autonomous forms of signature. His declaration of love at first sight of the city, as recorded in a letter of 1920, is one of 'limited liability' (BB XXVIII 102). And the contractual obligation between Brecht's cultural capital and Berlin as cultural capital remains an ambiguous one.

The chapter will navigate between Brecht as a figure of personal author-ship (naming or initialising his texts after himself) and the collective principle of the ensemble: Brecht as part of creative groupings and produced by as much as producing the cultural life of his time. In Jameson's terms, this is 'Brecht' as always also collectivised, as effect and as socio-cultural method.[4] Brecht's Berlin is mappable at once through his addresses and memorials, a place of personal inhabitation and investment, carrying his signature, and through a more generic or methodological kind of city, which has a special affinity with his project. The discussion in the *Geschichten vom Herrn Keuner* (Tales of Herr Keuner) of two cities known as A and B is indicative (BB XVIII 27). On one level, it may be tempting to read the letters as initials standing for the principal cities in Brecht's life, Augsburg and Berlin. This would follow the *à clef* principle of a signature text like the poem 'Vom armen B. B.' (Of Poor B. B.' (BB XI 119–20)), inscribing Berlin into the writer's monogram as his signature city. But the letters are more evidently understandable as ciphers for model cities, and Brecht's Berlin constantly tends in that direction. The resistance to individualist identification that informs Brecht's project extends to a pro-grammatic pursuit of the city as model or methodical. This is the city of the famous 'Straßenszene' (Street Scene) essay, where typical urban experience comes together 'at some street corner' (BB XXII.i 371) in an ensemble of location, personal and group action, and demonstration. Brecht's Berlin serves, therefore, as a site of experiment and engagement between the individual and the ensemble: a person and a population, a house and housing, a street and the streets, a city and cities. At the same time, the city has a particular relation to cultural mediation in the age of culture's technical reproducibility. The ensemble to be considered here is also that of the media in which Brecht works. And, in its relationship to Berlin, this

---

[3] See Michael Rutschky and Juergen Teller, *Der verborgene Brecht: Ein Berliner Stadtrundgang*, ed. Inge Gellert and Klara Wallner (Zurich/Berlin/New York: Scalo, 1997), p. 65.
[4] Fredric Jameson, *Brecht and Method* (London/New York: Verso, 1998), pp. 10–11.

ensemble of means of production is always marked by effects of contradiction, of troubled accommodation.

'UNINHABITABLE AND YET UNLEAVABLE'

The heading is drawn from the poem 'Untergang der Städte Sodom und
Gomorra' (Fall of the Cities of Sodom and Gomorrah). It appeals to one of
the discursive commonplaces of Berlin in the Weimar period, the fleshpot
city as latter-day Sodom: 'unbewohnbar/Und doch unverlaßbar, ganz wie
London/Und Berlin war Sodom und Gomorra' (uninhabitable/And yet
unleavable, just like London/And Berlin was Sodom and Gomorrah (BB xiv
247)). The adversative couple 'unbewohnbar' and 'unverlaßbar' are thus put
in series with two other couples, the one – Sodom and Gomorrah – an
archetypal urban collocation, the other – London und Berlin – less routine
and yet deemed completely comparable in these terms to the cities of the
plain. This is characteristic for Brecht's mobilisation of Berlin: its attractions
and its impossibilities are at once singular and in series, linked to other cities
both ancient and modern. As if to mark this combination of singularity and
plurality, Sodom and Gomorrah are yoked together in the singular verb.
The internal rhyme-word 'war' resonates both with Gomorrah, artificially
drawing out its final syllable and thereby subjecting the poetic diction to an
effect of *Verfremdung* (defamiliarisation), and with the repetition of the
suffix of functionality – 'bar' – turned here into two forms of urban
dysfunction. Through this elaborate sequencing, the city of Berlin is
included by implication in the prognosis of 'Fall of the Cities'.

The relationship between Brecht and Berlin, this functional and dysfunctional city, is something of a curiosity. The uninhabitable but unleavable
city is the key location for his life, writing, and theatre-work, and yet its role
is also abstracted or effaced. As Michael Bienert notes in his literary
travelogue, the city is rarely named in Brecht's writing.[5] And when it is, it
tends to be 'generalised and defamiliarised',[6] as in 'Untergang der Städte
Sodom und Gomorra', where it is subject to the sort of generalisation and
Verfremdung noted above. *Verfremdung* is here understandable as a technical
showing of alienation, of the city's functional (or dysfunctional) character as
uninhabitable. It seems, to adapt a well-known formulation from Brecht's
urban poetry, that what remains of the city as experiential site is that which

---

[5] Michael Bienert, *Mit Brecht durch Berlin: Ein literarischer Reiseführer* (Frankfurt am Main: Insel,
  1998), p. 11.
[6] *Ibid.*, p. 17.

has passed through it, the wind of 'Vom armen B. B.', rather than any settled sense of habitation or inhabitation. This would be to follow Marie Neumüllers in her account of Brecht's city-texts as aligned with Augé's dialectics of space and non-space,[7] where any sense of location is understandable only as a function of passage. The wind that serves as a key element in Brecht's construction of the city is an effect both of place and of non-place, always in transition. The wind that blows through Berlin is also the wind of the proverbially windy city Chicago or that which Brecht imagines blowing the ruins of wartime Berlin over to California and reassembling them in Santa Monica (BB XXIII 48). Brecht's Berlin is located between situation and transition, specificity and generality (as generic city).

If Berlin has a privileged status among Brecht's cities, it owes this, paradoxically, to its constant changeability, as Brecht writes in 1928 (BB XXI 267). It is perhaps just this principle of changeability that makes Berlin available as a template for transformation into the city or cities *per se*. But the transformations of what the poem 'Über Deutschland' calls 'many-citied Berlin' (BB XIV 453) are as much on the side of loss, abjection, or melancholia as on the side of activist betterment. It is perhaps appropriate that an urbanist, the GDR architect Henselmann, should see in his friend and collaborator Brecht not an 'actionist' but a 'melancholic revolutionary'.[8] Brecht's treatments and transmutations of Berlin are typically cast between political actionism and left melancholy.

This ambivalence can be traced in some of the key transformations that Berlin undergoes. The city becomes, or – as a city of performance – performs as, the London of *Die Dreigroschenoper* (The Threepenny Opera). The performance of London in the cynical Berlin cabaret-style makes it act as a mirror, according to Canetti, for its self-indulgent Berlin audience, rather than as a locus of critical change.[9] Its Soho scenes accordingly reflect, in Adorno's critique, not the proletarian terrain of the Weidendammer Bridge, in the vicinity of the Schiffbauerdamm, but the bourgeois mores of the Kurfürstendamm.[10] Or Berlin is projected into the fantasy frontier city of Mahagonny, for if Mahagonny is construed as 'kein Ort' (no place (BB II 331)), the key place it is not is Scheffler's frontier

---

[7] Marie Neumüllers, 'Mahagonny, das ist kein Ort', *mahagonny.com: the brechtyearbook* 29 (2004), ed. Marc Silberman and Florian Vassen, 43–53; p. 42.

[8] See Susanne von Götz, '"Ich habe der Arbeiterklasse ins Antlitz geschaut": Ein Gespräch mit Hermann Henselmann, Architekt der Stalinallee, über Brecht und den 17. Juni 1953', *Der Tagesspiegel*, 17 June 1993.

[9] Elias Canetti, *Die Fackel im Ohr* (Berlin: Volk und Welt, 1983), p. 344.

[10] Theodor Wiesengrund Adorno, 'Zur Dreigroschenoper', *Die Musik: Monatsschrift* 21.1 (1928/9), 424–8; p. 427.

city, Berlin. And, as if following Walther Rathenau's famous comparison, Berlin also becomes the Euro-American hybrid of Berlin-Chicago as allegory of the modern metropolis.[11] This is allegory as an other (market)place for trading words and a place of exchange for speaking otherwise. The 'Speicherbrandprozeß' (warehouse-fire trial) of *Arturo Ui* (BB VII 63–71) as a transposition of the sham Reichstag-fire trial, figures just such a site for speaking otherwise. It is an allegorical treatment of a historical process of public speaking, of propagandistic rhetoric and corrupt juridical pronouncement, transposed from the burnt-out Berlin parliament to the burnt-out architecture of the Chicago marketplace.

In each of these cases, Berlin is a foundation for transposition, seen and spoken otherwise and used as a site for seeing and speaking otherwise. This principle should alert us to the dangers of making ready assumptions about the city's role in Brecht's work, where it will often appear in modes of disguise – in allegorical form. And the principle of allegory here implies the element of speaking otherwise inherent in the project for change, but, following Benjamin, it also bespeaks the catastrophic conception of history which threatens to subvert that project in the direction of melancholia.

The argument here will review Benjamin's contention that Brecht displayed lack of feeling for the décor of the city, combined with an extreme sensitivity to the city-dweller's 'specific modes of reaction' (WB II.ii 557). It is certainly the case that Brecht has a preoccupation with human experience and behaviour over scenic effects, as marked in his focus upon the human cost of the spectacle of Berlin in ruins after the Second World War (BB XXVII 279). Rather than engaging in detailed topographical exploration, representations of Berlin in his work are accordingly often abstracted towards a more topological modelling of space: an analytic system of typical rather than particular sites. Yet, it also seems appropriate to suggest a more dialectical – more Benjaminian – analysis of the relationship between the details of urban environment and social experience. How are Brecht's comments regarding the cityscape to be squared with his *plaidoyers* for the retention of trees in the urban environment, as in 'Die Pappel vom Karlsplatz' (The Poplar on the Karlsplatz (BB XII 295)),[12] with his interventions on public sculptures and other aspects of post-war city-planning, or with his indulgence, albeit self-ironic, in the 'decent' and 'pleasant' proportions of bourgeois building culture when describing his apartment in the Chausseestraße

[11] Rathenau declared that 'Spree-Athens' is dead and 'Spree-Chicago' rising up (*Die schönste Stadt*, p. 23).
[12] This, notwithstanding the flaw in Brecht's urban knowledge: 'Karlsplatz' is a misnomer for 'Karlplatz'.

(BB XXX 232) and the 'noble' construction of the villa in Buckow (BB XXVII 330)? Or, indeed, with the extension of this aesthetic requirement to the working environment of the theatre, on the highly decorative model of the Theater am Schiffbauerdamm (BB XV 255)? What sort of relationship obtains between this concern for designs for living and working and the demands of the street, the exterior dimension of city living? And to what extent might issues of urban architecture and topography, as derived from Berlin, indeed inform both his writing and his ideological and aesthetic principles of performance?

While Benjamin's account supports the idea of Brecht the sociologist, analysing the reactions of the city-dweller as if in psycho-technical laboratory conditions, here, as so often with Brecht, contradictions are in play. His early responses to Berlin recurrently focus on the powerful impact of the urban environment, its traffic and architecture. He describes the city in a letter of 1923 to Arnolt Bronnen as an ensemble or montage of attractions, incorporating swimming, shouting, drinking cocoa, the Friedrichstraße, Aschinger's restaurant, the Charité hospital, the Gleisdreieck junction, the UFA film company, and the Wannsee lake (BB XXVIII 192). The Charité, where Brecht was treated for malnutrition in 1922, introduces a wry *memento mori* into the ensemble of urban activity, consumption, and attraction. Marieluise Fleißer gives an account of the writer as semiologist of this urban ensemble, open to the 'signs of the city'.[13] He is seen as *flâneur* and *bricoleur*, 'using his eyes' to read the streets as he walked them and to collect their signage.[14] These signs can be configured as street-performance and hence function as models of everyday theatre, transferable to the stage, as propounded in 'Über alltägliches Theater' (On Everyday Theatre (BB XII 319–22)). Fleißer relates how, on his wandering through Berlin, Brecht witnesses a street-scene between a prostitute and a 'fat pimp', who gives her directions in how to comport herself.[15] Social *gestus* in its most express form – the body performing to sell itself – is thus a kind of street-theatre, subject to directorial styling. And the signs that Brecht reads are not just those of human reaction, but also of the material landscape that elicits and frames reaction.

In one of his short prose pieces in the feuilleton style from the mid 1920s, 'Kritik' (Criticism), Brecht describes a theatrical encounter with a girl standing beneath an archway in the Münzstraße. While she is in a site of

---

[13] Günther Rühle (ed.), *Materialien zum Leben und Schreiben der Marieluise Fleißer* (Frankfurt am Main: Suhrkamp, 1973), p. 156.
[14] *Ibid.*, p. 153.   [15] *Ibid.*

prostitution, she offers another kind of service, gratuitous fashion advice, enacted through an elaborately gestic performance of the body's relationship to the street: '"*Lang* ist modern! Nicht kurz!! Bitte!!!"' ("*Long* is modern! Not short!! Please!!!" (BB XIX 279)).[16] It is the prostitute who now plays the role of actor-director. The pavement is appropriated as a teaching-stage here, set before a proscenium arch. It is used to give the measure of what is appropriate everyday behaviour on that same stage. The street-scene of fashion criticism can work as a model for the methods of critical theatre. Following Benjamin's account of the prostitute as a representative figure of 'dialectics at a standstill', allied to the dialectical passage-space of the arcades as at once house and street (WB V.i 55), Brecht here figures the prostitute as embodied advertisement in a sort of passage-space between house and street and in a dialectical role between director and actor. The street-scene can be aligned with the sort of everyday performances on the streets of Berlin that Brecht describes as a model for his poetic *gestus* in the essay 'Über reimlose Lyrik mit unregelmäßigen Rhythmen' (On Rhymeless Poetry with Irregular Rhythms (BB XXII.i 361)). The addresses of Berlin may only rarely be explicitly present in his writing, but the sights and sounds, the behaviours and voices of the city inhabit its gestic fabric.

Fleißer describes Brecht as seeking to immerse himself in the stimulation of the city, riding on the top of a bus to be 'eye-to-eye' with advertisements.[17] When he goes out to study modes of social reaction, he is also eye-to-eye with Weimar surfaces, the culture of illumination and façade that galvanised Berlin in the 1920s. The sorts of behaviours that he sees at work amongst those surfaces are both generic performances by inhabitants of the capitalist metropolis and more specific modes of reaction, which are produced by the particular 'format' of Berlin (BB XXVIII 101). It is at once the city of mass entertainment, focused for Brecht especially on the institution of the Sportpalast, which finds its way into his writing in various forms, and the city of mass movement on the streets.

While Brecht took in the city with the methodology of the *flâneur*, he was no self-effacing observer, constructing himself rather as part of the Berlin spectacle. Portraits from the 1920s attest to this. His trademark shiny leather jacket was fashioned, it seems, as another kind of specular Weimar surface, as in Rudolf Schlichter's *Neue Sachlichkeit* portrait of 1926, taking

---

[16] I have corrected the published version here. In the manuscript, held in the Bertolt-Brecht-Archiv (BBA) of the Akademie der Künste in Berlin, 'Nicht kurz' is followed by two exclamation marks not one, part of a mounting series (BBA 51/50).

[17] Rühle (ed.), *Materialien*, p. 153.

the urban industrial surfaces of a car as its background. And his body-image and voice were strategically projected, more than life-size, into the city of light and its architectures of publicity, as represented in George Grosz's 1927 satirical cartoon of Brecht as propagandist and publicity object for the Ullstein publishing house, where he is set, as if one of the city's cultural monuments, in outsized form in front of the publicity façade of its massive new headquarters.[18] One benefit of his liaison with the Ullstein house was the glossy car given to him by one of their major corporate advertisers, Steyr. This is Brecht as eye-to-eye with the business of (self-)advertising.

If this suggests that the fashion victim of 'Kritik' has become a self-fashioning man who is at home – or a proficient visitor – in the city and its cultural, media, consumption, and transport networks, another of the *feuilleton* pieces from 1926 presents a different picture. In 'Meine längste Reise' (My Longest Journey (BB XIX 283–5)), the narrator is at a loss in his negotiation of Berlin's public transport system. Fleißer describes Brecht as feeling antipathy towards the underground,[19] and this text gives an account of the anomie it induces. The narrator takes the underground from the Kaiserhof station to Nollendorfplatz, but finds himself transported on an allegorical journey well beyond his nominal goal. He has reached the end of his credit, has forfeited his meal ticket for Aschinger's restaurant, been given to understand that the city puts no value upon him. He gets out at the terminus, Reichskanzlerplatz, and returns on foot to his original destination, but still arrives too early at a place where nothing much awaits him. The text ends with the change of fortunes that soon came along, but also with the thought that these might change back at any time. The 'extraordinarily long journey' remains as a spectre of the sort of disorder, the lack of agency and orientation that might return on the Berlin network.

It is not only the underground that can lead to disorientation. One of Brecht's late poems provides an image that can serve as emblematic for the negotiation of urban topography in his work:

> 'Hier ist die Karte, da ist die Straße
> Sieh hier die Biegung, sieh da das Gefäll!'
> 'Gib mir die Karte, da will ich gehen.
> Nach der Karte
> Geht es sich schnell.'   (BB XV 286)

('Here is the map, there is the street / See here the bend, there the slope!' / 'Give me the map, that's where I want to go. / You can go quickly / By the map.')

---

[18] See Bienert, *Mit Brecht*, p. 61.   [19] *Ibid.*

The map provides an image of the street that offers facility of negotiation. Its two-dimensionality, however, is incommensurate with its object: the map represents turns, while the street also displays vertical contours. The second voice in the poem is made to fix upon the abstraction of the map as alternative urban space, as exposed in the double meanings that emerge in the response. The 'da' in 'da will ich gehen' becomes readable as the map itself, substituted for the 'da' that was the street, and 'Nach der Karte' readable as 'to the map', rather than according to it. This is indeed a self-reflexive journey ('Geht es sich'), a topographical short-circuit avoiding the gradients of the streets and quickly completed. The map stands here for maps of all kinds: for a map of Berlin, certainly, but also for other modes of abstracted representation. Brecht's project is constantly caught in the tension between the demands of real space and time and the guiding medium of their negotiation: the map, the image, or the formula. The gravitation between the map or plan and the demands of real terrain in his negotiation of the city of Berlin is also transferable, *mutatis mutandis*, onto the general orientation and mediation of his project, especially in its allegorical turns.

COHABITATION: BRECHT AND BENJAMIN

Before considering in more detail Brecht's mapping of urban exteriors, it is worth looking at his understanding of interior, domestic space. The two dimensions of living space are always dialectically involved with each other, not least through the mediation of the space of the theatre: the 'Haus' as an inside space also incorporating the outside. Domestic space for Brecht was always also work-place, and as such a kind of studio-theatre: an experimental space for testing theatrical and other work in progress. The function of living-space in the theatre thereby reflects back on the viability of living-space proper. He writes of the stage-set of an apartment that it is constructed not for habitation as such but to demonstrate inhabitants inhabiting it (BB XXII.i 260), and something of this instrumental function, and concomitant failure of function, is bound to be transferred to the writer's living practices in both internal and external spaces.

As we saw, Benjamin foregrounds Brecht's lack of attachment to the urban environment as 'décor', the terrain for so much of his own investigation, where urban façade and interior are dialectically entwined. Brecht and Benjamin both make records of a conversation they hold in June 1931, while staying in the south of France, exploring what appears to be Benjamin's home territory – living habits – from a place of proto-emigration.

It is a striking example of what might be called the cohabitation of this somewhat odd couple, the common space that is constructed out of their dialogue and that displays ambivalences on both sides. In Benjamin's account (WB VI 435–6), Brecht shows the sort of investment in styles and spaces of living that might be expected from Benjamin, who in his turn shows a 'Brechtian' critical distance from such concerns. Not for nothing is Brecht an exemplary figure for Benjamin's construction of the 'destructive character' and the principle of 'clearing out', of strategic vandalism, that goes with it (WB IV.i 396). Brecht causes surprise, however, by going against habit with his personal engagement in this subject, while Benjamin conversely recedes from his habitual private investment in it. The dialogue is thus 'außergewöhnlich' (extraordinary or 'extra-habitual' (WB VI 435)) indeed, outside their normal habitat, their spaces of habit. And the curious exchange of roles gives an indication both of the destructive character that subtends Benjamin's attachment to bourgeois standards of living and the attachment to those standards that Brecht finds himself imitating in spite of himself.

The curiously crossed debate provides room for unlikely forms of hospitality and accommodation between the two men, but also for the intervention of the spectre of the inhospitable host and the unwanted guest. Ultimately, these are also internalised roles. For Benjamin, the unwanted guest is represented in his writings on being at home in Berlin, both inside and on the streets, by the uncanny alter ego of the *bucklichte Männlein*. And Brecht, too, is subject to splitting. In an autobiographical note from the late 1920s, he styles himself as vagrant, unable to habituate himself to cities. The passage from habitation to habitation leads to a state of self-inhabitation ('sich selber zu bewohnen'), which extends the splitting between habit and passing through to his sense of self as provisional (BB XXVI 293–4). The split is a lasting one. In the poem 'Ein neues Haus' (A New House), written about the Weissensee villa, Brecht's first settled habitation after returning from exile to the ruins of Berlin, this condition is nicely caught in the ambiguity of the lines: 'Immer noch / Liegt auf dem Schrank mit den Manuskripten / Mein Koffer.' (Still / Lying on the cupboard with the manuscripts / Is my suitcase (BB XV 205)). The situation of the writer is always in transit, and the manuscripts are hence readable here as either in the cupboard, on the cupboard with the suitcase, or in the suitcase on the cupboard. Brecht, his work, and his Berlin habitations are in this sense always in a version of the 'Koffer in Berlin' mode, subject to an uncanny sense of removability. If, writing in 1953 from his retreat in Buckow, he describes a sense of existence as 'verfremdet', or estranged, by the events of the workers' uprising of the 17 June (BB XXVII 346), this is a mark of the sorts of accommodations, internal and external, that he has made. The feeling of living in a land that is still 'unheimlich' (BB XXVII 350), as he notes in 1954, extends to the split subjectivity that he inhabits.

The common denominator in Brecht's sequence of places to live in Berlin and elsewhere is a sense of never being properly at home, and this failure of home-making corresponds, in turn, to the fraught condition of the models for living that he constructs in his work. From exile in Paris in 1934, Benjamin sends Brecht a reproduction of Chardin's *Castle of Cards*, a work of art in the age of its technical reproducibility, with the ironic commentary that it is a 'building scheme' sent to him for training purposes by the 'master'.[20] This card demonstrating a card game serves as a playful *mise-en-abyme* for the relationship between Brecht and Benjamin, players of cards, chess, and ideas. The two men, master-builders both, each according to their method, construct their allegorical houses of cards. These are in the mode of interior building models for living outside. But they also correspond to another image that Brecht considers in his writings on *Verfremdung*, Brueghel's *The Tower of Babel*. The image is described as representing the tower as 'built crooked' and always provisional (BB XXII.i 273). Though the Brechtian and Benjaminian building projects are mediated by effects of *Verfremdung*, showing awareness of their own constructedness, they are always also liable to collapse into ruins, if not for internal reasons then through the intervention of the catastrophic wind of history, which may be all that will remain of them.

POETIC ACCOMMODATIONS

The debate that Brecht and Benjamin play out on internal accommodations also provides ground for thinking outwards into urban topography. Before turning to how this might figure in Brecht's work in the open-house of the theatre, it is worth considering its function in his poetry, and especially with regard to the critical dialogue that Benjamin establishes with it. This is writing that is often ill-accommodated, at odds with its location, as in one of Brecht's most famous lyrics of divided location: 'Schwierige Zeiten' (Difficult Times) of 1955. The poetic subject is caught in a bi-focal space here, between the interior – the scene of writing – and what he sees through his window. Forms of 'Gewohnheit' or habit, writing on the one hand and admiring nature on the other, are in conflict. The poem attributes the first

---

[20] Benjamin, *Gesammelte Briefe*, vol. IV, p. 335.

of these habits to adult life and the second to the poet's childhood world, and the second draft makes explicit what is only implicit in the final version: that the world of writerly compulsion is 'in Berlin'.[21] This is Berlin, however, not as part of the conventional metropolitan–provincial opposition, but as a site of withdrawal from the city. It is telling that 'in Berlin' is replaced in the final version of the poem by 'im Garten' (BB xv 294). The refusal to look clearly outwards through the window puts a block not only on the garden scene and its pastoral recall, but also on the city of the poet in difficult times, in Berlin but unable to be of it. The excluded site of the scene outside the window also becomes the elegiac material of the poem, and what it displaces is the here and now that presses upon the writer. The poem characterises the poet, therefore, as in a double exile as he inhabits the scene of writing, ill at home in it, unhabituated.

If 'Schwierige Zeiten' allows only for the domestic habit of writing, Brecht's earlier poetry at first ironically inhabits and then evicts itself from the interior. The poems of *Bertolt Brechts Hauspostille* (Bertolt Brecht's Domestic Breviary) are written and rewritten over the period in which Brecht moved to Berlin. It is indicative that the first version of what was to become 'Vom armen B. B.', the signature poem of the collection, was written on the night train heading south after an unsuccessful attempt at establishing himself in the capital in the winter of 1921–2. This is poetry in the transitional mode, on the move between locations. It is programmed to act in the mode of the breviary as bourgeois domestic companion text, but to use that form only to vandalise and evacuate its structures. The collection includes the exodus of the men of Mahagonny to that fantasy no-place of a city, Berlin by any other name. The seductive but homeless character of Mahagonny-Berlin is also found in the poem of urban vagrancy 'Gegen Verführung' (Against Seduction), for which Benjamin supplies a commentary. The opening stanza of the poem opens the structure of the house up, with the nightwind felt in the doorway (BB xi 116). This is the house as already conforming to the abandonment of 'Vom armen B. B.', feeling the wind that will be all that is left of it, and without the prospect of the most fundamental of domestic habits, that of returning home. Benjamin's commentary enacts another version of the dialogue on forms of living, as he feels drawn to gloss the poem through the discourse of the ruin, the collapsed house, offering no habitation.

The other poems from the *Hauspostille* treated in Benjamin's commentary extend this picture of evacuation from the vandalised home, moving

---

[21] BBA 202.

into more transitory habitats. 'Von den Sündern in der Hölle' (Of the Sinners in Hell (BB XI 118–19)) is a mock-elegy, incorporating amongst the dear departed the poet himself. In Benjamin's commentary this is the poet as the product of his original habitat, Catholic Bavaria, constructing a kind of 'Marterl' or wayside shrine, a site of memory for the dead. The poet's passage to Berlin, far removed from this habitat and its compulsive habits of imitation, helps to explain the radical displacement that the ritual structures undergo here. As Benjamin suggests, the dead in the fires of hell are both memorialised here and invoked as passers-by before their own memorial sites (WB II.ii 550). Brecht constructs, in other words, a performative version of the 'Marterl', the memorial stone as the final home or property of the dead, and makes it into a place of nomadic passage. His own memorial takes the form of a 'Hundestein' or dog's stone, one marked by the needs of passing vagrant animals.

This litany against old habits of habitation is perhaps most famously figured in the mock-martyric stations of 'Vom armen B. B.' It appears in the second stanza, where the poetic persona's assertion of home territory, that he is 'daheim' in the 'asphalt city', rings untrue: an infelicitous speech act yoking the adoptive asphalt city Berlin to the vernacular 'daheim' of his Bavarian origins. His place as he passes through the stations of the poem is interstitial, at once inside and outside any habitable structures. He imitates the habits of the city-dweller, but remains unhabituated, inviting others into his home, but without offering firm foundations. As a specimen of his species – 'a light breed' – the poetic subject identifies with the builders of cities and their medial networks, but here too the foundations are not firm: the 'indestructible' cities of Manhattan or Berlin are built not to last, or only to last in what passes through them: the wind. Benjamin's suggestion that the city might find a new habitation in the wind, redeeming the negation in a dialectical *Aufhebung* or sublation, remains uncertain.

Against this nihilistic framework, the Babylonian city is emptied out and vandalised by a provisional generation not followed by anything of account. As a representative of this generation without the successors who could make sense of their forerunning, the destructive character of Brecht's 'I' is caught in a condition of fundamental displacement. Benjamin notes the heaping of prepositions of place (WB II.ii 554), an accumulation that also extends to temporal siting, as the subject is caught between inside and outside, past and present. If the sequence is, as Benjamin comments, 'ungewöhnlich' (unusually) confusing, then it resonates with the loss of orientation through *habitus*, of the 'gewöhnlich' or habitual. Speirs argues that the line 'Aus den schwarzen Wäldern' can be read as 'made out of the black woods',[22] thus preparing for the identificatory figures of trees that run through Brecht's poetry. In that case, the tree-poet is here displaced from the woods into the city, from one cold habitat not properly his to another, as he is transplanted into asphalt.

The poet is constructed in Benjamin's commentary as a topographical figure combining the wind-blown door of 'Gegen die Verführung' and the 'Hundestein' of 'Von den Sündern in der Hölle'. He becomes a metaphorical gate through which the reader might pass and bearing 'B. B.' as a worn inscription (WB II.ii 554). It seems most appropriate to construe this as the city-gate through which the 'armer B. B.' passes, without achieving a settled place inside. It stands as a signature structure of entry for the reader as 'passer-by' but, like the dead figures of 'Von den Sündern', it seems that, in following the poet through the gate that carries his monogram, the reader is also made to identify with it, as a memorial for lost self. Out of this figure of self-effacement and passing over Benjamin constructs the possibility of a more active kind of gate, one that resists the routine passing of its own efforts and of the reader through it. In order to block such access, it seems that the gate has to fall, but only thereby does it come to stand in a meaningful way (WB II.ii 554). The uncertainty of Benjamin's recuperative move, taking the ruin as 'provisional', a necessary preamble to the engagement of the later poetry, is nicely caught in this figure of standing through falling. It provides a suitably ambivalent shape for the gate through, or past, which to pass to Brecht's later city poetry, as the writer who is resident, but also vagrant, in Berlin turns from the genre of the home breviary to that of the city-primer in the *Lesebuch für Städtebewohner* (Primer for City Dwellers): a reader of city life in poems, but also a guide to the reading of the city and its modes of habitation.

The category of the vandal from the Brecht–Benjamin dialogue can be aligned with the reduction of living patterns to pure transition that Brecht dramatises in the poems of the *Lesebuch*. For Benjamin, these are poems of revolutionary necessity and of exile, reading as prescient of the emigrations forced onto the city dwellers in Berlin and elsewhere by the rise of National Socialism. The anti-habitual *habitus* assumed by the transient protagonists of these poems is thus, in Benjamin's terms, a kind of 'crypto-emigration' (WB II.ii 556). For the inner emigrant the assumption of living-space in the city is merged, that is, with the underground, secretive space of the crypt.

[22] Ronald Speirs, 'Vom armen B. B.', *Brecht Handbuch*, ed. Jan Knopf, 5 vols. (Stuttgart: Metzler, 2001–3), vol. II, pp. 104–9; pp. 106–7.

It is perhaps a necessary consequence of this encryption that the cityscape presented here is under disguise, neither it nor its topographical features identified in other than generic terms.

Benjamin's dramatisation of the implications of the ballad 'Vom armen B. B.' through the allegorical figure of the fallen gate implies a removal of personal trace, here in the already partially effaced memorial signature. And the removal of tracks becomes the prime *gestus* of the *Lesebuch*, as instanced in the refrain of its opening poem: 'Verwisch die Spuren!' (Erase the traces!). It marks a new form of *habitus*, which works by removing all old habits of engagement with the city and other inhabitants. This extends to the final place of the crypto-emigrant, an unknown fighter encrypted without a tombstone (BB XI 157). The poem prompts Benjamin's account of Brecht as without feeling for the décor of the city (the 'ocean of houses', the 'breath-taking tempo of traffic', and the entertainment industry) and yet hyper-sensitive to urban social behaviours, so producing an unprecedented form of city poetry (WB II.ii 556–7). The reduction of urban *habitus* in these poems to a handbook of survival strategies, all turning on an erasure of traces of habits, also involves an erasing of the habitual forms of city poetry. A sequence of *topoi* familiar from Berlin poems of the first decades of the twentieth century is subjected to extreme reduction and abstraction here: the 'ocean of houses' is abstracted into any house that is available for temporary lodging; the tempo of urban traffic is reduced to the station as a site of arrival in the city but also as the place of separation from the other; and the entertainment industry is displaced into an establishment carrying the name of another city. The 'Stadt Hamburg' is readable either as the city itself or as a hotel or inn with that name, a generic place of temporary accommodation and entertainment. Hamburg is a city particularly associated with emigration, and – as a city of entertainment and accommodation in transit – peculiarly suited to encryption as a hotel in another city: a place for crypto-emigration.

While the *Lesebuch* is concerned with the urban *habitus* in its most transient effects, the traces under erasure and the smoke dispersing from the chimney, Brecht's later poetry maintains its equivocal relationship to the urban environment. This can be pursued through Benjamin's commentary, as it extends to the *Deutsche Kriegsfibel* (German War Primer). Benjamin takes up the motif of inscription in the built environment when he describes this text as lapidary. But the implication of the lapidary style here is less that of memorialisation as setting in stone than brevity; and when the material demands of chiselling in stone are removed, that brevity becomes a mark of haste, of writing that can only afford to adopt cursory forms and short habits. The style of inscription is thus exemplified for Benjamin in a more transitory form of public writing, in Brecht's verse:

> Auf der Mauer stand mit Kreide:
> Sie wollen den Krieg.
> Der es geschrieben hat
> Ist schon gefallen.   (BB XII 12)

(On the wall there stood in chalk: / They want war. / He who wrote it / Has already fallen.)

Benjamin suggests that the first line here could be a signature at the head of all the poems in the *Deutsche Kriegsfibel*: memorial inscriptions not cut in stone but chalked on the palisades (WB II.ii 564). The chalked inscription is thus the counter-figure to the walls painted in his colours by the antagonist of the collection, the 'decorator' Hitler. The transmutation of the wall into a fence in Benjamin's gloss projects the logic of transition into the architectural grounding of the inscriptions. The texts turn on the paradox of appearing to be written to last in their meaning and yet with the *gestus* of graffiti. Just as the city-gate that Benjamin employs as allegory for the *Hauspostille* has to fall in order to stand in the way, so here the writer of what stands on the wall has already fallen: the topography of urban resistance is marked out as provisional, but persistent in its effects.

What though, finally, of Berlin in Brecht's poetry when he is no longer in the position of the urban resistance fighter, but writing on the side of the metropolitan establishment? When he returned to Berlin after the war, the fabric of the city and its topography was in ruins, and the perceived function of the poet was no longer to write graffiti on the walls of the prevailing ideology but to point up the false designs according to which they were constructed by its predecessor. The primary *gestus* of showing, not least as deployed in the exposure of false habits of body and mind, is here redeployed to show false building habits, as enacted in the poem addressed to Helene Weigel for the 1949 premiere of *Mother Courage* at the Deutsches Theater. The poem calls her onto the stage of the 'Trümmerstadt' or city of ruins in order to point out the 'false construction formula' on the 'fallen house' (BB XV 203). The collapsed house here is at once the Deutsches Theater, representing the Berlin theatre houses put to abuse by the Nazis, and the house in a more generic sense in the 'Trümmerstadt' as city without houses and now the *tabula rasa* stage for a potential new kind of political theatre.

Brecht was all too aware that the ideological substructures of the ruined houses persist; as he wrote in the foreword to the *Antigonemodell*, what is so bad about ruins is that the house is gone, but the building plans remain (BB XXV 74). While Brecht was determined to point up the false formula, the deictic *gestus* was soon to be turned back upon him. The building of the Stalinallee as architectural display-ground for the GDR resurrected the spectre of urban planning and building as the theatre of totalitarian ideology. And here Brecht was on the side of the 'false construction formula'. He supported the building of Socialist 'palaces for living' in a style that emulated the buildings of the Prussian *ancien régime* and a building politics that mimicked that of that National Socialist regime by expurgating any internationalist Bauhaus influences in the pursuit of an organically German style (BB XXIII 203–4). Having excoriated the 'decorator' Hitler's designs for the 'deutsches Haus', a 'shit-house' parading as new-build (BB XI 215), Brecht here proves less perspicacious in questions of ideological housing. While Hitler's constructions are built out of damage, tearing (BB XI 217), the Stalinallee project foreshadows another project for a wall built out of the torn state of Berlin. Its houses are part of the same historical sequence as the allegorical German house of 'O Deutschland, bleiche Mutter!' (O Germany, pale mother! (BB XI 253–4)), offering only ambivalent habitation for her shameful children.

Fired up by the Stalinallee project, the Brecht who had been described as having no interest in urban décor became avidly involved in architectural debates with the chief architect, Hermann Henselmann, visiting the building-site and writing essays on urban design. Where his early city poetry had advocated the mode of graffiti, he now had his verses celebrating the GDR building project set in stone and bronze on two of the key buildings in the Stalinallee project. The verse on the Hochhaus an der Weberwiese proclaims it as part of the new workers' city of peace, built for its builders (BB XV 254). As Henselmann remarks of Brecht, he aspired to be the 'house-poet' of the builders of cities.[23] The house-poet's encomium for solid social housing has to be read, however, against the sort of provisionality of buildings that Brecht always espoused and that achieves new poignancy in the age of weapons of mass destruction (BB XVIII 42). Urban development remains a site of contradiction for the house-poet in this time of extreme political pressure.

That the verses for the Stalinallee project might be a kind of false construction formula is suggested by the poems Brecht wrote from his retreat in Buckow following the putting down of the workers' revolt led by the Stalinallee builders, when he intervened on the side of the regime.

---

[23] Hermann Henselmann, 'Brecht und die Stadt', *Die Weltbühne*, 25 September 1973.

Brecht sees the ideological space of the 'street' being co-opted here by other groups than the workers and manipulated by the intervention of the 'Bürgersteig', or pavement, the space of the unreconstructed bourgeoisie.[24] Brecht witnesses the Columbushaus on the Potsdamer Platz on fire, is reminded of the fateful burning of the Reichstag, and argues that workers responsible for building would not use fire as a weapon, then as now. And yet, in this situation of confusion on the street, his own topographical placement becomes uncertain, and he sanctions the intervention of the regime against the uprising. The scenes of the brutal putting down of the workers' uprising on the streets of East Berlin on 17 June thus come to imitate those witnessed by Brecht in the 'Blutmai' or Blood-May of 1929, when police battled with KPD (Kommunistische Partei Deutschlands) protestors outside the Karl-Liebknecht-Haus on the Bülowplatz.

In the poem 'Böser Morgen' (Wicked Morning), written in the aftermath of 17 June, the *gestus* of showing is turned back upon the poetic persona, as if he were indeed identified with the false formula. In a dream, the broken fingers of workers point out his diseased condition (BB XII 310). And in 'Die Kelle' (The Trowel (BB XV 270)), the persona dreams of himself as a construction worker on the Stalinallee, projected from his retreat into the building- and battle-site of Berlin and having half of his trowel shot out of his hand. Having embraced the party-line, partly, it seems, in order to secure the future of his own 'house', the Theater am Schiffbauerdamm as quarters for the Berliner Ensemble, Brecht's dream-poems expose his accommodation. It seems that dream enters Brecht's writing here as an embodiment of the return of the repressed, bringing the domain of the unconscious into the political arena of his work under the sign of *Entstellung*, of displacement and disfigurement. The disfigurement of the fingers that point at him in 'Böser Morgen' serves to show *Entstellung* being shown, to perform a *gestus* of exposure in a theatre of self-indictment.

In Brecht's discussions with Benjamin, Kafka serves as a contrapuntal figure, associated with the principles of the 'unheimlich' (WB VI 527) and of 'Entstellungen' (WB VI 433), the sort of socio-psychical nightmares that fascinate Brecht but that have to be kept at bay in his own project. The dreams of uncanny displacement in Berlin that we saw in Kafka's diaries are also uncannily close to a text like 'Meine längste Reise'. Benjamin writes that *Der Prozeß* (The Trial) is informed for Brecht by a nightmarish fear of the expansion of cities and their ambivalent social structures (WB VI 528–9). When Brecht is trying to awaken from the nightmare of history and his own

---

[24] See the letter to Peter Suhrkamp of 1 July 1953 (BB XXX 183).

accommodations with it, it comes to haunt him in the shape of the Berlin builders exposing his own role in the rebuilding of the metropolitan nightmare and its 'false building formulas'. The builders use the dream to enter the private space of Brecht's retreat and point to his imbrication in the Kafkaesque *Entstellungen* behind the building project of the capital of the GDR. Buckow, Brecht's extra-urban working- and living-space, is here what Wilfried Schoeller calls the 'echo space' and 'counter-location' for the difficult accommodations he makes in Berlin.[25] In 'Böser Morgen', the poet is one of a sequence of disfigured elements exposed in the landscape of that other place. In the 'Adresse des sterbenden Dichters an die Jugend' (Address by the Dying Poet to the Young) of 1939, Brecht adopted the persona of the dying poet to talk of the need to rid the cities of plague in order to make them habitable once more (BB XIV 456); now he is cast in the nightmare role of the bearer of contagion, removed from the city but indicative of its diseased condition.

THEATRICAL ACCOMMODATIONS

The nightmares of the modern city and the accommodations, physical, psychological, and ideological that its inhabitants make are a recurrent theme of Brecht's theatre. Responding to the draft of Max Frisch's play *Als der Krieg zu Ende war* (When the War Was Over (1947)), set against the backdrop of Berlin in ruins, Brecht constructs a commentary under the title 'Berliner Thema' (BB XX 197). The Berlin theme here is just that range of accommodations, as they figure in the straitened conditions of the immediate post-war period, and the theme in question is at work in all of Brecht's Berlin theatre and the different versions of the urban nightmare that they present.

Generally, the city takes an allegorical form here. If the term 'allegory' is associated with the marketplace as site for public speaking in another mode, Brecht's allegorical cities, and not least the dystopian/utopian city of Mahagonny, are such other marketplaces: projected scenes for playing out and speaking against the nightmares of capitalist exchange and exploitation. While Berlin was the real place in which Brecht experienced the modern marketplace most intensely, it rarely appears explicitly in his plays. Three exceptions will be the focus of this section, each of them motivated by the specific historical experience of the city, the singular but also historically representative nightmares of Berlin.

---

[25] Schoeller, *Nach Berlin!*, p. 45.

In *Trommeln in der Nacht* (Drums in the Night (1922)) the city takes one of its most familiar forms for Brecht, that of the battlefield (BB XXVII 70), located in a particular form of the modern marketplace as site of communication: the newspaper quarter, metonymically known as 'die Zeitungen' (The Papers). While the play never enters the barricaded site of the Spartacist battles in the newspaper quarter, as it passes from the domestic scene to public places, it makes recurrent reference to it. Several of the characters are involved in the newspaper industry, and trade in its discourse. The reality of the historical site of class warfare is ironically concealed behind the flimsy apparatus of bourgeois false consciousness, as marked in the *mise-en-scène* for the opening scene in the manuscript for the 1922 performance. The set appears provisional and the revolutionary action behind the scenes 'thin and ghostlike' (BB I 554). In conjunction with stage designer Caspar Neher, Brecht constructs theatrical space here as layered, with the revolution displaced into a gap between the cardboard walls of the domestic scene and the backcloth depicting the city 'in childlike fashion'.

The bourgeois melodrama played out in front of the concealed historical drama remains in an artificial, pantomimic mode. If, as the text suggests, the opening act is under the sign of Africa, the battle-place from which the ghostly Kragler returns to Berlin, the scenes we see can indeed seem only like thin and ghostlike theatrical interpositions. The play skirts around the action of the revolution, moving on to the Piccadillybar, and thereby to a place ironically renamed for the purposes of the drama: the Piccadillybar, which became known as the Deutsches Kaffeehaus 'Vaterland' in the nationalist zeal of 1914, here reverts to its more cosmopolitan pre-war name. And while later scenes take the action out onto the street, the locations remain generic and transitional: the 'path to the suburbs' of act three or the bridge of act five. One version of the heading of the third act has it located on a 'path to the newspaper quarter',[26] which gives an extra twist to the provisional nature of the setting, suggesting that it is on a course of engagement with, or evasion of, the political action within the city.

In the revised 1953 version of the play, Brecht writes another character into its fourth act: a young worker as counterpart to Kragler, representing intervention in the historical action that goes on behind the scenes and helping to satisfy the demands of the Socialist Realist agenda. And with that new activist character comes a more concrete engagement with the topographical specifics of the city, as locations and institutions from the

[26] Bertolt Brecht, *Gesammelte Werke in acht Bänden* (Frankfurt am Main: Suhrkamp. 1967), vol. I, p. 102.

Hausvogteiplatz and Brecht's home street, the Chausseestraße, to Siemens, Mosse, and Ullstein come to be named. Of course Berlin has become more properly Brecht's home territory by 1953, albeit interrupted by the enforced exile of the National Socialist period and the voluntary exile to the Buckow villa. It seems, though, that the topography which is sketched into the later version of the play is not simply local colour, but a response to demand for the embedding of drama in historical realities. In the event, the play remains uncomfortably cast between the historical-topographical real and the pantomime dimension of the painted cityscape and the lantern moon.

Furcht und Elend des Dritten Reiches (Fear and Misery of the Third Reich) is written under more direct political pressure, and, notwithstanding its episodic form, adopts a more conventional build in its dramatic style. What Benjamin calls its traditional dramaturgic construction (WB II.ii 516) corresponds in turn to the use of locality. Those scenes that are set in Berlin, whether in interior or exterior space, are given degrees of topographical determination. Brecht responds to Lukács's approval of his return towards dramatic theatre here by suggesting that epic has the flexibility to incorporate real space in this way (BB XXVI 318). Realistic topography, both interior and exterior, provides a framework for a montage of *gestus* typical for life under dictatorship, and is thereby turned towards the tableau principle of the epic style. The drama of the play turns on the life-and-death implications of revealing real locations and committing to living in them, while its epic element relies on the tableau-like showing of *gestus*: the kinds of behaviour that are used for persecution and survival in this time and place of fear and abjection. The tension between these two modes is fundamental to the effect of the play.

The first scene, 'Volksgemeinschaft' (Community of the *Volk*), introduces the principle of the dual topography of dramatic and epic modes. It represents two SS officers, coming from the celebrations after Hitler's inauguration as Reich Chancellor and getting lost in the capital to which they lay claim. While the date is given, the location is a generic one – 'The Street' – a location that had become during the street-battles of the Weimar Republic a metonymic representation of the workers who militate on it. It is the same allegorical street as is described in the motto verse for the second scene as (perhaps) retaining a memory of injustices done to its betrayed inhabitants (BB IV 344). The SS men find themselves in this 'street', remote from the power-base of the Reich Chancellery, and in a scene of grotesque disorientation, only emphasised by the use of the Berlin vernacular (BB IV 342). At a loss in this topography, they enact a paranoid pantomime, which culminates in shooting willy-nilly at the enemy territory, prompted by an innocent call from one side of the street and finding a victim on the opposite side. The scene presents a burlesque picture of the sort of *habitus* of vandalism characterising a regime of total violence that fails to know the city it inhabits.

The third scene, 'Das Kreidekreuz' (The Chalk Cross), a theatrical battle of wits between an SA-man out to entrap agitators and a Worker, explores further the forms of living in the city that are imposed by the Nazi regime. When places in Berlin are identified, it is in disguise. The SA-man suggests that his next destination will be in Reinickendorf or Rummelsburg, or maybe Lichterfelde (BB IV 345). His resistance to the perceived trick of being made to reveal the location of his operations also plays a trick back on him, ironically serving to reveal their indiscriminate topographical spread. Rummelsburg recurs as the putative home *Kiez* or neighbourhood of the Worker when he is drawn into performing a scene from the 'Stempelstelle' (dole office or 'stamp-station') in the Münzstraße: a mock-*Lehrstück*, designed by the SA-man, as actor-director, to show the infallibility of the Nazi surveillance network. The interview between him and the Worker is in a double site, combining and confusing the domestic space that they temporarily inhabit with the projected performance space of the 'Stempelstelle' and incorporating a performance style derived from habits of dissimulation and counter-dissimulation. The Worker then moves scene from the Münzstraße to the nearby Alexanderplatz in order to perform a routine of dissidence in the person of a proletarian woman and responding to it with the role of the informer, garnered as it were from the second scene of the play. He runs from the 'Alex', as scene of this dissident performance, apparently back to the same place, but the 'Alex' serves here as a double site, naming the square both as home-space of proletarian dissidence and of the police headquarters, now under the control of the Nazis.[27] He thus runs from the Alex to the Alex and back to the Alex, only to find that the woman he aims to expose has gone.

This trick parable of the escape of the dissident from surveillance is in turn outmanoeuvred by the SA-man's performance of the professional trick of placing the chalk cross on the back of the Worker: a stamp from the 'Stempelstelle' that will mark him out wherever he seeks to disappear in the city.[28] If dissidents use chalk to mark the city with their transitory texts of protest when on the run, so they can be marked and traced in transit in

---

[27] The location of the Polizeipräsidium is marked by a memorial to the victims of the Nazi reign there.
[28] This marking out for hunting down as criminal is inevitably reminiscent of the M chalked on the back of Peter Lorre in Lang's *M*.

their turn. Having established his 'Stempelstelle' *Lehrstück* as a means of exposing dissident tricks, the SA-man exposes his own secret practices: the appearance of winning out is subverted, as indicated when he tricks himself into spoiling his earlier trick, revealing in an unguarded moment that his next 'visit' will indeed be to Reinickendorf.

One of the scenes visited as a secondary site of the performance in the 'Stempelstelle' *Lehrstück* is the concentration camp: suggested but then ironically rejected as the scene for a discussion between a deposed Weimar functionary and Dr Ley, head of the German Labour Front (BB IV 352). In the following scenes, the concentration camp is indeed visited, and in Scene 4 this takes the form of Berlin's local camp at Oranienburg, forerunner of Sachsenhausen and the destination for many Berlin political dissidents. While the camp is not identified in the first version of the play, for the 1945 performance in New York it is given date and place: Konzentrationslager Oranienburg, 1934. The scene replays the performance set-up of the third scene, as the weary SS-guard allows the prisoner to whip the ground to trick the *Gruppenführer* into thinking he is still being beaten. Here, though, the trick fails, and the beating is intensified. Whereas the worker in the earlier scene still had some freedom to outmanoeuvre the system, toying with the camp as a site for his dissident performance but remaining on the relatively safer territory of the streets of Berlin, here that performance is staged as an endgame in the camp outside the city.

That the performer might be interchangeable in each case is suggested by the prospect of return to the Oranienburg camp in Scene 6, set in the Charité in Berlin. Here, a victim of beating at Oranienburg is brought to the hospital to be stitched up and returned to the labour camp. The surgeon's claim to want to expose the working environment of his patients in order better to treat them is silenced before the 'occupational illness' of the internee. One of the other patients mocks the surgeon's performance, asking where the patient is from and to where he will return (BB IV 380). The answer is finally given by one of the surgeon's assistants: 'Worker. Delivered from Oranienburg' (BB IV 381). His destination can only be the same as his provenance. The typical Worker of Scene 3 still free to perform acts of dissidence, incarcerated in Scene 4 and hospitalised in Scene 6, is to be made ready to return to his 'place of work'. The performance that could still range over the Berlin's topography in the earlier scene is now reduced to scenes without agency in the carceral loop between the city's extramural labour camp and its hospital. It thereby displays the transposition from city to camp posited by Agamben as the topographical condition of the state of exception.

The final dramatic accommodation with Berlin to be considered here is not a play proper, but its prelude: the 1948 'Vorspiel' that Brecht wrote for his version of *Antigone*, set in the ruined capital as 'Viewpoint of the world' (BB XXVII 293). Antigone has come to serve as a key embodiment for the working through of the crimes of the Nazi period in post-war Germany, a figure of active mourning in resistance to the postulation of a national 'inability to mourn'.[29] She has also been embraced as a model agent in many contemporary theories of ethics. For post-war Berlin she stands for the possibility of mourning for the victims of war and of the death camps, for those who have lain unburied and unmourned both inside and outside the city walls. In the aftermath of the war, Brecht felt that Berlin had to become another Thebes, to be made the framing site for his *Antigone*. While the collapse of the great city comes at the end of Sophocles' *Antigone*, as sequel to its drama of personal mourning, here it is also set before it in an anticipatory act of memorialisation. This scene from the latter-day 'Trümmerstadt' becomes the ruined gate through or past which the viewer passes into the mythical terrain of the gated city of Thebes, which will become in its turn by the end of the drama 'the collapsing city' (BB VIII 241).

The prelude is set outside, not yet in the space and time of the drama proper, but it is also internally split. The set is riven by a crack that marks this, and the title board lowered at the start of it, reading 'BERLIN. APRIL 1945. TAGESANBRUCH' (Daybreak) introduces a break into the temporality of the scene by splitting off the 'BRUCH'. Both the place and the time of this prelude are breached. It is cast between inside and out, before and after, in a condition of spatial and temporal liminality. Brecht employs here his signature epic method of splitting the action between drama in the present tense and narration in the past, between the present site of the action and a perspective outside it. The two sisters come up out of the air-raid cellar into their apartment and find the door open, taking it to be have been blown open by the fire-storm outside. The evidence, however, is of another cause:

DIE ZWEITE Schwester, woher kommt da im Staub die Spur?
DIE ERSTE Von einem, der hinauflief, ist es nur.   (BB VIII 195)

(THE SECOND Sister, whence comes the trace there in the dust? / THE FIRST It is just from one who ran upstairs.)

The trace of what has been here becomes profoundly ambiguous in the manuscript versions of the prelude. In the original version, the second part

---

[29] See Alexander Mitscherlich and Margarete Mitscherlich, *Die Unfähigkeit zu trauern: Grundlagen kollektiven Verhaltens*, 2nd edn (Munich: Piper, 1977).

of the first line read as 'ein Staub die Spur?' (a dust the trace).[30] That is, dust –
the key material for *Antigone* as for the ruined city – is in the original version
the minimal stuff of the trace rather than the material in which it is left. The
variants collapse figure and ground into the anti-material of which they are
made: dust to dust. Dust is, after all, as likely to cover tracks as to reveal
them. The dust, which in *Antigone* is both the corporeal material of death
and that which is used by Antigone, with her epithet of 'collector of dust'
(BB VIII 200), in her work of mourning, of covering the dead, modulates
here between a sign of life and a sign of death.

The following line is also at variance with the manuscript version, where
'hinauflief' is corrected to read 'hinauslief' (ran out).[31] The intruder who has
come from without and run upstairs is counterbalanced here with one who
has run out of the house. Inside and out are thus confounded in the textual
adjustments, and the trace is doubly uncertain. It points towards the scene
of death outside, and the sisters fail to identify and follow it in time. While
the first seems to want to adopt the role of latter-day Antigone, the dissident
who goes outside the city to challenge the power within, both she and her
sister are caught inside, and the possibility of intervention, after the event
and at pain of death, remains only in the suspension of the final lines.
Caught between the possibilities of killing her brother's killer, of going
outside to cut his body down for appropriate mourning, or of staying inside
and in silence, this latter-day Antigone, or Anti-Antigone, represents the
ethical as a fraught and broken project for post-war Berlin. She is a figure in
an allegorical constellation: caught at the threshold to the agonistic space
outside, the Berlin-Thebes behind the 'Vorspielwand' or prelude wall, with
the open door as city-gate and frame for the hidden corpse.

BERLIN IN LIGHTS – BERLIN REQUIEM

As an alternative to the Berlin prelude for *Antigone*, Brecht and Neher
considered a board representing a modern 'Trümmerstadt' (BB XXV 78).
The implication is that Berlin-Thebes, the archetype of the city in ruins, can
be represented by an image of any ruined city of modernity. The ruined city
is also a city without recognisable identity, one that has lost its topographical
bearings and so become interchangeable. This is the limit representation of
a city that gravitates between the glamorous and fast-moving city of light of
the Weimar years and a darker, more morbid city-image, as seen in two

---

[30] BBA 1071/12. This is hand-corrected in BBA 593.   [31] BBA 593.

Berlin projects that Brecht and Weill pursued together: the performance for the 'Berlin im Licht' (Berlin in Light) festival of 1928 and the songs for the dead that are collected in the cantata for radio, *Das Berliner Requiem*, written in the same year. The one image implies the other; the city of light is also a city of darkness. As the text that Brecht drafted for the 'Berlin im Licht' piece has it, the city is beyond the powers of the sun, and anybody without a streetlamp will never see it in the light (BB XIV 12). While Brecht is drawn into the corporate celebration of the electric city, the text he proposes for the advertising campaign is ironically twisted into an exposure of light as commodity: having and not having, seeing and not seeing in the city of visual spectacle. It is perhaps a sign of the power of the 'city of light' ideology that his critical subtext is absent from the version of the text that Weill ultimately used when the song was performed at the Krolloper, and the instrumental version, performed in front of one of the cathedrals of light – the KaDeWe department store on the Wittenbergplatz – does not resist its commercial function.

While the Brecht–Weill ensemble contributes to the city of light image of Weimar Berlin, their *Berliner Requiem*, with its shadowy visions of deaths in the city of light, also prefigures the city's collapse into a kind of anti-spectacle without light. Its texts are bound to the past, to the darker days following the First World War, and suggest an attachment to death, and the political causes of death, that subsists in the Berlin of the late 1920s. The *Requiem*, which takes its base in Berlin and mourns individual Berliners, becomes understandable as a requiem for what will have been: the city as a whole. Where 'Berlin im Licht' was attuned to the celebration of the city of light and its medial regime, the *Berliner Requiem*, composed to fit the specifications of the new genre of radio music and the demands of the mass medium, proved unpalatable for the radio stations. They had commissioned a requiem for sports heroes and were given instead a requiem for the victims of war and political violence.

The exemplary case here is the mourning of Rosa Luxemburg, which is enacted in several different versions within the *Requiem*, contributing to a project on the part of many leftist artists and commentators to bring the deaths of Luxemburg and Karl Liebknecht at the hands of the *Freikorps* militia to light, exposing what happened and where. In the texts to the songs 'Vom ertrunkenen Mädchen' (Of the Drowned Girl) and the 'Marterl', 'Hier ruht die Jungfrau' (Here Lies the Maiden), Luxemburg becomes identified with the sort of epitaphic inscription that is characteristic of the *Hauspostille* collection. She becomes a figure of allegory for lost life in the city, her memorial designed to be a site of breakage and discomfort, intrinsically divided from where she lies. As the poem 'Grabschrift 1919' (Epitaph 1919) has it:

> Die rote Rosa nun auch verschwand.
> Wo sie liegt, ist unbekannt.

(Red Rosa also disappeared now. / Where she lies is not known.)   (BB XI 205)

Nils Grosch suggests that the version of this poem that appears as an alternative text to the 'Marterl' in Weill's *Song-Album* for voice and piano of 1929 was probably written to be sung to the same melody. The text of the 'Grabschrift 1919' poem is varied here, as follows:

> Die rote Rosa schon lang verschwand.
> Die ist tot, ihr Aufenthaltsort ist unbekannt.[32]

(Red Rosa disappeared long since. / She is dead, her domicile is unknown.)

Whether the text, intended to mark the tenth anniversary of Luxemburg's death, was reworked by Brecht or improvised by Weill after Brecht is a matter of conjecture. Grosch notes that it fails to fit the scheme neatly, with an infelicitous emphasis on the third syllable of 'Aufenthaltsort'.[33] It might be more appropriate, however, to understand this as a characteristic effect of 'Verfremdung' in the relation of text and music, one that shifts the emphasis from the 'proper place' – the '-ort' in 'Aufenthaltsort' – onto 'halt' and thereby to a sort of premature 'hold' or 'stop'. This misplacement and mistiming is all too consistent with the requiem for an arrested figure whose barely identifiable body was dragged from the Landwehrkanal only after her funeral. Both place and time are out of joint here. From the perspective of 1929, Luxemburg has now been long gone, but the later poem still records the whereabouts of the long-buried figure as unknown. Emphasis is given to this with the stretching of the act of disappearance through the ungrammatical 'schon lang verschwand' (literally, 'disappeared for a long time already'), so that it is sustained as a melancholic condition of continued loss.

The defamiliarisation of 'Aufenthaltsort' highlights the irony of applying the term for the living to the dead: when Luxemburg was still alive her whereabouts had to remain unknown, following the sort of nomadic principle set out in the *Lesebuch für Städtebewohner*, and in her death a different kind of unknown location is applied to her corpse in a mocking

---

[32] Kurt Weill, 'Marterl', *Song-Album* (Vienna and Leipzig: Universal-Edition, 1929), pp. 8–10.
[33] Nils Grosch, '"Notiz" zum *Berliner Requiem*: Aspekte seiner Entstehung und Aufführung', *Kurt Weill-Studien* 1 (1996), 55–71; p. 69.

citation of juridical language. The disruption of the 'Aufenthaltsort' also foreshadows the fate of Mies van der Rohe's memorial to Luxemburg and Liebknecht in the Friedrichsfelde cemetery, constructed in 1926, destroyed by the Nazis in 1933, and, to Brecht's dismay (BB XXVII 296), deemed unsuitable to be rebuilt after the war by the East German authorities. Luxemburg's grave, however, became the site for an annual state commemoration and remains – like Brecht's – one of the most visited of personal memorials in Berlin, both of them sites not least of left melancholia, of nostalgia for the lost political topography of 'Red Berlin'.

The tension between the city of light and that of requiem runs right through Brecht's Berlin career, and it is in evidence not least in his dealings with the media of light: advertising, photography, and film. He takes one cue for this from Erich Mendelsohn's photographs of American cities, selecting *Amerika: Bilderbuch eines Architekten* (America: An Architect's Picturebook) as one of his books of 1926 for the Berlin magazine *Das Tage-Buch*. He describes images that evoke the deceptive impression that the great cities are habitable, using light to obscure their uninhabitable condition. Brecht is particularly drawn to an image of the 'gate' to the district of light within the city of light that is Broadway, with a sign reading 'Danger', and prompting him to think of what will be said of such urban circuses when their time is up (BB XXI 187–8). The seductions of the theatre and entertainment district are set under the sign of danger and have to be resisted by recognition of their mortality: of what will remain of them in the wind when the city falls.

Mendelsohn's picture-book is aware of the signs of danger and draws out the ruination that is always part of the allegorical work in his portraits of the marketplace of the American megalopolis. The texts that accompany his images serve to literarise them in the sense that Benjamin applies to the allegorical image. The caption for the Broadway photograph, in the section of his book entitled 'The Gigantic' records the gate to Broadway as a giant *memento mori*, figuring the 'quicksand' of human masses in a centrifugal funnel powered by money.[34] The 1928 edition of the text makes the allegorical fashioning of the image more explicit by lifting the emblematic danger-sign out of the image and adding it as an apotropaic gesture to the end of the accompanying text. The dangers beyond the gate are also figured in the section of the book entitled 'The Grotesque', where the city-of-light image of Broadway by night is subjected to an uncanny double exposure,

---

[34] Erich Mendelsohn, *Amerika: Bilderbuch eines Architekten* (Berlin: Mosse, 1926), p. 31.

with a text headed 'Unheimlich', as the contours of the houses are erased.[35] The city of light casts uncanny shadow-effects, 'un-heimlich' also in its erasure of the contours of habitation, exposing the uninhabitability that Brecht recognises behind appearances to the contrary.

The allegorical operations of the Mendelsohn picture-book are extendable to more general issues for Brecht in the representation of the *Stadtbild*, the city as inherently mediated by image. The painted backdrop of *Trommeln in der Nacht* or the tableau of the 'Trümmerstadt' proposed as a prelude to *Antigone* both point to this accommodation of the city in the medium of the image. In each case, the image is accompanied by instructive captions, which work against its cooption by seductive 'appearance', and the text of the drama acts as an extended performance of literarisation upon the city-image. The principle of literarisation extends across all aspects of the politics of urban representation. Literarisation, the textual effect, is understandable here as a principle of formulation that is applied to the architecture of representation. As Benjamin, following Brecht, puts it, literarisation means the permeation of the 'shaped' ('des Gestalteten') by the 'formulated' ('mit Formuliertem' (WB II.ii 524)). The media of image and text have the potential to be co-worked into a latter-day version of the *Orbis pictus*, as envisaged in Brecht's *Ruhrepos* (Epos of the Ruhr) project (BB XXI 205–6). And the city provides both an extraordinarily rich and dynamic convergence of text and image and a panoply of false forms. The *Urbis pictus*, as it were, falls all too easily into uncritical depictions in either medium, as in the poems submitted for the 1926 competition in the journal *Die literarische Welt*, which Brecht judges to be thoroughly refuted as unreconstructed bourgeois culture by the evidence of the city photographs also published by them (BB XXI 192). It is the photographs rather than the poems that here function to formulate social critique.

In the essay 'Über die Verbindung der Lyrik mit der Architektur' (On the Connection between Poetry and Architecture), Brecht describes photographs of the Russian revolutions of 1905 and 1917 and the literarisation of the 'Straßenbild' they display (BB XXII.i 140). The street-image becomes here a medium for the instructive text, written onto buildings, or indeed for second-order images in the films projected onto the walls of houses (BB XXII.i 140). These inscriptions or imagings are seen as 'emblems', re-presenting the *polis* through a kind of utilitarian emblematics that is always in transition. But on his 1935 visit to Moscow, Brecht laments the fact that the buildings of the new city, the marble walls of the underground stations or

---

[35] *Ibid.*, p. 44.

the tombs of the great revolutionaries in the wall of the Kremlin carry no such inscriptions (BB XXII.i 141). The emblematics of the revolutionary city, requiring renewed forms of productive writing and imaging are replaced here by a fixed form of *Straßen-* or *Stadtbild*. It is the counterpart to the form of totalised image resisting inscriptions that Brecht finds in the West in the 1950s, as reported by Henselmann.[36] The poet who sponsored the dissident inscriptions of Berlin graffiti artists on the run in his early work now sees the unamenability of Western architecture to graffiti as marking a lack of habitable urban space.

The text–image mediation around the *Stadtbild* of Berlin is further explored in the *Kriegsfibel* and Brecht's journals. The photo-epigrammatic *Kriegsfibel* is constructed after the manner of the emblem text, albeit subject to techniques of *Verfremdung* in the age of technical reproducibility. The emblem or epigram is refunctioned here, detached from its aesthetic and social conventions and put into the mode of the graffiti text, following the logic of the 'Auf der Mauer stand mit Kreide' verse from the *Deutsche Kriegsfibel*. In his absence from the scenes depicted in the images, the dissident writer constructs a sort of virtual inscription upon the material found in pictures of the war. The text's images with epigrammatic sub-scriptions in verse function in the allegorical mode, one designed above all to make the pictures speak or be read otherwise, to locate them in another discursive site. This is allegory refunctioned: where the baroque allegorist would disguise the object of representation in order to speak otherwise about it, Brecht is concerned to strip back the forms of ideological duplicity and duping that he finds represented in the journalistic images. As Ruth Berlau puts it in her foreword, the programme of the text is to develop a critically resistant mode of reading images, as mass mediated by illustrated magazines (BB XII 129). The inserted captions serve to literarise the image, making it understandable as the critically readable text it is. Brecht's refunctioned version of the allegory is designed to expose the structuration of mythologies, in a way that Barthes would later develop in his model readings of popular cultural imagery.

Two Berlin images can serve to show how the allegorical principle works here. The first is of the stone horse in front of the Reich Chancellery building (BB XII 187). The accompanying poem addresses the horse as sick, subject to an unsuccessful 'horse cure' over the eight years of the Nazi regime, but made to fix its view unerringly upon 'the dark future'

---

[36] See Erdmut Wizisla, *22 Versuche, eine Arbeit zu beschreiben* (Berlin: Akademie der Künste, 1998), p. 118.

(BB XII 186). The epigram is understandable as a graffiti text for its plinth. This is the horse as falsely constructed counterpart to others which Brecht seeks to memorialise in Berlin: those abused in Kleist's *Michael Kohlhaas*,[37] or the one that is sacrificed to hunger on the Frankfurter Allee in the poem 'O Falladah' (BB XIV 142–4). The sick horse of stone represents the allegorical principle of transience or ruination cast in material designed for intransience. It is the ruin in whole form. Or rather, in half form, for the text addresses only this horse looking to the future and thereby exposes by omission the other one to which it is yoked in the forecourt of the building, a horse trotting and looking in the other direction, which we might gloss as the dark past. The prospect presented here is of the horse's rear in a strategy often employed by sculptors of animal statues to represent the scatological other of the heroic image (such as Rauch's equestrian sculpture of Frederick the Great on Unter den Linden, with less favoured figures from the arts and sciences located under the horse's tail).

   The dark future into which the horse, as ruin or corpse-in-the-making, looks is represented in another Berlin image from the *Kriegsfibel*. The connection between the two is made by the text, through the application of the verb 'schinden' (to knacker) to the woman shown searching in the ruins of a house razed by allied bombing (BB XII 173). This photo-epigram complies with the isotopic model of above and below that Anya Feddersen recognises as an organising structure of the *Kriegsfibel*.[38] Following the bombers 'over Berlin' recorded in the accompanying Swedish newspaper text, the image is taken obliquely from above, while the woman searches in the remains of a structure that has been collapsed into rubble below. The apostrophic text tells her that her search for survivors at a lost address is in vain and should be redirected towards those 'dark powers' who have brought this upon her and reside elsewhere in Berlin (BB XII 172). The text is as it were graffiti for her to find either on a wall that still stands or on one that has already fallen. The image is followed by a gallery of leading Nazis, as if to identify those she has to seek. The first of them shows Hitler holding his December 1940 speech at the Rheinmetall-Borsig armaments factory, one of the Berlin addresses to which she might look. The logic of the accompanying epigram is that the cannons behind Hitler are addressed back at the city that has wreaked upon others the sort of catastrophic damage

---

[37] This misappropriated, sick horse suggests the sculpture of Kohlhaas with his horses that Brecht discussed with Henselmann for the Stalinallee, as a memorial for freedom fighters. The historical Kohlhaas was executed on the site of today's Strausberger Platz.

[38] Anya Feddersen, 'Kriegsfibel', *Brecht Handbuch*, ed. Jan Knopf, 5 vols. (Stuttgart: Metzler, 2001–3), vol. II, pp. 382–97; p. 388.

witnessed in the previous image. The image immediately preceding that of the woman in the rubble is an aerial view of bomb damage inflicted by Germany, so that the sequence appears to give a close-up, displacing the ruination of foreign territory back onto Berlin. At the end of the series of pictures of Nazi officials, the woman is given the ultimate address at which to find the cause of her misery and that of the collection in which she appears, in the form of the image of the Chancellery with sick horse, and inscribed upon it is another graffiti-epigram for her to read.

The photograph of the 'Trümmerfrau' *avant la lettre* corresponds in turn to other war images collected by Brecht in his journal. In the entry of 21 September 1940, he notes adjacent features in the *Berliner Illustrirte* on a blitzed London and the 'Baumeister' or master builders of Germany (BB XXVI 425). This number of the magazine makes an uncanny juxtaposition of the aerial images of bombsite ruins in London with those of the new town projected by Bauhaus architect turned Nazi master builder Herbert Rimpl, following the ideological model of Germania-Berlin as projected by Speer. The architects gathered around their models become readable in this context as military strategists planning air-raids. But the sequence of images inevitably also casts the pall of future destruction back over the construction plans of the master builders with their false construction formulas.[39] The aerial photograph is vested here with a particular form of the morbidity that such as Benjamin and Barthes have associated with the photographic medium. The reduction of the city image to its horizontal contours elides its vertical projection and draws the intact city towards the flattened. It is the counterpart of another medium of representation to which Brecht alludes in an ironic assessment of the 'Trümmerstadt' as anti-aesthetic spectacle, an etching ('Radierung') by Churchill after an idea by Hitler (BB XXVII 281). The two artistically disposed war leaders have collaborated in the work of making the Berlin *Stadtbild* not so much into an etching, as an erasure ('Radierung' in its other sense).

WHO OWNS BERLIN?

The photographic and other images considered here are in the mode of the tableau, held in display for critical viewing. This principle also informs Brecht's concern with the medium of the moving image, as exemplified in *Kuhle Wampe, oder Wem gehört die Welt?* (Kuhle Wampe, or Who Owns the

---

[39] This is expressed most brutally in the clipping from September 1943 in Brecht's journal, citing the US Secretary of the Treasury: 'we want to blast the city of Berlin off the face of the map' (BB XXVII 172).

World?), the film of 1932, publicised as 'Bert-Brecht-Film',[40] but made with an ensemble including director Slatan Dudow and composer Hanns Eisler. Brecht not only had principal responsibility for the screenplay and direction of dialogue but was also fully engaged on the 'construction-site' of the film.[41] For Brecht, the appeal of early film, in the mode of the cinema of attractions, lies in its placative style, which gives him impulses for the pacing, perspective, and performance style of the epic theatre. This is film conceived as always displaying its own processes of showing, constructed as 'a sequence of tableaux' (BB XXI 211). As Benjamin puts it, in language that recalls his accounts of the anachronistic viewing technology of the Kaiserpanorama, epic theatre proceeds like early film, sporadically, through effects of shock (WB II.ii 537). As such, early film is of a piece with Benjamin's account of urban modernity, and in *Kuhle Wampe*, the impact of the city is coordinated with both interruptive filmic style and the performance principles of epic theatre, imported back into the medium that helped to inspire them. What is created here is, to cite Benjamin once more, intervals (WB II.ii 538): breaks within the representation, and between the representation and the spectator, which should be understood in both temporal and spatial terms.

Kuhle Wampe embraces the principle of the interval in its overall disposition. It anachronistically adopts methods from silent cinema, making the medium behave in a manner it has outgrown. This is a city film from the early 1930s that begins as if it were silent. And while it appears to be a work of cinematic naturalism, and hence more directly located in its Berlin setting than anything considered so far, it is always also on stage, or what Benjamin calls a podium (WB II.ii 539). This is the stage as interval space, corresponding to the tableau as a form of representation that is set off in a frame and defined by critical gaps in its representation. At the same time, as a parodic version of the 'Wochenendfilm' or weekend-film genre, originally called *Weekend Kuhle Wampe*, the film exposes the ideology of the weekend as interval in working life: a space for entertainment and leisure that shores up the workings of the capitalist system. It has a particular, ironic relation to Siodmak's *Menschen am Sonntag* (People on Sunday (1930)), which shows Berlin as a city of everyday working activity and its natural outskirts as a site of weekend recreation, a carnival space. *Menschen am Sonntag* is directly cited in the scene where Fritz, working under a car, is called to the phone to

---

[40] 'Ein Bert-Brecht-Film soll gedreht werden', *Film-Kurier* 157 (8 July 1931).
[41] 'Brecht führt Dialog-Regie', *Film-Kurier* 229 (30 September 1931).

speak to Anni (in *Menschen* it is Annie), and Fritz is indeed the character in the film most suited to being called into the world of the earlier film.

The image of the Brandenburg Gate that opens *Kuhle Wampe* can also be read as a strategically refunctioned quotation from *Menschen*, where the weekenders travel through the Gate on their way to the space of recreation. *Kuhle Wampe* at once adopts elements of the docu-fiction style of the earlier film and works to refunction it: where work is turned into unemployment, the race for recreational pleasure is turned into a racing for jobs or for political change. While the protagonists of *Menschen* work in the entertainment and consumer sectors, their emblematic sites in the urban marketplace – the street as scene of commercial interaction and transportation, the shop window, the cinema – are reworked in *Kuhle Wampe*, as we shall see. For the unemployed in *Kuhle Wampe*, made to work ceaselessly in the vain search for work or stuck in meaningless leisure-time, the weekend as interval in or outside the everyday ceases to have meaning. By projecting the temporal interval of the weekend into the 'weekend colony' location of Kuhle Wampe as chronotope, the film puts the generic idea of the weekend-film on display and establishes a critical interval between it as consumer spectacle and the spectator who is to be activated.

The opening image establishes the location of the film in classic tableau style, fixing on the Brandenburg Gate as iconic topographical entry-point to the city.[42] The screenplay had envisaged the film opening with images of another kind of ironic site of display: a delicatessen shop window. Shop windows, including that of a delicatessen, become part of the general *mise-en-scène* instead.[43] In either event the entrance image was designed to represent a place of non-entry. The film was initially to be called *Ante Portas*, indicating the para-urban location of the Kuhle Wampe campsite, and it is therefore appropriate that it should begin its narrative before this city gate. It is a curious establishing image, however, failing to meet standard cinematographic requirements. The base of the gate is not shown, so it gives an undercut and dislocated impression. The iconic structure of Prussian state and military power, as emblematised by the Quadriga figure mounted upon it, is thus deprived of its foundation. The gate, so subject to triumphal appropriations and remodellings from all sides over its history, is strategically misappropriated here. The Quadriga as allegory of racing Victory is frozen in the posture of the chase, an ironic, emblematic

[42] It figures at the start of Wilder's *One, Two, Three*, here too to satirical effect, as a site of illicit border traffic.
[43] When the family drive out to Kuhle Wampe, they pass a delicatessen shop.

introduction to the unsuccessful hunts for work and home through Berlin's streets that will follow.

Like the ruined gate that Benjamin suggests as the allegorical figure for the *Hauspostille* collection, this representation of the triumphal gate is detached from its accustomed ideological grounding, a signature structure that is set up for a fall. As political allegory, it is a framework for speaking otherwise, not in the discourse of triumphalism, for which the gate has been appropriated from all sides. It becomes, therefore, a suitable gate for the entry into the city of the jobless. It is akin to the arch with the grave beneath it in the 'Gedicht vom Unbekannten Soldaten unter dem Triumphbogen' (Poem of the Unknown Soldier beneath the Triumphal Arch (BB XI 202–3)), a poem used for the *Berliner Requiem*. Like the iconic Arc de Triomphe, appropriated from Paris for Berlin in the *Requiem*, and refunctioned in its allegorical role to be exposed as a monument to triumphalism built upon savage sacrifice, the Brandenburg Gate is constructed as an ironic frame for the narrative of urban dispossession and mortality that the film will relate. The corpse that will be produced by the film and is in waiting behind the entrance portal, the 'One Less Unemployed' of the first act, is the counterpart to the defaced soldier buried under the arch.

Rather than leading to the representative thoroughfare of Unter den Linden, to the nearby Potsdamer Platz, or to other iconic architectures in its vicinity (the Reichstag or the Siegessäule), the tourist image accordingly leads to the less cinegenic aspects of the city of light: its dark factories and *Hinterhöfe*. In Lefebvre's terms, it moves strategically from representations of space to representational spaces (see p. 4). The cropped picture of the Gate functions as a counter-example for the use of the postcard image in film, standardly designed to set the spectacle up in much the same way as 'local colour' is used in conventional theatre (BB XXII.i 229). This establishing image is rather concerned with framing a process of understanding. The proffering of the incomplete postcard image subjects the standard opening *gestus* to an effect of 'Verfremdung', equivalent to that of the incomplete set in epic theatre. It is a strategically false start for a work that will resist the generic standards of the postcard film, creating a basis for a montage of city images separated by intervals.

The first cut, from the Brandenburg Gate to a factory landscape, is mediated by a fade, sustaining an ironic visual matching between the uprights of the Gate and factory chimneys, but thereafter the images are separated by pronounced cuts, the sort of shock effects that Benjamin sees in the aesthetics of filmic montage. The camera begins to move in response to the mobility of the train within the city image, but is halted without

reaching an aim, and this broken motion is followed by a crudely syncopated sequence of still or semi-still pictures of the urban environment.
While the factory images or the train imply a dynamic, working city,
reminiscent of the transportation and industrial images from the start of
Ruttmann's *Berlin* (see Chapter 3), the intervention of the bleak, unpopu-
lated *Hinterhöfe* interrupts this with a morbid immobility. Specifically, the
upwardly angled shots preview the perspective of those gathering around
the body of young Böhnike and looking up to the window from which he
has jumped. The accompanying music by Eisler propels the sense of expect-
ation that the film is going somewhere, but the disengaged imagetrack
resists any sense of productive goal. An intermedial interval opens up in
the film medium, as sound and image produce, Eisler argues, a kind of shock
eliciting resistance rather than empathy.[44] When music and image seem to
become more consonant, in the urban dynamics of the following section,
the dissonant effect of the interval in the establishing sequence remains with
the viewer as a block to the empathic excitement of the city symphony in its
high tempo mode.

As I have argued in detail elsewhere,[45] the following sequence, featuring a
form of bike race on the city streets, is informed by the tableau principle, the
image literarised by the texts that are interposed in the form of newspaper
titles, the *Litfaßsäule* (advertising column), or factory signs. The first part of
the scene turns on acts of reading on the street, organised around the
Litfaßsäule, but it also constructs the street as a text for critical reading. As
an iconic figure for street-reading, the *Litfaßsäule* functions as a key element
in the ensemble of texts that run through the film, texts that demand to be
read (such as the jobs pages) or that have to be passed by (as when the job-
hunters speed past a cinema, oblivious to the irony of the film title *Dienst ist
Dienst* (Duty is Duty)). While the camera is mobilised with the street-race,
it is also recurrently brought back to the static position of the tableau, as
when it focuses on the sign announcing that workers are not being
employed, indicating that the race for work is always held in a stultified
framework of joblessness.

The race is (in more than one sense) *held* in a topography that is not
designed to be recognisable in anything but generic terms. It starts in an
open space, as Berliners in search of work gather to get a copy of a jobs
paper. In the screenplay, this is not a purely arbitrary site, but identified as

---

[44] Hanns Eisler, cited in *Kuhle Wampe oder Wem gehört die Welt?: Protokoll*, ed. Wolfgang Gersch and
Werner Hecht (Frankfurt am Main: Suhrkamp, 1969), p. 99.

[45] Andrew J. Webber, *The European Avant-garde, 1900–1940* (Cambridge: Polity, 2004), pp. 138–43.

the Criminal Court in Moabit, where authority is housed in a palace in an area of proletarian hardship. It represents the rule of law in its intervention in the lives of the jobless workers 'in the name of the people' (this, the refrain in the judgement ritual of the tribunal later in the film). As such it is at once a typical place, a scene of gathering as in many other places in Berlin (BB XIX 443), and a particularly loaded, exemplary one. Both the protagonists of the film and the film itself are destined to come under juridical control. It seems that, in the event, another, more open site is used for filming. The only clue to its location is the address on a passing cart – 'Berlin O. Mainzerstr. 24' – indicating the working-class and industrial eastern district of Friedrichshain. This address, which may or may not be in the vicinity of the scene, can be understood above all as a mobile or migratory effect, serving as a reminder that the addresses given in the film are always transitory, subject to eviction procedures, and that they can be located in many places. In the background of the scene is a group of street-workers, in ironic counterpoint to those who will have to work the streets so hard only in order not to find work. The street is at once a site for work and a screen for the projection of the search for work as a play of racing shadows. The recurrent image of the body-shadow on the street prefigures the body in the *Hinterhof*, which will end this act with a death in a space between the domestic and the public, at once individual and typical: 'One Less Unemployed'.

The next sequence mimics the first by having Anni walk the streets in her quest to retain the family flat. The urban topography that was a hunting-ground for work is now one for habitation. Anni, a young woman in the style of the 'new woman' of Weimar Berlin, dynamically walks the streets, but as in the bike-race, the rhythm is one of a search from address to address, each time ending in failure. The sequence is accentuated by the accompaniment of the street-scenes by a soundtrack of traffic noise and the silence of the encounters with the mute figures of authority, performing their shrugging *gestus* as tableau in the stylised mode of silent film. As with the parallel sequence of the 'Hunt for Work', montage is used here as a rhetorical tool for making everyday behaviours critically readable, a means, as Marc Silberman argues, of 'inscribing' in everyday actions 'the conditions of their construction'.[46]

The critical inscription that Silberman describes here is achieved partly by the deployment of literal inscriptions, effects of literarisation. The addresses

---

[46] Marc Silberman, *German Cinema: Texts in Context* (Detroit: Wayne State University Press, 1995), p. 43.

that Anni visits in her search for help thus resonate with the handwritten sign used to block the search for work at the factory gate. Here the sign becomes typical rather than contingent, and its message of negation is carried over into the generic signs in front of the doors that are opened and then closed to Anni. A further element in this network of inscriptions is the certificate recording Anni's loss of work, which is shown to the camera later in the film and gives the family an address: Triftstraße, Berlin N. Here, the personal information in the document serves only to underline its typical character (the scenes were in fact filmed in the Müllerstraße in Wedding). The typical tenement address works much like the location of 'Wedding. Köslinerstraße. Hinterhaus' given for the performance of the eviction *Lehrstück* by the 'Rotes Sprachrohr' (Red Megaphone) troupe at the sports festival.[47] In both cases, the concealed 'rear-house' location is projected into the public domain as a lost address, typical of many others. The certificate takes its place in a sequence of generic insertions of documentary information: newspaper headlines recording the mounting numbers of the unemployed or the anonymous address-plates of the offices that Anni visits in search of help, all of which serve to turn the individual towards the general. This is the city film in the *Neue Sachlichkeit* mode of the *Querschnitt* or 'cross-section', cut through the space and activities of the everyday. The streets that Anni walks, like those that her brother cycled before her or those that the bands of young workers march through later in the film, are, precisely, typical, representative of a state of affairs generalised across the topography of Berlin.

Kuhle Wampe itself is conceived as a colony: a space of inhabitation outside the city, *ante portas*, and one where the weekend, as time outside the workaday order, becomes a generalised condition. As the family drives off from their old address, the word 'FREI' (free) above an entrance is framed in the corner of the screen. It seems to be an ironically laden sign of what might be to come, not least given that – as the screenplay emphasises – the car follows the route of the ambulance that carried Anni's dead brother away earlier (BB XIX 475). The move to the ostensible freedom of Kuhle Wampe is mediated by a sort of ethnographic, documentary voice-over, serving to distance the viewer from this new site for domestic life and drama. The freedom of the colony as place of escape or rescue is not to be taken as read. It can be understood as a heterotopian site in Foucault's sense: a paraurban place outside the normal order, which at once reflects and inverts it. It is cast

---

[47] As Bienert points out (*Mit Brecht*, pp. 94–5), the Kösliner Straße scenario refers to an attempted eviction of members of a Communist street-cell, as described in Neukrantz's *Barrikaden am Wedding*.

in the style of an idyll, but exposed as an 'other place' that merely reproduces the disorders within the city.

This is played out in the drama of the unplanned pregnancy and the farce of the engagement party. When Anni and Fritz walk from the camp to the tramstop, she is prematurely returned to the city as site of life-and-death spectacle in a vision, described in the screenplay as a 'children psychosis' (BB XIX 491). The sequence focuses on shop-windows as sites of display, a version of the imagery that was intended to introduce the film in the screenplay conception. The special relationship of the window-display to the urban spectacle of film is revealed in the subsequent sequence, where Fritz and Kurt are seen entering a cinema against the backdrop of advertising images and texts. The films advertised include a number of the popular German genre films of the day, as well as a work with a particular, and particularly morbid, relationship to the shop-window: Lang's *M*.

The shop-window is the classic site for the Weimar culture of spectacle, and here it is used to create a heterotopian display: the shop-window images of birth are converted into those of death and lead to a recurrence of the image of the premature death on the street of Anni's brother. When Anni was engaged in her 'Hunt for an Apartment', shop-windows formed an incidental part of the background track of street-images, and now they are refigured into a hallucinatory foreground. As it alternates between human figures and wax dolls, the sequence engages a key form of the uncanny for the Weimar discourse of the city street (as discussed in Chapter 3, p. 168). And the uncanny means here a return of the repressed in the form of a traumatic after-effect. The death of the brother, which seems to have passed so dispassionately in the film's narrative, recurs here on Anni's mindscreen in a flashback to the death scene. In this context, Anni's unemployment document, which is constructed into the montage, could easily be taken to be a premonitory death certificate. In the logic of the montage, joblessness becomes the conduit between life and death. The city of light in the *Neue Sachlichkeit* mode is also the city of requiem, cast in a visionary mode more appropriate to Expressionism.[48] The city's commodity culture sustains the nightmare of death in life: the shop-window serves as counterpart to the window as medium of the brother's suicide and framework for the spectacle it creates. Children, both real and as commodity images, act as linking figures between the two scenes, and the 'children psychosis' is

[48] The *contre-jour* shots of landscape and architecture that cameraman Günter Krampf used to uncanny effect in Murnau's *Nosferatu* (1922) are redeployed here for a different mode of 'Un-heimlichkeit'.

twisted, not least in the light of the reference to the psychotic childkiller in *M.*, towards aborted life.

In the final part of the film, the false colonial structure of the opposition between the city and the camp colony is dialectically *aufgehoben* or sublated, at once suspended and lifted to another level. Here, both the city and the colony outside the gates occur in revised form. The young workers are shown as pioneers working for the Socialist cause, distributing their advertising to all sections of the city, as charted on the city-map on the wall and literarised in the textual display of the wall newspaper.[49] Their working of the topography of the city is then projected into a different form of colonisation of the space beyond it, as they take over the lake and the fields outside the city as the site for their sporting competitions and agitprop theatre. If Kuhle Wampe was the scene for the father to indulge in the vicarious pleasures of the account of Mata Hari's performance at the Wintergarten variety in the newspaper, here, literarisation takes the form of young pioneers reading Hegel.

While the final scene seeks to sustain that mode of ideological reading, the train back into town is not simply available as a vehicle for it. The newspaper recurs here as an ambivalent medium of information, providing the basis for a debate between left and right on global economics. The question at the end of the film as to who will change the world is answered from the left in apparently unequivocal form: 'Those who don't like it!' But this also opens up the possibility that the ranks of the dissatisfied might just as easily be the agents of a right-wing revolution, in pursuit of the other kind of colonial project that their spokesman in the train back to Berlin would like to see. While the final cut of the film shows more of the young workers streaming back towards the city to the marching rhythm of the 'Solidarity Song', the screenplay suggests a more haunting form of accompaniment, as the song fades out, 'thin, ghostly and menacing' (BB XIX 571). The terms of its description echo those used to evoke the revolutionary action as thin and ghostly behind the scenes of *Trommeln in der Nacht* (BB I 554). The question is whether this reprise at the end of the film is the ghost of revolution stalking a Berlin that is threatened by it, or a marching song that is already functioning as requiem, threatening to be overwhelmed by the march of history in another direction. 'Whose street is the street? – Whose world is the world?' asks the song. The ownership of the streets of Berlin, and of the world at large, is in the balance.

---

[49] Brecht's involvement in this scene is documented by a photograph. See Werner Hecht, *Brecht Chronik: 1898–1956* (Frankfurt am Main: Suhrkamp, 1997), p. 312.

AFTER BRECHT: HEINER MÜLLER

> When the bridges, when the arches
> Are sucked up by the steppe
> And the castle seeps into the sand.[50]

If Brecht is, in some part at least, an invoker of ghosts in Berlin, from Kragler in *Trommeln in der Nacht* to the ending of *Kuhle Wampe*, Heiner Müller, his principal legatee at the Berliner Ensemble and on the German and international theatre scene, gives new life to those ghosts. The year 2006 saw both the fiftieth anniversary of Brecht's death and the tenth anniversary of Müller's, and this gave rise to graveside ceremonies and to celebratory-cum-melancholic reviews of their lives and works, and of death in them. The anniversary event for Müller at the Berliner Ensemble was *Vorsicht Optimist: 100 Fragen an Heiner Müller* (Beware Optimist: 100 Questions to Heiner Müller), a 'Séance' by Moritz von Uslar and Thomas Oberender, directed by Philipp Tiedemann. The ghosts of Müller are summoned here as a group of lemurs and questioned talk-show-style on the first and last things of life. The little set of wings on the shoulders of each of the Müller figures marks them out as so many under-endowed, stage-bound versions of the angel of history, which Müller famously adapted from Benjamin. With this spectacle, the Berliner Ensemble wrily exposes itself as what it in part is: a theatrical ghost-house in the baroque style, haunted by the *genius loci* of Brecht, and that of Müller after him. And in both cases the caution about optimism in the title of the Müller séance implies its contrary: the melancholic dispositions of these angels of history.

Müller's response to the Brecht legacy is, famously, to follow the Brechtian principle of refunctioning for other times and needs. In response to the edifice of political theatre that Brecht and company constructed out of the ruins of National Socialist Berlin, Müller looks underground. He cites an early post-war text of Brecht's pointing out that new houses, not least theatre-houses, are being built before the cellars have been cleared out. Brecht will have been thinking of such underground sites as the Gestapo cellar, which he visited in the company of an ex-internee, Günter Weissenborn, an experience of the city's topography of terror that he could only meet with stony silence, as if in imitation of the walls.[51] Müller compares Brecht's reference to the unexcavated cellars to Thomas Mann's pronouncement that the German *Stadtbild* shows the incompletion of any

---

[50]   From Gottfried Benn's poem 'Berlin', read by actor Ulrich Mühe (†) at Müller's funeral.
[51]   Günther Weisenborn, 'Mit Brecht im Gestapo-Keller', *Sonntag*, 10 January 1965.

historical era and the failure of its revolutions (HM VIII 225–6). In this analysis, Hitler's Germania might have been the absolute *Stadtbild*, but Berlin is divided instead into the contending, totalising city-images of capitalism and Communism. Müller sees Brecht as driven by the imperative of the moment to become complicit in neglecting the excavation of the cellars so that the people's palaces on the Eastern side could stand. Brecht's post-war theatre work was perhaps 'a heroic effort to clear out the cellars', but his work had to proceed without endangering 'the statics of the new buildings' (HM VIII 227).

This leaves Müller with the melancholy project of having to continue to dig out the 'bodies in the cellar' and thereby to betray Brecht's historical accommodations in order not to betray his legacy. When Müller gives Brecht an afterlife on stage, in his short drama *Nachleben Brechts Beischlaf Auferstehung In Berlin* (Brecht's Afterlife Lovemaking Resurrection in Berlin), he is seated high above a sky-scraper on top of a pile of ruins, refuse, and corpses (HM V 209). The apotheosis at the end of the drama, when the words 'BRECHT IS RESURRECTED' appear in lights on the Alexanderplatz high-rise, returns this latter-day image of the city of light to the spectacle of burning and ruination, as the theatre that houses it is described as collapsing in flames (HM V 212). And the 'transcendent' device of the final curtain bringing down the letters 'A.U.S.' ('aus' as 'finished'), indicates that the drama of Brecht's afterlife and resurrection is always already finished off by a catastrophic world order (for A.U.S. read an out-of-order U.S.A).

Müller's refunctioning of Brecht involves a teasing out of the author's dialogues with Benjamin and their triangulation with Kafka. The model of *Entstellung* that is represented for Brecht by Kafka, as mediated by Benjamin, and that haunted the construction of his works, is incorporated into Müller's revision of Brecht's project. He returns to Benjamin's question as to whether Brecht or Kafka manages to create a 'more spacious' work and concludes that Kafka's penal colony has better survived subsequent historical developments than the dialectical 'ideal construction' of the 'Lehrstücke' (HM VIII 224). Into the idealised space of the *Lehrstück* Müller introduces the psycho-social disfigurements of fantasy and dream, after Kafka or Artaud, the sorts of phantasmatic spaces described by Fiebach in his reading of Müller.[52] It is the space that Müller emblematically projects

---

[52] Joachim Fiebach, 'Nach Brecht – von Brecht aus – von ihm fort?: Heiner Müllers Texte seit den siebziger Jahren', *Brecht 88: Anregungen zum Dialog über die Vernunft am Jahrtausendende*, ed. Wolfgang Heise (Berlin: Henschelverlag, 1987), pp. 171–88; p. 171.

in his reworking of the dialectical standstill of Benjamin's angel of history:[53] a figure cast between the memorial stone angel and the violently mobilised body, its limbs and organs besieged on all sides by the wind and debris of history, in a condition of radical *Entstellung* (HM 1 53). Müller's subsequent reworkings of the angel of history, first in the 'Engel der Verzweiflung' (Angel of Despair) text, written for *Der Auftrag* (The Mission), and then in the poem 'Glückloser Engel 2' (Unfortunate Angel 2), associate the fraught figure with negative ground: the *Abgrund* or abyss. The latter text explicitly locates the angel in post-*Wende* Berlin, but as a site of chronotopical dislocation: 'Between city and city/After the Wall the abyss' (HM 1 236). The serial, emblematic angel has been retracted into an effect of *mise-en-abyme*: the 'standing place' of the first version has become an abysmal anti-ground for the angelic figure, and the melancholic subject can only hear the beating of its wings in the wind of history, now blowing in other directions.

In Müller's theatre, poetry, and prose, Berlin is a paradigmatic site, or *Schauplatz*, for the *Trauerspiel* of twentieth-century history, as well as for more personal dramas of mourning and melancholia. Its theatrical *locus classicus* is *Germania Tod in Berlin* (Germania Death in Berlin), started in 1950, published in 1978, and first performed at the Berliner Ensemble only in 1989. Here, decisive scenes of the twentieth-century history of Germany as played out in Berlin are reviewed. The review structure incorporates a network of intertextual links, invoking Berlin dramas from *Trommeln in der Nacht* to Toller's *Hoppla! Wir leben* (Hoppla! We're Alive (1927)), and combining these with references to a variety of dramatic sites and genres, from the uncanny fantasy stage of Hoffmann's Berlin (as marked in the 'Nachtstück' or 'night-piece' scene), to Berlin as revolutionary sepulchre in Heym's 1910 poem 'Berlin VIII', and the Führerbunker as cellar-theatre cabaret in the guignol style. With its leitmotif of building-work, as organised around the Stalinallee project,[54] the play asks what can be constructed out of the massive spectacle of destruction that is the German drama set in Berlin. In particular, it performs the removal and installation of memorials, with the suggestion that the sculpture of Frederick the Great as 'old Fritz' on Unter den Linden is to be replaced by that of a building-worker from the Stalinallee. The memorial is conceived as a figure of death in life in this drama of ghosts from Germany's present, its history, and its mythology. Thus, the workers' memorial is built as ruin, with the broken body of the

---

[53] See also Webber, *European Avant-garde*, pp. 5–8.
[54] The Heiner-Müller-Archiv (Akademie der Künste, Berlin), includes a photograph of one of Henselmann's Stalinallee drawings (ref. 6693).

stoned mason seen as fit to take the place of Frederick (HM IV 364). The disposition of Benjamin's baroque *Trauerspiel* is introduced into the wandering *Schauplatz* of the drama by the 'skull salesman', who offers for sale an eighteenth-century skull, complete with a *memento mori* inscription for a new home (HM IV 350).

This uncanny incorporation of the *memento mori* into the home is also characteristic for Müller's dramatisation of Berlin in his poetic writings, where historical development is marked by a recurrent principle of mortification. In the early post-war texts, Berlin emerges as an elegiac space of falling into ruin. In the first stanza of 'Berliner Elegien' (Berlin Elegies), it is introduced as a place of repeated falling and felling, so that when in the second stanza, set in the Osthafen or East Harbour, the ruins are illuminated from the building-site, the light *falls* from the scaffolding onto ruins, mediating between destruction and reconstruction, collapsing the one into the other (HM I 89). The poet is preoccupied with writing verses against the singing of sad songs, but his own elegiac verses are always also in that mode. In this they follow the Brechtian model. The mixing of the city and the woods in the first stanza, only for both to be felled, and the reference to the old man whistling with a 'Holunderblatt' (elder leaf) in the last, conjure up Brecht's own Berlin elegies, from 'Vom armen B. B.' to 'Schwierige Zeiten'. Brecht's elegiac voice is an object of and model for Müller's own.

While Müller's early elegies still propose the possibility of rebuilding, as a couple in 'Berliner Elegien' are seen embracing 'between the ruin wall and scaffolding' (HM I 89), we have seen that by the time of 'Glückloser Engel 2' that space has been transformed into no-man's land, between the two cities of Berlin and between the Wall and the abyss. The post-*Wende* city, the 'unreal capital' of 'Ajax zum Beispiel' (Ajax for Instance), is built upon the remains of the Holocaust. The subject's gaze falls upon the Mercedes star, turning melancholically 'over the tooth-gold of Auschwitz', and the unexcavated cellars haunt the reconstructed capital with their voices of ash and bonemeal (HM I 292). The emblem of the Berlin marketplace is thus spoken otherwise in Müller's allegory. The crypto-suicidal gaze of the poet, which 'falls out of the window' upon the Mercedes star on the Europa-Center, and is thereby relayed to the insignia of the Holocaust, follows the logic of falling that we saw in 'Berliner Elegien'. The fall into ruin links the post-war building-site as elegiac space to that of the post-Wall capital.

In the face of this ruin, Müller sets out to re-turn the *Wende*, and so to appropriate the *Abgrund* as ground for new aesthetico-political constructions. In 'Bautzen oder Babylon' (Bautzen or Babylon), he seeks to propose Berlin not only as the fulcrum between East and West, but as having the potential to reach beyond Eurocentric interests (HM VIII 395). And in 'Berlin twohearted city', he propounds the sort of art that finds the breaches in the sanitisation of the city and the world order and opens up a different kind of abyss, that of freedom (HM VIII 372). Müller's own disposition here is, however, also 'twohearted': the text has verses by Becher, representing the poet as ruined wall and mourning tree over the abyss, as its epigraph, another of the sad songs that he seeks to resist (HM VIII 372). This melancholic abyss thus appears to pre-empt and annul that projected in the manifesto for artistic freedom in the twohearted city.

Writing in the 1970s, Müller had already dubbed Berlin a dead city. In the poem 'Gestern an einem sonnigen Nachmittag' (Yesterday on a Sunny Afternoon), the body of his wife becomes the allegorical corpse upon which the 'dead city' is built, and which he feels the drive to dig up (HM I 200). It is the personal counterpart to the corpse of Rosa Luxemburg, as remembered, after Brecht, in *Germania Tod in Berlin*, the paradise of her Eden resonating ironically with the Hotel Eden where Luxemburg was brutalised before being thrown into the Landwehrkanal (HM IV 376). The home town has become uncanny, a place of returns from the dead. In Müller's last years, the return home is freighted with a more general sense of alienation, and his home-space of the Berliner Ensemble and the city streets also play host to uncanniness. One of his last poems, 'Ibsen oder der Tod als Embryo Fahrt durch eine fremde Stadt' (Ibsen or Death as Embryo Drive through a Strange City), sees the poet in the canteen of the Berliner Ensemble 'after Brecht': 'Im Theater nach Brecht' (HM I 284). As he drives back home through the 'strange city', he considers the discussion of the alienated Ibsen in the canteen, and how he created an explosive late *oeuvre* under the shadow of death: the uncanny, mortified embryo of the title.

While Müller's return to his and Brecht's theatre creates some possibility for renewed creativity, in the sober valedictory poem of 1994, 'Fremder Blick: Abschied von Berlin' (Alien Look: Departure from Berlin), the incarcerated writer, shut out of the city, has a play in his head but no audience for it:

> Aus meiner Zelle vor dem leeren Blatt
> Im Kopf ein Drama für kein Publikum
> Taub sind die Sieger die Besiegten stumm
> Ein fremder Blick auf eine fremde Stadt
> Graugelb die Wolken ziehn am Fenster hin
> Weißgrau die Tauben scheißen auf Berlin   (HM I 287)

(From my cell before the empty sheet / In my head a drama for no audience / Deaf are the victors the vanquished dumb / A strange look upon a strange city / Grey-yellow the clouds draw past the window / White-grey the pigeons shit on Berlin)

The introductory 'Aus' originally read 'In',[55] locating the scene of writing in an inside-out space, between interior and exterior, incorporation and excretion. His goodbye to Berlin is enacted through a collapsing of the abject features of the poetic landscape: the 'strange look' into the 'strange city'; the 'grey-yellow' of the clouds chiastically into the 'white-grey' of the pigeons (or, metonymically, of their shit).[56] And the pigeons themselves are made to resonate with the deafness of the victors ('Tauben'/'Taub'), suggesting that these too are shitting on Berlin. This is what is left of the angels of history. While for 'Berliner Elegien' they took the form of 'deadly swarms' dropping bombs (HM I 89), invoking such winged monsters as the imperial eagle, they are now banalised and excremental.

Müller owned a photograph of 1957 by Arno Fischer, depicting the façade of a Berlin ruin, not by chance the headquarters of the Reich Association of the German Aviation Industry (see Figure 4).[57] Beneath one gaping window is an effaced version of the imperial Eagle, clutching a swastika, on the ledge of the other perches a single pigeon. The pigeon is the abject, urban embodiment of the allegorical dove of peace, such as that copied from Picasso on the curtain of the Berliner Ensemble, or the one on a wall in the Nikolaiviertel, the successor to the Nazi eagle, proclaiming the capital of the GDR as 'City of Peace' (this is one of the detached icons that feature in Sophie Calle's *Entfernung*, as discussed in Chapter 1). Fischer's photograph allegorises the city as in the balance between imperialist violence and a potential for peace, always assuming that the subaltern pigeon is capable of carrying the allegorical load of its counterpart on the curtain of Brecht and Müller's theatre. The Berlin pigeons of Müller's poem drop dirt on what in 'Mommsens Block' he calls the 'wieder bereinigten Hauptstadt Berlin': the capital not 'reunited again' ('wieder vereinigt') but 'sanitised again' (HM I 262). And this scatological covering of the city includes one of its key tourist sites, Brecht's grave, as invoked in the act of *prosopopoeia* in Müller's late reprise of *Germania Tod in Berlin*: *Germania 3 Gespenster am toten Mann* (Germania 3 Ghosts at the Dead Man). Here, Brecht's voice from beyond the grave is ventriloquised into the phantom review of his posterity, giving

---

[55] Heiner-Müller-Archiv, Akademie der Künste Berlin (ref. 2851).
[56] A version dated '15.12.94', in a frail hand, replaces 'Weissgrau' with 'Grauweiss' (Heiner-Müller-Archiv, ref. 2850).
[57] Heiner-Müller-Archiv, ref. 6685.

4 Headquarters of Reich Association of the German Aviation Industry, Arno Fischer (1957).

instructions for his gravestone: birds should shit on it (HM V 288). The ghost of Brecht demands an obliteration of his name and his memory, reducing what is left of him in the sandy city of Berlin to 'a trace in the sand'. In one of his last texts, Müller duly figures himself in turn, after Brecht's 'dog's stone' as an abjected memorial, albeit a (still) living one, pissed upon by passing dogs.[58]

Müller's performance of his farewell from Berlin, and his resurrection of the ghost of Brecht in order also to perform the same for him, indicate that there is persistence to the creativity produced under the sign of historical melancholy. In his personal archive, Müller kept the last part of Marlene Dietrich's autobiography, *Ich bin, Gott sei Dank, Berlinerin* (I am, Thank God, A Berlin Woman), and highlighted the final paragraph with its acknowledgement of 'the persistence of mourning'.[59] It seems he shares the belief of this ultimate performer from and of Berlin in *Trauer* as the condition of *Spiel*. The catastrophic view of history fixes Müller the

[58] Jotted on the front page of *Neues Deutschland*, 8 June 1995 (Heiner-Müller-Archiv, ref. 4489).
[59] Heiner-Müller-Archiv (ref. 5757).

performance writer in a place of aporia, but this is also a site of production, however abject. The bird shitting on the city follows the sort of aporetic logic that de Man applies in his reading of allegory. The allegorical angel of history is spoken otherwise here, and this second-order allegory at once recognises impossibility and still makes a performance of it. De Man calls this kind of allegory meta-figural: 'it is an allegory of a figure ... which relapses into the figure it deconstructs.'[60] The angel, the bird, and the city are in such a meta-figural constellation, the one relapsing into the other. But, following the logic of the aporia in de Man's account, the constellation 'persists in performing what it has shown to be impossible to do',[61] not least a productive relationship to the city of Berlin. It is, following an epigram of Müller's from 1983, Berlin as at once the last part of a history that has not yet deserved the name and a potential starting-point: 'If history should take place, Berlin will be the beginning' (HM VIII 270).

[60] De Man, *Allegories of Reading*, p. 275. [61] *Ibid.*

CHAPTER 3

Berlin symphonies: movements and stills

A super-picture-house that never ends.[1]

This chapter considers a sequence of works representing the topographical and architectural ambiguities of Berlin in still and moving images, orchestrated around Walther Ruttmann's classic film *Berlin: Die Sinfonie der Grosstadt* (Berlin: The Symphony of the City (1927)). While convention sees such city symphonies as present-time, future-oriented studies in dynamic mass movement, the argument here is that the film also demands to be read against that grain. It contains troubling counter-rhythms, points of individual fixture, slippage, or reversal. The more melancholic dynamics of Thomas Schadt's re-orchestration of the city symphony, *Berlin: Sinfonie einer Großstadt* (Berlin: Symphony of a City (2002)), will provide a counterpoint to Ruttmann's film, highlighting the unsettling counter-rhythmic elements in the composition of the original. While the city symphony model seems to appeal to the dynamic experience of the moment, to a present day as embodying the propulsion of everyday life, it will be shown here to have a more complex relationship to the passage of time, to chronography. This is, as it were, set in two compound tenses: the future perfect, focusing on the melancholic experience of what *will have been*; and the peculiarly loaded version of the perfect tense that describes the temporal experience of trauma, with its attachment to what *has been*, to experience that is at once irrecoverably absent and yet doggedly, fixedly asserting a claim to presence. And this troubled relationship to time will be seen to be coordinated with a disconcerted sense of space and place, of topography. The city symphony constructs a topographical order for its composition, a

---

[1] From 'Berlin, die Symphonie der Großstadt', a satirical poem from the late 1920s, figuring Berlin as 'Überkintopp' (Berlin Filmmuseum, provenance unknown).

navigation of space calibrated against its temporal progression, but the film's spatial regime, too, is marked by symptomatic effects of disordering. The discussion will tease out the accidental, the melancholic, and the traumatic as they intervene in and disrupt the chronotopographical composition of the film.

Ruttmann's *Berlin* film has to be seen against the background of the avant-gardist trend towards an absolute cinema, whereby the medium would free itself from the literary apparatus of drama and narrative and explore its own technical and aesthetic specificity.[2] In the terms used by Moholy-Nagy, it was to become properly 'filmic',[3] self-standing rather than supplementary, realising the inherent dynamic capacity of the apparatus. If this new, autonomous cinematic art was to relate to any other medium, it was music: the film image would work in the mode of a compositional structure, through repetition with variation and the dialectical energy of contrapuntal organisation. Movement, as motor of contrastive effects of shape and light, was thus the stuff of the new filmic mode of composition. Ruttmann was the champion of this filmic avant-garde in the early 1920s, and his *Opus* series a laboratory for the new aesthetic programme. Walter Schobert has argued that the Berlin Symphony should be seen less as an exercise in documentary work than as a continuation of the experiments with light and rhythm in the earlier, abstract shorts.[4]

The montage structure of the film of the city certainly gives the opportunity for an elaborate, abstracted study in both sequential and variable motions of figures against ground. And this image-track works dialectically with Edmund Meisel's film music, in which the montage principle is also at work, creating a contrapuntal acoustic space.[5] A consequence of the understanding of the film as above all a more extended exercise in audio-visual experimentation is a tendency away from the sort of political responsibility that the material object of the film – a metropolis in a time of massive socio-political upheaval – might seem to demand. This is the basis of the sort of critique that has been levelled at it, by such as Siegfried Kracauer and pioneering documentary filmmaker John Grierson, as a film that fails to engage with the realities of Berlin life. Certainly, the film seems content to represent poverty as just another aspect of the urban spectacle, to organise

[2] Walter Ruttmann, 'Der neue Film', *Illustrierter Film-Kurier*, 658 (1927).
[3] László Moholy-Nagy, *Malerei, Fotografie, Film* (Mainz/Berlin: Florian Kupferberg, 1967), p. 120.
[4] Walter Schobert, *The German Avant-Garde Film of the 1920s* (Munich: Goethe-Institut, 1989), p. 14.
[5] See Inge Münz-Koenen, 'Großstadtbilder im filmischen Gedächtnis: Vom *Rausch der Bewegung* (1927) zum *Gefühl des Augenblicks* (2002)', *Der Bilderatlas im Wechsel der Künste und Medien*, ed. Sabine Flach *et al.* (Munich: Fink, 2005), pp. 271–92; p. 279.

the images of other races in the film around the carnivalesque figures of colonialist commerce, and to collude with the logic of women as objects of display, on and off the street.[6]

Ruttmann's film appears in this analysis as an extension of the sort of photographic image famously critiqued by Brecht, and after him by Benjamin: a representation of the outside of an AEG or Krupps factory that effaces both the functional apparatus of capital and consumption, which sustains the image from without, and that of labour, which sustains it from within. The factory is thus rendered as an aesthetic surface, an object of contemplation, mimicking social realism but inevitably remaining at the level of the fetish. On the face of it, Ruttmann's film seems open to this kind of reading. It is perhaps no coincidence that the film does indeed record the workers' entry into, and emergence from, the factory, a key *topos* of early documentary film from the Lumière brothers onwards. And while Ruttmann's camera also goes inside factories, it apparently does so in order to orchestrate the mechanical energy of the production system into the cinematic spectacle rather than to expose the iniquities of its human apparatus: the passage to and from work and the industrial machinery at work are above all studies in movement, never articulated into a critical representation of the world of industrialised labour. While the moving camera of film is in principle able to probe the structures that lie behind the surface image of Brecht's factory photograph, it may also be effectively stalled at the gates, as in *Kuhle Wampe*. It may merely serve the sort of attachment to the aesthetic surface that Janet Ward has described in her work on Weimar visual culture. Urban photography may appear to address social reality in an indexical fashion, and so attach itself to that reality, but it is also liable to resolve the depth and texture of social realities into effects of light, form, and surface. And when it is adopted as a paradigm for filmmaking, as in the case of Ruttmann's *Berlin*, it can serve to elide the documentary potential of the camera into formalistic experiment.

In a similar vein to Kracauer, though with less critical edge, Thomas Schadt argues that Ruttmann's film is 'free of historical burdens and compulsions',[7] a film disposed to the future, and that his own film, by contrast, could not but be freighted with all the heavy historical traces that had intervened between 1927 and the millennium, so displaying what

---

[6] See Anke Gleber, 'The Woman and the Camera – Walking in Berlin: Observations on Walter Ruttmann, Verena Stefan, and Helke Sander', *Berlin in Focus: Cultural Transformations in Germany*, ed. Barbara Becker-Cantarino (Westport: Greenwood, 1996), pp. 105–24.

[7] Thomas Schadt, 'Die Bilder hinter den Bildern', *Berlin: Sinfonie einer Großstadt* (Berlin: Nicolai, 2002), pp. 11–17; p. 13.

became in actuality of Ruttmann's future. Inge Münz-Koenen supports Schadt's perspective in her account of his project's historical and social amplification of Ruttmann's 'pure surface'.[8] My reading here will reassess the understanding of Ruttmann's film as unencumbered by history or politics, arguing that this 'absolute film' is in fact substantially marked by the contingencies, pressures, and memory traces of material history. Equally, Schadt's film – notwithstanding its foregrounding of historical legacy and political activism – remains uncomfortably attached to a more absolute form of aesthetic disposition, where the political and historical are resolved back into surface effect. While Schadt may be anxious not to have his film understood as a remake of Ruttmann's, the two works are closer to each other in their aesthetic-political disposition than might be assumed.

FIRST MOVEMENT:
TYPOGRAPHY – PHOTOGRAPHY – TOPOGRAPHY

It seems appropriate to approach Ruttmann's film – as indeed he and many of his contemporaries approached their experiments with the film medium – through the still images of graphic art and photography, and their convergence in the avant-garde praxis of photomontage. Such films as *Berlin: Die Sinfonie der Grosstadt* have to be understood through the medial complex that surrounds them, not least the graphic images projected in posters and other publicity material. Three migrants, El Lissitzky, Moholy-Nagy, and Umbo (Otto Umbehr), who helped to shape the Berlin avant-garde of the 1920s, will serve to introduce this contextual framework. A significant effect of the rise of the film medium was a galvanisation of other media, pictorial and literary, towards filmic effects of mobile extension in time and space, creating effects of chronographic and topographic projection. The 'New Seeing' ('Neues Sehen'), which became a key slogan of the avant-garde around the Bauhaus, proclaiming new forms of optical discipline, was substantially informed by a transfer of the 'filmic', in Moholy-Nagy's definition, to cultural perception at large. That is, film was to be established as an autonomous form only to be yoked to other new versions of old forms of representation.

Thus, Russian Constructivist El Lissitzky developed his concept of the 'Proun': graphic – and not least typographic – art which is projected into a new time-space continuum. For El Lissitzky, the typographic image would be cast into topography; his short statement 'Topographie der Typographie'

---

[8] Münz-Koenen, 'Großstadtbilder', p. 286.

(Topography of Typography (1923)) conceives of the book as three-dimensional space, with the language of print projected into that of architectonics (e.g. with 'Bogen' signifying both sheet of paper and arch).[9] In his theory and praxis, he projects the poster into the urban environment and artwork into the installation space as 'Prounenraum'. The new exhibition aesthetic required a new optics consonant with the complexity and mobility of modern urban experience. Conventional aesthetic contemplation in two dimensions would thus be converted into an active negotiation of the third spatial dimension and this in turn would open up a new temporal experience of the work of art. The medial mobility of this architectural and topographical modelling of graphic art is nicely envisioned as exchange on the urban transport system, with the 'Proun' as 'transfer station' between painting and architecture.[10] It thus emulates the topographical movement of film as prime vehicle in the transfer of the new urbanist optics.

In his film-scenario in storyboard form, *Dynamik der Gross-stadt* (Dynamics of the City), often seen as an influence on Ruttmann's film, Moholy-Nagy projects the new typo-topography more explicitly into cinematographic form. The scenario develops from an early sketch in ideographic form into an orchestrated structure incorporating typographic experiment, photography, and photomontage. As film-text, the work incorporates the whole space of the page as if on screen, suspending, as Dimendberg argues, conventional graphic relations between figure and ground.[11] As an exercise in dynamics – with the Weimar Berlin watchword 'Tempo Tempo' as leitmotif – the intermedial film-text strains at the limits of its printed form. One embodiment of the metropolitan tempo is the tiger, a figure dialectically split between the unimpeded onrush that might seem to embody the affinity of urban and cinematic dynamics and the 'constriction' of the cage and the page.[12] The carceral turning of the wild animal in its urban setting can serve as an emblem of the ambivalent construction of the urban film-text and, at the same time, suggest a projection of that constraint into the apparently unimpeded form that the text would be assumed to take on the screen. The city film is akin to the vehicles of its transport system, rushing openly but also containing and

---

[9] See Sophie Lissitzky-Küppers, *El Lissitzky: Maler Architekt Typograf Fotograf* (Dresden: VEB Verlag der Kunst, 1967), p. 356.

[10] *Ibid.*, p. 325.

[11] Edward Dimendberg, 'Transfiguring the Urban Gray: László Moholy-Nagy's Film Scenario "Dynamic of the Metropolis"', *Camera Obscura, Camera Lucida: Essays in Honour of Annette Michelson*, ed. Richard Allen and Malcolm Turvey (Amsterdam: Amsterdam University Press, 2003), pp. 109–26; p. 114.

[12] Moholy-Nagy, *Malerei*, p. 123.

contained, made to stop, turn, and circulate. Moholy-Nagy's dynamics are recurrently held up in the processes of construction (of houses or zeppelins) and in sites of deferment (shunting yards, sidings). The film displays procedures of preparation in order to control its shock-effects; the tiger is designed to get the audience used to illogical surprise.[13] This is then redeployed through the work by the repeated, disconcerting appearance of the lion's head.[14] The surprise inherent in the rush of images will be broken by the counter-surprise of hold-up.

The film-text moves at variable speeds and in multiple depths of field and directions, repeatedly going into frame-hold or slow motion, into extreme close-up or long shot, into reverse or spiral. And at its end it is relayed into potentially infinite rerun, quicker each time, by the typographical doubling up of the full-stop into a colon.[15] What the quick-time replay emphasises is the texture of slowing and holding in this dynamic notation, and especially those points at which the vitality of the spectacle is subjected to mortification. The glass of water, which is a key prop throughout, providing the film with effects of stillness/containment and flow/overflow, materiality and transparency, introduces by metonymic logic a scene of death by water. Out of the prospect of the stuff of life comes that of the mortuary:

> **Glas Wasser.**
> **Leichenschau (Morgue) von oben.**[16]
> (Glass of water. / Corpses on show (morgue) from above.)

The glass as a more or less immaterial body becomes a vehicle of inspection for the dead body, a scene that is reprised at the end in the spectacle of a cadaver swimming very slowly in the water.[17] The shadow-side of this transparently graphic and dynamic urban film-study is displayed here in the slowed mobility of the corpse, configured with a photograph of the semi-transparent body-image of a dead bird. Part of what the film wishes to surprise with is the event of death that is integral to the life of the city and always ready to strike unexpectedly. Elsewhere in the film-text, this traumatic impact is associated with transportation technologies, in each case perceived through glass and in association with water. While Moholy-Nagy argues that city-dwellers appear attuned to the optical and acoustic hypermobility of such spaces of urban convergence as the Potsdamer Platz, there is always the danger that they might revert to the condition of the man from the country, so overwhelmed by the assault of sound and image that he

[13] *Ibid.*   [14] *Ibid.*, p. 133.   [15] *Ibid.*, p. 135.   [16] *Ibid.*, p. 132.   [17] *Ibid.*, p. 135.

remains rooted to the spot before a tram.[18] The perpetual mobility of the city is always ready to be struck by mortal freezing.

The programmatic dynamics of Moholy-Nagy's film-text are set in counterpoint with the shock of the still and thus with the sort of mortuary effects that have been recognised as inherent to the work of stills photography by such key theorists as Benjamin, Barthes, and Sontag. In this sense, *Dynamik der Gross-stadt* should be considered in conjunction with Moholy-Nagy's short film-work with another title with programmatic implications for urban representation, *Berliner Stilleben* (Berlin Still Life (1926/32)). While *Berliner Stilleben* registers the motions of city life, as viewed both in its most representative spaces (with a sequence shot on the Potsdamer Platz) and in its more abject, marginal sites, it also bears an attachment to still life, to the stopping of vital energies. Streets are conduits for movement, human and mechanical, and are also held under a halting camera that scrutinises their material surfaces, exposing the scarring of the urban fabric. The camera modulates between face-to-face encounters with living subjects (an old woman performing a song-and-dance routine on the street looks into the camera, knowingly) and a more schematic, abstracted view of bodies and vehicles, both still and moving in urban space, often taken from Moholy-Nagy's trademark bird's eye perspective. As Sibyl Moholy-Nagy describes it, this is a film with a pronounced dimensional awareness, coordinating vertical and horizontal surfaces in its multi-perspectival negotiation of city-space.[19]

Living bodies alternate with inorganic ones, humans are juxtaposed with statues. Behind the filmic vision of busied life in the big city lies a series of more uncanny views of 'still life': a woman transfixed on a street before a heap of furniture, seeming to represent an interior turned out and made uninhabitable; children playing under the wheels of a stationary cart, intercut with dangerous shots of racing traffic; and the movement of the camera through a sequence of *Hinterhöfe* in a working-class area, recurrently held up in its penetration of this dark, recessive space. As Sibyl Moholy-Nagy notes, human and vehicular mobility is repeatedly robbed of direction by the camera's encounter with spatial blocks.[20] The high-speed transportation of the camera by a tram and the leitmotif of shots directed obliquely through the windscreens of vehicles, moving or still, involve the camera in the modulation between motion and immobilisation that

---

[18] *Ibid.*, p. 43.
[19] Sibyl Moholy-Nagy, *László Moholy-Nagy, ein Totalexperiment* (Berlin: Mann, 1973), p. 72.
[20] *Ibid.*

characterises the traffic system of the film. And when it follows a handcart into the *Hinterhöfe*, stretching back in a *mise-en-abyme* structure of frames within frames, the camera is subjected to the sort of uncanniness of spatial experience that Sibyl Moholy-Nagy sees in the buildings as 'uncanny stage', rising up between the human subjects of the film and leading into abject depths.[21]

There is thus a compositional crossover between the image-text of *Dynamik der Gross-stadt* and the cinematic logic of *Berliner Stilleben*, where the halting of the flow more than once takes the form of fixing upon textual tableaux, posters or inscriptions on buildings. This affinity also transfers to Ruttmann's *Berlin*, which is marked by such fixing on writing, too, in the form of signs and advertising. The repertoire of images that *Dynamik der Gross-stadt* has in common with Ruttmann's film – from the zoo animals, to the traffic of the Potsdamer Platz, the legs of dancing girls and soldiers, the jazz band, the shiny surfaces of the city of light, and the fireworks of the Lunapark – arguably transport with them the anti-filmic, still-life form they take in the film-text. As we will see, the mortuary scene from *Dynamik der Gross-stadt* can also be said to be there in Ruttmann's *Berlin*, though, much as in the still-life aesthetics of Moholy-Nagy's film, in a less explicit form.

If Moholy-Nagy's film of the metropolis is stilled in this way, it corresponds to the phenomenology of the photograph developed by Walter Benjamin in response to the experimental photo-aesthetics of such as Moholy-Nagy. Benjamin's genealogical account of photographic technology and aesthetics turns on the relationship between figures and the dimensions of time and space around them. In his account, photography is suspended between the capture of life and capture by death. In its representation of places and people, and the relationship between them, it can both confer degrees of immortality (e.g. to Schelling's clothes (WB II.i 373)) and provide an uncanny perspective on death (as in the stepmother of Dauthendey, whose gaze on the wedding photograph seems to foresee her suicide (WB II.i 371)). The photograph can both preserve what 'has lived' even in the anonymous shape of the fishwife and work more traumatically (as in the case of Mme Dauthendey) to catch the sort of image that Roland Barthes recognises as peculiar to the photograph, especially in its portrait form, that of a mortgaged future. It is what Barthes defines as the temporal *punctum* of the photographic image, the poignant indication

---

[21] *Ibid.*

of *what will have been*, combining future and past: '*This will be* and *this has been.*'[22]

Photography is thus cast between times and tenses. While it is a technology burdened by its history, never really of the moment, it also carries traces of an urgent presence, which Benjamin calls the contingent spark of the 'here and now' (WB II.i 371), that has singed it, marking the fetishistic, staged image with an unconscious truth. This burn-mark can be both vital and traumatically morbid. The memorial character of the early image with its long exposure is such that the subjects are at once bound into death and yet drawn into the duration of a living moment. David Octavius Hill's models are thus, either uncannily or transcendentally, 'at home' in the urban 'interior' of the cemetery (WB II.i 373). It is this that accounts for their aura, the capture of a visual space around the figure that holds them in the paradoxical spatial and temporal condition of remote proximity. Newer modes of photography tend towards the snapshot and the peeling away or decimation of the aura. Atget's evacuated Parisian street-scenes are seen as preparing the way for the photographic avant-garde and its isolation of images from the lived environment. A new photograph might feature a lifebuoy with the name of a city on it, and Atget's technique is to isolate the city from the romance of its name, sucking the aura out of it like water out of a sinking ship (WB II.i 378). It is a salvaging process designed to suspend the auratic distance, the 'peculiar mesh of space and time: singular appearance of a distance, however near it may be', and expose the reproducibility of the scene at close quarters, a space that is 'emptied out' (WB II.i 378). Benjamin sees this as the move to estrangement of the over-familiar city scene, which enables the Surrealists to discover the unconscious, the workings of chance, in their city photography, and – in a different mode – August Sander to transform the conventions of portraiture in his sociological anatomy of contemporary Germany (WB II.i 381).

Following Moholy-Nagy's analysis of the dialectics of cultural development, Benjamin sees the old forms, city scenes and portraits, as being superseded by, but also producing, and being reborn in avant-garde versions. A work like Moholy-Nagy's *Dynamik der Gross-stadt* thus responds to pictorial art by projecting it towards the techniques of film. In its exposure of its means of construction, it corresponds to the need identified by Brecht to reveal the institutional functions behind the photographic representation of the factory. And this, in turn, is elaborated in the

---

[22] Roland Barthes, *Camera Lucida: Reflections on Photography*, trans. Richard Howard (London: Vintage, 2000), p. 96.

experimental cinema of the Russian avant-gardists, and the debate between 'creative' and 'constructive' photography that informs their work (WB II.i 384).[23] While the logic of Benjamin's argument is to stress the constructivism of that cinematic project, there is a powerful undertow in his account towards what he here calls the 'creative', and which might be glossed as the iconic or the auratic.

Thus, the apogee of the new photography, the miniature camera ready to snap-shoot every aspect of city life and reveal the guilt-ridden character of the urban environment, is also in need of what Benjamin calls 'Beschriftung' (scripting), a literary or semiological inscription of the image to make it yield the sorts of criminological indices that it contains. The shock of the new remains approximate in its effect without this kind of detective work of reading and writing; its immediacy has to be held at a distance through the lens of the literary. Meanwhile, the old forms of photography and their alluring but ideologically suspect auratic effects, are not dead, any more than painting has been 'killed off' by the daguerreotype (WB II.i 384). These objects of nostalgic curiosity – as important it seems in the motivation of Benjamin's essay as the new 'post-auratic' techniques – are in a condition somewhere between redemptive galvanisation and the more uncanny state of the living dead. They are figured as golems, ready to be enlivened by the spark of difference between the old and the new, and to step out, coming closer and yet remaining unapproachable, as the aura demands (WB II.i 385).

SECOND MOVEMENT: UNCANNY STREETS

The combination of the creative and the constructive, whether in the still or the moving image, is certainly at work in Ruttmann's *Berlin*. We will turn to the film with the help of a final guiding figure. As well known as the film, is the imagery used to publicise it, and above all one particular image: the photomontage *Der rasende Reporter* (The Racing Reporter) by Umbo (see Figure 5). Umbo certainly typifies the creative-constructive dialectic. Much of his early work is in the old, academic genre of portraiture, lending an avant-garde twist to it through unconventional angles and extreme close-ups, but also with an attachment to time-honoured iconographic principles of shaping and lighting. He moves between highly posed studio-type shots, which give a sense of hold in time and space, and more spontaneous snapshots. When he transfers his perspective to the urban environment,

---

[23] See also Webber, *European Avant-Garde*, pp. 122–30, 144–56.

5   *Der rasende Reporter* (The Racing Reporter), Otto Umbehr (1926).

these contradictory elements are held in the mode of the photographer as *flâneur*. On the one hand, he spends time and covers ground in the expansive style of the *flâneur*, on the other he is ready to use new camera technology to take quick shots of the changing faces and dispositions of the city. Molderings describes the account of this project from Umbo's photographic notebook as a montage of city views that we might well compare to Ruttmann's film,[24] on which he indeed worked as assistant cameraman as

---

[24] Herbert Molderings, *Umbo: Otto Umbehr 1902–1980* (Düsseldorf: Richter Verlag, 1995), p. 86.

well as producing the publicity images in collaboration with Sasha Stone.[25] In 1926, when he produced the photomontage works for the film, Umbo was clearly in the service of the ascendant tendency of *Neue Sachlichkeit*, and two of these, *Perspektiven der Straße* (Perspectives of the Street) and *Der rasende Reporter*, are indeed exemplary works in this style. The first constructs a figure combining the shapes of tower and propeller, high-rise architecture and machinery, out of human acrobats. And the second mounts a photograph of the face of Egon Erwin Kisch, the eponymous 'racing reporter' onto a body constructed out of the machinery of an age dominated by new technologies of transportation and communication.

In *Der rasende Reporter* the artist creates a version of the emblematic figures of the baroque tradition, the incomplete bodies that Benjamin sees as exemplary forms of the allegory. Indeed, the figure, with its multiple prostheses, recalls in particular the sculptures and reliefs by Andreas Schlüter that decorate perhaps the model building of Berlin baroque, the Zeughaus on Unter den Linden, which indeed appears as part of the *mise-en-scène* of Ruttmann's film.[26] The emblematic figures of military prowess on the top of the building and its doors, made up entirely of body-armour and weapons of war around absent warriors, become in Umbo's design the allegorical machine-man of the new media age. The figure is at once one of enhanced power and of practical impossibility. The casting of this racing figure, made up of active machineries, in the seized up, cut-and-paste mode of the photomontage arguably only emphasises the sort of *vanitas* that shadows the model of baroque emblematics. There is, in other words, in this hyper-activated body a sort of death-cast, which recalls Benjamin's claim that the corpse, conceived as a compilation of parts, provides the most energetic form of allegory in the baroque tradition (WB I.i 391). Umbo's allegorical body-image casts the vital impulsion of its subscription, 'the racing reporter', into mortified form. This ambiguity is certainly drawn out, as we shall see, when the filmmaker is substituted for the reporter, and Ruttmann constructs his version of metropolitan reportage in a medium of photographic montage that is technically able to race. Here, the corpse is arguably dispersed throughout the film (in the artificial and damaged bodies, in the suicide scene, in the sequence tracking the hearse), though never directly put on display.

---

[25] See Jeanpaul Goergen, *Walther Ruttmann: Eine Dokumentation* (Berlin: Freunde der Deutschen Kinemathek, 1989), p. 114.
[26] The connection is also made in Sasha Stone's *Berlin in Bildern* (Vienna/Leipzig: Epstein, 1929), which includes an emblematic detail from the Zeughaus, the mask of a dying warrior, as well as an image of the Mossehaus, as discussed below.

6 *Unheimliche Straße* (Uncanny Street), Otto Umbehr (1928).

The soubriquet Umbo resonates with reconstructive and refunctioning principle of 'Umbau' (reconstruction), and indeed one of his most powerful Berlin images is *Der Alexanderplatz im Umbau* (The Alexanderplatz in Reconstruction (1928)), a photomontage collaboration with Sasha Stone. Like the fountain pen that forms the – slightly old-fashioned – arm of the 'rasende Reporter', disjointed at the elbow, his work tends to challenge, re- or deconstruct, the programme for which it is an apparent instrument. Working alongside and against the constructive principle is a more unruly, creative one, a vestigial attachment to a more expressive, spiritual mode. In one of his best-known sequences of images, Umbo takes the principle of urban 'Umbau' as an emblematic focus for that subversive procedure of recording. The three images, *Unheimliche Straße* (Uncanny Street) (Figure 6), *Mysterium der Straße* (Mystery of the Street), and *Schattenwunder* (Shadow Miracle) are street-scenes taken from above and turned through 90° in order to displace the point-of-view from a window over the street into a more mysterious site hovering above it. The implication of this turning is that the road and its shadows are uncannily projected into and under the building. This projection is equivalent in its effect to Moholy-Nagy's strategy in *Berliner Stilleben*, where the establishing scene, shot from a high window and emphasising the accompanying, active but lifeless figures of shadows cast on the street, prepares for penetration underneath and behind the building into the uncanny, shadowy spaces of the *Hinterhöfe*. In each case, the shadow projections gravitate between an uncanny topophobia and playfulness.

Each image in Umbo's triptych is dominated by the elongated shadows cast by bodies reduced to a minimum by the near-vertical perspective: the space of the street is preternaturally distended by these shadow effects. The photographer captures street-images in the documentary mode of *Neue Sachlichkeit*, indexical snapshots of the everyday street-scene, but invests them with the sort of shadow-life that characterises the representational worlds of Expressionism and Surrealism. This is a street being dug up, but what emerges is less an act of urban utility than of urban archaeology, digging up what is under the spatio-temporal surface. This, in turn, suggests an enigmatic, potentially uncanny exhumation and urban life as cast in the sort of melancholic still life that is familiar from the evacuated street-scenes of de Chirico.[27] A scene of working in stone, held in a freeze-frame, certainly conforms to the classic iconography of melancholy after Dürer. While the photographs appear to be a sequence of snapshots, what they capture is structures that seem uncannily predetermined, frozen in space and time. As Molderings points out, the street-diggers can seem to be performing the function of gravediggers, the pit they are digging can seem a street-grave.[28]

---

[27] See Webber, *European Avant-Garde*, p. 244.   [28] Molderings, *Umbo*, p. 99.

7 Overhead railway at the Dennewitzplatz from *Berlin: Die Sinfonie der Grosstadt* (Berlin: The Symphony of the City), Walther Ruttmann (1927).

And if the shadow-hole is readable in this way, it casts each of the other shadows in the photographs into a void condition, suggesting that the material world of the street is full of negative matter.

At the same time, the implication of the turning of the images is that the boundaries between architecture and street are uncannily crossed. The street and its shadow effects are projected through the building, under-cutting the support structure of the surveillant photographer. Umbo's street, in other words, follows the model of a Berlin spectacle featured in Ruttmann's film: the overhead railway cutting through a domestic building at Dennewitzplatz, making a rail tunnel out of a house (see Figure 7). And as Umbo repeats the projection of the street into the building through his three images, so the film repeats the footage of the train running through domestic architecture as if compulsively fixed upon the uncanny scandal of urban design. The uncanny passage of the railway through the house could be said to mimic the ghostly 'track', the incursion of street into building that

Benjamin sees in the arcades.[29] From this point of view, the urban excavations of the city built on sand, which are also a motif in the film, leaving rail tracks suspended over gaping holes in the ground, also have an uncanny effect on the reliability of the street as ground for pedestrians, architecture, and traffic.

In *Unheimliche Straße*, the uncanniness derives not least from a sort of double mutilation, operating along the axis of the gutter, which seems to act as a sort of mirror-line. The cyclist's body in suspended animation at the left of the image leans perilously towards its edge, his shadow splaying an invalid shape on the asphalt; and the pedestrian walking in the opposite direction, but with his shadow cast in the same direction, is decapitated in that virtual form by the abyssal shadow of the hole in the street. This figure seems to have followed a course along the pavement that could only have resulted in a gruesome street-accident, and his shadow projects him back into a fall into the pit or grave. It is the sort of street-accident, the fall in and from the street into subjacent space, which was foreseen in the discussion of *Irrungen, Wirrungen* in my Introduction. This accidental after-effect is also reprised in *Schattenwunder* where the head of one of the figures is fully cut off by the bottom edge of the image and so only cast into sight as a shadow, a negative simulacrum of itself. The representation of the potentially lethal accident that 'would have been' according to the visual logic of *Unheimliche Straße* is also projected into a sense of what 'will have been' in all three images, the *vanitas* that shadows the life of the street, its lacunae and reparations. Molderings argues that Umbo's perspective in these Berlin photographs is that of the *flâneur*, and this recalls the connection that Benjamin draws between that surveillant or voyeuristic perspective and the spectacle of urban crime and violence. The apparently arbitrary image, taken from a window over the street, transforms it into a kind of 'crime scene' under a forensic gaze.

The figure that carries on walking beyond the grave can be understood as a version of the survivor of trauma, following the account that Freud gives of the aftermath of a rail accident in *Moses and Monotheism* (SF XIV 171). The accident victim moves on from the scene of the accident or the crime apparently unharmed. But he is also understandable as an undead phantom, tracking through this urban shadow-picture and representing the principle of return, the revisiting of the psychical and motor symptoms that Freud sees as interrupting post-traumatic experience. In this reading, this image of

---

[29] Benjamin describes the arcade as 'The street which runs through houses Track of a ghost through the walls of houses' (WB v.ii 993), with the double space giving a typo-topographical sense of the phantom track.

body in urban street would be an avatar of the old photographs in Benjamin's account, spectral figures caught in the motion of stepping forward. Umbo's uncanny or mysterious street-scenes suggest a sequence of stills from a motion picture of Weimar Berlin that is also, in the manner of Moholy-Nagy's film of Berlin, a still life, like his *Dynamik der Gross-stadt* interrupted by mortuary images. A later series of Umbo's accompanies a piece by the arch-*flâneur* of Weimar Berlin, Franz Hessel, entitled 'Eine gefährliche Strasse' (A Dangerous Street) and devoted to another version of uncanny simulation, of still life in the city street, the serial displays of shop-window mannequins and their dismembered parts.[30] In both cases, the sort of 'Umbau' that Umbo carries out in his photographic work projects the observational *ratio* of *Neue Sachlichkeit* into a perspective more in line with those other successors of the nineteenth-century *flâneur*, the Surrealists. The work of photographic reconstruction presents the quotidian topography of Berlin as concealing more mysterious, uncanny, and potentially dangerous shadow-sites and -sights.

THIRD MOVEMENT: TRAUMATIC FAÇADES

In turning, now, to the two symphony films, the argument will be that they are marked by a similar sense of the mortal dangers of the street. As the publicity images for Ruttmann's film and the book of stills released in parallel with Schadt's show, these films are, notwithstanding the dynamic effects they produce or reproduce, particularly transferable into still forms. The largely fixed camera of both films maintains a relationship to the static economy of graphic representation,[31] and in particular to photography and typography, and so to the framed image or the page. One sequence in Ruttmann's film shows a photograph being taken in the park: the production of an image that acts to freeze the movement of the figures out walking; and another features images of the printed page of newspapers, spinning past as if on the press and yet also projecting crisis headlines into a visual hold. The *Litfaßsäule* is perhaps the key representation of the film's investment in this graphic principle and of its attachment to the more high-tech publicity media of the city of light. In one of its appearances in the film, a column is opened up to reveal an electrical substation concealed within, and some sequences were in fact filmed from inside a column, suggesting a coupling of the apparatus of technical reproduction with the graphic imagery of street advertising that is such a constant feature of the film.

---

[30] Published in *Das Illustrierte Blatt* 24, 15 June 1929, pp. 686–7.   [31] See Goergen, *Ruttmann*, p. 31.

The tension between mobile and still modes is established in the opening sequences of Ruttmann's film. The image-rush projected from the high-speed technological vehicle of the cine-train, an advanced version of the 'phantom rides' that were a generic feature of early cinema, gives way to a series of evacuated and static shots that could be stills. These images are reminiscent of Atget's Paris photographs and the impression of urban space as 'crime scene' that, following Benjamin, they give (WB VII.i 361). While the train careers at the city with the most advanced film-technical apparatus, its arrival in the station reminds us of Benjamin's argument in his *Berliner Chronik* that rail technology is already superannuated and the station most appropriate for the old medium of still photography, in particular the deficient photograph of the factory critiqued by Brecht (WB VI 470). If, as Benjamin suggests, film is better equipped to expose the functional structure of the urban, the halting of Ruttmann's film in the station appears to suggest a technological reversal and seizure of the apparatus. Having come to a stop in the station, the film presents the city troped as sleeping or 'dead', as Ruttmann describes it.[32] The futuristic impulsion is superseded here by a sense of time-lagging, presented in an oldfashioned, deadening cinematic style that could be that of the programme of screenings 'from twenty years ago' which accompanied the film at its première and was supposed to throw its innovations into relief. An unattributed essay on the film in the *bauhaus* journal is particularly critical of this 'unfilmic' sequence, its passive, static camerawork producing what it calls 'a dead point'.[33] If, as the satirical pastiche of Ruttmann's film cited in the epigraph to this chapter has it, Weimar Berlin is a 'Super-picture-house', this section converts the cinematic city back towards a gallery of photographs with a deathly cast.

When *Berlin* comes to awaken to new life and establish a more active *mise-en-scène* for the day in the life of the city, it is in the sort of uncanny, living-dead style that we saw in Umbo's shadowy street-scenes or in the waxwork fantasy of his 'gefährliche Strasse' collaboration with Hessel. The film focuses on the mannequins in shop-windows that will provide a simulation of the human form, both still and animate, throughout the film, and on doors and windows that sometimes appear to open without human agency. The hinge between the two opening sequences is provided by the arrival of the train at the Anhalter Bahnhof, a version of a generic

---

[32] Quoted by Schadt in the SWR (Südwestrundfunk) brochure (2001) for *Berlin: Sinfonie einer Großstadt*, p. 34.
[33] Anon., 'filmrhythmus, filmgestaltung', *bauhaus: vierteljahr-zeitschrift für gestaltung* 3.2 (April–June 1929), 5–11; p. 10.

scene for cinematic narrative that has a special status in the mythology of early film. As we saw in the Introduction, this primal scenario suggests a lethal danger in the harnessing of film and rail technologies, and its replaying here arguably carries mortifying after-effects.[34]

Ruttmann switches the logic of that traumatic scene by having the viewer impact visually with the city sign BERLIN, which comes at us as if to represent the cine-city taking over the oncoming threat of the cine-train. The impact of the city is deferred, however, as the initial visual dynamics yield to a static interlude, as if in recognition of Benjamin's playful allegorisation of 'Anhalter', speaking otherwise as 'Stopper'. The arrival of the train fails to engage directly with the technologically accelerated life of the metropolis, which is established only gradually out of the suspended animation of Ruttmann's 'dead city'. A recurrent feature of that awakened life, starting with the emergence of the Potsdam train from the Anhalter Bahnhof railway sheds, will be the image of the oncoming train or other vehicle, heading straight for the viewer or just diverted from frontal encounter. And another is the sequence of six shots of the overhead railway train entering into the tunnel passing through the house at Dennewitzplatz, and representing a repeated intrusion of transportation technology into living space. These features retain the impetus of the opening sequence, where technological mobility is uncannily divorced from human agency and appears to come back at the human domain with force. The repeated penetration of the train leads to a sequence of frenzied street and traffic shots, one of the points at which the visual regime of the city symphony threatens to exceed compositional control.

By first representing the dynamic city without movement, and especially the technologies of urban transportation, Ruttmann's film shifts it backwards in time. The streets of 1927 Berlin as represented here are fundamentally still those of the turn of the century, with the representative architectures of the imperial city and *Mietskasernen* ('rent barracks' or tenements) that are already showing their age. There is thus a powerful tension between the images purveyed in the advertisements for the film, incorporating high-rise futurist architectures on the American model, and the actual representation of the city in the film.[35] It is as though this were an elaboration of *Wenn Berlin New York wäre* (If Berlin were New York), from

---

[34] See also Andrew Webber, 'The Manipulation of Fantasy and Trauma in *Orlacs Hände*', *Words, Texts, Images*, ed. K. Kohl and R. Robertson (Oxford: Lang, 2002), pp. 153–74.

[35] The poster for the film represents the city through two stylised high-rise blocks, their flat rooflines suggesting an intervention in the debates around the Modernist *Flachdach* or flat-roof in late 1920s Germany.

Stone's series of hybridised photomontages of the city in its various elements. Iconic American urban scenery serves as a kind of prosthetic extension for the representation of Berlin as capital of modernity, akin to the prosthetic image of the 'American' racing reporter. An image from the film in the *Film-Kurier* brochure, taken from the sequence of empty street-scenes, serves only to highlight this disjuncture between the filmed city and its supplementation by an international currency of iconic images of the Modernist metropolis. In terms of Rathenau's famous pronouncement, this is Berlin as cast ambivalently between the 'dead' image of Spree-Athens and the new one of Spree-Chicago.[36] Indeed, the film as a whole avoids the more futuristic architectures, industrial and domestic, that were being developed in 1920s Berlin, albeit not on an American scale.[37]

The most striking exception to this pattern also proves the point that the film is as much attached to the sort of traumatic after-effects that go with the train entering the station as it is to the forward thrust of such technologies. Amongst the static street-images of houses largely from the late nineteenth-century *Gründerzeit* period, there is an immobile view of part of one of Berlin's Modernist masterpieces, the frontage of the headquarters of the Mosse Verlag, redesigned by Erich Mendelsohn in 1923 (see Figure 8). The old façade of the building had been one of the most notable examples of *Jugendstil* architecture in Berlin, featuring a naked female figure as an allegorical advertisement of the virtues of candour and wisdom embraced by the publishing house. For Mendelsohn, in post-imperial Berlin, to reconstruct this façade would be to hark back to the city-image of the age of the Kaiser, which had come to a catastrophic end. His design for the new façade emblazons a radically different vision of architectural truth onto the post-war remains of that city-image. However, if, as Benjamin believed, *Jugendstil* introduces the human body into advertising (WB v.i 250), the new design is also an effacement of that advertisement of the body. The damaged and removed body-image can be understood as an emblem for the corporeal/architectural violence that emerges in the history of the Mossehaus. It marks the same sort of uncanny danger that Mendelsohn saw in the photographs of the American metropolis.

Following Brecht's dictum on the factory photograph, the façade is a cover that requires critical penetration if it is to yield historical truth; all the

---

[36] Rathenau, *Die schönste Stadt*, p. 23.
[37] Examples include Berlin's first skyscraper, the Borsigturm (1924) and a number of low-rise housing projects under the 'Neues Bauen' (New Building) banner, such as the Hufeisen-Siedlung or Horseshoe Settlement (1925–7).

8 The Mossehaus from *Berlin: Die Sinfonie der Grosstadt* (Berlin: The Symphony of the City), Walther Ruttmann (1927).

more so when it is grafted onto a building with another kind of history. Ruttmann's camera gives the cue for such a move in this opening sequence by first settling on a drain-cover and then shifting its perspective down into the sewer below, where water flows in an unsettling of the immobility of the sequence. The indication is that, in spite of its attachment to urban surfaces, the film wishes to do socio-archaeological work, to penetrate spaces below and behind that are conventionally hidden, or abjected, and that harbour alternative perspectives. To use Lefebvre's terms, it is the irruption of the 'obscene' of the urban unconscious into the scene. This would be to convert the façade as symbol of urban modernity into a more allegorically disposed figure, one which represents the broken lines of history, incorporating the folded forms of the baroque structure that lies behind it and that it turns into a torso by replacing its facing or armature. The cue for this is perhaps given by the façade's alignment with the horizontal disposition of a classic baroque frontage on another well-known corner site elsewhere in Berlin, the Ephraimpalais in the Nikolaiviertel.[38] As recorded by Walther Kiaulehn, Berlin editor of the *Berliner Tageblatt*, the baroque style was certainly still at

[38] Ruttmann's 'dead city' sequence also features a baroque palace immediately before the sewer shot that leads to the Mossehaus.

work in the old-world interior behind Mendelsohn's streamlined façade.[39] And, in line with Benjamin's analysis, the allegorically laden baroque press-palace could be seen as a suitable *Schauplatz* for a modern form of mourning-play.

To contemporary viewers, the Modernist lines and blank windows of the Mossehaus façade also presented a catastrophic after-image, and – following the sewer shots – projection into another type of void. The reconstruction of the façade came about as the result of the damage inflicted by revolutionary street-battles in the wake of the First World War, when the building was at the heart of some of the most intense fighting between Spartacist insurgents and government troops. Indeed, the Mossehaus has a paradigmatic career throughout the twentieth century as a 'newspaper building' in another sense, recording the twists and turns of Berlin's political history in a part of the city where publishing houses of various ideological colours have both reported and enacted the great contests of the twentieth century.[40] In the film it is introduced as a dead façade in preparation for the featuring of newspaper production as a key element in the media-driven dynamics of the city.

The prime intention of Mendelsohn's first major intervention in the architectonic *Stadtbild* of Berlin was to deploy a more horizontal dynamic in order to create a 'participating mobile element', an architecture that would contribute to the transportation dynamic, of the metropolitan street.[41] The closed façade is opened up by the windows wrapped round it, as the sort of 'Durchgangsraum' or transit space that Benjamin saw in Mendelsohn's architectural innovations (WB III 196–7). This was architecture conceived on the model of musical composition, defined by rhythmic impetus, and thus peculiarly suited to participate in the orchestration of the city symphony. While the cropped and static representation of this building in the film signally fails to do justice to what Janet Ward calls its 'kinaesthetic cornering-effect',[42] it does perhaps do something to represent the history that subtends it. If, as the essay from *bauhaus* suggests, this contributes to a 'dead point' in the film's aesthetic regime, this is perhaps a cover for a more active engagement with the fabric of the city.

---

[39] Quoted in Bienert, *Mit Brecht*, p. 54.

[40] Having been severely damaged in the American bombing raid on the newspaper quarter on 3 February 1945, it was crudely reconstructed and served as a printing house for a number of GDR institutions. As part of the border-zone, it was the site of a notorious escape from East to West, when a border policeman was shot. The Mendelsohn frontage was restored in the early 1990s.

[41] See Martin Wörner *et al.* (eds.), *Architekturführer Berlin* (Berlin: Dietrich Reimer Verlag, 2001), p. 65.

[42] Ward, *Weimar Surfaces*, p. 67.

This would be to see Ruttmann, like Umbo, as a photographic *flâneur*, recording the urban 'crime scene' with his 'detective camera'.[43] Not only was the reconstruction of the building a response to, and effacement of, the marks of socio-political strife, but it was itself also afflicted by catastrophic damage. One of the most significant urban accidents of the period was the collapse of part of the building on 24 January 1923, which killed thirteen employees. The new technology of steel and concrete construction brought with it hazards that added to the death toll of the Mossehaus. Mendelsohn said that the design for the early post-war Einsteinturm in Potsdam, with its combination of technological and organic lines, derived from his experience in the trenches, and this principle could certainly also apply to the Mossehaus. But the technology of architecture, as derived from that of war, also arguably has traumatic impact entrenched within it, relayed in this case by the shots that riddled the surface of the newspaper building. Paul Virilio has argued that the Einsteinturm also carries with it the at once energetic and destructive prospect of the nuclear age,[44] and the Mossehaus too could be said to anticipate further violence. The representation of the dynamic building in the suspended animation of a static shot also uncannily engages the mobile medium of film with its cognate, still photography, and thus with the burden of mortality that is a feature of it. If, as Sabine Hake argues, the fast-moving linear frames of the opening sequence on the speeding train are a self-reflexive imaging of the racing film stock,[45] the immobile, blank, horizontal window series of the Mossehaus can be said to figure that stock as frozen in frame.

The image sequence in Ruttmann's film can be cross-referenced here with the work of the original 'racing reporter', Egon Erwin Kisch. While his epithet follows the image of technological acceleration on the American model, the nomadic journalist Kisch recurrently dwells on scenes that counter that ideology, from the time-locked spaces of the Kaiserpassage to the dead space of the mortuary. His essay on the Berlin mortuary, 'Dies ist das Haus der Opfer' (This is the House of Victims),[46] begins with an obituary to the Paris morgue, and is marked by a sense of the passage of these sites of mortal spectacle. It also provides the occasion for other forms

---

[43] See Ruttmann's interview for the *Berliner Zeitung* newspaper (20 September 1927).

[44] Quoted in Ward, *Weimar Surfaces*, p. 119.

[45] Sabine Hake, 'Urban Spectacle in Walter Ruttmann's *Berlin, Symphony of the Big City*', *Dancing on the Volcano: Essays on the Culture of the Weimar Republic*, ed. Thomas W. Kniesche and Stephen Brockmann (Columbia: Camden House, 1994), pp. 127–42; p. 136.

[46] Egon Erwin Kisch, 'Dies ist das Haus der Opfer', *Der rasende Reporter* (Berlin: Erich Reiss, 1925), pp. 258–61.

of obituary for the victims both of the violence that has continued after the war in the Spartacist uprising and of urban traffic and building accidents. It identifies, and carries out a redeeming autopsy on, the anonymised bodies of Rosa Luxemburg and Karl Liebknecht, their mutilations scandalising the official account of death by accidental drowning. And it also reviews the corpses of 'victims of Berlin's frantic tempo of acquisition', the thirty-five passengers killed in an accident of 1922 on Berlin's overloaded transport system as a result of the driving ideology of 'Tempo, Tempo'.

The account of the corpses from the Mossehaus accident on display in the morgue provokes a rereading of the representation of that building in Ruttmann's film. While Kisch compares the architecture of the mortuary to the glass and metal construction of another site of passing spectacle, the pavilion for beasts of prey at the Zoo, the steel and glass façade of the Mossehaus might also be seen to incorporate the logic of the morgue as *Leichenschauhaus* (literally, 'show-house for corpses'). As a building ravaged both by the street-fighting of the Spartacist revolt and by accident, it has a hidden affinity with that house of victims. The image of the façade as part of the *mise-en-scène* of quotidian awakening in Berlin thus carries both the melancholic weight of the historical violence that has filled the streets around it in recent years and the traumatic after-shock, or anticipation, of the sort of accident that can strike at any time and place into the everyday. It stands for both the *has been* and the *will have been* of historical experience.

If Ruttmann describes his collection of material for the film in the contemporary discourse of the tower of Babel (as featured in *Metropolis* and elsewhere),[47] the representation of the Mossehaus, piled up with other architectural images, arguably also participates in this dystopian urban fantasy. As 'participating mobile element', the Mossehaus is complicit in the damage done by urban dynamics, and it obliquely foresees the mortuary images that run through the film. Thus, when the camera looks through the windows of a tram and captures those of a hearse travelling in parallel with it, it puts a particular twist on the recourse to windows as sites of viewing, which is so fundamental to the disposition of the film. These two sets of mobile windows are configured into a logic of the spectacle of death attending that of high-speed life. Such urban casualties as those recorded by Kisch are recalled by this relaying of the transportation system with the perspective of the mortuary.

One review suggests that Ruttmann's film adopts the perspective of a traveller, casting an external eye on Berlin and following an 'American

---

[47] Interview in the *Berliner Zeitung*, 20 September 1927.

literary tempo',[48] but this overlooks the more 'un-American' activities in the film, elements such as the Mossehaus or the hearse, which arguably participate in a more intimate, knowing relationship with the life and death of the city. For Siegfried Kracauer, however, the film shows only false knowledge of its object. He sees it as wallowing in the orgiastic contrasts it records, rather than thinking their relationship in a properly dialectical fashion, so that the hearse, instead of serving as a vehicle for a critique of the sociopolitical system of the city, is merely a picturesque, fatalistic appendage.[49]

If this suggests a lack of a guiding critical knowledge, perhaps Bálasz's account of the film provides a way of gauging what or how the film really knows and gives to see. His reading of it works against the grain by suggesting that this exemplar of *Neue Sachlichkeit* in fact has an Expressionist disposition,[50] projecting the unconscious knowledge of the subject onto the cityscape. It may indeed be possible to understand the façade of the Mossehaus as such an image of psychical projection, caught in the uncertain, hypnagogic character of the awakening sequence of the film. For Benjamin, awakening is a key *topos* in the reading of urban culture, the point at which dreams, as 'what has been', are ready to be dialectically engaged with the present while also resisting it. The film arguably works in this double way, converting the dream-life of the city into waking, critical awareness and yet retaining persistent parts of what has been dreamt in a more primal, unconscious form of remembrance. Bálasz reverses the figure of the American travel reporter, suggesting that the film is designed less as a guide, signposting the city for the visitor, than in the mode of remembrance for the departed.[51] It is telling that the entrance into the city is figured by the camera tracking on a collision course towards the dislocated sign: BERLIN. As the luminous sign fills the screen, Berlin the city converges with Berlin the film as its projection in images of light. It is an encounter that will indeed be turned towards the past and departure in its reprise at the end of the film, when, as a final move in the spectacular display of urban light-effects, the city/film is put under the sign of closure: BERLIN ENDE.

The reading of the image of the Mossehaus as a memorial to its dead would certainly fit with Bálasz's counter-intuitive understanding of the film as turned towards the past and its physical and psychical burdens, but in a way that it does not fully know. It can be understood as an establishing

[48] Anon., '*Berlin: Die Sinfonie der Grosstadt*', *Kinematograph* 1075, 25 September 1927.
[49] *Frankfurter Zeitung*, 17 November 1927.
[50] Béla Bálasz, *Der Film: Werden und Wesen einer Kunst* (Vienna: Globus, 1972), p. 118.
[51] *Ibid.*, p. 163.

emblem for a network of images in the film, working allegorically in the way that Benjamin understands this, as an image of 'dialectics at a standstill', a 'mobile element' that has been held up in the force-field between impulsion and resistance. The mortuary site establishes a standstill framework for the representations of death and accident that run through the film, such as the hearse apparently ready to garner victims of traffic accidents as it runs alongside the tram. In common with other early city films,[52] *Berlin* at once orchestrates its symphonic picture of urban life, calibrating time and motion, chronographic and topographic dimensions, and exposes the accidental, having happened or waiting to happen, as a subversive counterpoint to its compositional design.

The controlling operations of the traffic police that recur in the film appeal to the idea of conducting the rhythms of the city and thus of its filmic symphony. This process is most clearly in evidence when the camera is held up directly in front of one traffic policeman, and the film is diverted into recording more marginal events, before being released once more into its forward dynamic. It effects a kind of dialectical standstill, in Benjamin's sense, holding the film up in order to show activity that its normal flow might miss. Whatever the achievements of these conductor figures, one of them pictured operating a set of traffic signals, in organising human and mechanical motion through the urban topography, there are elements that exceed their symphonic control. Pedestrians dodge dangerously between vehicles; emergency vehicles are shown speeding to the site of an accident; and a horse is filmed lying on its side after a fall, as if in reference to the distressed urban topography of Freud's Little Hans with his fear of falling horses. Neither the traffic police, nor the elaborate sequence of traffic and other street signs, can manage the motions of the film, its sometimes frantic crosscutting and superimposition of vehicular and human movements; hence its recurrent spinning out of kilter, as marked by the counter-sign and anti-topographical figure of the spiral.

The camera, whether borne along in the traffic by another vehicle or carried by a pedestrian, is also implicated in the risk that attaches to the transport system. In one short sequence, it comes to rest alongside the wheels of stationary vehicles, with an uncontrolled, swaying movement, as if overcome by the dizzying motions it has to record. At this point, the camera seems to suffer the sort of psychosomatic dysfunction that can interfere with the movements of the city-dweller. There is a haunting sequence in the latter part of the film when a female pedestrian moves in front of the camera,

---

[52] See Webber, *European Avant-Garde*, pp. 144–65.

as if transfixed by it, and appears ready to become a victim of the traffic speeding around her. This is a city-dweller caught in the transfixed condition of the visitor from the country on the Potsdamer Platz, described by Moholy-Nagy. She is one of the figures in the film, most drastically the woman who commits suicide, that trouble its representation of the mass movements of the city with their stray, idiosyncratic presences.[53]

The prospect of the accident is recurrently evoked. In particular, the film, apparently devoted to simply recording what was there in quotidian life and creating its symphonic effects purely through the editorial process, in fact stages the accidental intervention of violence or death. While the film's declared programme is to catch life unawares, the capture is, in various ways, a staged event.[54] Both the fight between two men on the street (a scene often created for the camera in early documentary cinema) and the sequence recording the suicide of the woman who jumps from the bridge are mounted in this way. The suicide, in particular, appears in the mode of another tradition of filmmaking, the extreme close-up of the crisis in the woman's features quoting the visual language of political melodrama in the style of Eisenstein.[55] It thereby introduces into the film an encounter with a personal case history that remains untold but also suggests a more general, socio-historical kind of distress that erupts here from the more regulated rhythms of urban life. Not for nothing is it crosscut with convergent images of the urban traffic system and the roller-coaster, suggesting an extrapolation of individual crisis into the dynamics of life at large. A submerged relationship might thus be inferred between this scene and that which records a political gathering, which is broken up when the speaker is taken away by the police. While the motivation behind the rally remains as unclear as that behind the suicide, it is held under the sign of mourning in the form of an emblematic flag with crape binding. If the suicide will end up joining the drowned corpses that Kisch records in his account of the 'house of victims', there might also be grounds for attaching her fate to that of another kind of death by drowning memorialised in that text and thus to one of the political victims that might be being mourned by the rally – Rosa Luxemburg.

Whether it be for Luxemburg or others, right or left, the memorial gathering marks the presence of a traumatic history in the film. Like the

---

[53] Another would be the man, trailing behind a family group early in the film, with two balls in tow. He recalls the protagonist of Kafka's story 'Blumfeld ein älterer Junggeselle' (Blumfeld an Elderly Bachelor), who is pursued in his urban dislocation by two celluloid balls.

[54] See Anon., 'Walter Ruttmanns Fahrkolonne', *Film-Kurier* 194, 20 August 1926.

[55] It recalls the distraught mother in the Odessa Steps sequence of *Battleship Potemkin*.

hearse, it represents that which has been and also acts as *memento mori* for that which will have been, for further mass engagements and their victims. While Ruttmann conceives the film as being driven by a contrapuntal relationship between man and machine, as in the emblematic shape of the racing reporter as 'cameraman', the shadow-side to this dialectical relationship is also in evidence. As Umbo's prosthetically enhanced cameraman is also a figure of dismemberment, so the images of bodies working mechanically in the film, from factory workers to marching soldiers and chorus girls, are undercut by isolated images of damaged bodies. The war-wounded may be seen only twice in the film, but their deficient bodies and the crude prostheses attached to them trouble the human machinery of the city. They correlate with the double-face of the streets presented in the film: on the one hand, crumbling, flaking, and under repair, on the other appealing to the late Weimar *topos* of the electrified 'city of light', its visual allure and technical energy reflected in glass façades and glossy asphalt. The human body and the corpus of the city,[56] both of them articulated with, and enhanced by, technical progress, and combining to mount the spectacle of urban modernity presented in the film, also show symptomatic signs of ravaging and impediment.

FOURTH MOVEMENT: SHADOWING RUTTMANN

How, then, does this reading of Ruttmann's symphony relate to Schadt's millennial version of the Berlin film project? Initially, their relationship is figured as one of reflection, but also of inversion. Schadt takes Ruttmann's cue in maintaining a largely still camera, producing tableau effects deriving from his interest in street photography.[57] Many of the shots, whether in urban panorama or portrait mode, are informed by the work of Heinrich Zille or August Sander,[58] and so are ready to form the photographic book of the film. While the camera often settles on individuals and groups, Schadt is more inclined than Ruttmann to introduce a purer, depopulated form of city image after the awakening sequence of the film, and thereby to subject the urban fabric to sustained scrutiny, interested as much in aesthetic composition as it is in social or historical revelation. The leitmotif of shadows, still or in motion, is indicative of this split attention to compositional effects and the implications of history.

---

[56] The city as body, with a recognisable Berlin physiognomy, is a regular trope in Weimar discourse and a recurrent feature of accounts of Ruttmann's film.
[57] Schadt, *Berlin: Sinfonie einer Großstadt*, p. 11.   [58] *Ibid.*, p. 14.

If Ruttmann's film shows a melancholic disposition in that early sequence, Schadt's seems more openly attached to this mood as it proceeds, notwithstanding the high-energy vitality of the Carnival of Cultures, Love Parade, or nightclub sequences. He also uses black and white, but thereby achieves an anachronistic effect that distances his film from the 'original' even as it refers to it. The strategy of filming on colour stock and then converting this to black and white gives the film a heightened, timeless visual quality, which mimics the impact of the technological innovations of Ruttmann's film. And Schadt slows the rhythm of the film, achieving a more contemplative pace, which challenges the visual training of the contemporary viewer in a way that imitates even as it inverts the accelerated shot changes that characterise the opening section of Ruttmann's film and are designed to challenge the limits of cinematic spectatorship in 1927. While Ruttmann approaches the city with the speeding technology of rail travel, Schadt dismisses this route as archaic in an age when travellers are most likely to come to it virtually via www.berlin.de.[59] Ruttmann's express train is reflected with an ironic twist by the more sedate, choreographic motions of the unmanned robotic vehicle carrying rolls of paper near the start of Schadt's film. The slow motions of the film are designed to work against the accelerated viewing habits of the early twenty-first century.

This relationship of reflection through inversion is established in the framing devices: the opening sequence of the first is replayed in the closing sequence of the second, and vice versa. The reflective surface of dark water that opens Ruttmann's film and closes Schadt's (reflecting, here, a reprise of the firework sequence from the start) creates a specular grounding for the inverted exchange of imagery. On one level, this chiastic structure indicates Schadt's programme, to commune with Ruttmann, relate to his model, but not simply to remake his film with a new stock of images, indeed to insist on the massive historical difference between the two. Equally, it might be argued that it illustrates a crossing that is likely to complicate any assertion of difference with dialectical tensions. As Münz-Koenen points out, the opening of Schadt's film, with its images of the millennium firework display over the Gendarmenmarkt, quoting the Lunapark fireworks at the end of Ruttmann's, is a curiously anachronistic spectacle for the establishing sequence.[60] The archaic technology of display works as historical flashback, corresponding to the inevitable associations with the spectacle of war in the explosive technology over the darkened city. The quotation

---

[59] *Berlin: Sinfonie einer Großstadt*, SWR brochure, p. 24.
[60] Münz-Koenen, 'Großstadtbilder', p. 292.

from Ruttmann is thus loaded after the fact, *nachträglich*, with traumatic impact. The programmatic turn back to show the catastrophic damage that was waiting to happen to Weimar Berlin in the Second World War reflects the sort of traumatic memory of war that was in fact already there for Ruttmann's film, though apparently not registered as such by Schadt.

Schadt's project is to highlight historical traces in the contemporary city, where the notion of trace embraces not only fragile marks or remnants, but also two more paradoxical forms: the concrete and apparently whole shapes of large-scale constructions that are also marked by traces in a more proper sense, the 'wounds and tearing' of historical violence,[61] and the negative, absent form of the more gaping wounds of the city's voids. He reconstructs a filmic architecture and topography which configures the memorial structures of the cityscape with its empty spaces and broken remainders, providing building materials that are cast between presence and absence.[62] And the logic of the film follows a similar pattern, focusing on key sites and events in a programmatic fashion, but also deriving a more incidental stock of filmic traces from the 'caesuras' in that programme, the times when Schadt and his assistant, Thomas Keller, were held up by conversations with passers-by on the purpose of their undertaking and their museum piece, Walter the filming cart,[63] or when the old-fashioned, decelerated, and personal process of filming opened up a dimension of 'Sehraum' (visual space) that might otherwise have been missed.[64] The gaps opened up in the filming process by the archaic technology correspond to those lacunae in the spatio-temporal continuity of the city that the film seeks to record. The filmic 'Sehraum' is extended into subjacent spaces that are not normally shown, projecting background sites into the foreground, which is conventionally preoccupied with the city's representative intersections.[65]

The film in fact uses, and crosses, two such ubiquitous visual crossing-points, the Reichstag and the Fernsehturm or TV Tower on the Alexanderplatz, as its organising base for the exploration of its alternative 'Sehraum': unfamiliar sights or familiar ones seen through unfamiliar perspectives. A dialectical relay is established between these two viewing platforms, producing a bifocal perspective on the city from above. The first, a stage for some of the defining scenes of Berlin's twentieth century and located on the cusp between East and West sides of the city, is now also a prime site for looking

[61] *Berlin: Sinfonie einer Großstadt*, SWR brochure, p. 29.   [62] *Ibid.*, p. 30.
[63] *Berlin: Sinfonie einer Großstadt*, SWR *Programm* (2001), p. 27.   [64] See *ibid.*, p. 20.
[65] Schadt in interview with Ole Lasse Hempel, 'Das lädierte Gesicht von Berlin', *Berliner Zeitung*, 31 May 2001.

over the cityscape; the second was established as, in every sense, televisual, a device for remote viewing: a panoptical viewing tower for the old East, looking over to the West, presenting a heroic architectural spectacle for viewers from both sides of the divide, and projecting television images across the territory of the GDR.

The Reichstag dome itself, a post-unification reconstruction of an old form, and designed to open up new possibilities of viewing both inside and outside the parliament building, is presented here as a viewing apparatus that challenges conventions of viewing. It is seen from a variety of angles, internal and external, from above and below, frontally and askance, with refractions and superimpositions. It is through this complex visual modelling that the camera's unconventional perspectives on the city are deployed. The operations of this viewing apparatus are aligned with the black-and-white images of its own history that are displayed in the dome or on sale in postcard form. These present an ironic *mise-en-abyme* of the film's procedure with contemporary Berlin, one that mimics the postcard style and works anachronistically in black and white and yet insists upon the configuration of historical and present-day views, of postcard and everyday perspectives. The viewing of the building's history through the visual apparatus of Foster's dome corresponds to Schadt's reviewing of Ruttmann through his early twenty-first-century lens.

The TV Tower is used for its provision of panoramic viewing, its rotation supplying a panning logic, enabling the camera to settle upon different sectors of the city, in the round. While the Reichstag is introduced via its fabric, both historical and modern, incorporating displays of historical images and the graffiti inscriptions of the Soviet occupying forces, the TV Tower is more virtually rendered as an architecturally disembodied, surveillant gaze, with the building present here only as one of the shadows that fall from the sky over Berlin. Together, the two monumental viewing structures correspond to the location work undertaken in different parts of the city by the film camera, which is both hidden and in evidence in its surveillance operations, at once a party to the media and information networks that it shows at work and asserting an alternative, more undercover point of view.

The return to the raised viewing apparatuses signals the release of further footage from the camera on the ground. The successive image sequences are both thematically distinct and interlinked in the overall compositional economy of the film, not least through the motif of re-construction. This is organised around the film's dual attention to architectural structures, covering a typology of walls in their diverse relationships to open and enclosed spaces, and to memorial figures of varying types. The two are coordinated in the opening sequence of the film through the silhouette of one of the cathedral buildings on the Gendarmenmarkt and the statue on top of it caught in the scatter of fireworks and serving to memorialise the damage done to bodies in the city. The baroque architecture and top-ography of Berlin is introduced here as a *Schauplatz* for the *Trauerspiel* of its history,[66] in Benjamin's sense, with the sculpted figure appearing as a kind of embattled angel of history.

This figure persists in the viewer's memory as the film proceeds through a montage of millennial revellers, often caught in smoky silhouette and in conjunction with fireworks, stroboscopes, or other dramatic lighting effects. Where Ruttmann's Weimar eye focused on waxworks and automata as counterparts to human activity in the city, Schadt's camera is drawn to such figures in stone or bronze, designed to represent historical remembrance and caught in another kind of uncanny tension with the contemporary life that populates other sequences of the film. They form the focus of Schadt's version of Benjamin's dialectical standstill: fixed, allegorically loaded images that are set into contradictory relations with each other or with their contextual sequences. Thus, the statuary of former eras, from the heroic sculptures of Bismarck's Prussia in the Siegesallee (Victory Avenue) to those of National Socialism and Communism, and standing for the dominant ideologies and the lost lives of other times, is brought into conjunction with those mourning the dead of 9/11, living bodies held still before walls in remembrance of the lost lives and collapsed walls of another city. As the sky-high architecture of New York was grafted onto Berlin in the publicity images for Ruttmann's film, so its destruction is memorialised here. The sequence is introduced by shots first of a stone Victory from the Schlossbrücke or Castle Bridge carrying the body of a dead warrior and then of a bronze Atlas figure with a globe on his shoulder, with America to the fore, suggesting that it is the memorial scene of another kind of imperial geopolitical order.

The common feature of these figures and constructions is loss, represent-ing absent bodies and destroyed buildings. Where walls still stand, they are often incomplete and abut void spaces, such as in the sequence depicting a series of *Brandmauern*. The remnants of the Wall with their psychedelic graffiti bodies represent in hyper-visible form the invisible partition that the Wall has become in the contemporary cityscape. The empty cells behind the walls of the Stasi detention centre at Hohenschönhausen, viewed from

---

[66] The sequence, equivalent to Ruttmann's 'dead city', includes a shot of the Old Library on the Bebelplatz, the baroque backdrop for the Nazi book-burnings.

the outside in and then from the inside out, recall the enforced isolation of dissidents, and the controlling of views that did not enjoy the freedom of the post-unification camera. The stone walls of the Olympic Stadium are shot as a receptacle for empty space, an apparently intact vestige of the fantasy city of Germania, an arena only for the stone figures of the National Socialist body-cult. By fixing on an entrance to the stadium marked with the numbers 36 and 37, the film obliquely signals the arena's attachment to the 1936 Olympics and thereby to the sort of politicised sporting spectacle that emerged between the sports and recreation shots of Ruttmann's film and his own. In the absence of living people, the stadium is suspended uncannily between times. The naked stone hyper-bodies of the past are partly veiled by a semi-transparent cover announcing 'investment in the future', as exemplified by the reconstruction of the stadium for new national and international spectacles, figured here by shots from a tennis tournament. The automatic head-movements of the crowd watching the tennis duel suggest that the ghosts of mass mimetic behaviour in the sporting arena of the 1936 Olympics are still there to be seen as a kind of body memory. The preparation of the stadium as showcase for the 2006 soccer World Cup leaves questions open about the city's investments in the past and the future.

The film works to open up spatio-temporal zones of meditation on what has been lost from the city. Thus, the sequence that considers the memorialisation of the city's Jewish inhabitants is framed by the passage of the shadows of clouds over the cityscape, as seen from the top of the TV Tower, itself following a shot through the glass of the Reichstag dome, with clouds reflected in it. The passing cloud stands for the passage of time over the city, for the meshing of chronographic and topographic dimensions; but it also provides a space for a perspective on what has been or threatens to be lost in the passage of history. The camera first looks down on the city, then moves from a ground-level view up into the sky down towards the gravestones of Berlin Jews and resistance fighters, before looking down through the grate of the latter, in a gesture reminiscent of Ruttmann's descent into the sewer. These blocks of stone with memorial inscriptions in an uninhabited space provide a further link in the chain of walls and figures. The inscriptions point up the crisis of representability that this part of the city's history involves: the play of light through the trees and stones, capturing cobwebs in front of a Jewish gravestone and a fern growing out of the resistance memorial, is made to do some delicate work of commemoration.

From this fragile image of growth from (the) underground, the camera switches to a leaden, horizontal shot of wasteland, a zero ground with a few bare sprigs of plant life between Brandenburger Tor and Potsdamer Platz, and the buildings under (re)construction beyond it. The visual blocks of the *Plattenbauten*, the GDR high-rises that provide the backdrop to the shot, match the gravestones of the previous sequence: a mortified architecture. This, the site of what will be the memorial for the murdered Jews of Europe and displaying, in anticipation of this, images of the National Socialist brutalisation of the Jewish population, is seen in ironic juxtaposition with sleek, semi-clad female figures on an advertising hoarding. The advertisement for the reality TV show 'GIRLSCAMP' indicates the unabashed power of capital to recuperate with its glossy publicity strategies the memories of other kinds of regimes of internment and surveillance. This open ground in the shadow of the corporate towers of the new Potsdamer Platz will come to be the site for a bodiless memorialisation of abjection on a mass scale: a monumental assembly of stelae that suggest fragmentary wall structures, broken blocks, or tombs without content or inscription, standing (in) for countless corpses. For now, it is an empty space, and the camera dwells on the shot of vacant ground as if in a mute and naked challenge to the representative project of representation that the memorial will undertake, its enactment of the supplanting of the city by the camp, after Agamben. At the end of the sequence, the camera returns to the Jewish graves, then travels up to the sky, before being projected downwards once more with a continuation of the view from the TV Tower of clouds passing over the city. And this, in turn, takes it to a neo-fascist demonstration, a parading of past brutalities in the present space of the city, with live bodies fashioned after their sculptural models in the Olympiastadion, in spite of the banner declaring 'No Space for Nazis'.

Ultimately, Schadt's film shows a Berlin caught between the weight of national history and the performative and medial energies of a cosmopolitan, postmodern metropolis. It is a city at once apparently at ease with itself in its love parades and yet still hampered by the historical and social divisions on show in parades of other kinds. Its necessary preoccupation with the past and its crimes can all too easily become a paranoid obsession; not for nothing are images from Fritz Lang's *M*, with a wide-eyed Peter Lorre as the hunted title figure, looking over his shoulder, projected into the later part of the film. From the proto-noir scenario of *M* to the thrillers of the Cold-War period, Berlin is particularly disposed towards filmic paranoia. Schadt's film repeatedly looks back over Berlin's shoulder, but does so in a more measured and melancholy way. While its attention to the burden of history is undoubtedly more explicitly part of the compositional programme than is the case for Ruttmann's symphony (Ruttmann's interfilmic quotation is from a Charlie Chaplin comedy), there is perhaps more communality in this respect than initially meets the eye. The unmarked façade of the Mossehaus might now be seen to stand for the brutality that drove its Jewish architect and so many others from the city, and left many projects unbuilt and many others destroyed. But it also has a relationship to other forms of historical violence that predate or accompany it, for what has already been at that point, even as it sets the scene for the unthinkable that is to come, for what will have been.

On the one hand, Schadt's filmic symphony intends to work contra-puntally against Ruttmann's, memorialising that which is lost from it. His camera is captured in a recurrent attitude of stalled analepsis and anamnesis, flashing back towards an irretrievable past through its mnemonic remnants in the present. Thus, the Anhalter Bahnhof that provides the entry structure into the city for Ruttmann's camera is one of the architectural fragments, the broken walls beyond refuge, which Schadt records with his. This is a façade that exhibits loss more openly than that of Ruttmann's Mossehaus. It is a classic version of the sort of ruined portal that Benjamin identifies as an exemplary form of allegorical construction. While Benjamin, in *Berliner Kindheit*, plays with the resonance of 'anhalten' as 'to stop' in the title of the station, what he does not envisage is that the station itself might go the way of ruin. The station that was a (non-)place of urban transition, has now become a more radical kind of non-place, a ruin representing terminal arrest. And the ruin functions as chronotopical figure, also a place of non-time. The allegorical figures on the top of the ruined portal represent Day and Night, set either side of a clock that has now been removed. Like the 'gate' from Fontane's *Irrungen, Wirrungen*, which helped to introduce this study, it is at once lifted out of time and marked out for transience by the absent clock. While the allegorical ensemble was designed to display the sempiternity of the station's activities, it is now arrested – *angehalten* – in the suspended temporality of the ruin. As such it is also a memorial for socio-cultural seizure. Between the everyday dynamics of the rail terminus of 1927 and the ruin of 2001 lies the place that formed part of the system of deportation under National Socialism and later the site of one of the city's memorials to victims of the Holocaust.[67]

On the other hand, Schadt's film can serve as a lens for revisiting the earlier work and seeing what is already lost there. In a sequence showing the mass movement of commuters, Schadt's camera catches a leg sticking out from behind a wall, a curious and poignant variation on the configuration of

---

[67] Deportations ran from the Anhalter Bahnhof, via Dresden, to Theresienstadt. In October 1995 the memorial was vandalised by neo-Nazis.

body and wall that operates throughout the film. It may be the leg of a drunk, or a corpse, or of some individual just sitting against the wall; we never see the body to which it belongs, and the passers-by, caught at knee height and by their shadows passing on the ground and over the abjected or 'obscene' limb, might not tell the difference. The mystery leg resonates with the shots from Ruttmann's film that isolate legs in motion (much like those of Schadt's commuters), not least the cine-legs of Charlie Chaplin. Here, it seems, the legs that sustain much of the energy of Ruttmann's film have been separated and immobilised in this figure that resists the flow of urban movement. It might also be possible, however, to think of this leg without a body as a counterpart to the body without one of its legs that we see briefly amongst the human traffic of Ruttmann's film, which we take to be a war invalid passing across the screen on crutches. This passing figure might remind us of the fact that that film has a history of its own, as well as a mortgaged future that it cannot yet know and which Schadt's counter-symphony records. Like the Mossehaus image, it can be said to embody the element of the individual, the corporeal, and the historical that Ruttmann's film might otherwise appear to elide.[68] The topographic and chronographic compositions of the two symphonies at once complement one another and also, contrapuntally, highlight the lacks in space and time that both bear in their representations of Berlin.

[68] Münz-Koenen, 'Großstadtbilder', p. 286.

CHAPTER 4

Berlin Alexanderplatz: alterations and reconstructions

Alexanderplatz, dear Alex, look what they've done to you.[1]

This chapter considers a model example of the kind of speaking otherwise of and in the city that characterises the account of Berlin in this volume. Its particular focus is Döblin's *Berlin Alexanderplatz: Die Geschichte vom Franz Biberkopf* (Berlin Alexanderplatz: The Story of Franz Biberkopf (1929)), and the multipart film for television that Fassbinder made of it. This is the story of a man who is subjected to various forms of alteration in a place that is exemplary for the allegorical principle: an 'other place' for speaking otherwise. As much as any other of Berlin's key sites, the Alexanderplatz is such a place, representing the paradox of having model status precisely in that it is especially subject to alteration in its spatial form and figurative identity over time. The constellation described by Kracauer in his 1932 essay 'Der neue Alexanderplatz' (The New Alexanderplatz) is exemplary here. The 'formless, open space' that was the square under reconstruction is succeeded by a model of organisation, with Behrens' twin office blocks creating a 'fortified wall'.[2] Yet, at the centre of this protected space is a traffic island, which he describes as no-man's land, with echoes of the square's role as revolutionary battleground after the First World War. The Alexanderplatz in Kracauer's description is caught between old and new, conflict and peace, chaos and order, openness and closure, marketplace glamour and abjection.

It is the destiny of the Alexanderplatz to modulate between oppositions in this way. Over the last century, it has been the object of a succession of architectural and topographical remodellings, proposed or actual, with designs from Mies van der Rohe and Mendelsohn for the 1929 competition, various GDR planning collectives in the 1964 competition, and Daniel Libeskind in 1993. Like the Potsdamer Platz, the Alexanderplatz was

---

[1] Alfred Döblin, 'Alexanderplatz' (1929), *Kleine Schriften III*, ed. Anthony Riley (Zurich: Walter, 1999), pp. 159–61; p. 159.
[2] Kracauer, 'Der neue Alexanderplatz', *Schriften*, vol. V.iii, pp. 150–4; pp. 150–1.

associated from the beginning of the city's boom-time in the late nineteenth century with the new urban dynamics of change and exchange. It featured in one of the earliest Skladanowsky films of Berlin attractions, *Leben und Treiben am Alexanderplatz* (Life and Activity on the Alexanderplatz (1896)), as a crossroads for multiple forms of transport and commercial activity. In its Weimar heyday, as seen in Döblin's novel, it epitomised the market-place, Berlin as aspiring capital of capital, as embodied in the palatial Tietz department store; but it also exposed the underside of the market dynamic: criminality and economic depression. When Döblin revisited black-market Berlin after the war, in 1947, it had become a place of ghosts in a haunted city.[3] As the most representative space of the capital of the GDR, the square was subsequently styled into a socialist version of the marketplace, with the massive Centrum department store and a series of other representative buildings allegorising the Socialist project in its technical, professional, social, and commercial aspects (the TV Tower, the House of the Teacher, the House of Health, the House of Travel, etc.). But it was also ready to become the very place in which that regime met its nemesis through public speaking, in the epoch-making shape of the mass rally for democratic change held there on 4 November 1989.

Since the *Wende*, the square has once more turned into a marketplace of late capitalism, incorporating as its trademark the retro-chic of GDR brutalist architecture. Now, as in the Weimar years, the Alexanderplatz is the *agora* of Berlin, a prime place for public speaking in its market and ideological forms, and through the allegorical principle a place for that speaking to take other forms. The 2005 performance of Döblin's novel under the direction of Franz Castorf on a container-stage in the condemned Palace of the Republic on the margin of the square was a fitting aftermath for the twentieth-century history of this representative place (see Figure 9). It transposed the allegorical spectacle of social anomie from Weimar to a post-*Wende* free market, staged in the melancholic palace-in-ruin of another, superseded historical order.

Döblin, who spent much of his life in the area around the Alexanderplatz, is particularly associated with this place. His role as doctor, dealing with both physiological and psychical disorders, put him in a diagnostic relation-ship to this urban territory and its population. At the same time, that relationship also had something of a case-history character in itself. In a text describing the arrival of his family, migrant Jews from the east, in Berlin, he describes the excitement of the encounter with the city as

---

[3] See Gerhard Schultze-Pfaelzer, 'Döblin sieht Gespenster', *Berlin am Mittag*, 22 November 1947.

9 Palace of the Republic with advertisement for Castorf's production of *Berlin Alexanderplatz*, July 2005.

'afterbirth',[4] in imagery which could indicate either breaking waters or childhood incontinence. And the subsequent journey through the city is described as taking the family in circles, so that they seem to arrive again and again at the same station. This 'Arrival in Berlin' is thus marked both by a particular, affective identification with the adoptive city and by symptomatic signs of trauma and uncanniness, suggesting that this representative writer of Berlin will always be in the ambivalent position of the migrant, never arriving properly in the city, always in an other place.

This condition is explored in the book in which the account of arrival appeared, in a group of texts under the title 'Erster Rückblick' (First Look Back): *Alfred Döblin: Im Buch – Zu Haus – Auf der Straße* (Alfred Döblin: In the Book – At Home – On the Street (1928)). Indicated by the photomontage by Sasha Stone on its cover (with images of Döblin at his writing desk and in his consultation room set into a view of the area around the Alexanderplatz),[5] the text represents Döblin as straddling the spaces of text, domestic interior – here also as clinic – and urban exterior. In the opening text, 'Dialog in der Münzstraße', that spatial disposition is exposed as

[4] Alfred Döblin, 'Erster Rückblick', *Schriften zu Leben und Werk*, ed. Erich Kleinschmidt (Olten: Walter, 1986), pp. 108–75; p. 110.
[5] The photograph, included in Stone's *Berlin in Bildern*, shows the Rotes Rathaus as seen from the Molkenmarkt.

psychically fraught. The café as scene for the dialogue functions here as a place between: between street and home, writing place and clinic.

Else Lasker-Schüler relates how she sought a diagnosis from Dr Döblin for a cardiac disorder which she attributed to a psychosomatic 'homesickness for the café',[6] and here we see another version of the café between condition and clinic, with roles reversed. The author is approached by somebody who appears to know him as a doctor, and the putative patient proceeds to subject him to a transferential version of the diagnosis that he has been given by other, psychoanalytically inclined practitioners, styled as 'Freud brothers'.[7] For Döblin, who was substantially involved in the development of psychoanalysis in Berlin, writing psychoanalytically inflected studies on hysteria and melancholy, but was free-thinking in his adaptation of Freudian tenets and methods in both clinical and literary practice,[8] the 'Freud brothers' are an ambivalently charged fraternity. Having undergone a training analysis with one of the leading lights of the Berlin Psychoanalytic Institute, Ernst Simmel, he is appropriately positioned to have the tables turned upon him by a Freudian patient.

When the analysand projects his own diagnosis of masochistic impotence onto the doctor, this takes a topographical form, as he suggests that Döblin is staying in the east of the city when he really wants to go west, into the terrain of the bourgeoisie, a notion that was just going through Dr Döblin's mind. The doctor's reaction to this diagnosis is suitably topographical in form: 'Ich [...] platze heraus, ich lache meilenlang' (I burst out, I laugh for miles).[9] Whether this explosive laughter, which indeed projects him westwards through the city to the Siegessäule,[10] is to be understood as symptomatic of an underlying *Platzangst* ('platze heraus'), an anxiety about his place in and around the Alexanderplatz, is a matter of conjecture. Certainly, one of the 'Freud brothers' might be inclined to read it in that way. The dialogue closes with the doctor's insistence that the Freudian defects being ascribed to him are only the stuff of his novels,[11] and that he is in fact firmly 'subscribed' to his tripartite territory of book, home, and the proletarian

---

[6] Else Lasker-Schüler, *Mein Herz: Ein Liebesroman mit Bildern und wirklich lebenden Menschen*, ed. Ricarda Dick (Frankfurt am Main: Jüdischer Verlag, 2003), p. 15.

[7] Döblin, 'Erster Rückblick', p. 109.

[8] See Veronika Fuechtner, '"Arzt und Dichter": Döblin's Medical, Psychiatric, and Psychoanalytical Work', *A Companion to the Works of Alfred Döblin*, ed. Roland Dollinger *et al.* (Rochester: Camden House, 2004), pp. 111–39.

[9] Döblin, 'Erster Rückblick', p. 109.   [10] *Ibid.*

[11] One reader of the text, Gerhart Hauptmann, made a similar diagnosis, writing 'Hysterie' in his copy (held in the Hauptmann collection, Staatsbibliothek Berlin).

streets around the Alexanderplatz.[12] This being at home in the book of his life seems, however, to be haunted by a more uncanny sense of the urban unhomely, of the other place, which is indeed recurrently the subject of his books, and not least *Berlin Alexanderplatz* as the book which seems particularly 'at home' in the territory in question.

Berlin Alexanderplatz presents a particular kind of topographical case history: a story that maps a person and a place in a fraught historical conjunction. It is deeply engaged with both place and person and yet also holds these at a certain distance, not least through the aesthetic method of montage. In his discussion of *Berlin Alexanderplatz*, Walter Benjamin recognises montage as the distinguishing feature of the work,[13] organising Döblin's radical transformation of the novel genre into a new form of epic narration. He sees Döblin as turning the modern novel out of the constraining, private regime of the book into the epic mode of public speech. In this it follows the possibilities opened up by the cultural scandal of Dada, in its demonstrative exploitation of everyday material, and the best of documentary filmmaking, also concerned with manifestation on the city street.[14] The speech of this new epic narrative takes the form of montage in order to give voice to the multiplicity and contradictions of the modern condition at large. Montage always works through breaks in continuity, but – as Benjamin insists – Döblin's montage is never wilful. It is sociological document and aesthetic form, its multiple parts organised around recurrent motifs, both documentary and formal. As we shall see, the key function in the montage is the exchange between location and dislocation in the relation between place and person, the two elements of the novel's title.

It is the elaborate use of montage, juxtaposing elements of inner and outer worlds, that has drawn comparison between the novel and Joyce's epochal work, *Ulysses*. Joyce and Döblin are seen by Brecht as pioneering narrative exponents of the modern epic mode and its principles of defamiliarisation. *Berlin Alexanderplatz* follows the logic of Brecht's description of Döblin's radicalisation of writing practices in 'Über Alfred Döblin' (On Alfred Döblin), producing a form of decentred work that influences the structural logic of Brecht's own works of epic theatre: a work where part and whole are dialectically related, at once reciprocal and separate. This applies, in particular, to the internal and external perspectives of the text, the exploration of psychology through environment, which Brecht calls the amplification of the introspective through the 'construction of the

---

[12] Döblin, 'Erster Rückblick', p. 110.
[13] Walter Benjamin, 'Krisis des Romans: Zu Döblins "Berlin Alexanderplatz"' (WB III 230–6).
[14] The marching rhythm of 'dada' (*BA* 292) may well be a playful nod to that movement's street works.

extraspective' (BB XXIII 23). The discussion here of *Berlin Alexanderplatz* will turn on this methodological interaction between introspective and extraspective dimensions: the construction of character in and through the mediation of environment. When Benjamin suggests that Biberkopf constantly invokes his destiny by painting the 'devil on the wall al fresco' (WB III 235), 'al fresco' is telling. The protagonist's fate is indeed primarily inscribed on the external surfaces of the open-air city. And, if the epic work is, according to Brecht, decentred, this also applies to both the central site and the central figure of *Berlin Alexanderplatz*, each of them at once focal and dispersed, subject to structures of displacement and substitution.

The title *Berlin Alexanderplatz* appears ready to be taken as read, a simple signpost. The naming of the novel after a place-name suggests from the start a concern with toponymy. And, indeed, *Berlin Alexanderplatz* is preoccupied with place-names as it charts the peregrinations of its protagonist on the streets of Berlin, reads addresses from a telephone book (*BA* 52–3), or lists the stops of a bus route or a tramline that it encounters. The eponymous place is one with a particular resonance: the Alexanderplatz is a key *topos* in the map of part actual and part figurative sites that make up the 'myth Berlin', not least in the exuberant but also deeply fraught city life of the mythical Weimar years. If mass modernity came relatively late to the German-speaking countries, in the Weimar period the metropolis as prime site of that modernity became the privileged place of narrative of all scales, and not least the novel. While Fontanopolis was still in transition towards the status of modern metropolis, the Berlin of the 1920s fully embraced that status, as *Weltstadt* or world city. Here is a novel that puts epic city-writing on the German map and German city-writing on the international map.

Berlin Alexanderplatz exemplifies the at once real and mythical territory of Weimar Berlin, not least through its relationship to other media. It is not, of course, the first novel to be serialised in a newspaper and so to adopt a certain kind of episodic logic in accordance with that mediation. However, this novel also thematises newspapers as medium, shows their economy of circulation, their ideological power, their penetration of mass consciousness at a time when the news media are more prolific and potent than ever before. At the same time, it has a fundamental relationship to the new technological media of urban modernity, responding to the challenge they pose for the time-honoured art of literature. In 'Erster Rückblick', Döblin describes having his hand read by a palmist, who recognises in him a sort of medium for 'disturbances and moods'.[15] And this medial character is clearly

---

[15] Döblin, 'Erster Rückblick', p. 137.

transferable to the mediation of the disorders and modalities of the city. Soon after its publication, the novel was both recast by Döblin in radio drama form (*Die Geschichte vom Franz Biberkopf* (1930)) and made into a film by Phil Jutzi (*Berlin Alexanderplatz: Die Geschichte Franz Biberkopfs* (1931)), and the new media of radio and cinema are presupposed in the form of the narrative, its broadcasting of the polyphonic voices and 'sound waves' (*BA* 87) of the city, and the adoption of a highly visualised montage technique in its narrative perspective. The novel cultivates a form of what Döblin as early as 1913 in his 'Berliner Programm' called 'Kinostil' (cine-style),[16] the sort of intensive sequencing of image that is demanded by the accelerated and complex *mise-en-scène* of modernity. By the late 1920s, the speed and convolution of urban experience were all the more intense, and film technique massively advanced. The development of sound film enabled a coordination of sight and sound in the representation of the spectacle of modernity. Early reviews described the novel as a 'written film',[17] a sort of 'talkie' in narrative form.[18] The novel is seen and heard as a city symphony, a sound-cinema counterpart to Ruttmann's *Berlin*, and as such a landmark work of the new media age.[19]

The novel focuses its mapping of the metropolis and its medial networks upon one of its ordinary residents. The subtitle of the novel, introducing the protagonist Biberkopf, aligns it with a pseudonymous title like Hesse's *Der Steppenwolf*. Like *Steppenwolf*, it applies a mythical man-animal name to its protagonist, representing the modern human condition in the allegorical form of a beast that is astray in the city. The particularly allegorical genre of the animal fable is related here to that of the psychoanalytic case history. As Hesse's novel is the case history of a kind of Wolf Man, so Döblin's is the case history of a man with animality hybridised into his psyche – a Beaverhead indeed. As much as the works of Hesse, Kafka, Mann, or Musil, Döblin's novel is informed by an, albeit ambivalently charged attachment to psychoanalytic thinking and method,[20] and the symbolic fact of becoming animal in the head embodies that attachment in a particular allegorical form. There will be more to say about the name Biberkopf in this respect in due course.

[16] Alfred Döblin, 'An Romanautoren und ihre Kritiker: Berliner Programm', *Schriften zu Ästhetik, Poetik und Literatur*, ed. Erich Kleinschmidt (Olten: Walter, 1989), pp. 119–23; p. 121.

[17] Review by Herbert Ihering, *Berliner Börsen-Courier*, 9 October 1931.

[18] Review by Kurt Pinthus, *8 Uhr-Abendblatt*, 9 October 1931.

[19] See Dietrich Scheunemann, *Romankrise: Die Entstehung der modernen Romanpoetik in Deutschland* (Heidelberg: Quelle & Meyer, 1978), pp. 167–74.

[20] See the letter to Julius Petersen of 18 September 1931, in Alfred Döblin, *Briefe*, ed. Walter Muschg (Olten: Walter, 1970), p. 165.

Franz Biberkopf is a proletarian figure, and his story thereby breaks with the bourgeois privilege of the novel tradition, especially in its *Bildungsroman* form. As Benjamin suggests, the milieu of petty criminals in which Biberkopf moves is a parallel social order to the petite bourgeoisie. When Benjamin calls this threepenny opera the final, dizzying ('schwindelnde') step of the bourgeois *Bildungsroman* (WB III 236), the term 'schwindelnd' is nicely readable as both dizzying and swindling, resonating with the 'Schwindel' with which life regales Biberkopf according to the prologue (*BA* 11). This suggests that Döblin's version of the *Bildungsroman* is both vertiginous (not least in its implantation of the genre into the dizzying space of the modern city) and double-dealing in its contract with the reader. As a sympathetic ethnographer of the criminal underclass,[21] the bourgeois writer finds himself in a transferential relationship with his object, and drawing his bourgeois readership into complicity. It is as much a novel in the picaresque tradition, a *Schelmenroman*, as it is a *Bildungsroman*, describing the adventures and misadventures of an itinerant rogue seeking rehabilitation but always prone to recidivism. While the institutions and discourses of medicine and the law make their judgements upon him, their diagnostic and corrective measures remain external to his case. Part of what the novel aims to do is to open up the complications of the sort of case that Döblin as a doctor working with the police encountered, and which he sees as exemplary of the broader psycho-topography of the Alexanderplatz, its case history.

If the novel's subtitle speaks otherwise, how should we view its title proper? We should reconsider the claim that *Berlin Alexanderplatz* has a place-name for its title. It is the name less of the square itself than of its position in the transport system, a place of transit, as heard or seen by a traveller.[22] The title puts this focal square of the city, known not least for its railway station, under the sign of transition: arrival, departure, or transfer. The protagonist of the novel is a one-time transport worker, and the novel itself is a work of transport, with repeated recourse to forms of transportation, both public and private. Individual and mass movement is a key feature of the Alexanderplatz, and it is not by chance that Biberkopf has to travel to the Alexanderplatz as his proper location at the start of the novel. Under the railway, underground, or tramway sign, 'Berlin Alexanderplatz',

[21] See Döblin, 'Mein Buch "Berlin Alexanderplatz"', *Schriften zum Leben und Werk*, pp. 215–17; p. 215.
[22] This is operative in the reference to *Berlin Alexanderplatz* in Hannes Stoehr's film *Berlin is in Germany* (2001), where an ex-convict from East Berlin, returning to the city from prison after the *Wende*, hears the announcement: 'Berlin Alexanderplatz'.

the place in question is transformed into one of Augé's non-places: a site of flow, intersection, and exchange rather than of stable topographical identity. The Alexanderplatz of 1929 is already in this sense the non-place of today's super-modern city.

If this novel is a landmark of the arrival of German culture in metropolitan modernity, it marks that arrival as subject to transition and displacement. The stimulation and the alienation, vitality and morbidity, inherent in the urban conditions of transition and displacement are its prime concern. We follow the exemplary urban trajectory of Biberkopf between the intensive, life-giving pleasures of the city streets, in which he steeps himself (*BA* 132) and the grinding inhumanity and mortal dangers that render the streets a site of suffering and impediment, as when he is paralysed on a kerbside by urban paranoia (*BA* 282).[23] The novel is strung between what can be called, after Bachelard, its topophilic tendencies,[24] taking pleasure in place, and insistent effects of topophobia.

Döblin's novel is a key document of what can be called Berlin's imaginary, its mythological archive, establishing the Alexanderplatz and the territory around it as a constitutive, ambiguous site. In today's Berlin, words from the novel are displayed on the unprepossessing GDR *Plattenbau*, the 'House of the Electro-industry', on one side of the square, encouraging the contemporary city-dweller or visitor to see a correlation between the place and the book of the place. In terms of Benjamin's reading, this gesture nicely represents the conversion of the book into epic, public form, inscribing the fate of Biberkopf al fresco onto a wall. It reminds us that *Berlin Alexanderplatz* emerges out of a Weimar culture that is instrumental in establishing a connection between urban environment and text. The work of such as Benjamin and Franz Hessel establishes the city as a complex and shifting sign system, a montage of text and image, both literal and metaphorical, requiring constant critical acts of reading.

This is the logic that informs the only actual intermedial montage of the text, the famous point at which Biberkopf's entry into the city is represented by a sequence of iconic institutional images (*BA* 49–50). The sequence is introduced by the emblematic figure of the Berlin bear, representing the city and – as popular etymology would have it at least – constructed into its name.[25] The bear certainly seems an appropriate stand-in for this bearish

[23] See Sabine Hake, 'Urban Paranoia in Alfred Döblin's *Berlin Alexanderplatz*', *The German Quarterly* 67 (1994), 347–68.

[24] Bachelard, *Poétique de l'espace*, p. 17.

[25] In fact, the name Berlin comes from the Slavic 'berl' (swamp).

Berliner, seeming to represent both the city and Biberkopf's act of entry into it. The sequence is followed first by a town planning document, concerned – suitably enough – with the attachment of a sign to a street-wall and then by a complex account of one of the key sites of the novel, the Rosenthaler Platz. It is a bewildering montage of that square's activities, and the fluctuating networks of meteorological, technological, and human traffic in which it stands,[26] its complexity in ironic counterpoint to the code of icons and the planning document. In fact, notwithstanding their fixed representative character, the icons entertain various cross-references, from the factory representing commerce to the money-bags of finance and tax, or the street-level images such as that of the Potsdamer Platz with its landmark traffic-light column, standing for 'traffic', and the 'underground construction', which at once lays foundations for traffic systems and undercuts and interrupts them. The images work in the manner of a primer, guiding the city-reader in his negotiation of the urban image-text. To enter the city is to enter the variations of this pictographic text. We can only speculate, with Alexander Honold, on whether it is part of the text's play with established models of novel-writing that this Berlin book culminates in the asylum at Berlin-Buch.[27] There is always potential for the book of the great city to go mad with the dynamic and crossed networks of urban intercourse.

The city had never been more publicly imaged and textualised than in this period, and the illuminated commercial signs of the 'City of Light' and the *Litfaßsäule*, often itself illuminated, are key features of this highlighted metropolitan word-image text. In the investigation of the case of Mieze's murder, both the police and Biberkopf resort to the *Litfaßsäule* to see and read what is happening. When the detectives cannot track down Reinhold, we read that if anything should happen: 'dann wird mans schon sehn, dann wirds an der Litfaßsäule stehn' (we'll see it then, it'll be on the advertising column then (*BA* 345)). The rhyming of 'sehn' and 'stehn' here is a common feature of this novel full of jingles of one kind or another, not least rhyming couplets in the *Moritat* or street-ballad style. It establishes the advertising column, indeed advertises it, as a place for standing and seeing, a medial equivalent of the ballad of dark deeds performed on the street. Biberkopf, too, needs to stand and see and read (*BA* 384). Rather than simply recording urban events, the text-image column comes to take on the character of 'an

---

[26] See David B. Dollenmayer, 'An Urban Montage and Its Significance in Döblin's *Berlin Alexanderplatz*', *The German Quarterly*, 53.3 (May, 1980), 317–36.

[27] Alexander Honold, 'Der Krieg und die Großstadt: *Berlin Alexanderplatz* und ein Trauma der Moderne', *Internationales Alfred-Döblin-Kolloquium Berlin 2001*, ed. Hartmut Egge and Gabriele Prauß (Berne: Lang, 2003), pp. 191–211; p. 208.

event' in itself (*BA* 237). It is the same metonymic logic as operates when the protagonist registers 'signs that were cinemas' (*BA* 31)); in the medial networks of the city, the medium or the sign takes the place of what it represents. The cover, designed by Georg Salter for the first edition of *Berlin Alexanderplatz*, itself of course an advertising image, represents the conjunction of space, text, and figure that is at work in the novel. Typography and topography are merged here to contextualise the stations of Biberkopf's story, as if in a stylised map of the text.

The Alexanderplatz is the focus of the text's orientation, but always in transition to such other places as feature on the cover. While close to the official centre of the city, the Alexanderplatz is also off-centre. Carrying the name of the Russian Tsar Alexander I, it seems disposed to look to the east, and so represents what is other to the comfortable bourgeois enclaves of the city's west side. The novel makes an ideological shift to the territory and concerns of proletariat and petite bourgeoisie and the mobile territory between the two. At the same time, this focal space of the workers' and petit-bourgeois districts of Berlin East is shown to be surrounded by underworld and migrant sub-cultures. As we saw in Chapter 2, the 'Alex' was also, metonymically, the familiar name for the police headquarters that stood there. 'Alex' is, as it were, both the Berlin criminal and the Berlin policeman.

When Benjamin suggests that the Alexanderplatz is a cruel 'regent' (on the model, perhaps of the tsar), regulating the surrounding domain as 'Bannkreis' (WB III 234), the sort of dialectic between control, fascination, and exclusion or exception that we saw in his elaboration of *Bannraum* and *Bannkreis* is at work. The fascination of this place in the novel is that it is at once, in Lefebvre's terms, a 'representation of space' and a 'representational space'. It is both the place of those representative structures that establish the city's dominant codes of order through frontal representation and of more localised sites of minority or underground culture.[28] Döblin's novel exposes the Alexanderplatz and its surroundings, from the frontal impact of its representative buildings to the dark rear spaces of the *Hinterhof*, as a hybrid of these two types of urban topography and thereby reveals the unfamiliar faces of the familiar place. Not for nothing does Biberkopf's return to the Alexanderplatz begin with a scene from the conventionally hidden representational space of the courtyards that make up its hinterland, suggesting an inversion of the representational hierarchy of spatial organisation.

---

[28] Lefebvre, *Production of Space*, p. 33.

One of the buildings that establishes the function of the Alexanderplatz as space of representation is the palatial *Polizeipräsidium*, described as a 'panoptical building' (*BA* 419). In a sketch for the preface, Döblin calls it an 'unheimliche Haus' (*BA* 818), and it seems that it does indeed inhabit the square as a representation of its uncanniness: of that which is disturbingly unconscious to it. This uncanniness resides not least in the building's traumatic history as scene of some of the worst bloodshed in the 1918 revolution, with the lifting of the Spartacist occupation of a building 'marked by death', as Döblin describes it in his *November 1918*.[29] This architectural uncanniness supports Benjamin's reading of Döblin as heir to E. T. A. Hoffmann in his cultivation of the Berlin novel (WB VII.i 90); the 'uncanny house' is a corollary of Hoffmann's 'deserted house', inhabited by a dark history. The uncanny panoptical building is emblematic of a sense of otherness that dwells on the Alexanderplatz. It fails properly to see the city that Döblin in his preface to Mario von Bucovich's photographic album of the city calls invisible,[30] and which his own detective work aims to reveal. The tension between 'representation of space' and 'representational space' in the field of the law is the same as applies to the counterpoint between the façade of the great Tietz department-store – with its spectacular windows for total viewing – and the more minoritised and undercover forms of trade that operate on and around the square.

UNDER ALTERATION

The detachable, familiar form of Alex is read by Alexander Honold as a figure of amputation, indicative of the symptomatic conditions of post-war trauma and repetition compulsion that he traces in the novel, as embodied in the invalid Biberkopf.[31] If it is indeed to be understood in this way, what the removal of the appendage leaves as corollary of the body of the amputee Biberkopf is '-anderplatz', a truncated form that can be read as 'other-place' If this seems fanciful, it is worth noting that Döblin recurrently associates the place and what occurs on and around it with 'andere' (other) and its cognates. Other is the watchword of the novel, and the Alex/anderplatz the representative place for encounters with otherness in Berlin. This involves the migrant, the criminal, and the homosexual as types of urban other, the

---

[29] Alfred Döblin, *Karl und Rosa* (*November 1918, dritter Teil*), ed. Werner Stauffacher (Olten: Walter, 1991), p. 505.
[30] Alfred Döblin, 'Geleitwort' in Mario von Bucovich, *Berlin* (Berlin: Albertus, 1928), pp. viii–ix.
[31] Honold, 'Der Krieg', p. 209.

underworld or otherworld figures that populate Döblin's novel, and also the principle of change for which the Alexanderplatz stands. As one of the historic marketplaces of the city, it is marked out as a place of exchange, of traffic of all kinds. It is in its character as a place of social, cultural, and ideological exchange that Ernst Bloch saw the exemplary function of the Alexanderplatz in Döblin's novel. The place of exchange demands mediation in a literary form that is mobile and various, that of montage, which has its true 'place' ('Platz') in the 'almost groundless exchangeability' of the Alex.[32] This mode of representation, which works through exchange, marks the 'Platz' out as indeed an '-anderplatz', a place of transformation that allegorically names its function.[33]

Alexander is, of course, not only the name of a Russian tsar, but also that of one of the epic adventurers of the ancient world. Its root is *andra* – man. Simon Goldhill has shown the ambiguity that is built into that root in Greek poetics, through the opening of *The Odyssey* where the hero is introduced under the mask of the first word *andra*, standing for 'man's place'.[34] *Andra* here is qualified by *polutropon* (with many turns), installing the model man Odysseus into a circuit of exchange, of place, speech, and identity. *Polutropos* is also the epithet of Hermes as an emblematic figure representing many-turning 'problems of exchange'.[35] Under the sign of exchange, Döblin's modern epic, like Joyce's *Ulysses*, can be said to pastiche the Odyssean model (the *Odyssey* is indeed one of its explicit mythical intertexts (*BA* 135)). Like Joyce, Döblin maps out an epic journey for his latter-day Odysseus within the compacted topography of the city. And in its primary placement on the Alexanderplatz, the novel signals the place of its representative man as one of many turns. The topography of the place is also a tropography, a system of rhetorical turns, and these apply not least, as we will see, to the category of manhood as transacted on and around the '-anderplatz'.

The physical terrain of and around the Alexanderplatz is the appropriate framework for the changes of person and place in the metropolitan Odyssey. We have already encountered the photomontage by Umbo and Stone with the title *The Alexanderplatz in Reconstruction*, and this is indeed

---

[32] Bloch, 'Berlin aus der Landschaft gesehen'.

[33] This follows the same punning principle as the jingle about the girl who beams ('strahlt') because she comes from Stralau (*BA* 150), or the case of a 'Frau Eugenie Groß, Berlin' (*BA* 125), following repeated mention of addresses in Groß-Berlin or Greater Berlin.

[34] Simon Goldhill, *The Poet's Voice: Essays on Poetics and Greek Literature* (Cambridge: Cambridge University Press, 1991), p. 2.

[35] *Ibid.*, p. 3.

something of a collocation: reconstruction and the Alex belong together. The work suitably casts the environmental montage in the form of photo-montage, shifting normal planes and perspectives into new relationships, in a technique akin to Döblin's textual montage. Throughout its twentieth-century history and until the present day, this is a paradigmatic place of reconstruction and resurfacing in a city that has been subject to constant remodelling. A series of photographs from Döblin's own album features more conventional variations on the same sort of scene of excavation,[36] which is indeed a signature scene for the novel. Along with the images of scenes from around the Alexanderplatz that Döblin included in the manu-script of the novel, the photographs can be understood as an implied presence in the novel, a latent iconotextual dimension displaying the open-ing up of subliminal space.

While the novel has often been compared to film-work, it can also be related to the technology of the still image. Thus, in a scene that Kaemmerling scrutinises for its filmic structure,[37] when Biberkopf first observes Mieze apparently seeking trade on the other side of the Alexanderplatz and then joins her, it is perhaps indicative that the sequence begins in front of a 'photographer's display-case' (*BA* 262).[38] While Kaemmerling sees the mont-age dynamic of the sequence, with its exchange of points of view and abrupt syntactical forms, as cinematic in structure, it would also be possible to read it as modulating in intermedial fashion between the moving and the fixed image, cinematography and still photography, or photomontage. It is a form designed to make the dynamics and statics of the scene visible, tracking and fixing the two aspects of urban life. It registers the turns and other movements that are a recurrent feature of this sequence, and the standing still that interrupts it (as when Biberkopf, occupying the position of the camera in his imaging of Mieze, is 'arrested at a distance' (*BA* 262)). The traffic represents the dynamic principle, and such fixed features of the street spectacle as the advertising column, where the two stand as they wait for the traffic to pass, the static. At the end of the scene, this standstill is experienced as shocking as Mieze stands still and alone in a mortal freeze-frame, and a fearful Biberkopf then gets her moving once more (*BA* 263). It is a 'photograph' as *memento mori* and an adumbration of what is to come,

---

[36] See Jochen Meyer (ed.), *Alfred Döblin 1878–1978: Eine Austellung des Deutschen Literaturarchivs im Schiller-Nationalmuseum Marbach am Neckar* (Marbach: Deutsche Schillergesellschaft, 1978), p. 232.
[37] Ekkehard Kaemmerling, 'Die filmische Schreibweise', *Materialien zu Alfred Döblin: 'Berlin Alexanderplatz'*, ed. Matthias Prangel (Frankfurt am Main: Suhrkamp, 1975), pp. 185–98; p. 187.
[38] In the first floor of the Aschinger building, before which Mieze stands, was a prominently advertised photographic studio.

or – to follow Barthes in his elaboration of the mortified temporality of photographs – of what will have been. While Barthes sees film as overcoming the fixture of still photography by its protensive or future-bound dynamic,[39] here we see that dynamic held up in the frame of the future perfect (Mieze will indeed *have been* by the end of the narrative).

Like so many of the scenes in the novel, this is accompanied by images of excavation and of demolition (the condemned Hahn department store). Such snapshot images have a particularly emblematic character in their function of making the unseen visible and linking this with the hollowing out that attends the dynamics of construction. Not for nothing does the scene take place against the backdrop of a construction fence, a leitmotif of the novel and permanent structure of impermanence on the Alexanderplatz. The digging-work constantly opens up perspectives on what is conventionally concealed, on subliminal material and structures, and in this it indicates that the novel is strategically aimed at exposing such insights. This is what we saw Brecht call the exploration of introspective dimensions via the extraspective. It represents Döblin's attachment to the archaeological methodology of psychoanalysis, undertaken on both collective and individual levels, and opened up in particular in the interaction between interior monologue and the external sights and voices of the city. There is a cross-mapping at work between psyche and city through unconscious and underground as two types of other *Schauplatz*, following Freud's allegorical toponymy of the unconscious. Döblin describes this in an account of a Berlin street-scene, when he passes a generator in a cellar, which 'digs' him up and leaves him walking on 'as if in a dream'.[40]

HAND SIGNALS – STREET SIGNS

The mapping of psyche onto urban topography in *Berlin Alexanderplatz* follows a more general pattern in Döblin's work. Daniel Libeskind describes his fascination with Döblin's handprint and the perception, though he is no 'occult architect', that it represents the matrix of Berlin and its lifelines.[41] In another piece on his design for the Alexanderplatz, this fantasy becomes a reality for Libeskind, when he suggests that when asked to describe the Alexanderplatz, Döblin presented an imprint of his left hand.[42] What is

[39] Barthes, *Camera Lucida*, p. 140.
[40] Döblin, 'Berlin und die Künstler', *Schriften zu Leben und Werk*, pp. 37–9; p. 39.
[41] Daniel Libeskind, *The Space of Encounter* (London: Thames & Hudson, 2001), p. 197.
[42] *Ibid.*, pp. 194–5.

implied here is a linkage between the mind, urban space, and the mark of bodily identity. Libeskind's fascination with this apocryphal scenario focuses on the choice of the left hand (he seems to be thinking here of Döblin's pseudonym 'Linke Poot' or 'Left Paw'), and suggests it might gesture in the direction of leftist politics. An imprint of the author's left hand is reproduced in 'Erster Rückblick',[43] and alongside the palmist who reads the hand as that of a medium, is the diagnosis of a graphologist, who sees Döblin's writing (another form of 'hand-print') as revealing an ambivalent cast between discipline and fantasy, with special access to the 'collective unconscious'.[44] Libeskind's account of Döblin's hand-gesture suggests a link between the lines of the hand and the urban map, a link that is as resonant with palmistry and criminology as it is with politics. It is the same logic as in the visual matching of the magnified fingerprint and the maps and plans used by the detectives in their psycho-topographical mappings of the Berlin underworld in Fritz Lang's *M*.

The criminological link extends to the psychological in Döblin's text *Die beiden Freundinnen und ihr Giftmord* (The Two Girlfriends and Their Murder by Poisoning (1924)). Here the mapping of identity is undertaken through a series of charts of psychical zones, in an appendix presented as a 'spatial representation' of the psychical changes in Elli Link, her husband, and her lover, Margarete Bende.[45] For Döblin, this topological form of representation corresponds to the 'spatial character' of the psyche.[46] Most of the diagrams represent the psyche as a circle, with its key complexes (maternal love, homosexuality, etc.) as smaller circles within or overlapping its periphery. An alternative mode of metapsychological mapping shows Elli Link's 'front against Margarete' and 'front against Link' as what appears to be a schematic corner housing block, made up of units for each of the key complexes, with homosexuality as the corner unit where the two fronts or façades meet. This housing block inhabited by fraught psychical complexes represents the domestic world as an uncanny site.

In Döblin's study, the eccentricity of the social outsider's psychical map, the transgressing of normative boundaries, correlates with that of handwriting. The symptomatological reading of the hand of the doctor-author is here applied to the case study. The psycho-topographical and graphological models share the feature of a dangerous inclination towards the left (marked

---

[43] Döblin, 'Erster Rückblick', between pp. 112 and 113.   [44] Döblin, 'Erster Rückblick', p. 136.
[45] Alfred Döblin, *Die beiden Freundinnen und ihr Giftmord* (Berlin: Die Schmiede, 1924). No page numbers in appendix.
[46] *Ibid.*, p. 111

also it seems in the invented name of Link, often used in its genitive form of Links). Link's psycho-diagram does indeed exceed the periphery on the left-hand side, and when Margarete Bende takes his place after collaborating with his wife Elli in his murder, so her left-leaning handwriting follows the same pattern, as described in a further appendix. The left follows a conventional encoding as the side of transgression, suggesting that the sort of relationship between environment and character that Döblin recognises here also extends to the form of writing. Elli Link's handwriting thus takes an architectonic form in his analysis, with its 'arcades' between letters representing the enclosure of her instinctual drives, and its vowels 'bolted to'.[47] He finds the cross-mapping between space and character – the symbiosis with houses, streets, and squares, as he calls it – a compelling dark truth.[48] And the relaying from psychical imaging (*Seelenbild*), via cityscape (*Stadtbild*), to handwriting (*Schriftbild*) appears to be no less dark a truth for Döblin.

In *Berlin Alexanderplatz*, Döblin explores the darker spaces of such cross-mappings in both lateral and vertical dimensions: the novel is preoccupied with other spaces behind, beyond, and beneath the eponymous square. It is through such spaces that the relationship between introspective and extraspective, psychical and urban dimensions is explored. While 1920s Berlin is conventionally associated with the glamorous sheen of Weimar surfaces, the 'hundred shiny window-panes' that Biberkopf encounters on his re-entry to the city (*BA* 16) or the illuminated signs 'that were cinemas' on the Münzstraße (*BA* 31), here we see those surfaces opened up for inspection and always ready to undermine the sleek glamour of appearance.

This breaking up of surface and volatile collapsing of layers applies at once to the city and its people, with the two regularly cross-referenced. It is in the subversive nature of the substratum to be projected above ground, so that Biberkopf, whose psychological house is not in order (with something amiss in his 'upper room' (*BA* 118)), is haunted by the possibility of the roofs of houses falling down on him like the proverbially unsettled sand upon which Berlin is built (*BA* 131). And the steam ram, driving rails into the ground on the Alexanderplatz, is described as if it were a building, a storey high (*BA* 165) and liable to fall on your head (*BA* 171). The threat is that the protagonist might be hit on the head as 'Hauptgebäude' (*BA* 314), as if the 'head-building' were under demolition.[49] The threat of the hammer that

---

[47] *Ibid.*, appendix.　　[48] *Ibid.*, p. 114.

[49] When Döblin revisits the ruined Alexanderplatz after the war, the logic is switched in the description of the erstwhile retail palace Tietz, now a ruin as corpse. See Döblin, *Schicksalsreise*, p. 343.

hangs over Biberkopf, and strikes when he is left lying on the road with his head in the gutter (*BA* 201), follows this logic of his construction, or destruction, into the fabric of the city, as he falls on his head into the city (*BA* 64). These urban reworkings of Biberkopf's head take up the distress that he felt upon first re-entering the city, where *Platzangst* becomes explosive, as the head threatens to burst ('platzen' (*BA* 15)). The head is under constant threat both from the psychical distress that is internal to it, in its own space, and the pressure of the space without, the one acting upon the other. 'Achtung Baustelle' (Beware Building Site (*BA* 132)) thus seems to apply to all levels of the urban environment and to the place of the city-dweller within it, who is always subject to pressures of bursting and collapse from that environment. Franz Biberkopf once worked in cement as well as in transportation, and he is thus doubly built into this construction site. Under the pressure of what comes to bear upon him, Biberkopf is transformed into 'another element' (*BA* 414).

The paradox of the place, its identity resting in change, is also that of the person. Biberkopf himself is the object of decimation and reconstruction, most graphically when his body is broken on the surface of a road. When he is apparently on his feet and in place, standing again on the Alexanderplatz like a building or a piece of street furniture,[50] he is always marked out for demolition work. After his ostensible street accident, we read that he is 'made of stone' (*BA* 223) and lying still as iron (*BA* 224). The man of the city has been constructed into urban materials for building and breaking up. When his fate is programmatically set out in the prologue to the novel, it is accordingly in the language of urban reconstruction. Biberkopf will by the end of the novel stand once more upon the Alexanderplatz, altered ('verändert'), in keeping with the principle of the place, beaten and bent into shape (*BA* 11).

The story of Biberkopf is cast between this sort of urban materialism – as the object of inanimate forces – and the sort of creaturely life that is implied in his name, through the beaver as builder-animal, a suitable emblematic figure for *homo faber*. But the novel's appeal to the creaturely is not simply constructive. It is in keeping with the model of creaturely life developed by Eric Santner,[51] after Benjamin and Agamben, representing the attachment of the human to the contingency of the creature. This is the recurrent logic of urban life in the novel, always ready to be reduced to bare life, unto death.

---

[50] Early in the novel pedestrians are seen as street lanterns in an ensemble with the houses (*BA* 16).
[51] Eric Santner, *On Creaturely Life: Rilke, Benjamin, Sebald* (Chicago: University of Chicago Press, 2006).

The corollary of the hammer that falls on streets or buildings – and on Biberkopf as a construct of stone and iron – is the slaughterhouse knife. As we shall see, the abattoir is the key heterotopia, or other space, of the city, the place in which the transaction of human life into its bare, creaturely other state is enacted.

The first few pages of the novel establish the relationship between person and place under the sign of otherness and transaction. Biberkopf's story begins at a gate on the edge of the city. Having served time outside the city limits in Tegel jail, he re-enters the city and rejoins his home territory as a migrant figure, still psychologically attached to the walls of the prison, as if to the city walls. For the ex-convict, the territories of Berlin as listed in the inventory attached to his 'area of exclusion' (*BA* 43) are always removed, even when the exclusion order is lifted. Biberkopf exists in a state of exception, in a form of urban experience that adumbrates the shift from the city to the para-urban camp that Agamben identifies as characteristic of modernity under the sign of the Holocaust. Thus, Döblin describes his vision of Biberkopf in an interview in 1931 as a migrant figure, entering the city from far away, from a suburb, a prison, or a concentration camp.[52] And, as we shall see, in his return to the city, Biberkopf comes to inhabit a series of potential identity positions – Jew, homosexual, Communist – that could indeed have condemned him to the sort of camp that was not yet knowable at that time, as well as the converse position of the National Socialist.

BERLIN-BABYLON

Biberkopf's encounters with the *Ostjuden*, early twentieth-century Berlin's principal immigrant community, at the start of the novel are telling here. His behaviour mimics that of itinerant Jews, and is described as such by one of them, his host Nachum, as he runs from house to house (*BA* 20). It is as though he is performing a version of the travelling Yiddish theatre shows that were staged in the *Hinterhöfe* of this area, though his performance is of another form of popular culture: German national songs. Nachum accepts Biberkopf back into Berlin in a fashion that imitates the historical entry of Jews into the city. As Jewish visitors and migrants to Berlin had had to enter the city through the Rosenthaler Tor, not far from the Alexanderplatz, a gated entrance administered by the resident Jewish community, so Biberkopf, who has been performing in a courtyard in the nearby

---

[52] 'Gespräch mit Alfred Döblin: Begegnungen mit Biberkopf', *LichtBildBühne*, 7 October 1931.

Sophienstraße, is received 'at the gate' (*BA* 18) by Nachum, who recognises him as one who has travelled from afar (*BA* 21). Biberkopf is an archetypal, indigenous Berliner, now in the position of the other. The encounter between the two reiterates the language of otherness, suggesting that Biberkopf is here in a condition of second-order alterity: the other of the Jew as other, the other guest (*BA* 19) of an itinerant host.

Nachum, the itinerant Jewish narrator, telling the picaresque story of another itinerant Jew, Zannowich, also triangulates Biberkopf with the Jewish narrator of his own picaresque adventures, Döblin. This opening excursion has a programmatic character. Like Kafka's novels, *Berlin Alexanderplatz* mounts an allegory of travel, transposing that time-honoured form for the exploration of identity to the dense, multicultural geography of the great city of modernity. And by its attachment to the category of the other, the scene establishes alterity as the native terrain of the novel. Biberkopf is aligned with the immigrant Jews as expatriated 'inhabitants of Babylon' (*BA* 21), introducing the leitmotif of Berlin as latter-day Babylon, a great city under the sign of ruin and expulsion. Like Kafka's K. in *Der Prozess* (*The Trial*), Biberkopf is always a stranger, a traveller or exile, on trial in his home town. There is a recurrent form of *Verfremdungseffekt* in *Berlin Alexanderplatz*, starting in its opening paragraph, where 'in Berlin' is repeated in a strangely excessive way. The story of 'Franz Biberkopf in Berlin' (*BA* 11) at once builds person into place, as though he inhabits it in a particularly essential way, and exposes the condition of being in the city as uncertain, requiring repeated confirmation. He will in fact have to re-enter the city repeatedly in order to be in it again. While he draws strength from the abject fate of Zannowich, the wandering Jew, in Nachum's story, the threat of such abjection will also attend his return to the Alexanderplatz proper.

Biberkopf's relationship to the city is also represented in his relationships to its cultural diversity. Not only does he first consort with the Jews of the Scheunenviertel, only to end up trafficking in the Nazi rag, the *Völkischer Beobachter*, but he is also at once drawn to and repelled by both homosexual and criminal subcultures. Indeed the two merge under the strictures of Paragraph 175, which criminalises homosexuality, and through the figure of Biberkopf's partner in crime, Reinhold. On the one hand, Biberkopf is drawn to the plight of homosexuals, to the extent that his lover, Lina, comes to doubt his sexuality. The marked repetition of the refrain, 'die gehen mir nichts an' (they have nothing to do with me), seems to suggest the opposite. Indeed, Fassbinder draws this out in the screenplay for his film version, where it is accompanied by its othering: 'Obwohl auf der anderen Seite'

(Although, on the other hand).[53] We will return to this crossing over to the other side in discussion of Biberkopf's relationship to Reinhold.

In keeping with the kind of linguistic confusion that is associated with Babylon, Biberkopf's resistance to a homosexual identification is nicely expressed in Yiddish.[54] Having read some minority interest magazines and decided to attend a homosexual rights meeting, Biberkopf's panicked reaction to this taboo territory is mimicked by the narrator, as he is left in a big 'Schamassel' at the less than 'kosher' business (*BA* 74). Biberkopf's ambivalent relations with the minority cultures of Berlin-Babylon are expressed in a confusion of tongues. The corollary of the experience of Jewish life as at once enclosed in the Scheunenviertel and vagrant is Biberkopf's discovery at the meeting of a new law in Chemnitz that bans 'those of the same sex' from public conveniences (*BA* 74); and in the dream that follows his discovery of the cultural topographical conditions of gay life, he tussles with a coachman who drives him in circles round the Rolandbrunnen fountain at the end of the Siegesallee.[55] The alignment of homosexual, Jewish, and criminal questions also appears in the headline in the right-wing *Berliner Arbeiter-Zeitung* vilifying a Czech Jew for seducing twenty boys (*BA* 282). Biberkopf's career involves dealing both in sexual reform publications and in the sort of mainstream press that likes nothing better than to combine the criminalisation of ethnic and sexual fringe groups.

If Berlin is allegorised as the catastrophic biblical city of Babylon – the monstrous fleshpot speaking in tongues and built for a fall – then the Alexanderplatz of the novel's title, a place of sex and other traffic, of cultural fluidity and linguistic variety, and of constant building, is its allegorical stage, its *Schauplatz*. As Werner Stauffacher has argued, location in the novel is always contingent for Döblin upon its linguistic mediation, modulating between actuality and invention (*BA* 865), and the Alexanderplatz serves above all as a scene for speaking otherwise, for drawing invention out of actuality. We can see how it serves as a place of allegorical representation at a point in the text that laments the fall of Babylon and other broken cities. We read that the yellow trams 'türmen' onto the square (*BA* 167), a curious

---

[53] Rainer Werner Fassbinder and Harry Baer, *Der Film* BERLIN *Alexanderplatz: Ein Arbeitsjournal* (Frankfurt am Main: Zweitausendeins, 1980), p. 64.

[54] Elsewhere, Yiddish functions as a form of criminal argot, with 'Ganofim' replacing 'Ganoven' (crooks (*BA* 69)).

[55] This monument is located on the edge of the Tiergarten, a prime gay cruising area, and the site of encounter between the 'bald-headed man' and his young lover in the story that Biberkopf reads (*BA* 75).

application of the colloquial 'türmen', which is used throughout the text to indicate breaking out of jail or 'scarpering' from the scene of a crime. Here the non-standard verb choice is taken up by the reference to bus 19 for the Turmstraße (Tower Street), so that the appearance of Babylon is doubly prepared through encoded reference to its landmark tower (which Alexander the Great failed to rebuild).[56] The non-standard verb also seems to suggest a topographical, or tropographical, projection out of the horizontal into the vertical, as though these trams were towering on the square.[57]

At the same time, the Babylonian spectacle of buildings in ruins is associated with another key allegorical site of the text. Another of the trams that crosses the square is from the Zentralviehhof (central livestock-yard), and this in its turn prepares for an associative network of traffic between urban destruction and the slaughterhouse. The Hahn department store is described as a gutted carcass (*BA* 167); its animal name ('Hahn' as cock) prepares it to present the spectacle of the slaughterhouse. We recall the scene on the Alex between Mieze and Biberkopf, where her death is foreseen, and both the Hahn store and the number 19 bus also feature. Mieze will indeed come to die in the style of the slaughterhouse. The key sites, processes, and language systems of the novel are inter-worked, and Döblin's montage technique thereby shows the sociological and formal design that lends coherence to the panoply of apparently arbitrary encounters. The planning and construction of the metropolis is reflected in what Döblin called the 'Bau', or 'build', of the epic work.[58] Under the allegorical sign of Berlin-Babylon, however, that design is often, as here, working at the limit, shadowed by the threat of confusion and collapse.

As Alex, the Alexanderplatz takes the anthropomorphic form of allegory: the square as a representative Berlin figure, a latter-day Roland of Berlin. Its counterpart would be the allegorical figure of Berolina, the massive bronze figure of a Berlin girl, which stood on the Alexanderplatz until it was apparently hauled away and melted down for ammunition at the start of the Second World War. The allegorical piece of street 'furniture' (a bronze

---

[56] The Berlin–Babylon connection is also made in one of Döblin's feuilleton pieces, where the 'Turmbau Babylons' (Tower of Babylon) becomes 'Turmbau Berlins'. See 'Der nördliche Friedrichstraße', *Kleine Schriften II*, ed. Anthony Riley (Olten: Walter, 1990), pp. 370–4; p. 372.

[57] The logic is the same as in Benjamin's description of the Alexanderplatz, where the vertical impact of the rams is aligned with the horizontal impact, above and below ground, of transport systems (*WB* III 233).

[58] See 'Der Bau des epischen Werks', *Schriften zu Ästhetik, Politik und Literatur*, pp. 215–45.

'Möbel' as Döblin calls it (*BA* 818)) marks the square out as domesticated public space, her removal as a loss of that sense of interiority. Döblin's novel also works substantially in the mode of allegory. We are reminded here of the indicative etymology of the rhetorical or iconographic figure of allegory as an other place for speaking, or a place for speaking otherwise. In Döblin's novel, the Alex-ander-platz, throughout its history one of Berlin's key marketplaces, becomes such a place of exchange for Berlin. The allegorical play with 'Turm' and 'Hahn' provides examples of such an alteration in language. This speaking otherwise is seen both in the idiom of Franz Biberkopf (Walter Benjamin, we recall, takes him as a paradigm of modern metropolitan speaking in the Berlin style (WB VII.i 72)) and in the colloquium of other voices, both diegetic and extradiegetic, that run through the novel. Döblin's narrator speaks as a ventriloquist of such other voices and their non-standard lexicons and grammars.

When Döblin writes on the Alexanderplatz in a feuilleton piece of 1929, it is as a place of mobility – a building-site between market-hall and department store, railway- and police-station, seen from a bus as a place of departure and return. Here the 'dear Alex' is addressed in melancholic-familiar style in the other speech of Berlin: 'wie haben sie dir zugericht' (look what they've done to you).[59] The non-standard use of 'dir' for 'dich', marking the familiar form of address, is also emblematic of the familiar character of the Berlin dialect. It is the language of the marketplace and of the latter-day *agora* as the place of popular politics, of public speaking in its different forms. Biberkopf may profess to be no 'public speaker' (*BA* 70), but when he sells his wares he also speaks a version of the language of the demagogue with his appeal to proletarian politics. And he is a public speaker in another sense; he speaks through what Benjamin suggests is the megaphone of Berlin (WB III 233), the public colloquium of its popular voices. In this, he ranges from the adept speaker of salesman's patter to more impeded forms of speech, aligned with the motif of stuttering that runs symptomatically through the text, marking what is unspeakable. As the representative common man and *vox populi* in this public arena, subject of and to the economics and politics of a city in foment, Biberkopf is another sort of Berlin allegory, the city's everyman. His function is to be both the novel's primary speaker and the common ear that hears the many voices of the city: focal point and passing witness.

---

[59] Döblin, 'Alexanderplatz', p. 159.

MARKETPLACE AND SLAUGHTERHOUSE

In the modulation of focalising and vocalising roles, negotiating with others and with his environment, Biberkopf is a figure of exchange. He trades in material commodities and in ideological positions, adopting and promoting one after the other in an exchangeable system. Commerce is the driving force of the city, especially on and around the great marketplace that is the Alexanderplatz, and not least in the speech that is transacted there. Such transactions of speech on and around the square provide many of the set-piece scenes of the novel, and they are both mobilised and interrupted by the traffic that is another feature of the place. Passengers become pedestrians and then passengers again in other forms of transport, and as they pass from one side to the other, the same people are converted from one kind of mock-epic exodus into another, 'wanderers from the east' into wanderers from the north, south, or west (*BA* 168). The narrator can only speculate on the task of trying to tell the personal narratives of all these travellers across the Alex. Biberkopf, and those whom he encounters, with whom he negotiates, have to stand in for the masses. As a marketeer on and of that place, Biberkopf is caught up in all sorts of commercial transactions: doing commerce with the stuff of life (fruit), with information (newspapers), and with the body (women). He embodies the principle of exchange, as he exchanges one kind of goods for another. He operates in both the official economy and the unofficial, where dealing in fruit is a cover for the parallel black-market of crime.

A key complex in the urban marketplace is the 'Viehhof'/'Schlachthof' (livestock-yard/slaughterhouse), which represents the consumer system of the city as turning on a ritual economy of violence. They can be understood as extensions to the series of allegorical yards that Benjamin explored in his Berlin writings. The 'Viehhof', with its 'Viehstraßen' (livestock streets (*BA* 140)) acts as a kind of *mise-en-abyme* for the city, a representative site that reflects in its spaces of courtyard ('Hof'), market, and street what goes on in the city at large. The slaughterhouse is understandable as a heterotopia in Foucault's sense, an institutional site that at once represents the prevailing order and inverts or carnivalises it. It exposes the contradictions that haunt the fantasy of social control and surveillance that Foucault famously exemplified through the architecture and rhetoric of the panopticon (represented here by the police building). His examples for heterotopia include such sites of confinement as the prison and the asylum, and in *Berlin Alexanderplatz* those other places of the social order are indeed networked with the slaughterhouse. As a heterotopian system, they serve as extensions

of the allegorical function of the Alexanderplatz as other place. Alongside
the construction of human life in the city into its technology and architecture are its becoming animal and the reduction of life to the bare, biopolitical
life of the organism. The struggle between crime and the law in the novel is
represented as a kind of animal farm, where the 'Bullen' (police as 'bulls')
are up against underworld figures repeatedly described as oxen. In a process
of reciprocal montage, references to criminology are constructed into the
account of the abattoir (*BA* 139), while the world of urban crime is cast in
the terms of the slaughterhouse (Benjamin elaborates this in his account of
the novel's milieu, in the language of penning, trotting, and the evisceration
of the *Hinterhöfe* (WB III 233–4)).

As already suggested, it is arguably no coincidence that 'Biberkopf' is
named after an animal, or an animal part. Just as his arm is forfeited in a
traffic accident and exchanged for a prosthesis, so the head highlighted by
his name is subject to a system of exchange. The montage of the novel's
form correlates not only with the construction and mapping of the city but
also with a montage of the body, which relates in turn to the ideological
reconstruction of the human subject. As one of the chapter headings has it,
'Ein anderer Mensch kriegt auch einen anderen Kopf' (Another person also
gets another head (*BA* 246)), and a recurrent form of such alteration in the
novel is allegorical animal heads.

When Reinhold sacrifices Biberkopf, it is in the style of the animal
market allegory. His hand deals an 'iron blow' to the arm of Biberkopf,
whom he calls an ox ('Rindsvieh' (*BA* 211)). Biberkopf is the sacrificial
animal of the market-city, and also both perpetrator and victim of a form
of hyperbolic, but inwardly panicked masculinity. It is a version of the crisis
of traditional masculine identity in the wake of the First World War and in a
time of mass unemployment. The placement of a war memorial next to the
administrative offices of the slaughterhouse (*BA* 137) establishes the topographical presence of the battlefield in the post-war city. Biberkopf's amputation can be understood as an after-effect of, and indeed comes to be
performed as, the damage to male bodies done in the war, so that the
narrative's recurrent return to the Invalidenstraße gains symbolic weight. It
would thus be a symptom of the sort of persistent after-effects of the war
that Döblin diagnosed as the collective neurosis plaguing a sick nation in the
Weimar years.[60] Men like the members of the Pums band find alternative
work of a conventionally masculine type, but the bonds in this sort of
Männerbund or 'men's association' are fraught with insecurity and resentment.

---

[60] See Fuechtner, '"Arzt und Dichter"', p. 122.

They show themselves in versions of what Klaus Theweleit has called the *Männerphantasien* (male fantasies), which would take hold of the German imaginary under National Socialism.[61] When Reinhold takes Franz's arm from him, it is treated as a symbolic castration (making a eunuch of him (*BA* 242)). The love between the two men is a threat to the homosocial order of the criminal subculture. When it ceases to be displaced into the exchange of women, through their 'girl-trade', the economy of free exchange turned into one of theft, it comes to a crisis and the sacrificial slaughter first of the phallic arm and then of the woman that Biberkopf still enjoys, Mieze. The sexual order of the text is fundamentally destabilised by the 'other' that is desire between men. For Biberkopf, Reinhold is that other; as he dances with Eva he loves two absent partners: one is Mieze and 'der andere' (the other) Reinhold (*BA* 299). The status as other object of Franz's desire resonates with the particular language of otherness attached to homosexuality in Weimar Germany, as in Richard Oswald's controversial Aufklärungsfilm of 1919, *Anders als die Andern* (Other than the Others).[62]

For Reinhold, Biberkopf is also associated with another almost homophonic kind of other head – the 'Bubikopf' or bob: a masculine form of feminine styling, suggesting a subversive transaction of gender identities. All the more so, as 'Bube' (boy) collocates in the novel with 'schwul' (gay), thus transacting the 'Bubikopf' hairstyle in the direction of the 'Glatzkopf', the bald-headed man whose prosecution for gay sex rouses Biberkopf's sympathy. When Reinhold tries to describe what makes him stare at a woman, he explains that she might for instance have a 'Bubikopf', 'cut like this' ('so geschnitten' (*BA* 184)). Biberkopf meanwhile stares at Reinhold, followed by the fateful refrain on the Grim Reaper ('Schnitter' (*BA* 184)). The cutting here has a particular resonance with the haircut, emphasising the mortal triangulation of the two men and the women they style and exchange as objects of what Lacanian psychoanalysis would call the dialectical desire of the other. Biberkopf is at once subject to the desire of the other, Reinhold's desire, and desire *for* that other.

This ambiguous othering can only ultimately be contained, it seems, by the violence of the slaughterhouse, the exchanging of the human values of care for the other that run through the text with the bare life violence that also racks it. When Reinhold slaughters Mieze he is also exchanging himself

[61] Klaus Theweleit, *Männerphantasien*, 2 vols. (Reinbek: Rowohlt, 1980).
[62] As Jelavich notes, the actor who played the gay blackmail victim in Oswald's film, Conrad Veidt, was rejected as Reinhold in Jutzi's film, perhaps because of uncomfortable associations for the sanitised film version. See Peter Jelavich, *Berlin Alexanderplatz: Radio, Film, and the Death of Weimar Culture* (Berkeley: University of California Press, 2006), p. 213.

for Biberkopf, taking the place of the man who beat Mieze as if in a display for him and who carries the criminal history of his brutal manslaughter of Ida. This violence between men, also when inflicted upon the women transacted between them, is characteristic of the particular kind of heterotopian order that Fassbinder will see in Döblin's text, where love between men finds its particular place, both utopian and dystopian, in the other institutional spaces of the prison or the slaughterhouse.

The end of the novel is rife with the language of othering, preparing for the programmatic return of the other Franz Biberkopf to the Alexanderplatz, still a place of difference. Having been battled over by Death and the Whore of Babylon, with the male figure of Death triumphant, Biberkopf is reborn in the Berlin-Buch asylum. The identification with animals that has run through the novel as the measure of the brute otherness in human nature is now made fully explicit in Biberkopf's deathbed illumination – first seeing that he is an animal ('ein Vieh') then even negating that identification, as professed 'Untier' or monster (*BA* 442). At the end of his story, Biberkopf thus attributes himself to the same non- or 'unspecies' as Georg Samsa in Kafka's classic Modernist tale of personal alteration in withdrawal from the city, *Die Verwandlung*.[63] The other that he becomes at this point is of course himself, as emphasised by the double use of the term as he is exchanged: an 'anderer' lay in the bed – presumably the now defunct Biberkopf we once knew; and the 'andere' – presumably the new Biberkopf – has the same papers as Franz (*BA* 442). This figure of the self-same other is a classic version of the *Doppelgänger*, an uncanny embodiment of the alterity that inheres in identity and comes back upon it.[64] When he returns to stand once more on the Alexanderplatz, still under reconstruction, and the narrator records the encounter in free indirect speech, it seems that the changed place and the changed man are as one, converged in the 'er ist da': he or it is there (*BA* 449).

The other Biberkopf, once unable to read the city (*BA* 63), is apparently finally able to read the 'street sign' that is seen at the end of the text (*BA* 453), but with the sense of location or orientation it might give never revealed. And he seems able to take care in the congested traffic of words in the city, not to fall once more in case they run him over. There is always the possibility in this place of speaking otherwise that words can be lethal in their rhyming or other effects, so that the 'Autobus' may make you into

---

[63] See Andrew Webber, 'Kafka, *Die Verwandlung*', *Landmarks in German Short Prose*, ed. Peter Hutchinson (Oxford: Lang, 2003), pp. 175–90; p. 180.
[64] See Webber, *Doppelgänger*.

'Appelmus' (apple puree (*BA* 453–4)). And at the close of the text the marketplace has been exchanged for another place, a military parade-ground or battle-field, as the text falls back into a march (*BA* 454–5):

und rechts und links und rechts und links, marschieren, marschieren, wir ziehen in den Krieg … widebum, widebum, dem einen gehts grade, dem andern gehts krumm, der eine bleibt stehen, der andere fällt um, der eine rennt weiter, der andere liegt stumm, widebum, widebum.
(and right and left and right and left, marching, marching, we're off to war … vidibum, vidibum, for the one things go straight, for the other they go bent, the one stays standing, the other falls down, the one runs on, the other lies dumb, vidibum, vidibum.)

It is the transformation – in both 'right and left' directions – that had already come over the Alexanderplatz during the Spartacist uprising, would do so once more in the Second World War, again when the square was the endpoint of the May-Day march-past in the GDR era, and, more recently, as the rally-ground for the neo-Nazi party, NPD, whose plans to march from there through the centre of the city on 8 May 2005 were blocked by a mass anti-fascist demonstration. In the terms of the mass movements of the novel, the march to the left would be that to the memorials to Rosa Luxemburg and Karl Liebknecht in Friedrichsfelde (*BA* 87), while the march to the right is that of the *Stahlhelm* rally (*BA* 82). Whether the de-individualised Biberkopf, shoulder to shoulder in a mass march to war at the close of the text, will go left or right, will be the one who stands or the other who falls, remains open. The phonetic effects of Biberkopf's marching tune – its '*widebum, widebum*' – complete the soundscape of the city novel. They chime both with the 'Rumm rumm' that was the rhythm of the steam ram on the Alexanderplatz (*BA* 165) and with the 'Wumm-wumm' of the fateful storm in the woods, its march chaotically destructive and echoing with the impact of bombs from the air (*BA* 354). The march accommodates both the drive of the city and the drive of nature, battering human life from 'rumm' to '*krumm*',[65] each of them always echoing the compulsive rhythms of the death drive.[66] Natural history and urban technology, forces that Döblin saw as battling over Berlin in a 1921 sketch for a novel,[67] are marching together here. The 'wide-' of '*widebum*' in the allegorical march of bare life seems to speak otherwise, echoing with 'wieder' (again), marking the impact again

---

[65] This 'krumm' bends the figure into the stoop that Santner describes in his *On Creaturely Life*.
[66] Freud's *Beyond the Pleasure Principle*, which establishes the death drive, was reviewed rather ambivalently by Döblin in 'Psychoanalyse von Heute' (Psychoanalysis of Today (1923)), *Kleine Schriften II*, pp. 261–6; pp. 265–6.
[67] See Philip Brady, 'Symphony and Jungle-Noises', *Berlin*, ed. Derek Glass *et al.*, pp. 83–106; p. 92.

and again. And the '-bum' also chimes, negatively as it were, with 'stumm', with the mutism of the dead as ultimate other, lying dumb, and so with the deathly silence into which the repetitions and variations of the polyphonic urban text are about to fall. In this final allegorical vision the novel uncannily records the mortal march of history, its insistent noise and its falling silent, in this other place.

GARBAGE, THE CITY, AND DEATH: FASSBINDER'S RECONSTRUCTIONS

Döblin's intention in his collaboration with Phil Jutzi in the 1931 film of *Berlin Alexanderplatz* was to show how another kind of writing could be the basis of another kind of filmmaking.[68] In the event, Jutzi's film, with its socially, politically, and psychosexually sanitised version of the novel's narrative failed to achieve any other kind of impact;[69] and even in that form, it was soon subject to the constraints of the new political climate. Döblin's intention had been for the film to take advantage of the medium's al fresco character as a vehicle for the public space of his epic writing, giving the author the sense of stepping from his living room into an open landscape or an urban space of mass congregation.[70] And sound film would enable narrative discourse to take a form more appropriate to the city, imitating the built environment in the form of the 'concreted word'.[71] Jutzi's film achieves some of this concrete impact in its word and image dynamics in such scenes as the one where Heinrich George as Biberkopf is selling his tie-bands on the Alexanderplatz, and where his broadcast urban discourse has to compete with passing traffic, with the camera moving from extreme close-up to more distant panning. But the overall effect of the film is of an unmotivated dislocation between word and image, between narrative and scene, most strikingly where quite radical images of the urban environment around the Alexanderplatz are arbitrarily interspersed without any sense of the integral montage that is at work in the novel.

For the Jutzi film, the environment described in the novel was still more or less unchanged, enabling such location scenes as Heinrich George's *tour-de-force* performance as street salesman. The scene in question is

---

[68] See Alfred Döblin, *Berlin Alexanderplatz: Drehbuch von Alfred Döblin und Hans Wilhelm zu Phil Jutzis Film von 1931* (Munich: text+kritik, 1996), p. 237.

[69] As a contemporary review in *Der Vorstoss* (18 October 1931) put it, the film lacks both the psychoanalytic depth and the political critique of the novel.

[70] Döblin, *Berlin Alexanderplatz: Drehbuch*, p. 237.   [71] *Ibid.*, p. 238.

reconstructed in an article in *Die Filmwoche*, describing how the film crew recreated the effect of the square under reconstruction by building a false fence brought in from the Neubabelsberg studios and carrying the warning 'Achtung Baustelle!' (Beware Building-site!).[72] Film imitates life in a simulated form of reconstruction, converting public space into studio, construction fence into film-set. The scene follows the logic of the film as a whole: a star vehicle for George, who, in the poster advertising the film, is implanted as a one-armed colossus into the monumental transportation hub and construction site of the Alexanderplatz.[73] And the final scene of the film repeats that logic by setting its irrepressible entertainer version of Biberkopf back in the marketplace of the Alexanderplatz, this time selling a more allegorical commodity: 'Stehaufmännchen' or self-righting dolls, as if recuperating the spectacle of the fallen in the final life-and-death march of the novel.

For Fassbinder, returning to *Berlin Alexanderplatz* for his fourteen-part film series for television in 1980, the location of the novel has much more fundamentally become an other place, a 'concrete desert' in East Berlin,[74] and the relationship between location shooting and studio work is accordingly far from straightforward. His project creates cinematic extensions of the extensions that Döblin creates around the Alexanderplatz, but extensions that also emphasise confinement and separation from the original scene. A series of films produced by the GDR state film company, DEFA, had recorded the destruction of the old fabric around the Alexanderplatz, and its reconstruction in a new, monumental style, and for Fassbinder's project the area is now, both historically and politically, a no-go area. In the event, after elaborate scouting of potential location sites, only small parts of the series were filmed on location in West Berlin (for instance, in the Deutsche Oper underground station), while most were reconstructed in the generic 'Berlin Street', also known as the 'Bergmann Straße',[75] in the Bavaria studios outside Munich. In 'Umbau der Straße "Potemkin"' (Reconstruction of "Potemkin" Street), Fassbinder and his assistant, Harry Baer, describe the reconstruction of this Potemkin street after its use as a scene of post-war destruction in an American production and in

---

[72] Rudi Loewenthal, 'Der Alexanderplatz als Filmkulisse: Heinrich Georges fliegender Krawattenladen', *Die Filmwoche* 27 (1931), 848–50; p. 848.

[73] The poster is reproduced in *Berlin Alexanderplatz: Drehbuch*, p. 22.

[74] *Der Film B E R L I N A l e x a n d e r p l a t z*, p. 516.

[75] The street was nicknamed Bergmann Straße after both the street in Berlin Kreuzberg and Ingmar Bergman, who had used it for his Berlin film *The Serpent's Egg* (1977).

Schlöndorff's *Die Blechtrommel* (The Tin Drum), and then its destructive remodelling as street of death for the epilogue of their own film.

The Potemkin version of Berlin put certain constraints upon the representational range of the project. At every turn, the film represents spatial restraint. From its opening, when Biberkopf is caught on the prison threshold, unwilling to enter into the open space without, through the next scene in the *Hinterhof*, and the dark interior into which Nachum leads him, it binds itself back into studio mode. The scene that follows this opening sequence can be considered as emblematic in this sense. Rather than entering the cinema, as in the novel, Biberkopf first experiences a flashback to his killing of Ida, in mind-screen style, then enters the prostitute's room only for the cinema sign to continue flashing into the room. 'KINO' is presented here as an insistently artificial effect, a pink light that pulses through the *mise-en-scène*, projecting the exterior into the interior. Fassbinder might seem here to take the elision of cinema and light-sign in the novel literally by not opening up the cinema space, but having the sign 'KINO' projected into other spaces. The same pink light also pulses into Biberkopf's lodgings, where it highlights the word 'Druck' (printing), etched in the window, and understandable as an allegorical inscription or imprint of pressure (the other meaning of 'Druck') between the inside and the outside spheres of his existence. And later in the film, the same cinema sign, with its ironic reflection on the cinematic fantasy, illuminates an encounter between Reinhold and Biberkopf in the *film noir* style, on the street, but in another shadowy and constricted space.

The continuity of lighting-effect here emphasises the restricted space of the film's *mise-en-scène*, its preference for tight interiors and its intensive recycling of scenes. On the one hand this is determined by the practical lack of availability of the Alexanderplatz and other civic spaces around it that feature so centrally in the novel. The claim made in the book of the film that the Alexanderplatz was not in itself of importance for Döblin is debatable, but the square is certainly always to be understood in relation to the other spaces which surround it, and it is these other spaces that are the territory of Fassbinder's film-work. In his review of the film, Karsten Witte defines it as a work of spatial transformation, and Fassbinder as another 'transport worker', creating transformative movements out of that place.[76] Its location is at once confined and dynamic, multidimensional. Necessity also chimes with aesthetic virtue here: the failure to enter upon the open square

---

[76] Karsten Witte, 'Fassbinders Serie "Berlin Alexanderplatz" an einem Stück: Die Gewalt des Ganzen', *Frankfurter Rundschau*, 18 October 1983.

corresponds to a style of tight spatial work – stage-work we might say – with intrusive effects of artificial lighting and sound, which is the director's signature. Christian Schärf recognises the pragmatic constraints, but argues that the abstinence from open urban space has a clear reason: Fassbinder's interest in the interpersonal rather than urban space.[77] It might be more accurate, however, to see the interpersonal relations between Biberkopf and the *Berlin Alexanderplatz* ensemble as always constructed into the space of city, both internal and external, and caught up especially in the tension between the two. Thus composer Peer Raben describes the film's special kind of city image as representing the incarceration of people in urban space, but always through a topographical dialectic, with the constricted interior representing what lies outside, and light and sound effects projecting the exterior in.[78]

While the interiors are experienced on the model of the cage, as Raben says, or the cell, outside space is also strategically restricted. The film uses its limited spatial means with extraordinary ingenuity, reworking the possibilities of the Berlin Street in various ways. But it also displays the constraint with which it works. As Tom Tykwer describes it in his review of what he calls a 'nocturnal chamber-piece', the screen image is recurrently at once contained by its lighting and brought into claustrophobic focus by the camera's fixture on framing structures, which function as 'frames within frames' for the image.[79] Both in its narrative repetitions and in its iconographic framing, the film creates effects of *mise-en-abyme*, of structures reflected within structures. Thus it recurrently goes underground for scenes that are designed for the open air, embracing darkness and spatial containment, and in one such scene emphatically marks the displacement into the intensely framed space of an underground station by retaining the reference to street traffic in the voice-over.[80] It is the equivalent of the ironic inclusion of 'open brackets' and 'close brackets' in the voice-over text, a *Verfremdungseffekt* that specifically draws attention to restriction and separation, on topographic and typographic levels. The underground station serves as an ideal liminal space, between inside and out, passage and market, public and private space. And, while both underground and over-ground scenes are populated with extras and pervaded by traffic

[77] Christian Schärf, *Alfred Döblins 'Berlin Alexanderplatz': Roman und Film: Zu einer intermedialen Poetik der modernen Literatur* (Stuttgart: Steiner, 2001), p. 34.
[78] *Berlin Alexanderplatz: Ein WDR-Film in 13 Teilen und einem Epilog* (ARD publicity brochure, 1980), p. 8.
[79] Tom Tykwer, 'Wer in einer Menschenhaut wohnt', *Frankfurter Allgemeine Zeitung*, 8 February 2007.
[80] *Der Film BERLIN Alexanderplatz*, p. 67.

movements, evoking the bustle of the city in the novel, it is an elaborately
managed form of urban dynamics. While Fassbinder employs aesthetics of
montage, it is not the hyperactive, polyphonic version of the novel's urban
set-pieces.

PHANTOM RIDES, WALKS, AND STILLS

The sequence of images used to introduce each of the parts of the work is
telling. Its apparent purpose is to illustrate the dense metropolitan variety of
Berlin in 1928: stills of various aspects of urban life are blended into footage
of the turning wheels of a 1920s tram, against a soundtrack of Richard
Tauber singing Lehár's 'Friends, life is worth living'. The tram wheels seem
to impel the image-track, as if a form of projection machinery, but the
vehicle does not move and the album of images represents forms of city life
that may or may not be worth living: from a scene from the Spartakus revolt
around the Berolina statue on the Alexanderplatz to the unemployed on the
streets and the security forces keeping order; from a Heinrich Zille photograph of a couple at a dance to a peephole image of intercourse between a
man and a woman, which flashes up with an unclear, subliminal effect;
from scenes of destitution and imprisonment to those of mass entertainment. The images remain obscure and stilted, not properly dynamised by
tram-wheels that seem to turn endlessly upon themselves. If Fassbinder is
indeed a 'transport worker', the transport work achieved here – much as in
the 'photographic scene' between Biberkopf and Mieze discussed above – is
also arrested. The film fixes its transformative motions, representing the
kind of bound dynamics that Benjamin calls 'dialectics at a standstill' and
that he shows at work not least in the life-and-death dialectics of photographic media. Biberkopf is, after all, no longer a transport worker, and his
condition is to remain caught between mobility and standstill.

   The allegorical 'film' of urban variety, seen at the start of each part of the
series, is invariable. The screenplay describes the effect that the sequence is
designed to have as like the 'uncanny and estranging' effect of walking down
a street and hearing the same radio music playing out of many homes.[81] This
is another form of the inside–outside dialectic: the song heard from inside is
a counterpart to the sound motifs heard from outside described by Raben.
And the sound logic implies a set of images representing both interior and
exterior scenes and experienced as if internal scenes projected outwards. In
their fixed, automatic form both sound and image tracks impart a sense of

---

[81] *Der Film* BERLIN *Alexanderplatz*, p. 22.

the urban uncanny. One of the interior images flashed into the sequence is that of Döblin with a patient in his consultation room, and the implication is that the clinic is integral to the city represented here, a necessary adjunct to the psychopathologies of its everyday life.

The introductory sequence, with its montage of original images of the city, driven by its electrified transport system, seems to have to do the work that the film can or does not. The extensive tram-ride at the start of Jutzi's film of the novel is striking by its absence in the Fassbinder version, but the prelude is not designed to serve the same function of mobile, panoramic entry to the city. It rather appears to represent the original location of the work as a lost scene, which can be only artificially reconstructed in another place. To take up another of the images in the sequence, and one with a particular poignancy for the story of Franz Biberkopf – that of an amputee doing metalwork with a stylised metal arm of his own – the prelude works as a less than convincing prosthesis, displaying the kinds of lack and uncanniness that are at work in the body of the film as a whole. Rather than being transported by the spinning wheels of the tram, the images are as it were caught in those wheels, in a logic which corresponds to the traffic accident that haunts the transportation networks of the city and is staged in Biberkopf's 'accident'. The amputee cast in the turning wheels of the tram thus has an emblematic character.

In keeping with the Benjaminian dialectic, the fixed mobility of the prelude also shows symptomatic signs of *Entstellung* and of the uncanniness attached to that psychical disfigurement/displacement. The uncanny effect that Fassbinder describes is recognisable as a classic form of that psychical disturbance in Freud's account: the urban pedestrian's experience of involuntary return to the same place. A key aspect of the uncanny condition is that of recursive motion fixed in standstill, and the film shows its attachment to this condition each time it restarts with its gallery of ghostly photographic stills. The title sequence creates a template for the compulsive patterns of return in the film, charging familiar scenes with uncanniness. This automatic recursion is repeatedly displayed in the film's form, say when Biberkopf returns repeatedly to the 'Straße Babylon' to hear the story of the Whore of Babylon but never to take advantage of the services offered there, as though he had made a repeated mistake according to an unconscious drive. We are reminded of Freud's experience in the Italian town, coming back repeatedly to its red-light district (SF XII 249).

The uncanny effect of urban topography in the film is orchestrated by its camerawork. The taxi ride with Eva and Mieze is elaborately set up, with an image-stream through the rear-window and another reflected in the glass screen between the passengers and the driver, designed to create a sense of the life of the city street outside. While the account in the book of the film celebrates this elaborate visual trickery,[82] creating a sense of an extended drive in a studio-street only a couple of hundred metres long, the effect is in fact curiously artificial and excessive, trammelling the conversation between the two women with an uncanny sense of the outside being filmed into the interior. The sequence features the mediation by windows and mirrors that is such a distinctive feature of Fassbinder's work, where windows characteristically serve only to project the outside in and mirrors to emphasise spatial enclosure. This is cinematographic work as the equivalent of what Thomas Elsaesser calls the 'specular machinery', the apparatus of reflection, duplication, and substitution, which at once sustains the identity of the protagonist and dismantles it.[83] Another such distorting lens is at work in the scene where Biberkopf is selling on the street. We see him framed by a dead chicken hanging in from a shop entrance on the opposite side of the street (perhaps a visual joke referring to the Hahn department store) and by shop-window dummies (as if mocking his exuberant sales pitch). This *mise-en-scène* between the dead and the inanimate is then filmed through the window of a passing bus, with a distorting and distancing effect upon the street-scene, screening it both in the sense of display and of separation.

A similar effect is at work in the film's version of the 'cinematic' or 'photographic' meeting with Mieze in front of Aschinger's. The encounter takes place at one of the film's generic sites, removed from the Alexanderplatz location of the novel. Fassbinder adopts a toponymic authority over his version of the city by locating the scene at the junction of two streets named after figures that interest him and are possible objects of future film projects. He might, he says, have named a street after a favourite Berlin author, Fontane, but opted instead for Jean-Paul-Straße, after the eighteenth-century German writer, and Moses-Straße after Freud's *Moses and Monotheism*.[84] In this studio reconstruction-cum-invention of a Berlin street corner, the framing strategies so characteristic of Fassbinder's film-work give constant reminders of cinematic construction. Biberkopf's viewing of Mieze is mediated by the windscreen of a truck, behind which he hides as a kind of street-camera, an apparatus with viewing lens. His position has the effect of placing Mieze, repeatedly, in the framing device

[82] *Ibid.*, p. 540.
[83] Thomas Elsaesser, *Fassbinder's Germany: History Identity Subject* (Amsterdam: Amsterdam University Press, 1996), p. 233.
[84] See Robert Fischer (ed.), *Fassbinder über Fassbinder: Die ungekürzten Interviews* (Frankfurt am Main: Verlag der Autoren, 2004), p. 508.

of the steering-wheel, which might be read as a particularly uncanny emblem for both Biberkopf, who has lost his arm under the wheels of a car, and for Mieze, who will also be a traffic victim in the dreamlike distortions of the action of the film in its epilogue. As in the taxi-ride sequence, the screening effect is associated here with mirroring, as the metalwork on the front of the truck reflects the street-scene as if through an additional lens. This sort of framing, screening, and mirroring, with its *mise-en-abyme* effect, recurs both in this scene and the film as a whole. At the same time, Biberkopf's point of view is mediated by that of the other, an anonymous potential customer, standing perhaps in place of the photographic showcase in the novel, who repeatedly views Mieze at close quarters as she passes to and fro. This viewer's uncomfortable proximity serves to expose the remote camerawork of Biberkopf's surveillance.

As Mieze looks out for Biberkopf, she in her turn takes on the appearance of a photographic automaton, her eyes scanning the opposite side of the street while the camera pans too mechanically for a point-of-view shot across the scene. The mechanical character of this act of urban surveillance is emphasised by repetition in the image-track: identical shop-signs, a line of bags on the truck which conceals Biberkopf, and in particular the windows of a passing bus, giving the effect of photographic frames. Again, the film achieves a particular kind of 'transport work' here, with the means of transport representing movement in standstill. The mechanics of the viewing process are at once emphasised and subverted by a curious act of elision, as the image of the corner-shop is merged with that of the truck on the opposite corner. That the shop in question is a 'Herrenschneider' (gentleman's tailor, or – literally – cutter) reflects ironically on the cutting process here, in conjunction with the body of the amputee Biberkopf, cut out of view. It seems most likely that the elision is designed to cut out a perspective that would have revealed the studio construction of the Berlin Street. Its effect in the point-of-view logic is to suggest a blind-spot, an uncanny angle of failure in the frame sequence of the mechanical scan.

As Mieze paces up and down, behind her on a construction fence is a series of posters showing a walking figure in profile, as if to image this place – in the style of a photographic still – as a recurrent scene of street-walking. The photograph works in conjunction here with the prostitute as shop-window dummy, an image that is evoked by the repeated stilling of Mieze's animation on the street. She spots Biberkopf as another bus passes between them, and she is seen through its mediation transfixed on the street as if in a sequence of photographic frames, before coming back to life and joining him. As a near miss with a car emphasises, the encounter through the mediation of the bus is a kind of virtual street accident, a leitmotif of both novel and film. The repetition of the visual track of bus window-frames – clearly the same vehicle returning – highlights the convergence of the film's practical limitations, its economic recycling of space and vehicles in a tight studio setting, with its aesthetic and psycho-dramatic design. As emphasised from the close-up shots that introduce it, the outdoor scene is conceived, as is so often the case in Fassbinder's work, as a kind of externalised chamber drama, caught tightly in physical and psychical space.

The uncanny sense of living-death that is present in the scene as narrated in the novel, and relayed into the film's camerawork, returns more brutally when the scene is rehearsed in the epilogue. It is viewed once more from Biberkopf's vantage point, but with Reinhold's murder of Mieze taking place in the empty street. The epilogue is indeed constructed as a sequence of such returns to, reconstructions of, the film's scenes. As the generic Berliner Straße is reconstructed, or broken down, into what the screenplay calls a 'dead street',[85] the metropolis converted into a necropolis, so the rerunning of the scene of the reunion with Mieze as that of her murder converts that street-scene too into one of death. It exposes, after the fact, the uncanny otherness that was already there in the original scene. That scene was always an 'other scene', displaying the psychical constitution of the city-life of the protagonists as grounded in otherness. The Moses-Straße may be seen as an uncannily appropriate scene for this, given the character of *Moses and Monotheism* as a murder mystery, its account of post-traumatic disorder, and its exemplification of the principle of *Entstellung*, of the disfigurement and displacement of evidence, whether in cases of murder or in the operations of the psyche.

TURN AND CUT

Just as the intervention of glass screens and lenses in the visual field emphasises the constructed character of the film spectacle, so too do the movements of the camera. A particularly insistent – and always potentially uncanny – feature here is turning in circles. Fassbinder's return to Döblin recurrently turns round topographic locations; indeed the turning moment, as an organisational figure of confinement and repetition, can be understood as the tropographical signature of the film. The turning in circles that is the dominant figure of Hoffmann's *Sandmann* also works to uncanny effect here. It can be seen in the scene in the underground station – always a

---

[85] *Der Film BERLIN Alexanderplatz*, p. 496.

kind of living-death space – where the camera circles round Biberkopf and a group of associates, frozen waxwork-style; or, in the scene near the start of the epilogue, where the undead corpse of the hanged man is made to turn, as if representing his persistent tendency to return from the dead.

If these turning movements are always potentially uncanny in their repetition and their intermediate status between life and death, they can also be understood according to another kind of disorder, with a similar symptomatology: melancholy. The melancholic Reinhold, who keeps returning to Biberkopf, embodies that condition. The trope of 'Drehung' (turning) that runs through the screenplay applies not least to the choreography of the encounters between the two men. This is the case in the sequence of scenes in the toilet of the bar that Fassbinder introduces to the narrative, taking it into a form of restricted, behind-the-scenes queer-space, a particular kind of heterotopian other scene that recurs in his work.[86] It is as though he is recurrently flouting the ban that was put upon the association of men in toilets in Chemnitz, as recorded in the novel.

The turning around each other in the dimly lit and mirrored space of the toilet is also played out in more open spaces. Thus in the scene by the *Litfaßsäule* between Franz and Reinhold, with Cilly in attendance, the advertising column, as a structure designed to be circled around, plays the focal point for an elaborate performance of turning. As the two men negotiate over the handover of Cilly, they repeatedly turn. Meanwhile, in the background, a scene of civil unrest is played out on the open top of a bus, creating an ironic chorus-style backdrop of battling between men for the choreographic negotiation in the foreground. More particularly, the scene illustrates a particular feature of the film's cinematographic rhetoric, the 'Schnitt in die Drehung' (cut into the turn),[87] a particularly telling form of the signature trope of turning. The conjunction of turn and cut corresponds emblematically to the logic of the filmic narrative, as indeed to that of the novel on which it is based: patterns of return that are recurrently interrupted. Ultimately, the principle of interruption is linked to the unkindest cut of all and to Death as the final cutter. It is the economy of recursive violence, of returning and cutting or blocking, that leads Thomas Elsaesser to see *Berlin Alexanderplatz* as exemplary of what he calls the 'vicious circle' in Fassbinder's filmwork.[88] In the turning and cutting

---

[86] For discussion of heterotopian configurations in Fassbinder's *Querelle* and other films, see Andrew Webber, 'Unnatural Acts: Sexuality, Film, and the Law', *Sexuality Repositioned: Diversity and the Law*, ed. Belinda Brooks-Gordon *et al.* (Oxford: Hart, 2004), pp. 297–315.

[87] *Der Film BERLIN Alexanderplatz*, p. 145; see also p. 139.   [88] Elsaesser, *Fassbinder's Germany*, p. 222.

between Biberkopf and Reinhold, it takes the form of the sort of spectacle of the sadomasochistic ruination of masculinity that Kaja Silverman analyses in the film.[89] The loss of Biberkopf's arm as symbolic castration under the wheel of the car, or the image of the amputee in the wheels of the tram in the title sequence, exemplify the principle of turn and cut as a composite trope of Fassbinder's filmwork here and, more especially, his representations of damaged and damaging masculinity.

EPILOGUE: ANGELS OF HISTORY

The epilogue is styled as a second-, or perhaps third-order dream-work: Fassbinder's dream of the dream of the Franz Biberkopf of Alfred Döblin. Dream-work here involves the sort of Freudian principles that Fassbinder sees at work in Döblin's novel, as elements of the narrative are displaced and condensed, subject to *Entstellung*, to spatial and corporeal disfigurement.[90] It is a kind of afterlife for the story, one that is acutely bound into the uncanny and melancholic conditions of what went before. And while it might seem to suggest that the epilogue stands as a sort of unconscious to the main body of the film, it is more appropriate to say that the film, like the novel before it, is full of the 'other scenes' of the unconscious as part of its allegorical structure. While the case of Franz Biberkopf was always allegorically disposed, in the epilogue it is subject to a full-blown allegorical treatment. On the one hand, this is a kind of Last Judgement, with paranoid fantasies of torture and retribution, and on the other a case study of melancholy, a compulsive attempt to retrieve the lost, dead object.

As W. G. Sebald points out in his melancholic reading of the destructive character of Döblin's writing, the novel is introduced with the story of a body, that of Zannowich, a body not properly buried or mourned, and corresponding, Sebald argues, to Benjamin's model of the corpse as the allegorisation of physical life.[91] The abjected body dumped in the refuse heap of the city is understandable in this reading as a melancholic emblem for the text, the counterpart to the ruins that run through its depiction of the metropolis. It is the counterpart to the corpse outside the city of Polyneices in *Antigone*, or the abjected body of Rosa Luxemburg as lamented in the third part of Döblin's trilogy *November 1918*, where Antigone stands as

---

[89] Kaja Silverman, *Male Subjectivity at the Margins* (London/New York: Routledge, 1992), pp. 225–44, 270–96.
[90] *Der Film BERLIN Alexanderplatz*, p. 8.
[91] Winfried Georg Sebald, *Der Mythus der Zerstörung im Werk Döblins* (Stuttgart: Klett, 1980), p. 65.

an allegorical figure of mourning, the reclamation of individual and mass deaths from abjection. Such work of mourning is melancholy work in such times. Fassbinder too was working on a film on Rosa Luxemburg at the time of his death; and it is reasonable to assume that it would have carried on the particular kind of melancholic mourning-work against the grain that he contributed to the latter-day *Antigone* of the collaborative film made in a later time of German melancholy, *Deutschland im Herbst* (Germany in Autumn (1978)). In the dead city of the epilogue to *Berlin Alexanderplatz*, the corpse returns as melancholic object, desperately sought by Biberkopf as he digs in the grave or on the street, and then haunting his dream as Mieze reappears repeatedly as phantasm, only to be violated and lost again. The smearing of his own face with earth and the recurrent violence done to his body in the torture scenes of the epilogue mimic the fate of the lost body of Mieze in a form of melancholic incorporation.

The epilogue is accordingly attended by two angels, who embody the iconography of melancholy as established by Dürer and Benjamin, albeit in a travesty style that is Fassbinder's own. They sit at the graveside as Biberkopf digs for the body, and accompany the stations of his dream, less as guardians than as ironic commentators on his exemplary enactment of the human tragicomedy. The encircling that is a key feature of the cinematography is intensified here. One scene sees Biberkopf turning on the spot, with the angels revolving around him, while the camera in turn orbits round them on a circular track. The angels' circulation imitates the re-turning disposition of Benjamin's *angelus novus*: a form of inexorably moving forward that is always also turned back upon itself, fixated upon the losses of the past. As Döblin's novel makes an allegorical move into the battlefields of history at its end, so Fassbinder's angels of history make another kind of historical turn, returning upon what will have been after the time of the novel. For Fassbinder, the inevitable destiny of the reborn Biberkopf is to march to the right as National Socialist: the erstwhile 'transport worker' and 'killer',[92] going with the flows and counter-flows of Weimar Berlin, seems to predispose his avatar for that historical course. And the reckoning to which he is subject in the epilogue is accordingly also a post-Holocaust judgement. The abattoir, which was the appropriate hetero-topian space for the bare life of late Weimar Berlin is turned into another kind of other place here, where the torture of the bodies of Biberkopf or Mieze by the avenging Reinhold is merely a detail in a historical heap that inevitably summons up images of the final solution. In a scene that returns

---

[92] *Der Film* BERLIN *Alexanderplatz*, p. 8.

to the *Hinterhof* in the Jewish quarter, Mieze's body is taken out of the yard on a refuse cart in a reprise of the fate of the Jew Zannowich and of many others in the historical aftermath of Döblin's novel. Fassbinder's allegorical angels of history recite the march from the end of the novel with reference to mass conflicts from the Napoleonic Wars to the First World War. But the historical death drive that they record in the metropolis as necropolis turns above all upon the violence that is right behind them, in the imminent future, as they look back upon the destruction of the past from the historical threshold of Weimar Berlin.

CHAPTER 5

Berlin Wall: divisions and falls

Berlin is the problem of division.[1]

This chapter will consider four exemplary representations of Berlin in what might be called its postlapsarian state: the partitioning of the city that followed *Der Fall von Berlin* (The Fall of Berlin), to cite the title of the 1949 film. It was a fall that left the city as case (the other sense of *Fall* in German), a place racked by pathological and criminological after-effects. The city thus provided the set for a particular form of film noir, where the sorts of psycho- and sociopathic shadows that were cast in the pre-war city of Lang's *M* adopted a more broken form in the genre of *Trümmerfilme* or ruin films with their disintegrated architectures and bodies; and it furnished the fraught ground for similarly shadowy and disoriented scenarios in the *Trümmerliteratur* of the early post-war years. And the project of reconstruction out of those ruins was one fraught with ambivalence, as we saw in the case of Brecht. The configuration of the fallen city – as represented in the ruined cityscape and the persistent gaps even when it was rebuilt – and the Wall that came to organise its reconstruction through division is a key feature of the cultural topography of Berlin in the second half of the twentieth century. Following the *Wende*, as we shall see in the final chapter, the figures of the fall and the Wall converge, though not without remnants of the earlier configuration.

The first text to be considered here, Ingeborg Bachmann's *Ein Ort für Zufälle* (1964), represents the traumatic, fallen state behind the West Berlin of the *Wirtschaftswunder* years; the second, Wolf's 'Unter den Linden' (1969), responds with a less overtly traumatic, but nonetheless fraught view from the Eastern side of the Wall and the spaces for fantasy it allows; the third, Uwe Johnson's *Zwei Ansichten* (Two Views (1965)), adopts a bifocal view of the divided city; and Wenders' film *Der Himmel über*

---

[1] Maurice Blanchot, 'Berlin', *Modern Language Notes* 109.3 (1994), 345–55; p. 346.

229

Berlin (Wings of Desire – literally, the Sky/Heavens over Berlin (1987)), apparently lifted up over the city, is also bound into its ground and its underground, projecting its celestial visions out of a haunted and split city on the verge of its historical turn towards unification. In each case, utopian possibilities – material, political, or metaphysical – are entertained, but also subject to different versions of collapse: to satirical subversion, traumatic return, or melancholic fixture.

PLACE FOR COINCIDENCES

Ein Ort für Zufälle, the speech written by Bachmann to mark her receipt of the Georg-Büchner-Preis in 1964, is a satire on the grossly excessive culture of consumption in the West Berlin of the *Wirtschaftswunder* and the historical conditions of violence and division that provide its volatile foundations.[2] Bachmann is rarely considered as a satirist, but there is certainly reason to scrutinise what Sigrid Weigel calls the 'satirical quality' of her writing.[3] While Bachmann's texts may, *prima facie*, engage in satire only in rare cases, it remains a regulatory presence throughout her writing, attending and mocking her interest in possibilities of utopia as social structure and literary form. In *Ein Ort für Zufälle*, Berlin becomes the site for a particularly dystopian form of urban satire.

The reading of *Ein Ort für Zufälle* here will be approached through two cases of topographical coincidence. The first is that of one of Jelinek's satirical texts, the poem that appeared in the Introduction. What the text shows is that her satirical project is eminently exportable from the satirical terrain of Austria, and its capital, to an ambivalently invested neighbouring land and its capital. Jelinek's satirical eye for sport as an arena for the duplicities of culture in general follows Bachmann in a text with a close relationship to *Ein Ort für Zufälle*, *Sterben für Berlin* (Dying for Berlin), where opposing bands of football fans mount a 'battle' ('Kampf *(TP* 76)) that is understandable as a rerun of other battles to the death in and for Berlin. In both cases, topography functions in fraught and ambivalent ways. The psycho-topographical displacement (*Verschiebung*) that we saw at work in Jelinek's poem also operates in Bachmann's representation of Berlin. In

---

[2] See also Bachmann's poem 'Das deutsche Wunder' (The German Miracle), '*Ich weiß keine bessere Welt': Unveröffentlichte Gedichte*, ed. Heinz Bachmann *et al.* (Munich: Piper, 2000), pp. 13–34. The miracle in question is satirically constructed through a Berlin racked by post-war guilt and Cold-War paranoia.

[3] Sigrid Weigel, *Ingeborg Bachmann: Hinterlassenschaften unter Wahrung des Briefgeheimnisses* (Vienna: Paul Zsolnay, 1999), p. 189.

Ein Ort für Zufälle, Bachmann traces both existential and economic forms of displacement, as parts of Berlin's topography are seismically shifted (Potsdam slides into Tegel (*TP* 212)), its landmarks displaced, and the shops that serve the official economy of the post-war *Wirtschaftswunder* are overloaded with panic buying, slip, and collapse. At the same time, the sense of *Verschiebung* as postponement can serve to remind us that such displacements are after-effects, inevitable returns of the repressed.

The second case of topographical coincidence to be considered here follows the logic of Jelinek's displacement underground and finds it at work on the Alexanderplatz. This is a site that Bachmann marks as one of the definitive locations when she draws her toponymic map of literature, in the 'Umgang mit Namen' (Traffic with Names) lecture from her *Frankfurter Vorlesungen* (Frankfurt Lectures (IB IV 239)). Such names are 'zufällig' (coincidental), but they anchor within them the 'Vorfälle, Zufälle' (incidences, coincidences) that have befallen the place they designate (IB IV 240–1), as we saw in the case of the Alexanderplatz in Chapter 4. The *Ingeborg Bachmann Altar*, a 2006 installation by Thomas Hirschhorn in a passage in the underground complex at Berlin Alexanderplatz, nicely captures the ambivalence of Berlin for Bachmann, or Bachmann for Berlin. It is a performative memorial, encouraging passers-by to add their own sentimental tributes to those already collected, and creating in that sense a place for coincidences.[4]

The author who died before her time becomes here a sort of literary princess of hearts, as if taking up posthumously the fairy-tale persona that runs as a fantasy through her writings. The installation says something of the particular kind of quasi-martyric victimisation and idealisation to which Bachmann has been subject. She represents a sacrificial gift of death for those who survive her and provides a memorial site for votive gifts in return. The installation at once performs and mimics acts of mourning, resonating at once with the never sufficient mourning-work after the deaths of the many in the Holocaust and in war, and with the excessive public spectacles of mourning for one, the hyperbolic public version of more private grieving that followed the untimely death of Princess Diana (when Berlin, too, was decked with tributes). The altar at once serves as a tribute and satirises this, and as such it also re-enacts the kind of double bind that informs Bachmann's own acts of mourning for what has been lost and her exposure of the idealisations and commodifications that seek to redeem that loss. It

---

[4] As the website of the Neue Gesellschaft für bildende Kunst has it, the accumulation of mementos is regulated by chance ('zufällig'). See www.ngbk.de/typo3/index.php?id=37&no_cache=1&sword_list[.

re-enacts, in that sense, the strategies of *Ein Ort für Zufälle*, its challenge to routine forms of mourning-work. This is to see Bachmann as another kind of literary princess, a latter-day version of the dissident mourner Antigone, insisting upon attending to the victims of the tragedy of twentieth-century history. And, at the same time, it is to see her as performing the satire that is the counterpart to that tragic role in her work of cultural political resistance. In the cross-over performance between tragedy and satire lies an attempt at a representative work of mourning, while the gap between the two modes shows what Judith Butler sees as the crux of Antigone's political agency: the exposure of 'the limits to representation and representability'.[5]

Ein Ort für Zufälle gives an account of Bachmann's stay in Berlin, supported by the Ford Foundation, in 1963. If Berlin is here given the epithet of a place for coincidences, one of the forms this takes is through encounters with other writers. On one level, there were her contacts with such leading writers of the day as Günter Grass, Uwe Johnson, Allen Ginsberg, and Witold Gombrowicz, who was also a guest of the Ford Foundation. While Gombrowicz describes a sense of ambivalent enthralment on this strangely deserted 'island',[6] Bachmann sees their coincidental experience of the city as that of two lost and alien visitors who duly become sick in their different ways in and of a city that reeks of sickness and death (IB IV 326). The urban pathology that she diagnoses, the sickness of the city in its history and topography, came upon her in the form of the nervous breakdowns she suffered there, of which *Ein Ort für Zufälle* is, in part, the pathographic account. Personal symptomatology meshes here with the historical pathology of the city, which is revisited by past violence and trauma. Berlin is still both attacking and under attack from the air and on the ground: passenger and freight planes threaten the peace; buildings collapse in anticipation of an 'attack' (*TP* 211); the economic miracle is haunted by the ghosts of inflation (*TP* 210); mutilated figures as if out of the Berlin album of George Grosz populate the city, their disfigurement symptomatic of disorder that is 'inward' (*TP* 210); the execution site at Plötzensee is still in use (*TP* 219); and the S-Bahn train travels out of a collapsing Bellevue station in the direction of Wannsee (*TP* 211), the site of the conference that determined the mass deportation and murder of European Jewry.

In pursuing its pathography, both personal and municipal, the text also stages more or less explicit encounters with writers of other ages. It projects,

[5] Judith Butler, *Antigone's Claim: Kinship Between Life and Death* (New York: Columbia University Press, 2000), p. 2.
[6] Witold Gombrowicz, *Berliner Notizen* (Pfullingen: Neske, 1965), p. 72.

in particular, a network of satirical intertexts, ranging from Voltaire's *Candide*, through Büchner's satirical writings, to Kafka's 'Ein Landarzt' (A Country Doctor), understood here as a satirical treatment of the therapeutic project. Bachmann's satirical account of Berlin in the early 1960s enlists these intertextual resources in order to articulate her vision of postwar utopianism as dystopically twisted, a grotesque parody of the hopes she might have. The 'Ort für Zufälle' is exposed as a historically traumatised and collapsed non-place, following the resonance of 'falling to' that comes with 'Zufall' from Büchner's deployment of it. 'Zufall' is the term used for the psychical collapses of Büchner's Lenz in the eponymous novella, but it also implies the repeated physical falling to which he is subject. It is thus the symptom of an individual case, the 'Fall' of Lenz, and it is extendable at once to other personal cases, including that of the author of *Ein Ort für Zufälle*, who repeatedly 'falls' and is befallen in Berlin, and to the mass pathography of the place in question.

Repetition is intrinsic to the principle of 'Zufälle' as that which 'lies far back' but returns intermittently out of repression (*TP* 231). Having been expelled in the traumatic course of personal and collective history, madness falls back upon the individual and the masses from without in the particular conditions of this place and of the 'legacies of this time' (*TP* 229) that are chronotopically built into it. As Lenz was a stranger to the territory of his host Oberlin (*TP* 172), so Bachmann negotiates Berlin (with a lamenting resonance perhaps of 'O Berlin') as an alien and alienated topographer, but one whose own collapse brings her peculiarly close to the territory in question. Like Lenz, she walks on her head, as if always falling to the ground, both strange to the place and intimate with it, as its topographical scout ('Kundschafter' (*TP* 232)). It is a disposition that figures, or disfigures, her as what Sigrid Weigel calls a 'Symptomkörper' (symptomatic body), tracing in embodied form the contours of an 'entstellte Topographie' (disfigured topography),[7] a place whose truth is always under displacement.

The endemic sickness of this place, unamenable to treatment, is exposed by this disoriented topographer: the patient as symptomatic diagnostician of a social order that has not come to terms with the legacy of the unnatural disaster of war and the Holocaust. 'Es ist eine Katastrophe' (It's a catastrophe (*TP* 211)) is the commonplace that falls catastrophically short of registering the true character of what has occurred. This is catastrophe on a par with war, oppression, and the Lisbon earthquake, as pitched in grotesque accumulation against the doctrine of inflationary optimism in

---

[7] Weigel, *Ingeborg Bachmann*, pp. 373–83.

Candide.[8] With reference to that text's dystopian satire of a ravaged 'best of all possible worlds', *Ein Ort für Zufälle* asks whether habitable space can be found in the pathologically displaced 'world' of Berlin, which may in fact be the best that can be hoped for. The hyperbolic reiteration of Leibniz's formula in Voltaire's satirical text is reformulated as a pathologically obsessive, voiced or unvoiced speech act in Bachmann's latter-day, satirical version of the post-catastrophic world: 'It's still best here, you do best to stay here, you can bear it best here, there's nowhere better' (*TP* 214). The repeated formula is then repeated on the radio tower, broadcasting a new version of a much manipulated ideological message using the old propaganda machinery.

Berlin, as something close to the worst place to be or to have been in the mid-twentieth-century world, but converted here into the best possible or 'least worst' place, also reflects more widely upon that world at large. It arguably redounds, in particular, upon the homeland of the displaced author and its no longer annexed capital, as no better a place to be, in spite of its own post-war programmes of betterment. While the text originally went under the title *Deutsche Zufälle* (German Coincidences), and seems to assert specificity for its location in the German capital, it also teases with questions of locatability, suggesting the possibility of transfer to other places. In particular, the 'Zufälle' of the text are understandable, by extension, as the coincidence, the coming together or collapsing, that characterises the relationship between Berlin and what Kurt Bartsch has called its 'Gegenort' or counter-place, Vienna.[9] Beneath their palpable differences, the two cities share grounding in a dreadful recent history, which is subject to repression and elision. Displaced from one to the other, Bachmann is peculiarly able to register the displacements that underlie the post-war project of restoration and its construction of a best place to be.

If *Candide* is one intertext of *Ein Ort für Zufälle*, as marked by the language of betterment in a place shaken by the after-shocks of war and earthquake, two other satirical texts contribute to a wider intertextual network.[10] While the 'Zufälle' of the title are drawn in the first place from Büchner's *Lenz*, they also resonate with the wordplay of his *Leonce und*

---

[8] Part of what *Candide* rails against is despotism. Frederick II had the satirical *Diatribe of Doctor Akakia*, by his erstwhile favourite Voltaire, burned in the streets of Berlin, showing that book-burning has a history in this place of coincidences.

[9] In discussion at the 'Literaturforum im Brecht-Haus' in Berlin on 15 August 2006. Bartsch also aligns the two cities in his *Ingeborg Bachmann* (Stuttgart: Metzler, 1997), p. 135.

[10] *Ein Ort für Zufälle* is overlooked in Joachim Eberhardt's *'Es gibt für mich keine Zitate': Intertextualität im dichterischen Werk Ingeborg Bachmanns* (Tübingen: Niemeyer, 2002).

Lena, where 'Zufall' is played out into a system of collapsing possibilities. The satirical exposure of ideal worlds in *Leonce und Lena* is effected through an elaborate interplay of citation, reiteration and punning.[11] The very word 'Platz' provokes *Platzangst*, and the mock fairy-tale lovers 'fall together' under the sign of a 'Zufall', which may be playfully providential or coercive.[12] And the playing with linguistic coincidence in Bachmann's text is similarly cast between ludic performance and darker compulsion. The *Ort für Zufälle* is introduced by a mystery place within the place of the title, serving as a *mise-en-abyme* of the city. It is a paronomastic address where occurrence and emergence are mortified: 'ist zum Umkommen, kommt, kommt vor und hervor, ist etwas – in Berlin' (comes with death, comes, comes about and forth, is something – in Berlin (*TP* 206)). Bachmann here continues the melancholic serial puns of Büchner's Valerio exploring the sad business 'about the word to come' ('um das Wort kommen'), where neither 'umkommen' (to die) nor 'vorkommen' (to come about) happens to occur, but the former perhaps constitutes what is most sad about and around ('um') the word 'kommen'. The variations on 'vorkommen' that run through *Ein Ort für Zufälle* arguably remain cross-contaminated with their deadly counterpart, 'umkommen', as they happen or come forth in the city of mortal collapse.

The next satirical intertext exposes the fantasy of the recuperative treatment of psychical and somatic disorder. Here too, satire is effected, as is so often the case (witness the travels of Gulliver or Candide), by transposition to another place, one which is full of coincidences with, and so collapses back into, the place of origin. The traveller in question is Kafka's country doctor. This is a doctor called upon to treat a case in another place and finding that the case and its place are fraught with coincidence with the home that he has left. I have suggested elsewhere that Kafka's text is both a creative working of Freud's dream-work model, following an aesthetic of *Entstellung*, and a satirical exposé of psychoanalysis as therapeutic praxis.[13] The country doctor is displaced into transferential forms of his own pathological fantasies, and the diagnostic and therapeutic journey ends with the putative 'Weltverbesserer',[14] charged with making the world a better place, adrift in the wasteland.

---

[11] See Andrew Webber, 'Büchner, *Leonce und Lena*', *Landmarks in German Comedy*, ed. Peter Hutchinson, (Oxford: Lang, 2006), pp. 87–102.

[12] Georg Büchner, *Leonce und Lena*, *Werke und Briefe: Münchner Ausgabe*, ed. Karl Pörnbacher *et al.* (Munich: dtv, 1988), p. 188.

[13] See Webber, *Doppelgänger*, pp. 328–35; *European Avant-Garde*, pp. 173–5.

[14] Franz Kafka, 'Ein Landarzt', *Die Erzählungen und andere ausgewählte Prosa*, ed. Jürgen Born *et al.* (Frankfurt am Main: Fischer, 1996), pp. 253–60; p. 256.

In Bachmann's text, where physical and psychopathological disorder is rife, Kafka's country doctor can be seen to serve as a model for the satirical exposure of medicine in the city. The conjunction of two of the authors most attentively read by Bachmann, Kafka and Freud, plays into her text through Kafka's deeply ambivalent treatment of the therapeutic and epistemological powers of Freud's method. In *Ein Ort für Zufälle*, as in Kafka's 'Ein Landarzt', medical practice, or malpractice, stands for the shortcomings in the more general project of post-catastrophic recuperation. When Bachmann's patients are pinned to their beds with maladministered syringes, and the *Chefarzt* (consultant) thinks only of his card game, medicine stands allegorically for the coercions and false consciousness that characterise a society in restoration, and one not least with a recent history of terrible medical malpractice.[15] The 'Fehlläuten' (misringing) of the torturous night-bell, ushering in the nocturnal misadventure of the country doctor,[16] still rings through the equivalent bell of *Ein Ort für Zufälle*. It remains uncertain whether the camel that bears the patient-narrator of Bachmann's text off into the 'Sandwüste' (sandy wastes (*TP* 198)) of the Mark Brandenburg and remains oblivious to such institutional signals as the 'night bell' (*TP* 224) represents a real release from the predicament of the country doctor who has responded to the false signal of the bell and remains cast away in the 'Schneewüste' (snowy wastes).[17] In the more or less worst of possible worlds depicted in the two texts, exposed to the ordeals of what Kafka's text, without knowledge of what is yet to come, calls 'this most unhappy of ages',[18] the inherent impossibility of making good is a shared condition. The 'es ist niemals gutzumachen' (it can never be made good), marking the paralytic close of Kafka's narrative,[19] echoes in the same fixed condition in Bachmann's: 'es ist nie wieder gutzumachen' (it can never be made good once more (*TP* 213)).

One of the characteristics of satire is its transgression of the boundary between human and animal. The mythical figure that gave its name to the dramatic genre also embodied the attachment of humanity to animality. In Kafka's text, that principle takes the form of the 'Pferdeknecht', less a groom than a horse-man, incorporating the doctor's animal desires in a displaced and disfigured form. For Bachmann, the Berlin Zoo and the circus also open up a relationship between the human and the animal, but in a more

[15] My reading of 'Ein Landarzt' in *The Doppelgänger* suggested that its Freudian satire might relate in particular to the dream of Irma's injection from the *Interpretation of Dreams*. In one variant of the hospital scene from *Ein Ort für Zufälle*, the malpractising, strong-arm nurse is called Irma (*TP* 84).
[16] Kafka, 'Ein Landarzt', p. 260. [17] *Ibid.*, p. 259. [18] *Ibid.* [19] *Ibid.*, p. 260.

benevolent form – there seems to be no equivalent of the 'Pferdeknecht' in her text, a figure who might also be identified as a 'camel-man', as his horses are described as lowering their heads like camels.[20] In the illustrations made for the publication of *Ein Ort für Zufälle* in the *Quarthefte* series by Günter Grass, like Kafka an arch exponent of the satirical tradition in his hybrid-isations of human and animal forms, the potential for a reading of the text as a latter-day satyr drama in this sense emerges. Here, animal forms are mixed with both the human (parading soldiers becoming animal as Berlin bears) and the architectural. The camel is first figured in front of the Brandenburg Gate and the Wall (in Bachmann's text it carries the Siegessäule or Victory Column on its hump) and then, at the end of the text, has its humps shaped into North African buildings,[21] marking the transition from the immured territory of the Brandenburg Gate to the 'sandy wastes' of the Mark Brandenburg. If the camel is a 'dream animal' (*TP* 180), like the horses of 'Ein Landarzt', it transports the subject and her world into *Entstellung*, through forms of psychically laden displacement and condensation.

In *Ein Ort für Zufälle*, this *Entstellung* appears to be the positive counter-part to that which obtains in the nightmarish disfigurements of the Berlin cityscape, or indeed of Kafka's landscape. The escaped camel seems capable of carrying the brutalised, institutionalised subject into a freer territory, drawing benefit from the coincidence between the sandy grounding of Berlin and the open spaces of the desert. The text, in its various drafts, is, however, also in part a laboratory piece for the *Todesarten* (Types of Death) project, where the escape into the desert proves less positive. 'Zufall' is transmuted into 'Fall', the moment of traumatic collapse that defines the case study in *Der Fall Franza* (The Franza Case), as a 'journey through an illness' (IB III 341). The camel mediates the communication between Bachmann's Berlin and the Egyptian desert, dystopian and utopian spaces. As a sketch for *Ein Ort für Zufälle* has it, the text is conceived to transport the reader both into Berlin and into the desert (*TP* 181). The spatio-temporal displacement at work here follows the shifting between subject and scene. The self is less the visiting agent than aligned 'contrapuntally' (*TP* 181) with the city as that which is visited by sickness or nightmares. And it thus remains unclear whether the travelling of the subject, and of its contrapuntal partner the city, into the desert is merely a function of being visited by delirium. Under the effect of this travel, and the sand that sustains

---

[20] *Ibid.*, p. 254.
[21] Ingeborg Bachmann, *Ein Ort für Zufälle: Mit Zeichnungen von Günter Grass*, *Quarthefte* 6 (Berlin: Wagenbach, 1965), pp. 53, 11, 59.

it, Berlin is aligned with Cairo. Sand, figured throughout Berlin's cultural history as an unreliable medium upon which to build a city, ironically undermines the status it is given here as the best place to fix upon when the city is shifting and spinning. To fix visually upon the sand is one thing, assuming that it is not itself shifting, as sand is wont to do, but one version suggests being stuck in the sand (*TP* 214) and the other getting it in the eye (*TP* 198) and so being plagued by the sand-blindness of the desert.

In view of this ambiguous hybridisation of Berlin and the desert, the city becomes an archaeological site, so that the consultant can go down into the street in order to show arches with hieroglyphics to his patients (*TP* 207). But the archaeological remains are haunting. In one of the variants, the narrator asks what you could look for where there is only sand and 'Brandmauern' and appears to conclude: 'Gespenst, Gespenster' (ghost, ghosts (*TP* 180)). The *Brandmauern* of Berlin provide a particular kind of ghostly scene for historical remains: the firewalls of a city so associated with burnings become walls of fire or fired walls, sheltering only burnt fragments, as in the case of the 'Brandmauern' on the Lützowplatz, where the only finds are 'totally charred little bones' (*TP* 208).[22] The terrain is cleared for new building-sites, but the 'charred ground' (*TP* 208) is ghostly, with the violence of history burnt into it as a foundational absence.

The seismic shocking and shifting of the post-war city creates a new form of archaeological site, where shops become 'geschichtet zu einem Haufen' (layered in a heap (*TP* 215)) as they are buried in sand. In an earlier version of the text, as if by a trick of parapraxis, 'geschichtet' read 'geschlichtet' (smoothed (*TP* 198)), suggesting perhaps a glossing over of the heaping of history. The spectacle that is presented is one of reduction to impenetrable layers, with shop-windows at the top of the heap offering only obscure views. This layering is also a representation of the city's history (as 'Ge-schichte'), an archaeology collapsing over-ground and underground, with the 'aufgeschichtete[n] Glas' (piled up glass) eluding vision and suppressing speech (*TP* 216). Like burning, or the piles of shoes that are left by the collapse of the shops, piles of glass have a particular historical weight in post-Holocaust Berlin. The only element in the flattened and layered architecture that remains open is an old bar in Alt-Moabit, apparently 'die beste' (*TP* 216), the best of all possible Berlin bars. The

---

[22] In the poem 'Daß es gestern schlimmer war' (That it was worse yesterday), the subject suffers a fate like her counterpart in *Malina*, falling into the 'crack Berlin'. This 'crack in the wall' in a city cracked by a Wall, is figured as the mortal gap between two 'Brandmauern'. See Bachmann, *Ich weiß keine bessere Welt*, p. 131.

suggestion is that it survives the general clearance on account of its location. A metropolitan quarter carrying the name of an old desert land is sufficient, it seems, to preserve it, transfiguring the principle of place-names as 'zufällig' (IB IV 240) and preventing collapse in this case.

Bachmann's version of the satirical travel genre carries the immense burden of this historical accretion of layers, the weight of the city's 'Zufälle', or collapses, which at the same time represents the massive absence of that which has been lost from it and is inadequately seen or spoken in it. On the one hand, the camel, as the narrator's impossible 'Untier' (beast), 'Traumtier' (dream animal), and 'Stadttier' (city animal), at once emblematic of an alternative way of being in the city and embodying a recuperative foreign 'shore' (*TP* 180), seems ready to transport her and her fellow sufferers out of the city and into a utopian place of 'infinite relief' (*TP* 187). On the other, the more conventional forms of travel that might be offered by 'Scharnhorst Reisen' (Scharnhorst Travels), as advertised in the text, are less likely to lead to the free space of the desert. The travel agency carries, perhaps not by coincidence, the name of a battleship that was the pride of the Nazi fleet, launched by Hitler in 1936 and sunk in 1943. Such satirical turns bind the text back into the city and its disavowed history.

In her discussion of Musil's *Der Mann ohne Eigenschaften* (The Man without Qualities), Bachmann suggests that it is cast between confession, satire, and 'positive construction' (IB IV 24). If the latter element has to struggle to find space to stand in her text, as compared with the elaboration of the 'andere Zustand' (other condition) in Musil's, it is because any postive 'Zustand' is under much more pressure to collapse into 'Zufall' in a post-Holocaust, nuclear age.[23] This is particularly the case in the land that has been the scene of so much of the destruction, casting Bachmann into a most torturous 'Zustand' (TP 233). In *Ein Ort für Zufälle*, as one part of the hybrid satire is a positive construction – the surviving bar from Alt-Moabit and the utopian camel – another is confession. Bachmann's text is a pathographic *de profundis* for an author finding herself deeply sickened in her relationship to her place and time. The city of Vienna, which in *Malina* is at once a place for utopian travelling thanks to 'Zufall' (IB III 13) and an uncanny, psychopathological place of 'Platzangst' (IB III 170) and more pernicious forms of 'Zufall' (IB III 181), coincides here with Berlin as 'Ort für Zufälle'. Thus, the Austrian traveller also finds both her personal condition and that of her homeland in this other land, her home city, always ready to

---

[23] The two terms are collapsed when 'Zufälle' are glossed as an individual's physical and psychical 'Zustände' (*TP* 189).

be seen in itself as terminal, as 'Endstadt' (IB II 127), in this 'best possible' city of satire.

STREET OF DREAMS

Christa Wolf's 'Unter den Linden' can be understood as a counter-text to *Ein Ort für Zufälle*, prospecting the divided Berlin from the other side. When Wolf suggests that Bachmann's casebook is concerned with the borderline case ('Grenzfall') in every case ('Fall'),[24] she recognises a preoccupation that is also inherent to her own casework. And while the two texts engage only indirectly with the walled border, it is arguably the ultimate *Grenzfall*, the determining topographical fault-line that links and divides their territiories. The intertextual relationship with Bachmann professed in other Wolf texts takes a more implicit, or speculative, form here. The Bachmann invoked *in memoriam* in *Kindheitsmuster* (A Model Childhood (1976)) is the writer of physical and psychical damage, putting her writing hand into the fire in order to write of it.[25] And in the more recent Berlin text, *Leibhaftig* (In Person (2002)), the hospital anaesthetist who tends the patient-protagonist and accompanies her on her fantasised urban wanderings bears the 'resonant' name of Kora Bachmann.[26] The resonance here is above all with connotations of pathology and of death (Kora as goddess of the underworld) and with the death-marked space that characterises Bachmann's *Todesarten* project.[27]

For the patient in *Leibhaftig*, whose illness opens up her own internal 'Untergrund' (underground),[28] that space lies beneath Berlin. It is a labyrinthine network of subterranean spaces, from the Friedrichstraße underground station, through street excavations exposing the viscera of the city, to the cellar of her house with its archaeology of the National Socialist years, its incendiary history piled up, like the collapsed architectures in Bachmann's text, in the form of 'geschichtetes Brennholz' (layered firewood).[29] This is a *Kranken-geschichte* or case history in all senses. The going underground, into the dark historical foundations of the city, involves a deconstruction of its foundations, its ground. Like Thomas Mann's *Schwere Stunde* (Hard Hour), as analysed by the character with the telling

---

[24] Christa Wolf, 'Die zumutbare Wahrheit: Prosa der Ingeborg Bachmann', in *Werke*, ed. Sonja Hilzinger, 12 vols. (Munich: Luchterhand, 1999–2001), vol. IV, pp. 145–61; p. 152.

[25] Christa Wolf, *Kindheitsmuster* (Darmstadt: Luchterhand, 1979), p. 166.

[26] Wolf, *Leibhaftig* (Munich: Luchterhand, 2002), p. 55.

[27] Kora's hand is also associated with the hand in the fire (*ibid.* p. 141).

[28] *Ibid.*, p. 6.   [29] *Ibid.*, p. 114.

name of Urban, this proves to be 'Doppelbödig' (double-grounded), not least in its linguistic form. Urban, suffering as he does from 'Grundkummer' or grounding in grief, has a particular, uncanny attachment to the urban double-ground, so that his fate is to become one of the bodies in the cellars that the text explores. Wolf elsewhere explores the etymology of 'Kummer' and finds a network of meanings around distress and arrest;[30] and a similar duplicity of meaning is at work in 'Grund'. Consciousness is described here as going to ground ('es geht zum Grund') only to find its deathly double-meaning of ruination ('Zugrunde gehen').[31]

This is the same constellation as is used to describe 'what remains', at the end of the melancholy text of that name: 'Was meiner Stadt zugrunde liegt und woran sie zugrunde geht' (What is the foundation of my city and what will destroy it).[32] And the same double-grounding recurs once more, as we shall see, in 'Unter den Linden'. The image of the city for the narrator of *Was bleibt* has become allegorically one with the Stasi surveillance officers whom, from the window of her representative 'Berliner Zimmer', she watches watching her. And the 'Ort' of Berlin, under the pressure of the coercion enacted in it, has become a 'Nicht-Ort'.[33] The utopia that Wolf found lacking in *Kein Ort: Nirgends* (No Place, Nowhere (1979)) is also turned to negation, the *u-topos* or no-place, here. In *Leibhaftig*, as so often in the elegiac telling of the history and topography of this city, it is the body of Rosa Luxemburg that stands emblematically for that (non-) ground-ing in violence and destruction.[34] Her death by water is a counterpart to Bachmann's death by fire.[35] Wolf joins the ranks of those who remember the abjected body of Luxemburg, albeit in a context where the new version of the state mourns that loss, and the latter-day Antigone would seek other unmourned victims of her state's violence.

While *Leibhaftig* resonates directly with the pathological topography of *Ein Ort für Zufälle*, 'Unter den Linden' does so more obliquely. That the dreamscape of this representative boulevard is also a place for coincidence, which she berates as a 'Zufallsstraße' (chance street (*UL* 94)), may in its turn be just a coincidence. It is certainly excessively marked as such, when the narrator repeatedly insists upon the 'Zufall' of an encounter with her friend Max and his 'coincidental' companion (*UL* 64). And the coordination of the epithet 'zufällig' with the postlapsarian condition, 'after the fall'

---

[30] Christa Wolf, *Was bleibt* (Hamburg: Luchterhand, 1993), p. 15.   [31] Wolf, *Leibhaftig*, p. 31.
[32] Wolf, *Was bleibt*, p. 108.   [33] *Ibid.*, p. 34.   [34] Wolf, *Leibhaftig*, p. 20.
[35] Bachmann died in 1973 after her bed caught light, though there is speculation as to the circumstances and cause of her death.

(*UL* 94), might encourage us to think of Wolf as responding to Bachmann's drawing of collapse out of 'Zufall'. Similarly, 'Zufall' comes, with pride, 'before the fall' (*UL* 78) or demands testimony from the coincidental witness of an 'Unfall' or accident (*UL* 79). Here too, then, the place of 'Zufall' is also a place of potentially grievous falling; 'Zufall' and other forms of 'Fall' come together with a frequency that appears more than coincidental. The text's 'praise of coincidence' (*UL* 67) is accordingly shadowed by such potential collapses.

The symptoms that befall this dream-text are, however, more subtly marked than those of *Ein Ort für Zufälle*, not least because 'Unter den Linden' is working under effects of censorship and self-censorship. Its motto from Rahel Varnhagen on the human condition of being 'gekränkt' (offended) to the core suggests a text that is concerned with offended subjectivity, but also encodes the possibility for this to be understood as a form of pathology ('gekränkt' as 'sickened'). And by its invocation of a ghostly presence from pre-Holocaust Berlin, one who suffered from an earlier incarnation of anti-Semitism, the epigraph suggests *in absentia* the historical grief that subtends the Berlin street-scene. It is the narrator's destiny to be 'gekränkt' in her turn by her treatment on the bus (*UL* 55); and her expulsion from it in response to a kind of paranoid fantasy of being under trial in the city also resonates with historical versions of such persecution. It is perhaps not by chance that she alights in front of the State Opera House, at the historical site of the burning of the books, of the sort of fire into which Bachmann's hand reaches in order to write of it. When the narrator writes that 'Geschichte' pursues her (*UL* 57), this has to be understood in a double sense: the story of the girl whose case she reconstructs and history, as the archaeological *Ge-schichte* of a street like Unter den Linden.

This is a place that is always also under itself in the manner of the 'Platz' from Jelinek's poem. The 'unter' of 'Unter den Linden' in Wolf's text is indicative of its attachment to what lies under the surface. While the narrative seems to operate in terms of the appearance of this representative, tourist street, negotiating its sights in the mode of *flânerie*, its concern is with the psycho-topography that contends with official appearances, and according to which the street under the sign of 'unter' always leads 'into the deep' (*UL* 61). The Unter den Linden explored in the text is a second-order street, running beneath the everyday version, in the dimension of the unconscious. It is at once a place of personal dream for the narrating subject and of unconsciously inflected operations on a historical and political level. The wrong turn taken by the guardsman is an example of the parapraxis, the psycho-topographical lapsing, that affects representative acts in this para-street. His conjectural state of psychosomatic damage (as a victim of heat stress (*UL* 56)) correlates with the historical and political damage that underlies the oneiric street-scene, 'undamaged' as it may seem to be (*UL* 54). 'Wachablösung' (relief of the guard (*UL* 55)) works here in the manner of dream language, as a release from the need to guard, but also from the constraints of waking ('Wachen') and into the other space of dreams. But this other space is a ground of contestation between autonomy and heteronomy. It is under the surveillance of the 'dream censor' (*UL* 75), a psychical version of the censorship authorities that hold guard in the polis, and is haunted by the scenario of the trial. The guardsman's lapse, leaving his place unoccupied, is of the same order as that of the student who neglects her studies, and whose 'crime-scene' is visited in reconstruction, as if for a court (*UL* 58) by the dream-text.

The sort of underground that the narrator enters here is a virtual one, in the shape of the pool in the inner court of the old State Library, where she finds herself in her element, having reached the 'Grund' (*UL* 61). But this grounding is chimeric, leaving the narrator in an impossible, virtual space, a u-topian dimension. And it carries with it the uncanniness of the double ground. It is the utopian, potentially deadly element of Bachmann's latter-day water sprite in 'Undine geht' (Undine Goes (1961)), a text cited by Wolf in conjunction with the reference to the author's death by fire in *Kindheitsmuster*; or the dystopian urban element of Rosa Luxemburg in the Landwehrkanal as recalled in *Leibhaftig*. This non-place of fantasy or of death is uninhabitable, even in the dimension of dream, and she is accordingly drawn from the water by the allegorical figure of Pain and subjected once more to social incorporation. The State Library acts as a representative site of social regulation, a library of state; and here she is subject to the double-bind of inclusion through exclusion that is implied by being 'aus-gesetzt', ex-posed, to its authority. The library, with its *nomos*, its 'site-rules' (*UL* 62), imposes a state of exception upon the subject, who is allowed, indeed constrained, to enter, but always subject to the contingencies of laws that may change overnight, laws that are proved by the exception. While the statues of the Humboldt brothers in front of the university are benign representatives of Enlightenment traditions in Berlin, the institutions of state put learning under coercive regulation.

When the narrator is joined by the dream-figure of the golden fish, it is as if the space of the street is converted into the element of water which she had been forced to leave. The fish is the equivalent of Bachmann's camel as dream animal, incorporating the possibility of utopia into the fraught space of the city, and invoking the idea of Unter den Linden as a place of just distribution. But this utopian figure is subject to the distortions of urban reality: seen in reflection in a shop-window, he scares shoppers away, and the shops are stormed as young people seek to follow his fashion for gold. Wolf's Unter den Linden, with its 'Wunderfisch', is thus subject to a mirror-image of the dystopian *Wirtschaftswunder* in Bachmann's West Berlin. It is the golden fish's fate to go to ground in ruin – 'zugrundegehen', with the narrator asking 'Zu welchem Grund?' (To which ground? (*UL* 71)). It is perhaps akin to the ground that the narrator had found earlier in the pool, but one that they will not find together. This fish out of water is ultimately no more capable of transporting the subject out of the space of social regulation than Bachmann's displaced camel. It is telling that the allegorical fish is represented as black, turned from utopia to melancholy, in the illustration by Harald Metzkes that accompanied the first publication of the text.[36] The fish, like Bachmann's camel, also embodies a potential for psycho-pathology in the city: the case histories of a camel- and a fish-woman. Indeed, Wolf's fish-woman has a particular intertextual relation-ship to the classic Unter den Linden text, E. T. A. Hoffmann's *Das öde Haus*, which also frames the psycho-topographical case history of its pro-tagonist through dreams, mirror-images, underground spaces, and effects of 'Zufall', and features a magic goldfish in its repertoire of other-wordly figures. The ambivalence of Hoffmann's uncanny dream-street is reflected in Wolf's. The utopian vision of the fish in the shop-window has a counter-part in another kind of speculation, when – in an 'unguarded moment' – a 'landscape of ruins' appears in place of the reflection of the Lindenhotel. Both transcendence and ruin, utopia and melancholia, are prospects that haunt the space of the city and its 'street-traffic regulations' (*UL* 69): other places that inhabit it, but are not in themselves inhabitable.

The vision of the alternative place is crowded out by another double subjection to law on each side of the divided city: the narrating subject's arrest when on an incursion into West Berlin to distribute propaganda, and the rebuke for infringement of traffic law when, lost in memories of that incursion, she crosses the road on red. It carries the same implication as the scene before the Brandenburg Gate, where the narrator's 'protest' that she does not belong to the tour-group is cut off by its leader (*UL* 82). The potential for autonomous demonstration is pervasively controlled in the show-case street. The refusal of protest leads to the enactment of a scene from the trial set against the 'little wall' in front of the Gate (*UL* 85), an ironic substitute for the Wall behind it, and then to a desperate attempt on

[36] Christa Wolf, *Unter den Linden: Drei unwahrscheinliche Geschichten* (Berlin/Weimar: Aufbau, 1974).

the subject's part to find on this representative street an authority to which she might appeal (this as she passes the Soviet Embassy). In this court-space, dispersed through the street, the narrator comes to converge with the girl on trial for wasting the university's time, and subject to the sort of pathographic force that characterises *Ein Ort für Zufälle*, so that any doctor would have signed a sick-note for her (*UL* 89).

The 'Zufälle' that have more or less benign control of the earlier part of the narrative are here converted into 'Zustände' with the same mortal implications as in Bachmann, leading to death (*UL* 90). These personal 'Zustände' unto death combine with the political duress that rules the psycho-topography of the 'Zufallsstraße'. The closing recuperation of those pathological conditions found in Unter den Linden as place for coincidences is in the characteristic mode of the self-censor, or of the writer eluding censorship by pre-empting its logic. Thus, the waking or the guarded language that frames the narrative is also readable as though it had spilled out of the dream narrative: the realisation that 'hits' her and fills the body 'cell by cell' (*UL* 95) is ominous language for this text concerned with justice and force. In the light of this, the return of the text to its beginning at the end may have uncanny rather than recuperative implications. As with Rita in *Der geteilte Himmel*, Berlin is experienced here as an uncanny city.[37] The case that the text has made against the social conditions behind the personal case, the reasons (*Gründe*) that might lie at the base (*zugrundeliegen*) of such personal ruin (*Zugrundegehen*), are part of 'what remains' from Wolf's early work, exposed in the critical moments of its topographical exploration, and ready to return again – like the double-ground of *zugrunde* – in the later texts.

While Bachmann's and Wolf's texts explore the possibilities for transportation to other places that might lie in sand or water, and communicate through the traumatic possibilities of fire, what of the element of air, the 'Berliner Luft'? Another of the features from *Ein Ort für Zufälle* that recurs in *Leibhaftig* is the violence of aeroplanes flying over the hospital, freighted with memories of air-war. The elements (always with the implicit fire of air-war) are combined here. When the narrator of *Leibhaftig* sinks under the 'flood' and her consciousness goes to ground or into ruin ('Zugrunde gehen'), it is under the influence of the ear-rending noise of planes flying low. These insistent flying machines are also reminders in both texts of divided airspace, the equivalent of the Bahnhof Friedrichstraße as a site of separation and its 'Tränenbunker' or bunker of tears, which also appears in

---

[37] Wolf, *Der geteilte Himmel* (Munich: dtv, 1973), p. 168.

both texts. The 'Tränenbunker' is also envisioned in *Leibhaftig* as a place of transit for a Jew seeking an impossible other place to be in the 1930s,[38] just as the divided airspace resounds with the force of earlier flight patterns.

TALE OF TWO CITIES

Both the 'Berliner Luft' and the space for movement on the ground are rife with historical freight. Another Berlin text from the 1960s, Uwe Johnson's *Zwei Ansichten*, which views the horizontally divided city from both sides, also reveals the loaded divisions and interactions between vertical dimensions: air, ground, and underground. Where the texts by Bachmann and Wolf engaged with effects of 'Zufall', the lead term of Johnson's text is 'unverhofft' (unexpected), which proliferates throughout the text, as if in parody of the proverb 'unverhofft kommt oft' (the unexpected often happens). It occurs here most often in association with loss or shock rather than with the utopian possibility of coincidental occurrence or encounter that it might seem to suggest. While the metropolis is a classic site for chance encounter, in the case of Berlin coincidence in its darker aspect is inevitable, marking the recurrent impact of trauma, which – however much it might be expected – will always have an effect of shock.

Johnson's leitmotif of the unexpected is attached to the divided condition of the state and the city, so that a flight announcement of the passage into East German airspace can create, 'unverhofft', a fearful sense of penetration into alien space (*ZA* 133). The loss of his car by the male protagonist, the West German photographer B., leaving him with a sense of lack that is 'unverhofft' (*ZA* 10), introduces the theme of transportation problems that runs through the text. The theft of the car displaces him into air travel, which he finds 'unheimlich' (*ZA* 20), and into the negotiation of the city on foot and by public transport, which subjects him to disorientation. The aeroplanes in which he flies or which fly overhead constantly threaten to fall from the sky, or to take him as their target (*ZA* 74), so that the 'Fall' in question (*ZA* 81) extends to his own case of aerophobia. The airspace of Berlin is configured with the destruction of the city from the sky. The aeroplanes that he photographs coming into the city are thus seen to fit neatly into 'gaps in the ruins' (*ZA* 144). And when B. is travelling into the city by taxi after a traumatic flight, the element of the air itself has the impact of air attack and firestorm through the broken archaeology of the

---

[38] Wolf, *Leibhaftig*, p. 59.

city, as the air strikes hot into the car through bombed out gaps (*ZA* 69). The uncanniness of air travel is transferred into the failure to be at home in the city, both in motorised form, as here, and on foot. B.'s request for help to find the most convenient border crossing meets with a reaction from a policeman that is reminiscent of Kafka's dream of disorientation in Berlin that opened this study (*ZA* 19) (see p. 8). The end of the novel, suitably enough, has B. come to grief in a street accident, struck by a bus and landing with his head in the gutter in a fallen posture reminiscent of Franz Biberkopf before him (*ZA* 239). His fear of falling is finally realised, as he becomes a hospital case.

While B. is a stranger to the city, for the female protagonist D., too, the divided city of which she is a resident is experienced as strange. While she knows the city, remembers it, in its historical layering (*ZA* 41), she has to take on the position of being a stranger ('ortsfremd') in order to pass from one side to the other (*ZA* 223). Her transformation into another identity, strange to the city, also involves a discovery of a secret sub-city, a 'heimliche Stadt', running beneath the evident one (*ZA* 217). And for her, too, this secret dimension in the home town creates uncanny effects in a dreamlike scene, representing a knowledge that estranges her (*ZA* 220). As she waits for her transmission to the West, she is racked by uncanny dreams that expose her to the trauma of the border crossing in a variety of dimensions: underwater; underground; lying in sand; and in the transparent layers of a building between prison and hospital, where she is interrogated, and the 'Grenzverletzer' (those who have 'injured' the border) themselves lie wounded (*ZA* 204). The hospital is once again the elective symbolic territory for siting a case of sickness in and of Berlin; and as the anaesthetist Kora Bachmann becomes transferentially involved in the case of the first-person patient in *Leibhaftig*, so the nurse D. is intimately linked with a woman who has fallen ill over the division of the city. This patient's violent symptomatic behaviour is also marked as 'unverhofft' (*ZA* 121), and she will return, by an uncanny coincidence, to accompany D.'s flight from East Berlin. A similar coincidence seems to link D. with B. and his transportation problems, as – while she is waiting in the safe-house – she is jogged 'unverhofft' by the noise of motors on the street (*ZA* 222). The engine of B.'s new car, which has replaced the lost one, meanwhile 'dies', also 'unverhofft', as he drives to meet her (*ZA* 236). At the end of the text, D. appears to have overcome the transference with her patient and her divided connection with the case of B. She has survived the crossing and the humiliation of the transit camp that awaits her on the other side, and appears ready to live in the West, while B. lies sick in the hospital, a fallen figure. The two views of the divided lovers in the divided city remain, and the prospects are uncertain on either side.

The fraught airspace of *Zwei Ansichten*, with its ambivalent attachment to the situation on the ground, is also surveyed as allegorical 'geteilte Himmel' or divided sky in Wolf's 1963 text of that name and in the 1964 film by Konrad Wolf based upon it. The air over the divided city is the element that is indivisible and yet divided 'first of all'.[39] Peculiarly apt to support utopian flights, it is also susceptible to grounding and so to control, exclusion, and violence. The film quotes the experimental effects of Ruttmann's *Berlin* symphony,[40] but in a deconstructive fashion, using stylised light effects from the Weimar 'City of Light' to divide the protagonist from her fiancé as they separate, and a brief and less highly charged version of the train's approach to Berlin to represent her melancholic departure from the city. Another DEFA film, directed by Kurt Barthel and co-written by Christa and Gerhard Wolf, the unfinished *Fräulein Schmetterling* (Miss Butterfly (1965/6)), takes the principle of the utopian creature further by having its 'butterfly-woman' fly over the old streets under threat of demolition off the Alexanderplatz. But this allegorical figure of fantasy and dream, the Miss Butterfly of the GDR, is destined to be brought out of her element down to earth, and the film's investment in fantasy soon provoked the sort of 'dream censorship' that so often clipped the wings of DEFA's more imaginative filmmakers. As a victim of the backlash against the creative licence of DEFA's New Wave at the 11th Plenary of the SED (Sozialistische Einheitspartei Deutschlands or Socialist Unity Party of Germany), when Christa Wolf was a lone resistant voice, Fräulein Schmetterling appears as a fairy-tale version of the angel of history, ultimately another grounded denizen of Christa Wolf's melancholic Eastern landscape.[41] The film looks forward, coincidentally, to Kutluğ Ataman's 2004 installation piece, *A Butterfly Flaps its Wings*, projected onto the House of the Teacher on the Alexanderplatz. This mobile but pinned butterfly, conceived as a phantom or dreamlike reference to the 9/11 attack on New York and the new forms of urban aerophobia that go with it, might also be

---

[39] Wolf, *Der geteilte Himmel*, p. 187.

[40] See Daniela Berghahn, *Hollywood behind the Wall: The Cinema of East Germany* (Manchester: Manchester University Press, 2005), p. 78.

[41] Iris Radisch, in a review of Irina Liebmann's *Die freien Frauen* (The Free Women (2004)), a haunted tale of two cities – Berlin and Katowice, allegorises Wolf as the 'Melancholia' of the East, and Liebmann as snow queen of the post-*Wende* German winter. Iris Radisch, 'Die Schneekönigin', *Die Zeit* literatur (October 2004), 3.

understood more generally as an elegiac performance of the blockage of possibilities of free flight over the city of Berlin.

CITY OF FALLEN ANGELS

A no less fantastical project for imaginative control of Berlin's airspace than *Fräulein Schmetterling*, and sharing with it the motifs of flight and of the circus as alternative space for utopian fantasy, is Wenders' *Der Himmel über Berlin*. For Wenders, this film 'IN und ÜBER Berlin' (in and about/over Berlin) enters the air above the city in order to give a privileged view of it. He sees it as at once a unique city, unique both in its air (his version of the 'Berliner Luft') and underfoot, on the ground, and as an exemplary one, a representative 'ÜBERLEBENSORT' or place of survival in a fraught time of survival, an emblematic place of division in a time of global separation.[42] By adopting the conceit of the angels who watch over the inhabitants of the divided city, Wenders establishes an alternative, utopian form of control of the airspace. But his angels are in part derived from the model of Benjamin's angel of history, and as such cannot enjoy free flight, but are constantly trained upon traumatic disruption on the ground. He conceived of them as from the start in a fallen state, banished to Berlin as the most terrible city in the world at the end of the war.[43] The transcendental figures are attached to the ruins of history in the fallen city and, as such, always liable to fall once more in their turn.

By approaching the city from the air, *Der Himmel über Berlin* adopts a *topos* that runs through post-war filmmaking and writing, from Billy Wilder's *A Foreign Affair* (1948) and Carol Reed's *A Man Between* (1953) to Peter Schneider's novel *Der Mauerspringer* (The Wall Jumper (1982)), which opens by exploring the topography of the 'Siamese city' from the air and following the jagged line of the Wall.[44] The spectacle of destruction in the first case is already substantially repaired in the second and barely visible in the third. But, on closer inspection, Schneider's Berlin is characterised by 'tearing in the asphalt' with the past breaking through,[45] just as the sky over Berlin in his later *Paarungen* is seen as reflecting the torn concrete below.[46] The shadow of the aeroplane that the narrator of *Der Mauerspringer* sees passing over the city is akin to the shadow that falls upon the subject in

---

[42] Wim Wenders, 'Eine Beschreibung eines recht unbeschreiblichen Filmes: *Aus dem ersten Treatment zu "Der Himmel über Berlin"*, *Die Logik der Bilder: Essays und Gespräche*, ed. Michael Töteberg (Frankfurt am Main: Verlag der Autoren, 1988), pp. 93–104; p. 94.

[43] *Ibid.*, p. 99.   [44] Peter Schneider, *Der Mauerspringer* (Hamburg: Luchterhand, 1984), pp. 5–6.

[45] *Ibid.*, p. 7.   [46] Schneider, *Paarungen* (Reinbek: Rowohlt, 1992), p. 9.

Freud's formulation of the melancholic condition: it marks the city out as haunted by shades of the past, with an underlying depressive condition.

The approach from the air in *Der Himmel über Berlin* is also shadowed by the view of the war-torn city, and set to find its key scenes in the gaps left by the destruction. It is such empty spaces – 'Niemandsländer' or no-man's-lands as he calls them – that fascinate Wenders in his adopted city, a fascination that smacks of traumatophilia with its attachment to the 'wounds' of Berlin.[47] The lacunae in the 'Stadt-Bild' are sought out as particular places for finding true city-images,[48] with the distinctive backdrop of the *Brandmauern* as the history books of the cityscape.[49] Such scenes have a particular poignancy for Wenders because they are under the shadow of transience, places of historical witness that 'cannot survive',[50] and his film-work clings nostalgically to these places that will have been. In the original plans for the film, the early view of the contemporary city from the sky was also going to segue into one of the decimated post-war cityscape, the two mediated by the flap of angel's wing across the visual field, at once linking and dividing them.[51]

Der Himmel über Berlin combines flying machines – the aeroplane in which Peter Falk arrives, the British Army helicopter hovering over the Wall, the references to Blériot and, more obliquely, to Lilienthal – with the angels as flying camera figures.[52] The angels are one moment fantastic architectural features added to the top of Berlin's iconic monuments and memorial structures, the next swooping over the city and passing unhindered through such solid structures as the Wall. While the conceit of the angels allows Wenders free access to the divided city in the air and on the ground, their condition as separated from the human world they observe casts the topographical division into a different dimension. While they open up the psychical dimension of city space, hearing the inner voices of the people they home in on, this freedom of the psychical airwaves also emphasises the separation, the enclosure of individual mental space. The potential interference of the many voices heard in the heads of the citizens of Berlin projects into the film the possibility of a paranoid schizophrenic condition, an unbearable hearing of voices, which can be controlled only by the encapsulation of individual cases.

---

[47] Wim Wenders, *The Act of Seeing: Texte und Gespräche* (Frankfurt am Main: Verlag der Autoren, 1992), p. 123.
[48] *Ibid.*, p. 124.   [49] *Ibid.*, p. 133.   [50] *Ibid.*, p. 138.
[51] See Wenders' chronological account for participants in the project (1986), held in the Berlin Filmmuseum (no page numbers).
[52] The reference to flight pioneer Otto Lilienthal is through the Lilienthaler Chaussee.

This dialectic of opening and closure operates throughout the film. If *Der Himmel über Berlin* is indeed, as Wenders suggested, a vertical form of his favoured road-movie genre,[53] it projects the monumental dividing line that blocks the road network of Berlin into that vertical dimension. The angels draw near, but they are recurrently also withdrawn to points high above the city, the Siegessäule or the Gedächtniskirche (Memorial Church), with distant views of the roads below and their human life. Their predicament, like that of Berliners on either side of the Wall, is to be 'so near and yet so far', to invoke the title of Wenders' post-unification sequel, *In weiter Ferne, so nah!* (Faraway, So Close! (1993)). It is also a version of the formulation that Benjamin famously applied to aura – the singular experience of the visual object as at once proximate and profoundly distant. While the angels are endowed with such an aura as they come in close to human experience, it is always only in separation. We see this in the scene from the end of the film where Cassiel is cast in a glowing monochrome visual capsule, which the book of the film calls an 'aura of black-and-white', as he sits watching his fallen buddy Damiel training with Marion the trapeze artist in full colour.[54] The auratic mode of the black-and-white footage used for the angel's-eye views that organise the first part of the film, modulating between expansion and intimacy, is also inherently melancholic. It is a chiaroscuro space of haunted separation, embodied in particular in the saturnine figure of Cassiel, the 'angel of solitude and tears' as he is called in the library scene, an avatar of Dürer's Melancholia.

In the scene before Damiel's fall, the two angels walk towards the Wall from either side to meet in the death-strip, co-opted here as a site for coming to life. And an earlier scene has them walk over the Landwehrkanal and through the Wall, as if marking out a mirror-line of an axis to the monumental line of division. These are two of several sequences that divide the screen symmetrically between the two figures, suggesting at once a doubling and a polarity between them. The second scene in the death-strip leads to the division of the angelic perspective, hitherto balanced between pleasure and sadness over what they behold, into a schizoid condition of euphoria and melancholia. The separation also marks a move into a more discontinuous mode of filming. It draws out and dramatises the element of separation that had already been present in the earlier camerawork, notwithstanding its

[53] See Coco Fusco, 'Angels, History and Poetic Fantasy: An Interview with Wim Wenders', *Cineaste* 16.4 (1988), 14–17; p. 16.
[54] Wim Wenders and Peter Handke, *Der Himmel über Berlin: Ein Filmbuch* (Frankfurt am Main: Suhrkamp, 1990), p. 165.

effect of producing a spatio-temporal continuum.[55] Here, too, a distance was retained in both spatial and temporal dimensions. Wenders accordingly adapts his version of Benjamin's chronotopical formulation of aura, suggesting that the distant can come ever so near, but not right up to the present moment in time ('Bisher') or the present point in space ('bis her').[56]

This version of the auratic is the domain of the image, of stories only ever witnessed as visual effects. It is seen not as fully intact but, in the manner of the heaping of historical experience beheld by the angel of history, as a continuous sequence of discontinuous parts. As we shall see, the film operates under that angel's aegis. The imagistic mode is set against the domain of narrative, the actively experiential dimension coloured by flesh and blood into which Damiel falls, as if in an air-drop from the helicopter in the sky over Berlin. The armour that falls after him and strikes him on the head marks the fall into narrative as traumatic. It is associated as much with the armaments that have fallen from military aircraft over Berlin before as with more benevolent drops, and with those who have fallen from the sky into the city (the angels were originally conceived as airmen shot down over Berlin).[57]

The scene seems to recuperate the wound of the fall by having Damiel joyfully lick his blood with a new human appetite for taste and colour. The taste for blood might in fact seem to convert the angel dramatically into a vampire, referring to an earlier role of Bruno Ganz's in Werner Herzog's 1979 remake of F. W. Murnau's *Nosferatu*, where he plays the innocent husband who becomes an agent of vampirism. In this light, his fascination with Marion's neckline might indeed be viewed as less angelic than it seemed. The original plan for the film had included a host of demonic figures, werewolves from the Nazi past living underground and other Gothic spirits haunting the cityscape.[58] And this playful reference to the vampire might be seen in that context. At the same time, the scene occurs at a time when blood is the carrier of paranoid fears of contagion, as an AIDS poster seen on the *Brandmauer* behind the circus-ground off the Friedrichstraße reminds us.[59] The psychopathologies of everyday urban life revealed in the exploration of mental space in the opening sequence have their counterpart in this other form of sickness. *Der Himmel über Berlin* is perhaps not so far removed from the Gothic New York of the 1980s in Tony

[55] See Wenders' chronological account. [56] See *ibid*.
[57] Wenders, 'Eine Beschreibung', p. 97. [58] See the chronological account.
[59] In the first treatment, the fallen angel is besieged by dreams and human feelings like 'viruses' for one with deficient immunity ('Eine Beschreibung', p. 103).

Kushner's *Angels in America*. As Damiel walks on through the city, he is passed by an ambulance on an emergency, which he blithely allows to pass without any impulse for angelic intervention, a reminder that health emergencies and accidents still happen.[60]

The vampiric possibility would concur with another interfilmic reference, when – as Simon Ward has pointed out – Damiel is positioned in front of a West Berlin shop-window, eating an apple, in a quotation from Lang's *M*.[61] The urban bogeyman that we saw revisiting Schadt's *Berlin* symphony film has thus already returned here. Again, the reference may be playful or purely formal, or – as Ward suggests – it may be seen as contributing to the intertextual homage to Weimar culture in the film. But intertexual quotation will always be liable to carry the implications of the source text with it. In this light, the quotation from *M* may serve to suggest that Damiel, the fallen angel turned metropolitan *flâneur*, in fact has the makings of a criminal stalker. His encounters with children, in particular, would thus appear in a less innocent light and subvert the fairy-tale narrative that bears the film to its conclusion. What are we to make, for instance, of his gleeful performance of local knowledge when he leaves the Turkish boy who asks him the way to the Akazienstraße more lost than he was before? Is this child perhaps lost in the same way as the distressed child encountered in Cassiel's dark vision of the city as he plunges from the Siegessäule: one of what Emma Wilson has called cinema's missing children?[62]

What Damiel sees in the window is not a display of knives around a mirror, but a television showing a winking Peter Falk, which might also appear to implicate the actor-detective in Lang's dark scenario. And the role of Peter Falk, alias Columbo or Colombo, the benevolent and shrewd detective – a globe-trotting actor, an accidental tourist,[63] a *flâneur* ('Spazieren … Go spazieren!' as his Jewish grandmother told him), and a portraitist of people and the city – should also not be taken for granted. He could be understood as a Lucifer or as Mephistopheles in a version of the Faustian pact – an agent of evil who draws other angels out of their relative state of grace, aligned with the seductive Ripley in *Der amerikanische Freund* (The American Friend (1977)) or the criminal fallen angel Emit Flesti in *In*

---

[60] The scene is one of many that look forward to Tykwer's *Lola rennt*.
[61] In a paper for the Conference of University Teachers of German in Leeds (March 2006) entitled 'The Remembrance of Visual Culture Past in Wim Wenders' *Wings of Desire*'.
[62] Emma Wilson, *Cinema's Missing Children* (London: Wallflower, 2002).
[63] 'I wish you were here' is his refrain, to his grandmother and the angels, as he explores the city and records unlikely postcard sights.

weiter Ferne, so nah! His role as actor suggests a man of many parts, trying on hats and roles, and indeed at the point where he is searching for the right hat the book of the film slips into calling him Colombo.[64] His conversation on the film set with a young boy playing a Hitler Youth revolves, after all, around the theory that Hitler could have had a double played by an actor, and Falk's role in the film relies upon a confusion of his person with his screen role. If he is recognisable to people on the street as Colombo, presumably Bruno Ganz can be recognisable as, and confused with, the ambiguous protagonists of *Nosferatu* or *Der amerikanische Freund*. On an allegorical level, the screen-name, Colombo, may seem to put him on the side of the doves in the film (the 'colombe' evoked in the circus), but the name Falk has resonances rather of a hawk (the German pronounciation is used on the film set).[65]

If these references are indeed to be taken seriously, they would be symptomatic of the less benign fallen states of humanity to which the film is witness and which it might seem to redeem with its romance narrative framing. The prime allegorical site for this is the headquarters of the angels in the Western counterpart of Wolf's State Library, this too a place of reckoning. It is the library as archive of knowledge and experience, a place of humanistic optimism, but also of historical pessimism. As has been noted by Alice A. Kuzniar and Xavier Vila, the presiding genius of the Library, reflecting upon the status of the angels who watch over acts of reading and writing there, is Benjamin's angel of history, introduced in one of the trains of thought that provide the voice-over colloquium as the camera tracks around.[66] We do not see Klee's *Angelus novus*, nor the text that Benjamin wrote about it, but the mention of Benjamin's ownership of it evokes his theses on the concept of history, and in particular the reading of the *angelus* as angel of history. Curiously, the reference to the angel in the book of the film breaks off with a colon,[67] which, if it is not just a typographic error, is appropriate to the angel's function as a figure faced up to and focalising what follows in its wake, here in the tracking of texts and images in the library. The angel of history serves as it were to behold all that is accumulated by way of cultural historical evidence in this Berlin archive.

---

[64] Wenders and Handke, *Der Himmel über Berlin: Ein Filmbuch*, p. 67.
[65] Indeed, one character in *In weiter Ferne, so nah!* pronounces it 'Falke'.
[66] Alice A. Kuzniar and Xavier Vila, 'Witnessing Narration in: *Wings of Desire*', *Film Criticism* 16.3 (1992), 355–67.
[67] Wenders and Handke, *Der Himmel über Berlin: Ein Filmbuch*, p. 23.

If the angel of history is the opening image in the gallery, the closing ones are those that we see in August Sander's photographic archive, *Menschen des zwanzigsten Jahrhunderts* (People of the Twentieth Century), as viewed by the Homer figure.[68] He opens the book at the end, with the terminal images of persecution, mutilation, and death that as it were look back over Sander's album. There is the final image in the book from the section 'The Last People', a *memento mori* in the form of the laid out corpse of an old woman; the extraordinary image two from the end, of a woman mutilated by an explosion, her facial features erased and her eyes behind dark glasses while her body appears untouched, a radical *Entstellung* of the principle of portraiture that governs the album; and there are two of the pairs of images of persecuted Jews from the penultimate section of the album, figures who – to follow Barthes – will have been. Between the first images and the last, film footage of corpses lying in the ruins of the city is interspersed, apparently the victims of air-war, viewed as though on Homer's mind-screen as a supplement to the photographic album. The heaped corpses provide a particularly harrowing physical form for the ruins of history that Benjamin's angel must contemplate. The figures, or disfigures, of *Entstellung* from Sander's album, subjecting the composed genre of portrait photography to flight, mutilation, and death, stand allegorically as embodiments of ruin, in accordance with the corpse in Benjamin's analysis. And the moving picture extension of the photograph album incorporates that allegorical vision into the medium of film. While Barthes suggests that film mobilises the mortified stillness of photography through its forward dynamic, Wenders' symphony of the city suggests a melancholic incorporation of the moving image into the mode of the still album, much as we saw in the case of Ruttmann's *Berlin*.[69]

The scene showing Curt Bois, as Homer the 'angel of narration',[70] cast in the role of that archetypal Berlin entertainer, the Leiermann or organ-grinder, and playing 'Berliner Luft' on his music box at the edge of no-man's land, cannot rescue the air or ground of Berlin from these images of persecution and destruction. He senses that there are still points of passage into the land of narrative in the historical topography of the city, but the disorientating, negative space of what was once the Potsdamer Platz renders his narration confused and unheard except by the angels. Homer

---

[68] See August Sander, *Menschen des 20. Jahrhunderts: Portraitphotographien von 1892–1952*, ed. Gunther Sander (Munich: Schirmer/Mosel, 1980).

[69] See also Robert Phillip Kolker and Peter Beicken, *The Films of Wim Wenders: Cinema as Vision and Desire* (Cambridge: Cambridge University Press, 1993), p. 143. The link is sustained in Schadt's Berlin symphony, paying homage to Alekan's camerawork in *Der Himmel über Berlin*.

[70] In the chronological account, the Homer role was taken by the archangel Raphael.

seeks to fulfil the classical model of mnemonic recall here, doing the memory work of Simonides by establishing the place of what is lost in order to ascertain its historical identity. But his anamnestic quest for the lost architectures and experiences of the classic chronotope of the Potsdamer Platz in its Weimar heyday is waylaid by the spatial void of no-man's land.

The original conception of the library in which the angels meet was of a building in no-man's land torn open by bombing,[71] and in the images of the bodies from Sander's album and Homer's mind-screen that ruined building is a phantom presence in the light, intact, and 'airy' spaces of the new State Library.[72] The equivalent interior to the ruined library building in the film is the bunker in the Goebenstraße, with its massive, but internally broken architecture, inhabited by extras for the noirish film being shot there, a cast of underground survivors of the Holocaust and the war, or of the city's undead. The overwhelming mood of this space is melancholic fixation, as in the case of the old woman playing a Jew who recalls her wartime encounter with a Frenchman and his parting words: 'Berlin, das wird nicht mehr' (Berlin will no longer be). As she recalls this statement, contradicting the process of becoming that is supposed to be axiomatic for the city, documentary footage of the city in ruins plays on her mind-screen.

In accordance with what is thus seen from within it, the bunker has an image of the ruined city painted onto it, as if a poster fixed with sticky tape, and acting as a *mise-en-abyme*, an emblematic subversion of its massive protective presence. And, as the book of the film points out,[73] and the film shows, it has a palace of the people, a huge housing block known as the 'Sozialpalast', built around it. The palace and the ruin are thus configured through the bunker with its internal damage: an ensemble in the classic style of Benjamin's allegory. And this is linked, in its turn, to the other bunker near the Anhalter Bahnhof, an ensemble of the impenetrable and the ruined façade. As he passes it, Peter Falk recalls hearing a recollection of the Anhalter as the station where not trains but 'the station stops', the sort of speaking otherwise of the allegorical site that Benjamin recorded, an arrested condition that now takes on the form of ruin.

Critics have debated the extent to which Wenders really invests in the romantic resolution of the film. Roger Cook notes another filmic quotation in Marion's ecstatic discourse in the Hotel Esplanade when she appears to cite a line from the song of another 'angel', Dietrich as Lola Lola in *Der*

---

[71] The chronological account invokes a burnt-out library from a photograph of a building in London.
[72] See Wenders and Handke, *Der Himmel über Berlin: Ein Filmbuch*, p. 23.   [73] See *ibid.*, p. 64.

blaue Engel (The Blue Angel (1930)). For Cook this is evidence of Wenders playing with the available repertoire of romance in a knowing performance of the postmodern condition.[74] What the quotation would also suggest is an alternative kind of angel narrative, a distinctly fallen one, where the apparently angelic performer seduces the innocent 'angel' who falls for her and makes a pantomime chicken of him. This alternative, cynical styling of the Berlin angel is another shadow presence, a potential for mockery of romance as kitsch, in Wenders' postmodern city of angels. The fantasy world of his angels in Berlin is caught between the Gothic on the one hand and the burlesque on the other (here, too, the wings of the angel are accompanied by the circus-role of the chicken).

When Marion, in her set-piece speech in the Esplanade, invokes the 'Zufall' that has ruled her life hitherto, she claims to stand for the whole city, and through it the world. The speech seems to announce the end of that painful condition of contingency for her, and of the sort of psycho-pathology, the fear of accident, of falling from her flight, that has haunted her act and made her sick. And it extends to the more general recuperation of what Bachmann called the 'Ort für Zufälle', and a form of urban love story to supersede the melancholic sense of being bound to a history of loss, on personal and political levels, of Wolf's 'Unter den Linden'. This is allegory on a grandiose scale, a decisive union enacted on the 'Platz des Volkes' (Place of the People), with the people as one in their desire. Wenders described the initial incommensurability of Handke's texts with the film's location work in terms of monoliths that had fallen from the sky,[75] and in this scene we see that the *mise-en-scène* has been fashioned to fit the monumental, not to say totalitarian structure of the couple's discourse that appears to have fallen out of the sky over Berlin. The scene seems to want to overcome the kind of 'state boundaries' between people in their autonomous spheres, the psychical states of exception, which go through the head of the chauffeur as he drives the vintage car to the film set. But its dream of mass union is enacted between two individuals, with the city's inhabitants and their insistent fears and memories excluded. The states of exception that characterise the city and the psychical territories of its inhabitants, heaped up in the witnessing of the film, are excluded here as if by the decree of a

---

[74] Roger F. Cook, 'Angels, Fiction, and History in Berlin: *Wings of Desire*', *The Cinema of Wim Wenders: Image, Narrative, and the Postmodern Condition*, ed. Roger F. Cook and Gerd Gemünden (Detroit: Wayne State University Press, 1997), pp. 163–90; p. 178.

[75] Wenders, *Logik der Bilder*, p. 135.

total fantasy of union, as we cease to see Berlin through the melancholic eye of the angel of history.

Whether as crowning coincidence in the place of coincidences or historical necessity, the allegorical vision also previews the no less euphoric union, under the banner of the *Volk*, that would follow just two years later. The union of the circus angel who might always happen to fall and the fallen angel proper who could once pass through walls seems to foresee what seemed so distant but was in fact so near in 1987: the fall of the Berlin Wall. That critics have found that the euphoria of the scene in the Esplanade has something of the period style and tenor of the fantasies of the fascist era,[76] set as it is in a hotel that was once the haunt of Nazis, may have implications in turn for the mass versions of such euphoria that would be played out in the terrain of what was no-man's land in 1989. Certainly, what the euphoria of this historic fall into union played out in the ruins of the Wall excluded was the sort of ruins of history, the falls of Berlin, that went before and that still rack and divide the post-unification city.

It is the sort of fall that is envisioned by Cassiel as he jumps from the Siegessäule, on the model of the suicidal jump of the young man who wanted to fly from the top of the Europa-Center, which is in its turn modelled on the fall of an aeroplane circling over the city. Cassiel projects another version of the allegory of the angel of history as he beholds in his headlong fall an image-rush described as 'paranoid'.[77] The frantic sequence, seen as the 'fall' of the camera onto the city,[78] takes in views of late 1980s Berlin as a place of isolation, disorientation, and persecution and ends up by slowing into footage of the firestorms of the city at war. This paranoid view of a city never able to escape the ghosts of its history is one alternative to the film's unified ending. Another might be the brief appearance of one of the extras, the extra humans as the Peter Falk character calls them, in the bunker. Against the enraptured proclamations of Damiel and Marion, we might still hear the barely audible inner voice of the young woman having a yellow star sewn to her coat for her role in the film within the film, her gaze averted, and speaking in tongues to give her melancholic view of things: 'It will never change. Es wird sich nicht ändern', followed by 'the same sentence in Hebrew'.[79]

---

[76] See David Harvey, *The Condition of Postmodernity* (Oxford: Blackwell, 1989), p. 321; Kolker and Beicken, *Films of Wim Wenders*, p. 157.

[77] Wenders and Handke, *Der Himmel über Berlin: Ein Filmbuch*, p. 95. In the chronological account, Cassiel, who also fell to earth, was put in an asylum.

[78] *Ibid.*   [79] *Ibid.*, p. 69.

AFTER-IMAGES

In the spring of 1991, there was a major retrospective of Anselm Kiefer's work at the National Gallery in Berlin, which was seen as a corrective to the state of national euphoria after the fall of the Wall. This is counteractive allegorical work, taking possession of the national archive and iconography in order to place, speak, and see it otherwise. A provocative early photographic series by Kiefer was called *Besetzungen* (Occupations (1969)), and his work as a whole can be understood as exposing the cathexes or *Besetzungen* of German psycho-topographies, and mounting strategic counter-occupations. The main hall of the Museum of the Present in the Hamburger Bahnhof, another principal station of Berlin that has stopped, now serving as a focal site in its new cultural landscape, features key works by Kiefer. Stranded in the decommissioned railway hall are several allegorical canvases and installations, each of them heavily freighted with German history, and not least that of the city of Berlin. There is *Volkszählung* (Census (1991)), Kiefer's contribution to the alternative forms of national library that we have already encountered (we recall

10 *Mohn und Gedächtnis* (Poppy and Memory) / *Der Engel der Geschichte* (The Angel of History) and *Volkszählung* (Census), Anselm Kiefer (1989 and 1991), Hamburger Bahnhof.

Ullmann's void under the Bebelplatz): a melancholy structure with illegible books of lead, and set within it a glass polyhedron modelled after Dürer's iconography of Melancholy. This is a transparent version of the melancholic block, a repository enclosing a photographic archive in the form of film-strips, taking account of the living and the dead. We are reminded of the books, photographs, and films that are archived in Wenders' vision of the new State Library, but Kiefer's store of words and images, and his angel of Melancholy, remain virtual, implicit.

The angel appears, reconstructed, in a companion piece to *Volkszählung*, and one that featured in the 1991 exhibition: *Mohn und Gedächtnis* (Poppy and Memory (1989)), also known as *Der Engel der Geschichte* (The Angel of History) (see Figure 10). This is an aeroplane, lined with lead, which projects the suggestion of a hangar into the station, an air museum into the art museum. On its wings are poppy seeds and ledgers of lead, suggesting a version of the 'raisin bombers' that supplied West Berlin in the airlift, but here loaded with a mixed cargo of oblivion and the potential for memory. The poppy seeds, wiping out memory, can also be read as bombs, and the documents as the sort of propaganda material that is dropped from the sky. The seeds in Kiefer's work offer only uncertain prospect for growth. The angel of history carries an ambivalent load on its wings.

A third work, loaned to the museum in 2006, features what could be read as an image of *vanitas* for the glossy new museum of contemporary art, constructed out of the wartime ruins of the old terminus. It carries as title the biblical legend *Grass Will Grow over Your Cities*, written in the sky over a city now levelled to a leaden landscape. On a nearby wall is Kiefer's pronouncement on the human condition and the nature of history, taken from a 1995 interview for *Die Zeit*: rubble is the future because all that is passes.[80] It suggests at once an inevitable ruination of the palaces of the present, structures that will have been, but also the possibility of reclamation of the future out of ruins, which are also subject to the passage of time and may provide the materials for new constructions. Kiefer sees himself as a worker of ruins in this sense. Perhaps the grass that grows over the ruins of cities carries the seeds of hope in a melancholic world vision. It is a dialectic between the damage of the past and prospects for the future, between fall and rise, dystopia and utopia, cultural and natural history, which also characterises the representations of the Walled city from above and below in the literary and film works reviewed in this chapter.

---

[80] Anselm Kiefer, 'Der Mensch ist böse', *Die Zeit*, 3 March 2005.

CHAPTER 6

Berlin marathon: openings and closures

> When I went all out,
> Ran out in Berlin![1]
>
> Else Lasker-Schüler

While the last chapter considered representations of the Walled city in the wake of its great fall, this one explores aspects of the city's cultural topography following the fall of the Wall, embraced by many as a fall into unity and normality, perhaps into innocence. It is the time 'after the Wall', after this exceptional chronotopical imposition,[2] creating the conditions for a newfound freedom of the city. Thus, when Peter Falk returns to the city after unification to take a cameo role in Wenders' *In weiter Ferne, so nah!*, he is able to explore what was the blocked territory of the Eastern part of the city. However, when he asks a taxi driver from the West to take him to Rummelsburg on the Eastern side of the city, the driver is still in the psychotopographic condition of the 'Wall in the head'. While, in Berlin as place of coincidences, the American actor may happen to bear the name of a leading map company, he is stranded in the remapped city. The reopened topography is also subject to new kinds of blocking and disorientation.

Representations of Berlin in film and text after the *Wende* seek to reanimate the pre-war traditions of negotiating the city: the *flânerie* of Benjamin and Hessel and the exploratory, unfettered camerawork of Ruttmann. Authors like Günter Grass in *Ein weites Feld* or Cees Nooteboom in *Allerseelen* continue the epic practice of walking the city and of mapping its cultural archaeology. And filmmaker Thomas Schadt understands his reworking of Ruttmann's *Berlin* as a kind of Berlin marathon.[3] It is a more slow-paced version of the feat

---

[1] Else Lasker-Schüler, *Werke und Briefe: Kritische Ausgabe*, ed. Norbert Oellers *et al.* (Frankfurt am Main: Jüdischer Verlag, 1996–), vol. IV.i, p. 389. See also Webber, 'Inside Out', pp. 158–9.
[2] See, for example, Bodo Morshäuser on the transitional time zones before, during, and 'after the Wall', in his *Liebeserklärung an eine häßliche Stadt: Berliner Gefühle* (Frankfurt am Main: Suhrkamp, 1998), p. 119.
[3] See Schadt, *Berlin: Sinfonie einer Großstadt*, p. 15.

achieved by the title character in Tom Tykwer's *Lola rennt* (Run Lola run) (1998) as marathon woman. Whether walking or running, such explorations are rarely free-flowing, however, invariably characterised by an uncertain compromise between innocence or ignorance and the burdensome knowledge of their surroundings.

This chapter takes as its focus the treatment of space in Berlin films since the *Wende*, asking how this city, so freighted with historical meaning, and yet also subject to clearance of its historical fabric, is figured after unification. The focus of the chapter is on key topographic structures, hinging or blocking the relationship between the inside and outside of urban experience: walls, doors, and windows. Through readings of the representation of these features as framing devices in several films of divergent styles, it will show the special ambivalence attached to the negotiation of both interior and exterior space in the filmic representation of Berlin. What emerges after the historical 'turn' is a cinema apparently divided between entrenchment or return on the one hand and a turn towards new freedom of movement on the other. Whatever their surface mood and character, however, each of these films in fact articulates an ambiguous relationship between these two modes, and the architectural and topographical framing features provide a focus for that double-bind. The second half of the chapter is devoted to more extended readings of two films that, in their running through Berlin, present particularly acute parallel performances of its divided condition between old and new: Kutluğ Ataman's *Lola und Bilidikid* (1999) and Tykwer's *Lola rennt*.

BERLIN: OPEN CITY?

Cinema has played a fundamental role in fashioning Berlin's image and cultural self-understanding throughout the twentieth century and not least since 1989, where film has had much to say about Berlin as crucible for political and cultural upheavals. What emerges after that historical turn at once breaks with the past, responding to a new cultural-political situation, and displays historical continuities in a network of quotations and resonances from earlier film-making, references ranging from the satirical to the nostalgic, the melancholic, and the haunting. Film provides an instrument for gauging how the space of the city has been organised in ideological terms. The marshalling of narrative by the artificial eye of the camera allows film to provide a particularly compelling sense of orientation or disorientation, especially in the complex, interpenetrating space of the city. In Berlin films, this involves scanning the cityscape for its organising features, its points of reference, for what is lost and what is still there. The Wall is the most palpable example of a structure designed to demarcate ideological spaces, keep things in place, and it has provided a focus for a series of films in various genres. It is the most striking feature in a uniquely burdened and contested urban topography, but also represents the special susceptibility of Berlin's buildings and boundaries to dismantling or effacement.

Berlin has been both a stage and a screen for the drama of modern German history. In particular, it provided the setting for the motion pictures relayed around the globe of unification, both as a more or less spontaneous demonstration of people power and as a highly orchestrated form of official spectacle, using the Reichstag and the Brandenburg Gate for its *mise-en-scène*. This film of German unity was designed to counter the memory of Berlin as a stage for the ideological cult spectacles of totalitarian regimes, and yet the redemptive sequel also, inevitably, summons up the earlier versions. The films under discussion here can all be understood as producing active counter-images, alternative footage, to the global block-buster we might call 'Reunification: A Film out of Germany'.

Berlin is a city at once of monumental sites of memory, past structures that remain present and can continue to act as memorials, and of sites of removal or displacement, Huyssen's voids of Berlin. These voids, both physical and ideological, also relate to those spaces that may have buildings and life in them but are effaced from the city in its representative sense: *terra incognita* on the city map, where alternative cultural meanings are pro-duced. Both the voids and these hidden spaces have the potential to act as counter-sites to the official sites or realms of the city's memory. The absent spaces of the cityscape can thus become a medium for coming to terms with and drawing attention to traumas past and present. The films under review here are interested at once in the (filmic) memories attached to Berlin and in exposing the sort of past and present experience that has been and continues to be elided by the master or official narrative of twentieth-century Berlin.

The Wall, an intrusive, monumental structure that was also a void, demarcating no-man's land at the centre of the divided city, is the prime site of memory here. As such, it works in ambivalent ways. On the one hand, it serves as a monumental emblem of containment and blocking; on the other, it provokes creative resistance. The Wall was of course a mon-umental canvas for graffiti and pop art, and it might also be viewed as a kind of film screen, a space for the projection of cultural fantasies about German identities on either side. When Jürgen Böttcher, in *Die Mauer*, projected footage from its history onto the Wall as it was dismantled, he exposed its more general function as screen: a structure of showing and of hiding, of screening off. The pocked and striated surface of the Wall has the effect of appearing before the images projected onto it here, as a veil or partial screen.

Several of the films discussed here revisit the space organised by the Wall to view it more dialectically: to see how there were certain kinds of freedom of movement in its shadow and, conversely, that forms of traumatic containment still operate after its removal. The Wall is metonymically linked here to a series of other boundary structures, whether closed or opened up: walls, doors, and windows. The window as glass wall is an exemplary form, as in the mediation of shots by glass partitions that we saw in Schadt's *Berlin*. These architectural features act as 'transitional objects' in the sense suggested by Henri Lefebvre,[4] borrowing D. W. Winnicott's psychoanalytic term to describe their dual character as opening up to other psycho-topographical spaces but also held in frame. They are cast between fixture and mobility: the potential to hold and organise space, whether positively or negatively, and the negotiation, whether in liberty or at a loss, of the void.

Michael Klier's *Ostkreuz* (1991) concerns the struggle of a young girl, Elfie, to make the money to allow her to move with her mother into a new flat. The film locates itself in a counter-space, off-centre in the post-*Wende* city. It takes its name from a place of intersection on the city's transportation system. For the purposes of the film this site of transit is an allegorical location, representing the condition of people from the East held up at a crossing-point in the city's economic and cultural networks, if not on a sort of urban crucifix. The film opens in an inverted, other space: a space that appears to be a marginal wasteland, but is located at what is designated once more to become the centre of the city. It is the territory without orientation of Wenders' Homer, where the Potsdamer Platz once was and will come to be again. Fringed by semi-derelict *Plattenbauten*, it gives the contemporary viewer who knows the Potsdamer Platz in its reconstructed form the uncanny impression of being elsewhere, in a site created by a topographic transplant from the city's Eastern edge, the hinterland of Ostkreuz or beyond. The erstwhile urban hub, set to be restored, is a place of difficult, stumbling acts of passage and encounter, a perpetual transit camp in the no-man's land between the old East and the West.

Stylistically, the film is marked by short, syncopated sequences, with intrusive cuts and gaps, repeatedly stopping the action, excising sections from the narrative, and subjecting the spectator to estrangement. It follows the Brechtian legacy in the New German Cinema, resisting the lure of

---

[4] Lefebvre, *Production of Space*, p. 209.

identification and aiming to elicit critical viewing. Its aim is to tell a story that would not conventionally be told, to give cinematic life to one of the voided spaces of post-unification Berlin, but to resist tragic or melodramatic cinematic formulas. The film is accordingly shot in a virtually monochromatic style, but not in the sort of black-and-white chic, the 'pseudo-poetry' that the director distrusts.[5] It also resists becoming a postcard film and offering the pleasure of heritage tourism to the viewer, but restricts itself largely to the austerity of the city's wastelands and to the architecture in transit of the containers where Elfie and her mother live. Its style is closest to that of Italian neo-realism, with a particular correspondence to Roberto Rossellini's *Germany Year Zero*, which explores the life that is left in Berlin, reduced to the degree zero, after the war. In *Ostkreuz*, a new form of *Trümmerfilm* or rubble film is shot in the wasteland at the empty centre of post-Cold-War Berlin. While the protagonist of Rossellini's film, Edmund, representing the orphan status of the post-war generation, killed himself by jumping from an opening where there was once a window (an architectonic leitmotif of the film), his namesake in Klier's film is abandoned, but finds some kind of alternative family relationship with Elfie. At the end of the film, Elfie is silhouetted against a window of the derelict building they have occupied together. Having blocked off one window to give themselves protection in their makeshift home, they retain this other empty and open frame on the world outside. It creates the effect of a screen within a screen, with Elfie as spectator, beholding a potential new space for her life's narrative. It remains open whether this *mise-en-abyme* effect frames a forward-looking space or one merely of frozen isolation. Elfie, at least, unlike Rossellini's Edmund, does not close her film by jumping to her death.

In the run-up to this final frame, the camera tracks past a run-down vestige of GDR film culture – the Kino Vorwärts (Forwards Cinema) in Berlin Karlshorst. It is possible that it is in this representative abandoned building that the protagonists take refuge – hence the screening effect of the window at the end; at any rate, it is under its sign. On the one hand this is an ironic acknowledgement of a 'Forwards' ideology that has led nowhere and is now evacuated. As the children pass in front of it, in a forward direction, so a figure in the uniform of the old regime walks past in the other direction. At the same time, and notwithstanding the intrusion of state ideology, DEFA produced, at its best, films to rival the masterworks of Italian neo-realism. And in *Ostkreuz* Klier is also setting an agenda for a new form of cinema, one represented emblematically in the abandoned but potentially

---

[5] Michael Klier, interview in *epd Film*, 8.8 (1991), 3–4; p. 4.

inhabitable architecture of the Kino Vorwärts and that has continuities with those traditions of socially engaged filmmaking.

The closing image of *Ostkreuz*, framed by a window and shot against the light, configuring openness and closure, matches that of Oskar Roehler's film *Die Unberührbare* (The Untouchable (2000)). Here, though, the protagonist, Hanna Flanders, does indeed follow the lead of Rossellini's Edmund. For Roehler, the figure of his mother, the untouchable title figure, serves ambivalent purposes. She joins the ranks of mother figures standing emblematically for the historical experience of Germany, like the one in Helma Sanders-Brahms's allegorical film of Germany at war, *Deutschland bleiche Mutter* (Germany Pale Mother (1979)). In *Die Unberührbare*, the mother is at once a grotesquely overproduced version of the consumer fetishism that she critiques, a woman at war with the world, and a figure of extreme vulnerability, experiencing the scars of German history with a hysterically heightened sense of trauma. She is as much a construction, or spectacle, as the celebration of unification that is broadcast into the opening sequence of the film on her television: she embodies in hyperbolic, allegorical form the condition of a nation that may be deeply scarred and alienated but conceals this in a show of glamorous self-possession.

Roehler's use of black and white as integral to a carefully posed and framed aesthetic is, it seems, elicited by the performance of the title figure. It works anachronistically to show a figure stranded by history, melancholically attached to nostalgia for a lost time and place. For Günter Blamberger, it is the style not only of old films, or of films when they turn to history, but also of a filmic landscape that corresponds to a reduced, monochromatic 'landscape of the soul' in another kind of latter-day *Trümmerfilm*.[6] These two types of ruined landscape and broken topography relate in their turn to the pantomime face of the untouchable protagonist: a study in black and white that records in its restrained mimic effects the anxieties and the pain behind the mummification of the mask. Space, both internal and external, provides the framing structure for this subtly agonised exploration of psychosomatic terrain. Blamberger contrasts this with the colourful, energetic negotiation of the city in *Lola rennt*: the two female performances in and of the post-*Wende* capital, so different in style and scope.[7]

---

[6] Günter Blamberger, '"Zeichen der Freiheit": Notizen zu Oskar Roehlers Film *Die Unberührbare*', in Oskar Roehler, *Die Unberührbare: Das Original-Drehbuch* (Cologne: Kiepenheuer & Witsch, 2002), pp. 155–64; p. 163.
[7] *Ibid.*, pp. 157–8.

The protagonist's status as an exile from historical place and moment means that *Die Unberührbare* is not a Berlin film as such; only its central section is actually set there. But the city – projected in virtual form into the establishing scene – is pivotal as the scene of Flanders' confrontation with Germany present and historical. When Berlin was divided, its polarisation allowed her to live in the West and abhor it by comparison with the East. Now East and West coalesce in a Germany that she cannot call her own and yet which holds a mirror up to her. The parodic mirroring of the Westernised condition of the East Germans in the figure of their critic is displayed in the sight of her stumbling around a wasteland in East Berlin in the masquerade of her cosmetics, wig, and coat by Dior. Dislocated in this other space, she allegorises the fraught historical condition of the reunified city.

Whether enclosed by the insistent framing of the film, not least by the doors and windows of her sequence of temporary domiciles, or stumbling in the open, this figure between doll and mummy, unable to live in the temporal or spatial present, experiences space as *unheimlich*. In her negotiation of internal and external spaces in Berlin, between conditions of claustrophobia and agoraphobia, she is subject to an uncanny sense of displacement, a kind of uneasy local knowledge that is fraught with disorientation and exclusion from community. The telephone kiosk outside the Zoo station represents the two conditions in conjunction: she is at once isolated and surrounded in this structure, which combines openness and closure in an architectural form between window, door, and wall.[8] Her desperate sense of displacement in the city is put on show. Similarly, the shots into the bungalow through closed windows in the opening sequence and elsewhere indicate that the protagonist is placed in separation, screened off. The windows as screens within the film screen are set in relay with the television screen, with an effect of *mise-en-abyme*, suggesting an intrusive form of estrangement. This is repeated in switched form in the point-of-view shot through windows into darkness when she is in East Berlin, described in the screenplay in the language of the uncanny.[9] And in the final scene, this is switched once more into its negative, as it were, as the camera detaches itself from the protagonist's point of view to look through an open window from within, a perspective that is blanked out by intense light.

---

[8] See also the ambiguous use of the telephone kiosk, as public–private communication structure with glass walls, in *Lola rennt*.
[9] Roehler, *Die Unberührbare*, p. 89.

While the dispossessed, the untouchables, of *Ostkreuz* seem to be ready to find a way of surviving what history has done to them, finding some form of relationship and domicile, the uncanny and untouchable Hanna Flanders is more radically alone at the end of her film. She is stripped of her make-up and costume, of the masquerade that she performed in relation to and defiance of the march of German history. A figure whose proper rite of sacrifice would be to fall or jump from the Berlin Wall in a public act of resistance, instead goes to her death in the isolation of a provincial sanatorium. The sequence gravitates between long shots of her isolation in empty space and intense close-up, as she is insistently framed by the uncanny architecture of the sanatorium, its walls and doors, stairs and window. When she tumbles out of the window into the void, her death not only mimics, at a geographical and historical distance, the suicidal self-sacrifice of the young Bönike in *Kuhle Wampe* and Rossellini's Edmund but also one of the forms of Wall-death in the divided Berlin. The figure of uncanny displacement is definitively turned out of her final *un-heimlich* domicile, reenacting – at a further remove – the uncannily compulsive fate of the protagonist in E. T. A. Hoffmann's *Sandmann*.

After the degrees of monochromatic brutalism that characterise the first two films here, we turn to the colourful, all-singing and dancing retrospective of life in East Berlin under the GDR, *Sonnenallee* (2000). The question to be asked of this film is whether it is any more than an exercise in the kind of crass commercialisation of socio-historical experience that is ultimately the death of Roehler's fatally nostalgic Hanna Flanders. Is the version of nostalgia for the GDR it constructs merely a product of what a review article in *Die Zeit* calls the 'nostalgia stall' of recent German film?[10] If, as Hanna responds to the teacher who accosts her in the bar in East Berlin, German and History – the two subjects he teaches – are a 'fatal mixture', how does a comic popular success like *Sonnenallee* deal with that combination? The answer is in another mode of stylised performance: burlesque. For Thomas Brussig, who wrote the screenplay, it is the only appropriate genre for the filming of the GDR.[11] This is comedy in a self-consciously theatrical, almost pantomimic style. It is a film that constantly draws attention to its own constructedness, whether in the stylised performances and set-piece encounters of its characters or in the setting that is prepared for the film. This is effected not least through its focus on artificially constructed communal and domestic spaces, set apart from more expansive urban topographies; the

[10] Katja Nicodemus, 'Unsere kleine Traumfabrik', *Die Zeit*, 28 August 2003.
[11] Leander Haußmann (ed.), *Sonnenallee: Das Buch zum Farbfilm* (Berlin: Quadriga, 1999), p. 12.

English version of the film's title, *Sun Alley*, is nicely wrong in this sense, suggesting the kind of marginal enclosure, the false form of urban top-ography, that is created by the blocking off of the thoroughfare by the Wall. Set, costumes, and props are minutely observed replicas of the original, but they make no pretence of being anything other than simulated, questioning the very idea of the original, as the simulacrum of a simulacrum. The Wall is here a monumental simulation in cardboard, ready to be removed like its historical counterpart when it is needed no more. Like the Berlin Street re-used by Fassbinder, the Babelsberg studio set for the focal scenes of the film will be recycled for the next retro-film that can make use of it.[12]

By insisting on its anti-realistic aesthetic at every turn, the film controls the uncritical pleasures of nostalgia and mockery that it might seem to purvey and that attracted negative comment in many of the reviews of the film. *Sonnenallee* at once trades in *Ostalgie*, the fetishistic nostalgia for the trappings of GDR culture that has developed to industrial proportions over recent years, and subverts it as a method of appropriation of the past. A telling moment in the film is when Micha, the young protagonist, bounding upstairs to the flat of his beloved Miriam, encounters a figure at the door of another flat. This is Winfried Glatzeder, who played Paul in Heiner Carow's DEFA tragicomedy *Die Legende von Paul und Paula* (The Legend of Paul and Paula (1974)). Glatzeder's appearance is on the one hand an act of film-cultural nostalgia, paying homage to DEFA at its finest via a film that could be seen as a model for *Sonnenallee*: a love story surrounded by domestic problems and challenging the tenets of Socialist Realism by adopting the stylised mode of burlesque, with a pop music soundtrack. Like the cultural contraband that circulates in *Sonnenallee*, the film was subject to the censorship of the regime, thus becoming still more of a cult object. At the same time, this staged encounter on the stairs has ironic knowledge of the element of contrivance that the films share. While *Sonnenallee* is shot in a reconstructed studio-set East Berlin of yesteryear, the artifice of the narrative in Carow's film is set against the 'unreal' destruction of the buildings of the past and the construction of new architectures in its 'real' location setting. The reappearance of Paul on the stairs recalls the scene where he is exiled from Paula's apartment and has to break down the door to be with her again, for the time being. Micha may have access to his Miriam, with promise of happiness ever after, but Paula, the Mother Courage of the GDR, was already lost at the end of her film. While *Sonnenallee* may trade

---

[12] The street-scenery was redeployed for Polanski's *The Pianist* (2002) and von Trotta's *Rosenstraße* (2003).

in nostalgia for the old East, it mediates this through critical distance, at once ironic and melancholic.

Sonnenallee is a film in colour, a film indeed that uses colour as if it still had novel appeal, hence the ironic anachronism of the book of the (colour-) film: *Sonnenallee: Das Buch zum Farbfilm*. Haußmann takes the grey that is the requisite colour of his Cold-War Berlin setting and uses it as a foil for heightened colouration, with the *taz* review announcing the end of the GDR in grey.[13] In its ending, however, the colour bleeds out of the film. Its climax, in keeping with the burlesque style, is a full-scale song and dance act, as the inhabitants of the 'shorter end' of the Sonnenallee of the 1970s rehearse the popular overwhelming of the Wall in 1989. The film, however, refuses to enter into the space that the dance routine aims to open up. Micha and Wuschel enact their version of the leap from the window or balcony that is part of the traumatic history of the Wall. The leap seems to transcend at once the fatal jumping and falling that informed the relationship between window and Wall and the blocking that characterised the walled-up windows of the border area. What they leap into, however, is not the light that opens up through the window-frame at the end of the other two films, but a grey void, a set that is emptied of its final theatre as the camera withdraws from it with its back to the West. The 'colour-film' turns to grey, to the ironic strains of the pop-song 'Du hast den Farbfilm vergessen' (You've forgotten the colour-film), suggesting that the formal aesthetic of the film, the mode of fantasy it has constructed, is bound up with unreliable memory. The exposure of an abandoned film-set, complete with tumble-weed, as the camera withdraws to the other side of the Wall, casts the process of Westernising as a move into the generic territory of the Western in a haunted form. It mounts a reversal of the fantastical transformation of Wenders' *Der Himmel über Berlin*, when the angel falls into colour film on the Western side of the Wall. At the end of *Sonnenallee*, the sober aftermath to the burlesque of nostalgia is the depopulated spectacle of melancholy.

This ambivalent treatment of the memory of the GDR, part false memory in the nostalgia generated by a new memory industry, part insistently traumatic and melancholic, also prevails in the hybrid structure and mood of Wolfgang Becker's *Good Bye, Lenin!* (2003). The combination of popular appeal and more critical edge there is already at work in his earlier film, *Das Leben ist eine Baustelle* (Life is a Building-Site (1997)). Indeed, there is a wry signature of continuity between them in the supermarket

---

[13] Christiane Kühl, 'Endlich Schluß mit Grau! DDR in Farbe', *taz*, 7 October 1999.

chicken that reappears in *Good Bye, Lenin!* as a grotesque embodiment of survivalist strategies in the consumer networks of the city between slaughterhouse and hypermarket. *Das Leben ist eine Baustelle* is perhaps the ultimate film of Berlin in the years of reconstruction following the *Wende* (with many of the interiors themselves reconstructed in the abandoned McNair barracks in Lichterfelde). Building-sites and refurbishments are a constant feature of the film, and always also representing reconstruction on other than physical levels. As Buddy remarks as he and Jan cross that most time-honoured of places of urban flux and searching, the Alexanderplatz: 'You can paint the walls ('Wände') differently, but you can't get rid of the memories.' The adage is nicely open to an alternative reading, a punning version of the speaking otherwise that we have seen operating at that place: the replacement of the symbolic 'Wände' of more localised reconstruction projects with the national reconstruction project of the *Wende*, which may also be painted in different ways but will remain unsettled by the past. Reconstruction in 'Building-site Berlin' is shadowed by memories of what went before. The reunified city presents itself as a place of progress, but the film is interested in those left behind in a more uncertain condition.

Das Leben ist eine Baustelle is a film about possibilities of relationship, between inhabitants of the city under construction, and between its past and present states. It moves between the domestic spaces of the city, its kitchens and bedrooms, and more public ones. Like *Ostkreuz*, it is a film about dislocation and the quest for a place to be at home in the city. The condition of displacement in both internal and external space is an ambivalent one, at once marked by the estrangement of urban exile and supporting the possibility for new encounter. The condition is figured topographically by the film's negotiation of urban space. The beginning of the film establishes a model for this: outside on the street a riot is being put down by the police, while inside Jan is having sex in a bedroom. In the intimate domestic scene he finds only alienation, while in the brutal street-scene he finds intimacy. The move between the two is figured by matching shots of windows and doors. As the lover he leaves looks from inside through the window onto the street, we see Jan standing on an underground train and the glazed door closing as he moves off on the transport system. When he is on the run from the police with the woman he literally bumps into, he is found hiding in somebody else's flat; and now he holds the broken glazed door of the shower cubicle, a nakedly ineffectual response to the riot-shields held by the police. The visual matching introduces us to a film about the search for a habitable space, and the broken door of the shower is a comic emblem of structures of access and enclosure, social and domestic, which provide no protection and transparently need mending.

Jan's transportation by the underground between these two flats in which he cannot be at home indicates its role in the film as a system of linkage but also of isolation and disjuncture between the different sites of the city. Relationships in the city, encounters and chases, are mediated and also blocked or frustrated by the transport system, and underground and tram serve a leitmotif function here. Not for nothing is the first date of Jan and Vera in an underground station: he appears to have missed her, but she makes a connection by a personal take-over of the public address system. The film bears the imprint of its screenwriter Tom Tykwer, a rehearsal for *Lola rennt* in its attachment to the idea of chance as a peculiar dimension of the filmed city. The transport network embodies at once regulation and chance, a system of sliding doors. Chance has it, for instance, that the itinerant Kristina is almost knocked down by what becomes her adoptive family in Berlin.

The near miss here, like the accidents that happen or narrowly fail to happen in *Lola rennt*, is an indication of the potential trauma in the system, in traffic, but also in the traffic between people. HIV/AIDS haunts the film as a contagion that circulates in the city; not for nothing does Jan encounter both an AIDS victim reduced to begging and his ex-lover Moni, apparently now also HIV-positive, in an underground train. The networks of sexual relations, intimate and passionate or more routine, also carry the subterranean possibility of infection. Berlin in the nineties is a city seen as under plague conditions. Jan and Vera pass a hoarding – one of the many improvised walls blocking the space of 'Building-site Berlin'– with the graffiti slogan, 'Die Liebe in den Zeiten der Kohl-Ära' (Love in the Time of Kohl-Era). It is a subversive appropriation of the *Baustelle* as *Schaustelle* or 'building-site-seeing' logic, creating visual effects against the grain of the official spectacle. While the Wall and its graffiti are now dismantled, this mock wall provides a canvas for new forms of resistance and provocation; the slogan is clearly designed to suggest both the real fear of the HIV virus and the life-and-death struggle for love under the political conditions, diagnosed as pathological, of the reunified Berlin.

At its end, Becker's film is reminiscent of the ending of *Ostkreuz*, with the members of an alternative family, their status and relationships uncertain, in a bright icy scene set apart from the recognisable topography of Berlin. More particularly, the closing scene of skating on a frozen pond is a quotation from another film altogether, the provocative 1981 film on the Berlin gay-scene, Frank Ripploh's *Taxi zum Klo* (Taxi to the Loo). While

Becker's is a resolutely heterosexual buddy film, it thus carries a sort of memorial at its end to Berlin as a city providing unusual liberties for other sexualities. The promiscuous vitality of *Taxi zum Klo* is as it were a victim of the virus remembered here. The final scene of *Das Leben ist eine Baustelle* is thus, like the film as a whole, suspended between vitality and community and a more melancholic, death-touched modality.

RUN LOLAS RUN

The end of *Das Leben ist eine Baustelle* also provides a link to the next film, with a different take on marginal inhabitants of Berlin, Kutluğ Ataman's *Lola und Bilidikid*. Here too, existences at the margins of the new Berlin are enabled by the continuation of one of the city's key traditions, not least in filmic terms, that of performance. But just as Buddy's crooning mixes nostalgia with melancholy, the acts of performance in Ataman's film are ambivalent in their implications. Ataman is interested in the crossing of two of Berlin's subcultures, Turkish and gay, which converge in the transgender Turkish cabaret culture in Kreuzberg. All the characters in the film are engaged in acts of performance in relation to the requirements of the dominant culture. Performance is here best understood in the way that is theorised by Judith Butler: in its model form, the drag act, performance is seen at once as an opportunity for challenging the rule of heterosexist culture and yet as an act that is substantially conditioned by the terms of that culture. It at once exposes and partakes in the melancholic condition of always failing to achieve a personally adequate performance. Ataman's work, in film and video, is constantly preoccupied by drag acts of one kind or another – whether transgender or what can be called ethnic drag – the imitative performances that are played out by minority cultures in relation to majority ones. When the group of Turkish drag artistes, the 'Gastarbeiterinnen' (Female Guest-workers), perform their versions of migrant women living in Berlin, they are exposing at once the masquerade of femininity and that of ethnic otherness. Ataman sees the performance of identity as tightly prescribed and melancholically conditioned, but also explores possibilities for subjects to take control of their performances and counter the normative.

Lola und Bilidikid announces in its title another kind of crossing, that of two film genres, the musical with its performance of femininity as a stage act (following cabaret acts from Marlene Dietrich as Lola Lola in the Weimar classic *Der blaue Engel* (The Blue Angel (1930)) to Fassbinder's *Lola* (1981)) and the Western, with the young gay Turks like Bilidikid compensating for their unacceptable sexuality by playing out hyberbolic forms of masculinity. While the film certainly derives pleasures from the allure and swagger of these two alternative forms of performance, it ultimately questions their viability as modes of survival. Both of the title figures are sacrificed in their masquerade roles. While the end of the film appears to show the potential for performing more freely, that this freedom is vulnerable is shown in a key scene. Here, the film revisits one of Berlin's sites of memory, the Olympic Stadium, and mounts a parodied form of the racist and masculinist supremacy cult of 1936, as three of the young protagonist Murat's classmates first enact a performance of their version of Nazi ideology and then queer-bash him in the stadium toilets. The scene is an example of how the film explores counter-spaces, scenes behind doors and walls – here the monumental walls of the Nazi arena – providing alternative spaces to perform. Ataman conceives the film through a dual topography, gravitating between the overground world and the underground: an ambivalent, covert world, which has spaces at once for alternative, liberating forms of identity performance and for the abject spectacle of xenophobic and homophobic violence.

The urban performances of *Lola und Bilidikid* will be read here in conjunction with those of a much better known film, and one that has taken on an emblematic character for the fashionable image of post-*Wende* Berlin: *Lola rennt*. In another key sequence from *Lola und Bilidikid*, the iconic figure of Tykwer's Lola that has run around the world as an allegorical representative of the New Berlin is deployed in a different form, mocked up by the young Turkish protagonist, in drag and wearing a red wig, on the run from a group of queer-bashers. While Tykwer's Lola runs in an elaborate, metaphysically inclined game of chance, Ataman's version, for all its indulgence in drag performance and melodrama, is running for life or death in a more real, political sense. It is a performance that reiterates that of another Lola: Lasker-Schüler, the exponent of ethnic and transgender drag, on the streets of Berlin as city of cabaret. The reading of both films here extends my analysis elsewhere of Lasker-Schüler's strategies of performance in Berlin, combining and complicating categories of ethnicity, gender, and sexuality.[14] At the end of her time in Berlin, Lasker-Schüler, running for her life, reaches the limits of her performance. And while Tykwer's Lola may be given the ability to run in the way that women never do in film, it is a performance which is undone by the end of the film and the restoration of her man to the requisite position of agency, walking by her side, where he belongs, along the street.

---

[14] See Webber, 'Inside Out'.

The Lola performances to be considered here are a revision not just of conventional female roles but specifically of a key tradition of female masquerade, as screened by Josef von Sternberg or Fassbinder. Their Lolas are women who achieve degrees of agency in their destinies, but always through their fixed and commodified role as stage artists. Ataman's Lola appears to revive the Berlin cabaret tradition, in a hybridised Turkish form that challenges both race laws and gender regulations. This Lola puts the figure back on the stage designed for her, but only in order radically to question the established heterosexual model of female performer and male gaze. This also means mobilising the generic hybridity that is indicated in the film's title. The cabaret film meets the Western here, and thus two gendered models of spectacular performance, the one female, enclosed, and static, the other male, open, and dynamic, are set against each other. And out of this engagement, the binary logic of gender difference upon which they rely is put into question. While cabaret can feature in Westerns as a distraction for the male gaze within and upon the films, offering a hyperbolically feminised supplement to the hyperbolically homosocial world of the genre, here a queered version of that gender model is established.

To make Lola run is to animate the cabaret act, turning theatre into sport in the open. In *Lola rennt* it is the pursuit of a goal in a contest with the clock, in *Lola und Bilidikid* a pursuit to the death of a figure marked as other in ethnic terms and queer in gender and sexual terms. By subjecting its protagonist to an ordeal of gender performance in the Olympic Stadium as theatre of sport, *Lola und Bilidikid* invokes a different genealogy from cabaret or Western films. Since Leni Riefenstahl's films of the 1936 Olympics, the stadium has become an intrinsically cinematic site, a site of filmic memory and of a spectacular inaugurating moment in the genre of the sports film. Just as these new Lola films redefine the cabaret acts of the earlier ones, so the racing performances of their title figures redefine the logic of the Olympic site. Tykwer's Lola runs free from the historically laden sites of Berlin on a course that seems designed not to bring the city's twentieth-century past into play. The film's technologically driven synchronic layering virtually cuts out the dimension of cultural memory. In particular, Lola's Olympian feat never takes her to the heroic place and architecture designed for the display of such epic achievements; she runs her three-leg marathon largely on streets designed to stage the everyday. Ataman's Lola does not enter the Olympic Stadium either, but the brother who comes to perform her in the film's denouement does. His Olympic experience is, however, as we shall see, a radical counter-performance to those established by Riefenstahl.

Ataman's film crosses categories of identity. The binary logic that seeks to control the positions of self-same and other in the domains of ethnicity, gender, and sexuality is exposed where these become confused with each other. This is focused on an exemplary figure of dissimulation: the macho Turkish man who sleeps with Turkish men and German prostitutes, both dressed in forms of female drag, behind the back of a wife who is confined to another, domestic masquerade of femininity. In one variation of this figure, Murat's older brother Osman, he can both 'play the Turk' as an act of comedy, an Orientalised demotic speaker of German, and 'play the Turk' as an act of coercion in his imposition of patriarchal authority in a culture where the role is marked as foreign, where Turkish men compensate for ethnic discrimination by reverse-discrimination against German men seen as effeminised. The film's drag-performers act to expose the hypocrisy of men who want to have it both ways: the cabaret performance of feminine masquerades through ethnic stereotypes is above all directed at their male counterparts. The stage act of the 'Gastarbeiterinnen' combines gender drag with 'ethnic drag' and shows the collusion of the two orders.[15]

The transvestite cabaret of ethnic difference in *Lola und Bilidikid* can be compared to that analysed by Butler in her *Bodies that Matter*, through Jennie Livingston's film *Paris is Burning*, which focuses on the drag balls mounted by transgender black and Latino performers in Harlem.[16] In her reading of the film, Butler seeks to correct the critique of bell hooks, who had seen the drag performances as a misogynist aping of heterosexist positions and the film as colluding in racial and gender subjection. Butler wants to see the drag performances rather as ambivalent, at once an appropriation of heteronormative logic and working towards its subversion. This dialectic opens up for Butler a certain space for bypassing the violence of racial and sexual subjection, but it also shows how that space is repeatedly brought back to the need to pass, to conform to the interlocked norms of race, class, gender, and sexuality. The death of drag artist and prostitute Venus Xtravaganza, apparently at the hands of a client, is thus put down to her failure to achieve a total act of passing as woman. To resist the rule of subjection is to risk the vengeful violence of abjection.

The drag act of *Lola und Bilidikid* is also deeply ambivalent in Butler's sense. Ataman's understanding of identity in this film, as in such video work

---

[15] See also Katrin Sieg, 'Ethnic Drag and National Identity: Multicultural Crises, Crossings, and Interventions', *The Imperialist Imagination: German Colonialism and its Legacy*, ed. Sara Friedrichsmeyer *et al.* (Ann Arbor: University of Michigan Press, 1998), pp. 259–319.

[16] Judith Butler, *Bodies that Matter: On the Discursive Limits of 'Sex'* (New York/London: Routledge, 1993), pp. 121–40.

as *Women Who Wear Wigs* (1999),[17] follows the fundamental structure of performativity as construed by Butler, a form of 'speech act' which is subject to rigorous and injurious prescription but also open to strategies of resignification. As he puts it: 'Identity is a dress that other people put on you … but then talking is a form of rebellion.'[18] What Ataman does in *Lola und Bilidikid* is to organise the resignification of identity through the mode of melodrama, which in its classic form, in the so-called 'women's films' of the 1950s, served to fix the suffering caused by the straightening of sexual and gender identities. Ataman's project is to resignify the generic specifications of melodrama, to transfer the women's film into a form where the women who wear wigs may or may not be biologically female, where gender is open to more mobile forms of reconstruction.

The core tension of the film's melodrama is the impossible demand at once to appropriate and to rebel against hegemonic norms. The macho Bili thus requires the impossible of Lola: that she should actually be a woman, pass totally into the heterosexual family, rather than ostentatiously by-passing that structure in her queer performance of styles of femininity. The demand is as impossible for Lola, who wants to be a man in a gay relationship, as it is for the deluded Bili, who needs this too but desires otherwise. In the denouement of the film, when Bili castrates one of the youths he takes to be responsible for Lola's death, he merely mimes the sort of violence which led to the mutilation and killing of Venus Xtravaganza. He cannot make Lola have the operation or take a knife to her himself so that she will become a woman he could never really desire, and he exacts the castration he wanted of her from her putative killer.

Yet the film is not contained by this violent double bind; it rather develops in terms of ambivalence in Butler's sense. While it certainly produces spectacles of abjection, it also opens up alternative spaces, unlikely relationships and communities. The abject takes as its site the darkened and underground spaces of the city, deserted noir-style streets and buildings, and not least the toilet as a recurrent site of sex. In the establishing scene, we encounter Berlin in a key site of memory, under the sign of the iconic winged angel of victory on the Siegessäule. The imperialist icon, which was appropriated from above by Wenders for his angels, is here re-appropriated as a figure of aegis over the nocturnal cruising grounds around the column,

---

[17] The four-channel piece *Women Who Wear Wigs* represents the speech acts of four Turkish women who wear wigs for political, sexual, theatrical, or medical reasons. Another work, *It's a Vicious Circle* (2002) reconstructs the performances required of a black man in Berlin.

[18] Ataman in interview with Nira Ratnam in *The Observer*, 29 December 2002.

which has been counter-colonised by the Berlin gay scene.[19] A new, potentially liberating world is opened up to the young Murat, but one that is shot in the generic style of horror (with lightning flashes and looming figures) and experienced as dark, disorientating, and threatening.

The establishing shot marks this out as a Berlin film and also points towards the film's dual topography. The iconic architecture of the city's imperial memory is crosscut with more obscure, subcultural spaces, which give evidence of a persistent state of cultural imperialism and colonisation. While the opening shot might seem to set the film in the genre of the postcard movie, it proceeds to deconstruct the postcard image.[20] The film is established through its split into upper world and underworld, working along a double axis. The divided city Berlin is conducive to this topographic doubling. As a place of segregation, destruction, and renewal, Berlin provides the ideal split 'stage' for the film's performances of division and transformation.[21] The river performs the symbolic function of marking this separation and flux.[22] The dualism is also incorporated into the cinematic styling: 'In the underworld, the camera is all frantic, hand-held and in gritty, true colours, while the upper world is more ordered.'[23] The relation between the spaces and their respective formal signatures is, however, dialectically complicated: 'sometimes, the two worlds go into each other so that a dolly shot suddenly becomes hand-held'.[24] The underworld level corresponds to the upper on something like the model of the Foucauldian heterotopia, a counter-site in which the sites of culture are 'simultaneously represented, contested, and inverted'.[25] In the film, over-ground figures, both human and topical, regularly go underground in states of inversion.

The scenes shot in the Olympic Stadium, a deserted master-site of memory, display this heterotopian organisation of city space. Ataman turns from the panoptically organised site of spectacle in Riefenstahl's marshalling of the stadium as heroic film set and goes into its underside. The stadium as site of spectacle serves as a foil of epic scale to the intimate stage of the cabaret club, both arenas for the performance of Butlerian ambivalence. Both sites of open display are shown to incorporate a more

---

[19] The Berlin gay magazine *Siegessäule* cheekily appropriates the column as a communal gay erection.
[20] In his interview on the DVD, the production designer, John de Minico, stresses that the film resists the postcard or documentary modes of city filming.
[21] As described by Ataman in interview on the DVD.   [22] As Ataman told me.
[23] Ataman in interview: http://www.german-cinema.de/magazine/1998/01/prodreport/4-produkt_E. html.
[24] *Ibid.*   [25] Foucault, 'Of Other Spaces', p. 24.

hidden form of spectacle, a version of the closet.[26] As Bili, the unfaithful 'husband', went behind the scenes at the cabaret club while Lola was performing on stage as 'Gastarbeiterin', first to be given oral sex and then to brutalise the man who fails to pay the price, so the spectacle mounted in the spectatorial void of the Olympic Stadium leads into a closet scene in the toilets which mimics the earlier one. What the two scenes show is that the prescribed spectacle, whether on the sub-cultural stage or in the super-cultural arena, contains by implication the repressive logic of the closet.

Taking the Berlin Olympic Stadium as a paradigm, Henning Eichberg has argued that stadiums are constructed according to a dual model: their dominant logic is that of the pyramid, built up towards an exalted specta-torial position, in relay with the eye of God at the apex of the pyramid. Here, this position is adopted by the tribune of the *Führer* as focal point in the axial organisation of the complex, the viewing platform for the dis-ciplinary and consecrating gaze of what Susan Sontag calls the 'Super-Spectator'.[27] At the same time, Eichberg argues, the pyramid is constructed upon and sustained by a labyrinthine underground. The burial chamber provides the model for cryptic spaces that subtend the spectacular super-structure. In the case of the Berlin stadium, the panoptical fantasy is staged by the use of searchlights, vaulting over the structure as a 'cathedral of light', and by the incorporation of the camera as a metaphorical cannon, trained on every move in the first televised games.[28] The Reich Sports Field, designed by Werner March, with the close involvement of Hitler and his court architect, Albert Speer, was conceived within the sacralised ideological framework of the 'World Capital Germania'. It can be understood as a defining site in the cultic enactment of false state and race memory that Paul Connerton has seen as a key feature of the Nazi regime.[29] Like Speer's 'cathedral of light' projected over the Nuremberg rally-ground, as described by Paul Virilio, it is a composite architecture of stone and light designed as a theatre of dreams.[30] It was an arena for display of the total power of the imperial state, not least a ritual arena of war, complete with a monumental

---

[26] An intermediary film is Szabó's *Mephisto* (1981), after the 1936 novel by Klaus Mann, where the Gustav Gründgens figure as court player to the Nazi regime and sexual masquerader is exposed in the spotlights of the stadium.

[27] Susan Sontag, 'Fascinating Fascism', *Under the Sign of Saturn* (New York: Farrar, Straus and Giroux, 1980), pp. 73–105; p. 87.

[28] Henning Eichberg, 'Stadium, Pyramid, Labyrinth: Eye and Body on the Move', *The Stadium and the City*, ed. John Bale and Olof Moen (Keele: Keele University Press, 1995), pp. 323–47; pp. 324–5.

[29] Paul Connerton, *How Societies Remember* (Cambridge: Cambridge University Press, 1989), pp. 41–3.

[30] Paul Virilio, *The Vision Machine*, trans. Julie Rose (Bloomington/Indianapolis: Indiana University Press, 1994), p. 11.

parade ground and a hall consecrated to a death-cult of the fallen heroes of Germany. It thus functioned as a key site for the travesty of Olympian spectacle which Walter Benjamin, in his *Work of Art* essay, sees in the specular performance of the rituals of fascism (WB I.ii 469), taking over the topography of his home city as *Schauplatz* for its aestheticisation of politics.

A key contribution to this aestheticisation was of course made by Riefenstahl's films, which incorporate cinema as the spectacular medium of light into the architecture of stone and light. The cameras orchestrated by her made of the stadium an outdoor broadcast studio, a film theatre for a panoptical artificial eye with an unprecedented mobility, range, and control.[31] As the stadium uses hyper-modern structural technology clad in the rock of ages, so the film seeks to achieve a sense of a timeless penetration of space, a total presence, by effacing the technology that serves that effect. What it aims to achieve is the kind of pre-modern auratic effect which Benjamin sees as superseded by mass media technology, harnessing it to the mass sports and political events for which those media are mobilised (WB I.ii 467). It cultivates a simultaneous effect of intimate proximity and monumental distance, of specular viewing only through awe-struck subjection to the total power of the spectacle. In its hold on time and space, the film relays the desire to make the historical moment mythical, to raise the stadium as one-off site of an international festival to a sacred national place of eternal return. Filmed through the lens of myth (not least through the Apollonian capture of the sun over the cauldron), the *stadium* as spatial and temporal 'stage' is sublimated into a chronotopical site of totality.

As the stadium is constructed as a false memorialisation of the imperial German nation as heir to the suprematist myth of the Greeks, so the film is introduced by a metamorphosis of the memorial sculpture of Greek myth into the living body of contemporary Germany. If the panoptical film seems to achieve a mythical reach, however (and thereby to install itself as something of a film myth), it is also strategically blinded in its unswerving dedication to the surface of the spectacle, its official appearance, to the exclusion of historical truths. In its blind-spot are the acts of repression which enabled that spectacle: most notably the banning of Jews from German sporting institutions and the proposals to bar black competitors as the 'slave race' from this ritual co-opted by the Nordic master race from their adopted antecedents, the Ancient Greeks. In the event, the colour bar was lifted, and black athlete Jesse Owens famously became the key player in the theatrical agon of the sporting contest. While Riefenstahl's camera

---

[31] See Taylor Downing, *Olympia* (London: BFI, 1992).

records the act of cultural false memory in the ideological passing of the torch from Greece to Germany, it also comes to be fascinated by the sporting mastery of the 'slave' race. While the Nazis sought to remove the evidence of the Nuremberg race laws, the public baiting of Jews, from the streets of Berlin in preparation for the Olympics, the repressed returns at the centre of the spectacle.

Parallel to this exposure of the racial double bind is a sexual one. The persecution of Jews went hand in hand with the draconian enforcement of Paragraph 175 of the penal code, outlawing homosexual acts. Yet in the run-up to the Olympics, the regime saw that part of the tourist image of Berlin which had to be reconstructed around the games was the notorious sexual licence of Weimar cabaret culture. The official spectacle of the new Reich required the unofficial, and not least the queer, attractions of Berlin as side-show or counter-spectacle. Himmler ordered that several gay bars should be reopened and that 'foreign gentlemen' should not be arrested for transgression of Paragraph 175 without his express permission.[32] Implicit in this move was also an unknowing recognition of the homoerotic element in the logic of the sporting spectacle (as also in the logic of the National Socialist organisation),[33] a lure at once for sports and for sex tourists. The appropriation of the Greek festival of sporting combat also involved an incorporation of the 'Greek love' that was officially anathema to the regime. The pastiche of Greek figures in the sculptures installed around the stadium complex (in particular, pairs of heroically fashioned male figures in attitudes of sporting camaraderie) gives evidence of the queer potential involved in the homosocial embrace between Greek and German cultures. The metamorphosis of the sculptural form into the living in the prologue of the first film is particularly potent in this respect: the chaste sculptures of goddesses introduce the same function for the naked female form in the callisthenic interludes later in the film. The two male forms featured at the end of the sequence – the lubricious, openly reclining Barberinian faun and Myron's discus thrower – are both, on the other hand, highlighted as if with body-oil.[34] Their sensuality is recaptured in the scenes of swimming and showering in the prologue to the second film, where the glistening male bodies are entwined in frame, engaging in mutual massaging and beating with twigs.

[32] See David Clay Large, *Berlin: A Modern History* (London: Allen Lane, 2001), p. 295.

[33] See Hilmar Hoffmann, *Mythos Olympia: Autonomie und Unterwerfung von Sport und Kultur* (Berlin/ Weimar: Aufbau, 1995), p. 129.

[34] The hybrid species of the faun subverts the eugenic model established by the other Classical sculptures, prefiguring the physical appeal of the black athletes later in the film.

As the black athlete rebounds on the spectacle designed to marginalise him, so the ideological abjection of homosexuality is bound up with its return in alternative forms.

Ataman's cinematic return to the Olympic Stadium can be seen against this context of the repressions which haunt the official film of the official spectacle. Riefenstahl's panoptical style, which extends to the intimate behind-the-scenes sauna and showering shots, is rejoined here by Ataman's provocatively underground take on the stadium. Murat and his classmates, amongst them the three queer-bashers, are taken on an educational outing to the stadium, accompanied by a listless commentary on National Socialist architectural politics from their apathetic teacher. The three thugs, one sporting a hairstyle slicked down in the fashion of Hitler, take over the key ritual structure of the stadium, the cauldron, in a travestied performance of national supremacy at the apex of the pyramid. The sequence is shot in mock-epic style, adopting the same sort of aerial perspectives as Riefenstahl. When Murat joins them, he is abused as a 'camel-fucking' Turk, only for him to suggest, in what Butler would call the resignification of the injurious speech act, that one of the thugs is the camel looking for a fuck. This logic of the neo-fascist as closet queer is indeed exploited in the film, and when another member of the trio enters the toilets in the labyrinthine underside of the arena, Murat follows him. The toilets are heterotopian in the proper sense, the cryptic other space of inversion to which the film repeatedly returns. It is public and yet covert, a place for the encoded display of desire, its graffiti providing anti-iconic counter-texts and -images to the inscriptions and sculpted bodies which help ideologically to orchestrate the official space of the stadium. The camera is now handheld in the tight 'closet' space of the toilet, giving an intimate and tender close-up of a kiss between Murat and his classmate. As they start to have oral sex they are interrupted by the other two, who brutalise Murat, before their closeted friend makes a show of urinating over him.

The sequence shows how the ritual space of the stadium, designed for spectacular performance under the sacrificial flame, relies on secreted scenes of both covert desire and brutal abjection. The racial and sexual others which are abjected by the Nazis return to be abjected once more by neo-Nazis in a ritual of humiliation in this key site of collective memory. While Riefenstahl's spectacle is elaborately sanitised, organised around the focal figure of the hygienic body, whether in the arena or the showers, in *Lola und Bilidikid* the golden shower is a travesty enactment of the fascist ideology of hygiene and pollution, redolent of the grotesque interlinking of ritual cleansing and filthy brutality in the death camps. The camp which, following Agamben, has superseded the city as base model of modernity, is concealed here in the metropolitan arena.

From this scene of abjection, the film moves to the recuperative domestic rite of the bathing of Murat by his mother and a release of the truth hidden in the family home. As in Livingston's *Paris is Burning*, motherhood and sibling relations, both biological and adoptive, serve as a corrective to violence and exploitation between men across ethnic, sexual, class, and gender lines. The film ends with Murat's mother emancipating herself from Osman's authority, casting off her headscarf in a gesture which complements the donning of the wig by her other two sons. And in the *ancien régime* villa of the film's other mother figure, an upper-class matriarch, a scene is put together which counters the abjection of the sequence in the stadium. The wealthy German son, Friedrich, and the posturing Turkish hustler, Iskender, here find a space for an embrace with more utopian possibilities. As – 'incidentally' – an architect, Friedrich is participating in the post-unification reconstruction and reinvention of another key site of Berlin memory, the ideologically and architecture-historically contested area of the divided city between the Alexanderplatz and the Schlossplatz. His model for the rede-signing of this site is in the bedroom of the villa, and after a night of passion he and Iskender tumble over and wreak havoc upon it, bringing down another of Berlin's iconic structures, the bulbous TV Tower, in the process. In model form, the oversized queer bodies take over the key civic space, enacting a domestic, alternative reclamation of the streets, their own private Christopher Street Day Parade. Their playful display of an unath-letic, Turko-German form of the Olympic discipline of Graeco-Roman wrestling serves as a queer cooption of the dominant logic of sporting display and of the organisation of urban space. If the scene in the stadium stages an abject version of contact and combat between the German body and the ethnically other around queerness, here a counter-version is staged in the scaled-down architectural arena of another of Berlin's hyperbolic sites of memory.

In her essay 'Fascinating Fascism', devoted largely to Riefenstahl, Susan Sontag has noted how the fascist aesthetic has lent itself to camp treatment, suggesting a potentially dangerous accommodation.[35] In *Lola und Bilidikid*, camp, as embodied by the sisterhood of drag artists on the one hand and the aristocratic self-styling of Friedrich and his mother on the other, serves as a more resistant response to the return of fascism. It allows the film to finish with a recuperative return to its beginning and a renewed reclamation

[35] Sontag, 'Fascinating Fascism', p. 97.

of the imperial topography of Berlin under the sign of performative resignification, in Butler's sense. This is, for Ataman, Berlin the transvestite, a city that is constantly cross-dressing, reinventing and replaying itself.[36] The epilogue starts with a citation of perhaps the best-known queer book on Berlin, Isherwood's cabaret text *Goodbye to Berlin*, as two of the transvestite sisters bid what appears to be a purely rhetorical farewell to the city. They take the film back to the Siegessäule, in full costume and daylight, flirting with the taxi-driver as they play out their own version of Berlin Christopher Street Day or Love Parade. Here they perform a victory pageant right at the city's centre, in a space without walls that has been appropriated in their different ways by both Turkish and gay cultures. The taxi, which had been part of the film's system of oppression, constraining the lives of Turks in Berlin, becomes a vehicle for a more open negotiation of the city, with clear windows on the world and doors that open where the passengers wish. In its performative revisiting of Berlin's topography of terror, *Lola und Bilidikid* thus achieves something like *Paris is Burning* in Butler's account, finding 'occasional spaces' in which 'annihilating norms' can be 'mimed, reworked, resignified.'[37]

MARATHON WOMAN

As we have seen, Berlin is a city with a particular mythology, and this rests not least in its function as film-city, a one-time world centre of film production and an ongoing site for film scenarios. The cinema has served as a prime register of the city's mythologies, from the Berlin films of the Weimar period, and the Babylonian city-outside-the-city of the Babelsberg (literally Babylon Hill) studios, via Cold-War thrillers, to the cutting-edge contemporary style of the Berlin School. Mythologies always have a tendency to resist historical change, to posit themselves as timeless, notwithstanding the evidence of history – in the case of Berlin the transitory succession of empires which have contested control over the city in the twentieth century. Berlin is a site of mythical projections, but also, and in tension with this, its topography is intensely marked by the particular processes of its history.

The discussion here of *Lola rennt*, the film which put post-*Wende* Berlin back onto the international screen-map, is focused on this relation between mythology and history. The film plays with the conventional stations and

---

[36] This is how Ataman described the city's transformations to me.
[37] Butler, *Bodies that Matter*, pp. 124–5.

monstrous obstacles of mythical quest structures, as ironically introduced by the voice of Hans Paetsch, the narrator of fairy tales as 'administrator of myths'.[38] It is an archetypal story-line produced with new means; as Tykwer has it, the quest for the grail with 100,000 Marks as its object.[39] With its tortoise, its blind seer, its Cerberus, its Cyclops, its sirens, its Charybdis, and its Circe, it is a film that is figured more particularly as a reconstruction of Classical myth-narratives, not least as a mock version of Homer's quest epic, *The Odyssey*.[40] While the film relates to a model form of grand narrative, it does so in a way that is eclectic and synthetic; in *Lola rennt* the *topoi* of archaic mythology are syncretised with a multilayered, fast-forward picture of urban modernity.

Tykwer's film emerged at a time when German film was freeing itself from the often morbid attachment to history which was the legacy of the New German Cinema of the seventies and eighties. The post-*Wende* comedies and thrillers are generally prepared to release themselves from the need to frame their pictures with the historical attachment to the Nazi period and to follow more international guidelines. German film culture is now figured as *Baustelle*, as a site of new constructions, and nowhere does this apply more closely than to '*Baustelle* Berlin', where physical reconstruction operates in tandem with ideological and socio-cultural remodelling. *Baustelle* is here projected into a site of display, a cinematic *Schaustelle*.

In *Lola rennt*, Tykwer certainly releases his film from historicising conventions. This is Berlin shot in the style of a globalised media revolution and in the globally transferable and readily exportable genre of the thriller. As we are reminded by the key site of the 'Deutsche Transfer Bank', it is part of a global exchange of bankable film productions, the bank heist being a key example of such international currency. The film avoids the more obvious memorial sites of the city, adopting instead a montage of unlikely angles on secondary postcard settings and of more or less unglamorous local territory, recognisable as Berlin to those in the know, but not in the established form of the Angst-ridden, post-imperialist cityscape. It is telling that where landmark sites are used for the film, they are appropriated as places of play, with Lola running across the giant chequerboard of the Gendarmenmarkt and the museum building on Unter den Linden transformed into a casino for Lola to play in. And the splits still inherent in the post-unification capital are effaced

[38] Michael Töteberg (ed.), *Tom Tykwer: Lola rennt* (Reinbek: Rowohlt, 1998), p. 130.
[39] Tom Tykwer *et al.*, publicity brochure for *Lola rennt* (1998).
[40] See Andrew Webber, 'Gender and the City: *Lola rennt*', *German as a Foreign Language* 1 (2003), 1–16 (www.gfl.journal.de/1-2003/webber.html).

by Lola's taxi ride to the wrong Grunewaldstraße on the Eastern side of the city; the East and its historical specificity is thus merely, perhaps playfully, incorporated as a misdirected detour.

Notwithstanding the film's self-conscious, philosophical experimentation with spatial and temporal framing, then, its fixation upon clocks and appointments, it in fact effaces the political significance of time and place in order to retell a sort of new Odyssey, a timeless story taking place, as the publicity booklet has it, in 'Berlin. Jetzt' (Berlin. Now). If *Lola rennt* is indeed, as Stefan Arndt of the production company X-Filme claims, the absolute 'Berlin-Film',[41] it is a Berlin which is largely freed of its history. Tykwer claims that the historical experience of the late twentieth century is released from its binding to the past or the future, that it is fundamentally defined by contemporary situation; and in '*Baustelle* Berlin' this experience is at its most intense.[42] The most politically occupied city of the twentieth century is thus converted into a place open to the production of contemporary spectacle, seen by Tykwer as a sort of film studio where anything goes. While the mock-biographical entry for Lola in the book of the film tells us that she has three models, Pippi Longstocking, Madonna, and Sophie Scholl,[43] it is the fantasy powers of the first and the performance glamour of the second rather than the historical political resistance of the third which determine her role. The unlikely trio is brought together as a provocatively synthetic group of active female role models. They give the cue to approach the film through its treatment of gender, and its relationship thereby to the histories and mythologies of German and international film traditions. A key question will be whether the image of girl power that Lola projects represents a historically specific emancipation of the female role, or whether it is rather part of a more deep-rooted and controlling mythology of the feminine, and thereby of a gender order which is anything but free.

The incongruity of Lola's role models is characteristic of the styling of the film as a whole. Part of the film's appeal to the exchange values of international postmodernism lies in its eclectic incorporation and recycling of styles and its foregrounding of the idea of style, not least the international style of MTV and fashion publicity. Like commercials or pop videos, *Lola rennt* formulates its aesthetic not least by way of the free mixing of a variety of audio-visual media (incorporating standard 35mm stock, handheld camerawork, video, animation, black and white, heightened colouration, graining, split-screen in seventies Hollywood fashion, and postcards in the flip-book

---

[41] Tykwer *et al.*, publicity brochure for *Lola rennt*.   [42] *Ibid.*
[43] Töteberg (ed.), *Tom Tykwer: Lola rennt*, p. 118.

style). As a 'romantic-philosophical Action-Love-Experimental-Thriller',[44] it makes an appeal to a wide range of generic conventions from cinematic melodrama to the interactive computer game. And it operates through the citation of multiple filmic and other cultural references, as programmatically introduced by the disjunctive quotations from high-cultural poet T.S. Eliot and one-time national football coach Sepp Herberger in the introductory sequence. In its citation of film types and techniques it is designed as a centennial showcase for the historical variants of cinema's aesthetic technology, from the magic lantern to the Domino Compositor.[45]

A key part of the film's multilayered citational network lies in the specification of the female protagonist. Apart from her biographical 'models', Lola also appears to 'quote' many screen models; her identity as body and as cartoon is a confabulation of roles from Marlene Dietrich to Lara Croft and Tank Girl. Lola is a compelling new screen presence, but she is also a fabrication of styles, not least indeed a hair-style, as indicated by the *reductio ad absurdum* of the credits where 'Lola' is the name given to the protagonist's patent hair-design. Lola is thus also a 'look', set, along with the running gear, the Doc Martins, and the tattoo, to become a fashion statement to be quoted by self-styling followers of the film. Specifically, the Lola look seems designed to become a foundational icon of street-style for the New Berlin. The picture of the running Lola has provided, in the shape of Franka Potente, a frank and potent new figuration of the New Germany at the millennium, in particular of a dynamic, reconstructed Berlin, and not least Berlin as a city of film.

One of the ways in which Berlin has been figured as twentieth-century metropolis is as the sort of feminised figure (Berolina or Viktoria) that is the focus of many metropolitan and state mythologies. Mythologies need icons, and, as Sigrid Weigel has pointed out, the female figure is the preferred form for the foundational, mythic image of states and cities.[46] Weigel describes how these mythologies typically project an ambivalent image of the feminine, as monster or Babylonian whore on the one hand and succouring mother or virgin on the other. Lola is figured as both redeemer and criminal, child-like innocent and daunting femme fatale, and in this she corresponds to the sort of ambivalence which Weigel describes. As we shall see, the alluring surface of her film image incorporates darker aspects of threat. Weigel's

---

[44] *Ibid.*, p. 129.   [45] *Ibid.*, p. 131.

[46] Sigrid Weigel, '"Die Städte sind weiblich und nur dem Sieger hold": Zur Funktion des Weiblichen in Gründungsmythen und Städtedarstellungen', *Triumph und Scheitern in der Metropole: Zur Rolle der Weiblichkeit in der Geschichte Berlins*, ed. Sigrun Anselm and Barbara Beck (Berlin: Dietrich Reimer, 1987), pp. 207–27.

analysis can be turned in the direction of psychoanalysis, which leads us to understand the foundational mythical structures of both personal and cultural development as marked by trauma. If the ostensibly timeless and totalising structures of myth do indeed incorporate a genetic core of traumatic experience, their control over both personal and cultural histories is destined to be neurotically distorted, specifically to show symptoms of hysteria.[47] This is the version of myth, hysterical at base, which is at work in *Lola rennt*.

When Tykwer describes the origination of the *Lola rennt* project, he talks of an iconic image – the head of a female figure caught running in profile – which provokes the film's scenario and comes to function as its leitmotif. We recall that, as Friedrich Kittler has pointed out, the etymology in both German and English indicates that the *Hauptstadt* or capital city is conceived as the head of the body politic, and in the figuration of Lola as the film's template the capital is rendered energetic and mobile, endowed with a new physicality and style. The idea of the frantically racing figure appeals to Tykwer as embodying the fundamental emotional drive of the cinematic medium.[48] Here, however, the generically male function is appropriated for the female figure which is designed by film convention to be waiting or pursued rather than in pursuit. If we saw the alteration of the male hero in the mock-Odyssey of *Berlin Alexanderplatz*, in this rerunning of that mythical model, the 'many-turning' man is superseded by a street-wise woman, who also has to negotiate many turns, topographical and otherwise.

In practice, the film is substantially shaped by its pursuit of the body of Lola, an energetic urban body which performs the impossible acts required of it in the fantasy resolutions of the opening scenario. The idea of free movement is always, though, reliant on the dialectical energy that can be gained from resistance to it, from the freezing of frames, the interruption of one narrative strand and form of technology by another, the impacts and accidents which affect the circulation of people and traffic in the city. *Lola rennt* at once projects a fantasy of speed which seems to emancipate it from the heavy weight of Tykwer's earlier films, and yet interrupts the dynamic with scenes of hold-up and accident which invest it with indications of a traumatic load. Here again, the road accident and the intervention of emergency services are emblematic for the impact of trauma. And this sense of trauma is extrapolated into the collisions or near collisions of bodies with bodies or other objects, most dramatically vehicles and bullets,

---

[47] See Richard Falcon, '*Run Lola Run/Lola rennt*', *Sight and Sound* 9.11 (November, 1999), 52.
[48] Töteberg (ed.), *Tom Tykwer: Lola rennt*, p. 129.

the smashing of the ambulance into the pane of glass, and the near collision of the desperately running Lola with the glass of the camera lens. Lola's superhuman ability to shatter glass with her scream and to talk to Manni through glass is countered by the threat of trauma which glass represents as unseen obstacle. While the urban space of a city like Berlin has been seen by Benjamin and others as programmed for the shock and collision of traffic and crowds, in Tykwer's production of Berlin as a semi-evacuated studio-city, these traumatic coincidences are abstracted from the normal flow, their dangers highlighted.

If the idea of the running figure becomes a leitmotif for the film's structural development, the blaze of red which is Lola's hair has a more particular directive, signalling function in what Tykwer calls the 'colour dramaturgy' of the film.[49] The fashion statement of the 'Lola' look represents at once the physical energy of this body and its attachment to danger. It is correlated with the stop-and-go dynamics of the diegesis, as marked by the circulation of traffic and by street furniture: the emergency vehicle, racing and braking, the traffic-lights which signal a halt or are raced past. Lola appears as three-speed colour machine, in the red, blue, and green of her hair and clothes, a transmogrification of the iconic *Ampelmännchen* or traffic-light manikin into a new red-headed and green-legged body which runs against all traffic and pedestrian regulation, halting traffic and pedestrians alike, hitching lifts, and provoking collisions. The scenes in the bed are as if bathed in the stop-light, and thereby lifted out of the helter-skelter dynamic of the film. As carnal scenes of death as much as love, coloured as if by the seeping blood first of Lola and then of Manni, they are attached to the idea of the traumatic accident, a threat of total interruption which hangs over the myth of total love. The red arrows that help to impel Lola's race against time are thus countered not only by the red lights, but also by the red spiral as emblem of the race of life into death. The signs on the street and in shop windows link *Lola rennt* to such Weimar classics as Ruttmann's *Berlin* and Lang's *M*, where the spiral also emblematises urban motion that threatens to go out of control.

Lola and her red hairstyle are constructed in counterpoint to a whole series of the hallowed icons of the city's past. In filmic terms, this involves both the Maria of Fritz Lang's *Metropolis* (with Lola fashioned as an action doll and an animated 'miracle machine')[50] and Dietrich as Lola Lola. Both

---

[49] *Ibid.*, p. 134.
[50] Tom Tykwer, 'Werkstattgespräch' with Peter Kremski and Reinhard Wulf, *Filmbulletin* 229 (December, 2000), 33–40; p. 35.

of these embody the ambivalence of Weigel's foundational female figures, as redeeming angel and destructive vamp. If the iconic image comes first in the origination of the film, the name comes second. When Tykwer describes the generation of the film out of the fascinating image, he fails to mention how the figure was given its name (simply saying in the English commentary on the DVD 'it was there and I liked it'). Lola has many resonances, from the precocious sexuality of Lolita to the vampish cabaret act of Dietrich. Her performance of an action film form of femininity stands in a complicated relation to a network of female performances which, after the model of Dietrich, have adopted the name of Lola.

Dietrich's Lola Lola, one of the archetypal images of what Mulvey has famously called the 'to-be-looked-at-ness' of the female body on screen,[51] is an artist who, with her changes of costume and repertoire of characters, performs the performance of femininity. Her screen performance is also a highly self-conscious stage act, a *mise-en-abyme* of the film spectacle. It is a show based on artifice and add-on, showing and hiding, fantasy wigs and pantomime costumes. It corresponds to the performative principle that Butler identifies as the basis of gender identity, a repetitive citation of acts over time in order to pass as male or female. At the same time, it is a sort of drag act of femininity, excessive and staged, an impersonation. According to Butler, drag exposes the unnaturalness, the contingency, and the trouble inherent in all forms of gender performance.[52]

As an alluring figure of performativity, a diva rehearsing an act, Lola and her pianola, she is designed and destined to be reproduced and replayed. The doubling of her name is programmatic in this sense. Dietrich's Lola Lola becomes the embodiment of the performance culture of Weimar Berlin and is then reproduced in a host of filmic reprises from Fassbinder's *Lola*, to Visconti's *The Damned* and Fosse's *Cabaret*. The Dietrich image as performing a kind of fetishised hyper-femininity is thereby ready to be rehearsed in travesty acts. It is primed to be subjected to forms of impersonation and gender-bending and -blending in Dietrich's own later films (notably *Morocco*) and in the queer attendants and accessories of Fassbinder's *Lola*, of *Cabaret*, and *The Damned*, which expose the performance as camp. Dietrich's performance of Lola Lola also turns the performance of the ostensibly manly Professor Rath into a travesty, donning a wig. This suggests a model of

---

[51] Laura Mulvey, 'Visual Pleasure and Narrative Cinema', *Visual and Other Pleasures* (Basingstoke: Macmillan, 1989), pp. 14–28; p. 19.

[52] Judith Butler, *Gender Trouble: Feminism and the Subversion of Identity* (New York/London: Routledge, 1990), p. 137.

performative agency for the female star which, in line with Judith Butler's analysis of gender performativity, serves to expose more general trouble in the order of gender.

While *Lola rennt* is seemingly a film free of gender trouble of this kind, closer scrutiny shows otherwise. Tykwer's films seem to operate within a conventional binary and heterosexually secured structure of gender, but this is in fact always open to question. The focus in the opening scene on a collection of dolls can serve to make us aware of the conventional binarism of gender construction, but the presence of a Ken amongst the Barbies also questions the binary model. Lola is a doll dressed for action: as an exponent of girl-power, a sort of hybrid of Ken and Barbie. Conversely, the nicely named Manni clearly has trouble living up to his manful role; in the scene in the telephone kiosk he is reduced to a figure of impotence and need, certainly no phone-box 'Supermanni', and it is Lola who has to intervene in the role of animated super-heroic rescuer. Manni's uncertain masculinity is only emphasised by his role relative to the hyper-masculinity of Ronnie and his gang; this is a homosocial order of embraces and corporal punishments between men. Indeed, the masculine world of uniforms and muscled posturing in the film – like that of Ataman's Bili – may be understood as a sort of drag, a performance in which Manni struggles to pass.

Lola rennt appears to supersede the gender relations which were prevalent in the *Neue Deutsche Film* as much as in the Hollywood tradition, the objectification of the female figure which, in its most extreme forms, works through a melodramatic, hysterical fixation. It seems to offer a new brand of agency, where being bound to her man is no impediment to the protagonist's action heroism. In fact, Lola's construction is based on a complicated mythology. She is the princess who saves rather than being saved, a female grail knight, a Penelope who intervenes in her man's mock-Odyssey rather than staying at home; and more darkly she is Medusa with the evil eye that mortifies Schuster the guard and freezes on his lips the words Lolalola which would style her as princess-doll. Her activity is also, however, conditioned and driven by another version of hysteria.[53] The scream is the focus of the conversion of hysterical panic into energetic intervention.[54] Here, however, hysteria is also the condition of the male lead. He is thus introduced in a state of physical disorder and emotional incontinence, with his hysterical discourse as 'waterfall'.[55] While the film, at first sight, seems to represent a redressing of conventional gender roles in the late twentieth-century urban

[53] *Ibid.*, p. 119.   [54] See Tykwer *et al.*, publicity brochure for *Lola rennt*.
[55] Töteberg (ed.), *Tom Tykwer: Lola rennt*, p. 22.

culture of Berlin, it also suggests that what is being equalised is a struggle to overcome the shared, transgender condition of hysteria.

One of the playful snap-shot inserts in the film shows the two bank employees finding happiness together in a sadomasochistic relationship, with the telling clerk submitting to his dominatrix colleague. This represents in an uncharacteristically camp moment the potential for bending of the performative rules of gender which is more subtly at work throughout the film. It offers the basis for the link to *Lola und Bilidikid* with its more explicitly staged acts of gender, and asks questions about gender and sexuality in their relation to other forms of identity prescription. The red wig that is the trademark of Ataman's Lola and the symbolic object which prompts his brutal outing to and from his family marks the sort of gender performance that can never pass, but provocatively draws attention to its own masquerade. As this Lola performed a subcultural version of Dietrich's cabaret artiste, so his brother enacts a version of *Lola rennt* in his desperate race to escape those in pursuit. In both films the agency and power of the female or feminised figure is conditioned, as so often in the computer games which *Lola rennt* cites, by the controlling hand of male power and fantasy, by the need to perform for the male gaze.

This leads us to an interfilmic relationship staged explicitly by *Lola rennt*. As Tykwer's earlier film *Winterschläfer* (Winter Sleepers (1997)) tells its story of traumatic amnesia with reference to Hitchcock's *Spellbound*, *Lola rennt* is organised around motifs from another of Hitchcock's narratives of traumatic psychopathology, *Vertigo*. The signature of Hitchcock's film is inscribed throughout the film, in the *mise-en-scène* (especially the vertiginous return to the stairway in the three runs), in the iconography of the spiral, and, in particular, in the portrait on the wall of the casino. The film's producer was charged with improvising a painting of 'something from *Vertigo*' to go on the wall, and followed the logical path of painting the portrait which embodies Kim Novak's fixation with the traumatic case history of Carlotta Valdes. The copying of the portrait, drawing attention to the idea of the simulacrum and its ability to fascinate and support the forms of impersonation, the obsessive styling in the image of the other, which structure *Vertigo*, also provides a nice index of the citational performances of femininity. What emerges, however, is a sort of dream portrait that condenses the image of Carlotta with the back of Novak's head, which is the object of her obsessive attention with that of James Stewart's character, John Ferguson, and, by extension, of Hitchcock's fetishistic filmic gaze.

The mocked-up portrait represents a combination of the emblematic spiral with the idea of the fetishised hairpiece. The emergency encoded in

Lola's 'fiery red' shock of hair is thus linked to another sort of cinematic tradition: Dietrich's make-over from Lola Lola (with her femme fatale song warning of blonde women) and the blondes, or the blonde hair-dos, which fascinate Hitchcock's camera throughout his career. These fabricated cinematic blondes are designed to pass as natural, yet operate within a framework of intense theatricality and impersonation. Lola's hair is styled for a heroine who is designed to be natural, singing on the soundtrack but never a stage-act, and yet it could no more pass as natural than the red wig of her cabaret artist namesake in Ataman's film. Lola's 'Lola' hair-do challenges the artificial blonde extravagance of her Barbie dolls and yet still arguably functions as an attachment to dolling up. The call of her neurotic, housebound mother, repeated at the beginning of each run, suggesting that the alcoholic mother is also a shampoo-addict, marks the hold over the film of the need for styling.

Tykwer claims in the English-language commentary to the film that his aim was to make Franka Potente known to US audiences. He thus follows a model of *auteur* directors fashioning and marketing their female leads: Sternberg and Dietrich, Lang and his Maria (Brigitte Helm), Hitchcock and Novak. Each of these director's dolls, however, is based upon troubled forms of performance, where hyper-femininity exposes itself as masquerading, as stage-act or impersonation. In each case, too, this operates – as in *Lola rennt* – in association with a form of hystericised performance of manhood by the male lead. With Potente, Tykwer clearly wanted to create a new Lola who would redefine the allure of the doll and her to-be-looked-at-ness. But the sweating, screaming, tattooed Lola, with boots for high-heels, showing her underwear in a less staged fashion than Dietrich's Lola, is nonetheless an intensely styled cinematic construct.

At the same time, each of the films represents through its patterns of repetition, reenactment, and impersonation, a potentially dire threat to both male and female identities. The spiral hair-style borrowed from Hitchcock represents a danger that the film scenario might spiral in on itself, that repetition might become a desperate compulsion, and that the quest-run might spin into free-fall, following the film's effects of *mise-en-abyme*, as in the title sequence with its imitation of the animation graphics of the dream in *Vertigo*. The recurrent effects of circling in the camerawork, and the circle or spiral as iconographic motif, relate to a sense of post-traumatic disorder in Tykwer's protagonists, which he calls '*Post-Schock*'.[56] Trauma creates compulsive structures of return in this way. It seems that, no less than in

---

[56] Tykwer, 'Werkstattgespräch', p. 40.

the order of gender, citational practices in film can gravitate from the compulsory to the compulsive. The compulsion to repeat the repetition compulsions of Hitchcock's psycho-dramas can be said to expose a sort of uncanny fixation, haunting the controlled generic synthesis of Tykwer's film. The after-effects of *Vertigo* represent the fear of falling as an uncanny counterpart to urban *Platzangst* (we recall the cases of Little Hans and the *Sandmann*). The spiral as emblem of that fixation retains a hysterical presence throughout the film's performance, a reminder of the traumatic accidents, pursuits, and collapses to which the performative act may always be uncannily susceptible.

CROSSING-POINTS

Mama, something's sunk there.[57]

It was said that the city's appeal to film is partly as a place of coincidence, and this can be both productive and destructive, providential and – after the model of Bachmann's 'Zufälle' – traumatic in its psycho-topographical effects. The account of post-*Wende* film here concludes with a remarkable urban coincidence: *Lola und Bilidikid* and *Lola rennt* were shot at the same time, in different parts of Berlin, both figuring flame-haired Lola figures on the run in sequences which are sometimes uncannily alike. A particularly striking case is the sequence already mentioned where Ataman's Lola, reenacted by her brother Murat, runs through the abandoned factory building. As this Lola races past a sequence of window-frames, the *mise-en-scène* suggests a rerunning of the virtuoso sequence of Tykwer's Lola racing across the Oberbaum Bridge, framed by the more open window structures of the arcades. Apparently Tykwer and Ataman knew nothing of each other's projects, but the coincidence is significant. For Tykwer, the city is above all appealing as a place of orchestrated movement and exchange which is, however, also a site of unaccountable chance encounters and accidents. While the opening scene of his film is set in an unidentified sporting arena, it is characteristic of his staging of cabaret performance as epic running feat that it avoids the Olympic Stadium as site of memory. The marshalling of figures in that scene might be read as an ironic reworking of the mass choreographies of Riefenstahl, focusing instead on chance and individual resistance.

---

[57] A child seeing a navigating mast rising from the Spree by the Oberbaum Bridge (overheard by the author, August 2007).

Tykwer feels free to manipulate the city's topography and liberate it from the burden of history. Not for nothing is an aerial map of the city used as a sort of clapper-board at the end of the opening sequence; the city is here emblematically divided and then clapped together again, suggesting that the divisive memories of a fraught century can be superseded by the creative energy of the film, the Walled city converted into an open one. While Tykwer argues that *Das Leben ist eine Baustelle* shows a morbid Berlin still in the vortex of the fall of the Wall,[58] he sees *Lola rennt* as marking a new stage in the cultural history of the city. The film uses Berlin as what he calls in the publicity brochure for the film a kind of studio, not in the sense of an historical set for another retro-film, but as a site for new licence in experimental *mise-en-scène*. It is a space to be played with in a pressing present tense. It would be wrong, however, to assume that this Berlin film is just a glorified play-station. Lola's performance here may not be deadly in the way of her namesake in Ataman's film, but it certainly has a potential to be so. The pane of glass, a mobile window ready to block the street and cause accidents is emblematic of this, just as the window of the supermarket through which the voices of Lola and Manni can magically be heard before she enters by the sliding door is the emblem of the counter-possibility of special forms of communication across dividing lines in the city.

Lola rennt has of course been so successful a German export precisely because it is global in its reach – through its generic narrative moves, its music, its pace, and its technology. It suggests that perhaps Berlin is ready to become a different kind of film-studio, not for superficial entertainment, but for a type of performance both entertaining and serious that could in principle take place anywhere in the postmodern world but takes place here in Berlin because it provides a particular setting for filmic staging and movement. We could perhaps think of Lola's run as passing by the other figures that we have seen in this diverse group of Berlin films – like the characters she encounters, whose possible fates are then played out in alternative forms of mini-film. One point of convergence would be the Oberbaum Bridge, a key architectural feature in the last three films discussed. This is a bridge once part of the system of the Wall between East and West, as featured for instance in the drama of division in Frank Vogel's DEFA film ... *und deine Liebe auch* (... and Your Love Too (1962)), and now part of the 'History Mile' of the Berlin Wall. It represents both linkage and separation, open and closed architectures and topographies, a key site of both chance encounter and controlled transit. In 1997, a work entitled

---

[58] Töteberg (ed.), *Tom Tykwer: Lola rennt*, p. 135.

Übergänge (Crossings) was installed on it, a playful meditation on human and political transfers and transitions, both chance and guided, with randomly illuminated neon figures representing the game of 'stone, paper, scissors'.

When Tykwer's Lola runs over the bridge, following in the footsteps of Jan in *Das Leben ist eine Baustelle*, this is either a profoundly symbolic linking construction between divided spaces or merely a great cinematic opportunity, as Becker suggests,[59] just as it provides an exquisite crepuscular shot for the cover image of the book of Schadt's *Berlin* film. There is a possibility that on the same day that Tykwer was filming his Lola racing across the bridge, Ataman was also filming his, floating dead in the Spree with the bridge as backdrop. Here, Lola the victim in the Berlin waterways chimes with Rosa, as a further return of the *corpus delictus* of historical violence in the city. A young girl asks the dead Lola if s/he is a mermaid, suggesting that s/he remains an impossible, floating figure of hybridity to the end. Berlin film since 1989 is cast somewhere between these versions of the allegorical Lola figure: alluring and energetic or brutal and melancholic, vital and free-running or deadly still, related or divided.

In the publicity brochure for *Lola rennt*, Tykwer describes Berlin as uniquely 'synthetic and vital', but all the Berlin films discussed here have also shown elements of breakage in the synthesis, and of mortification in the life, of the city. As we saw in the case of Schadt's *Berlin*, the city provides the grounds for new urban symphonies, often tending towards a melancholic key. The musical documentary *Berlin, Babylon* (2001) shows the spectacle of construction – *Baustelle* as *Schaustelle* – but undermined by the established connection of the overreaching city with its Babylonian counterpart. It is another work that operates under the aegis of Benjamin's angel of history, always ready to see the building site as a heap of fragments rather than a new global city in the making. The city provides the territory for interwoven narratives, either enlivened or mortified by chance encounter, in films like Andreas Dresen's *Nachtgestalten* (Night Figures (1999)) or Vanessa Jopp's tragicomic *Komm näher* (Come Closer (2006)), where the *Imbißbude* or snack-stall as point of intersection is nicely named 'Check Point Curry'. Berlin is shown as a place to be exploited for its new opportunities, but also as a place of exploitation in its new globalised forms, as in the episodic theatre-film, *Stadt als Beute* (City as Booty (2005)) by Miriam Dehne, Esther Gronenborn, and Irene von Alberti, with its characters rehearsing roles in a burlesque anti-Capitalist (and anti-capital) drama in the theatre and on the itinerant stage of the city streets.

---

[59] See Wolfgang Becker *et al.*, publicity brochure for *Das Leben ist eine Baustelle* (1997).

The spectacle of exploitation is focused not least on the rites of passage of a new generation of lost children. Astray in Berlin as new capital of youth culture, excluded from its love parades, they follow in the footsteps of Rossellini's Edmund, and Klier's Elfie and Edmund. These are the alienated children of the suburban high-rises in Gronenborn's *alaska.de* (2000), with the newcomer fighting for control of a street-map in its opening sequence; the young mule running drugs on the streets in Detlev Buck's *Knallhart* (Hard as Nails (2006)), and gaining knowledge of the underworld version of the city's topography; the girl-gang militant from Wedding in Sylke Enders' *Kroko* (Croc (2003)); the boy who tries to guide his father out of his post-*Wende* depression in Robert Thalheim's *Netto* (Net Amount (2005)); or the phantom vagrant at large in the new city centre in Christian Petzoldt's *Gespenster* (Ghosts (2005)). And there is the boy from the East in Becker's *Good Bye, Lenin!*, who finds his father in a Wannsee villa, even as he loses his mother. Encountering his half-siblings watching television, the young protagonist introduces himself as Alex(ander) and is told to take a seat ('Platz'), as if to implant the iconic Eastern location of the Alexanderplatz allegorically in the affluent Western suburbs of a city still divided.

All of these scenarios are, at one level, evidence of Berlin's assumption of a new form of normality in its cinematic culture, of generic forms and narratives that could take place anywhere: urban thriller, social satire, or family melodrama. The coming-of-age genre is a particular vehicle for a similar rite of passage for the cultural life of the new capital. The recurrent story-line of disorientation and the attempt to navigate a challenging environment is a global one, as indicated by the networked title of *alaska. de* or the obsessive berating of the Sony Center in *Stadt als Beute*. But the post-*Wende* scenarios also carry with them a specificity of location, a particular historical and present disposition, that make the cinematic marathon of contemporary Berlin a cultural event unlike any other.

AFTERWORD

Goodbye to Berlin?

Farewell Berlin, and off we go.[1]

This book started with the journeys of the poet Ören from Berlin to Berlin, and with Kafka, a migrating visitor returning to the city in both life and dreams. Over the long twentieth century, this rhythm of coming and going has been a distinctive pattern of the city. From exiles from the National Socialist capital such as Brecht and Döblin, to the various forms of passage from one Berlin to the other in the time of the Walled city, and the movements to-and-fro of a latter-day migrant like Ören or Emine Özdamar and many others, arrival is turned towards departure, and departure doubled back into return. In other cases, the departure has been more definitive, with return available, if at all, only in memory or fantasy. An example would be Benjamin and the map of his life in the city, which we might imagine as one of the documents he carried in the case from Berlin that he lost in flight. Another would be Lasker-Schüler, with her exile poem 'Mein blaues Klavier' (My Blue Piano (1937)) evoking a home she no longer has, with an allegorical blue angel in the cabaret style of Dietrich's Lola Lola as its overarching emblematic figure.[2] Her angel as it were looks back at the city in both its cultural energy and its historical destructiveness, joining a host of such figures that we have witnessed in the texts and films considered here. For a city at once so culturally dynamic and so fraught in its modern historical experience, the act of return is also liable to be characterised by profound ambivalence: at once nostalgic and melancholically haunted, compulsive and resistant.

If a case has been made here for Berlin, less for good than for ill, as capital of the twentieth century, is it ready now to depart from that status and to be just another capital amongst capitals? Is it a place coming to be liked, both

[1] 'Adieu Berlin, abfahren wir', as sung in Jutzi's *Berlin Alexanderplatz.*
[2] See Webber, 'Inside Out', pp. 155–6.

by its nation and by others, one that encourages but does not demand return? Berlin on the threshold to the twenty-first century is as Janus-faced as the capital of Benjamin's childhood around 1900. It still has something of the contorted features of his allegorical figures, the melancholy angel and the *bucklichte Männlein*. It looks forward to new departures, but also remains attached to a perhaps uniquely traumatic past century, bearing the shadow of historical melancholy and feeling the potential for uncanny returns. Indeed, part of its appeal for early twenty-first-century tourism is the fetishistic allure of that attachment (the quest for Hitler's interred bunker or the fallen Wall). And, for a more critical topographer like the poet Durs Grünbein, it is the architectures of Germania, organised around the invisible central point of the Hitler bunker, that dominate his account of 'Berlin. Topographie' in 2001: recycled or ruined buildings along an axis from the Anhalter Bahnhof, via the administrative blocks of the Wilhelmstraße, to the Olympic Stadium, seen as still cast in the sort of unnaturally blazing light that characterises photographs of the ruins of 1945.[3]

In the shadow of this light, and with its focus on key sites in Grünbein's topography, the World Cup summer of 2006 could not help but feel somewhat uncanny. Berlin as the capital of another kind of allegorical land, which Sönke Wortmann's film of Germany's World Cup campaign called *Deutschland: ein Sommermärchen* (Germany: A Summer's Tale (2006)), had a sense of fairy-tale unreality about it. The city cannot quite believe that its passage through the darker seasons of its twentieth century, German autumns and winters, and the questionable signs of a new spring after unification, can now have entered a season of content: a time in which national colours can fly freely for all and the parade-ground in front of the Brandenburg Gate – in the territory under exception of the central *Bannkreis* or security ring – can be given over to an (inter)national fandom that in part celebrates the comeback of the host city as cosmopolis. The location shooting in the summer of 2007 for Bryan Singer's film on the Stauffenberg plot, *Valkyrie*, with its revival under another flag of one of Grünbein's undead, recycled buildings, the Reich Air Ministry on the Wilhelmstraße (see Figure 11), serves as a suitable uncanny counterpart to that fantasy of comeback. As Grass's *Ein weites Feld* reminds us, this is indeed an undead building, occupied first by Göring, then by the GDR House of Ministries, then by the Treuhand Agency, and now by the Finance Ministry. Its commandeering as film-set, with its GDR mural

---

[3] Durs Grünbein, *Das erste Jahr: Berliner Aufzeichnungen* (Frankfurt am Main: Suhrkamp, 2001), pp. 93–4.

11 Location work for Singer's *Valkyrie*, Wilhelmstraße, August 2007.

covered up and imperial eagles reinstalled, crowns its extraordinary history
of amenability to appropriation.

While this volume has done much to emphasise the traumatism, the
uncanniness, and the melancholia in the psycho-topographical disposition

of the city throughout the twentieth century, it has also wanted to show something of the extraordinary creativity that has been produced in and in spite of those conditions. In the twenty-first century, Berlin might indeed be in a position to turn Benjamin's angel round and to look forward, a city where, to recall the formulation coined by Heiner Müller and cited by Wenders,[4] history may find a starting place, one not compulsively heaped with a pre-history of impeding ruins. One of the implications of such a turn is the relinquishing of any claim to the title of capital of this century, opting instead to be one amongst others, aware of its place and its relations to other places. Late twentieth-century Berlin may have been one of the biggest building-sites on the globe, but what has emerged is far from the mega-lomaniac master-plan of the 1930s. It is an urban polity that is broadly open to what lies ahead and around, balancing present and future claims with those of its history.

In the early twentieth century, the market gate of Miletus was installed in Berlin, a piece of plundered ancient imperial architecture co-opted as cultural capital by the modern imperialist project. We saw Weiss's protagonists beholding the gate at a time when that imperialism had moved into its bid for global domination. It stood as an adequate allegorical representation of the triumphant historical march of Berlin, but also of the ruination that such historical movements bring with them and, ultimately, upon themselves. As such, it can be understood as a counterpart to that other triumphal gate, the Brandenburg Gate. This we have seen blocked and re-opened, damaged and redressed, appropriated for a range of ideological purposes and moments of historical spectacle. It has been a place of stand-off and procession, of euphoria and melancholia, serving variously as a plinth for Wenders' angels, an advertising hoarding, and a backdrop on one side for mass celebrations on the parade ground turned fan-mile and on another for the view over the memorial to the murdered Jews of Europe.

In the twenty-first century, the two gates are open to another type of city and other kinds of market. The *allos agora* that has been the leitmotif of this study is redefined here. The market is that of international corporate capital, of new economies of life-style, entertainment, and global tourism. The simulation of the Brandenburg Gate that was mounted over it as publicity for the telecom giant that sponsored its refurbishment is indication enough of this transformation into an object of international mediatisation and commerce. According to William Mitchell, the capital of the twenty-first century is the 'City of Bits', one dispersed across the new, mobile *agora* of

---

[4] Wenders, *Logik der Bilder*, pp. 96–7.

the 'Infobahn', operating in the global economic and information networks of neo-liberal commerce, the electronic media, and (post-)postmodern cultural exchange. This would be the virtual capital (its only actual rival probably Beijing)[5] that succeeds Paris as 'capital of the nineteenth century', and Berlin, proposed here as capital of the twentieth. Mitchell's charter for this new frontier capital or post-capital, located in the trans-global flows of information, is, nicely enough, made with reference to Miletus, the ancient city on a peninsula by the Maeander.[6] At the start of the twentieth-century with the rise of imperial Berlin as world city, it was an island in the Spree that became the site for a representative entrance to Miletus. At the start of the twenty-first century, the (market)place for that gate of a ruined city pieced together in Berlin is in the city of bits. The Miletus-Berlin version of the new tourist capital is a virtual location to be found, with other such bits, on the Infobahn.

In the age of the electronic network, Berlin remains, to follow the title of Grass's novel of the city, 'ein weites Feld', a wide open field that poses a special challenge to the cultural topographer. It is an urban field that takes both actual and virtual forms, an archaeological site of modernity to rival Freud's Rome, still bearing psycho-topographical evidence of the multiple occupancies that it has hosted since the days of Fontanopolis. Whether in the underground labyrinth of the Stasi agent in Wolfgang Hilbig's "*Ich*" ('I' (1993)), the archaeological city-walks of Cees Nooteboom's *Allerseelen*, the haunted houses of the Scheunenviertel in Irina Liebmann's Berlin novels, the scarred corporeal topography of Thomas Hettche's *Nox* (1995), the nomadic party-sites of Tanja Dückers' *Spielzone* (Play Zone (1999)), or the satirical new Berlin-Sodom in the occupied Potsdamer Platz high-rise of Lukas Hammerstein's *120 Tage von Berlin* (120 Days of Berlin (2003)), those occupancies still bear to varying degrees upon the writing of the city at the millennium, just as upon its filming. As we saw in the last chapter, they do not exert total control over its present or future, but they persist in the city's cultural topography.

As charted in *Ein weites Feld*, the archives, ministries, and monuments of Berlin are being returned to their place in the past and yet still liable to return in recycled forms. Berlin is a city with more freedom of movement than it has had for many decades, but that movement is still shadowed by the ghosts of past controls. These are embodied in the diurnal and nocturnal

---

[5] Beijing featured as 'Capital of the Twenty-First Century' in *Die Zeit*, 19 July 2007.
[6] William J. Mitchell, *City of Bits: Space, Place, and the Infobahn* (Cambridge, Mass.: MIT Press, 1995), p. 24.

shadow of the agent Hoftaller who accompanies the latter-day Fontane figure on his wanderings through the city in Grass's novel, more *bucklichte Männlein* than angel of history, representing the melancholy distortions of the subject's and the city's accommodations with history. It is a shadow figure to match the uncanny one that we saw accompanying Kafka in the Berlin of his dreams. The triadic figure of subject, city, and shadow, combining nostalgia with the forceful grip of the past, creative remembrance with melancholy, seems an appropriate allegorical constellation for Berlin reaching the end of its long twentieth century. If subject and shadow bid goodbye to Berlin at the end of the novel, it perhaps indicates a possibility of liberation for the city from the ghosts of its archives and ministries, the prospect of achieving forms of remembrance that do not fall into historical repetition, following the circulating motion of the paternoster lift. The burning of that allegorical lift in Berlin's twentieth-century 'house of ministries' might suggest a positive recycling of the historically fuelled element of fire in Berlin, a breaking of the destructive and repressive cycle. It seems to indicate a possibility for this novel and for the chronotope or *Zeitraum* of the city in the long twentieth century that it allegorises as wide open field indeed to be spoken and seen otherwise, not always in dialogue with the shadows. Berlin is not a place that can easily be enjoyed without melancholy, without a binding sense of what has been lost by it. But it does seem to be becoming once more a city whose psychopathologies are the more routine ones of everyday life, one in which the inhabitant, the visitor, or the angel of history might also find grounds and pause for cultural topographic pleasure in the present moment and in future prospects.

Bibliography

Adorno, Theodor Wiesengrund, 'Zur Dreigroschenoper', *Die Musik: Monatsschrift* 21.1 (1928/9), 424–8

Agamben, Giorgio, *Homo Sacer: Sovereign Power and Bare Life*, trans. Daniel Heller-Roazen (Stanford: Stanford University Press, 1998)

    State of Exception, trans. Kevin Attell (Chicago/London: University of Chicago Press, 2005)

Assmann, Aleida, *Erinnerungsräume: Formen und Wandlungen des kulturellen Gedächtnisses* (Munich: C. H. Beck, 1999)

Ataman, Kutluğ, interview, www.german-cinema.de/magazine/1998/01/prodreport/4-produkt_E.html

    interview, *The Observer*, 29 December 2002

Augé, Marc, *Non-Places: Introduction to an Anthropology of Supermodernity*, trans. John Howe (New York/London: Verso, 1995)

Bachelard, Gaston, *La Poétique de l'espace*, 4th edn (Paris: Presses universitaires de France, 1964)

Bachmann, Ingeborg, *Ein Ort für Zufälle: Mit Zeichnungen von Günter Grass*, Quarthefte 6 (Berlin: Wagenbach, 1965)

    Werke, ed. Christine Koschel *et al.*, 4 vols. (Munich: Piper, 1978)

    Ein Ort für Zufälle, *'Todesarten'-Projekt: Kritische Ausgabe*, ed. Robert Pichl *et al.*, 4 vols. (Munich/Zurich: Piper, 1995), vol. 1

    'Ich weiß keine bessere Welt': Unveröffentlichte Gedichte, ed. Heinz Bachmann *et al.* (Munich: Piper, 2000)

Bálasz, Béla, *Der Film: Werden und Wesen einer Kunst* (Vienna: Globus, 1972)

Barthes, Roland, 'Semiology and Urbanism', *The Semiotic Challenge*, trans. Richard Howard (Oxford: Blackwell, 1988), pp. 191–201

    Camera Lucida: Reflections on Photography, trans. Richard Howard (London: Vintage, 2000)

Bartsch, Kurt, *Ingeborg Bachmann* (Stuttgart: Metzler, 1997)

Becker, Wolfgang, *et al.*, publicity brochure for *Das Leben ist eine Baustelle* (1997)

Benjamin, Walter, *Berliner Kindheit um neunzehnhundert* (Frankfurt am Main: Suhrkamp, 1950)

    Gesammelte Schriften, ed. Rolf Tiedemann, and Hermann Schweppenhäuser, 7 vols. (Frankfurt am Main: Suhrkamp, 1991)

Gesammelte Briefe, ed. Christian Gödde and Henri Lonitz, 6 vols. (Frankfurt am Main: Suhrkamp, 1995–2000)

Berghahn, Daniela, *Hollywood behind the Wall: The Cinema of East Germany* (Manchester: Manchester University Press, 2005)

Berlin Alexanderplatz: Ein WDR-Film in 13 Teilen und einem Epilog (ARD publicity brochure, 1980)

'Berlin Alexanderplatz', *Der Vorstoss*, 18 October 1931

'Berlin: Comeback einer Weltstadt', *Der Spiegel* 12 (19 March 2007)

'*Berlin: Die Sinfonie der Grosstadt*', *Kinematograph* 1075 (25 September 1927)

'*Berlin: Die Sinfonie der Grosstadt*', *Frankfurter Zeitung*, 17 November 1927

Bienert, Michael, *Mit Brecht durch Berlin: Ein literarischer Reiseführer* (Frankfurt am Main: Insel, 1998)

Biermann, Wolf, '"Ein Kuss in meiner Seele": Dankrede für Ehrenbürgerschaft', *Die Zeit*, 29 March 2007

Blamberger, Günter, '"Zeichen der Freiheit": Notizen zu Oskar Roehlers Film *Die Unberührbare*', in Oskar Roehler, *Die Unberührbare: Das Original-Drehbuch* (Cologne: Kiepenheuer & Witsch, 2002), pp. 155–64

Blanchot, Maurice, 'Berlin', *Modern Language Notes* 109.3 (1994), 345–55

Bloch, Ernst, 'Berlin aus der Landschaft gesehen', *Frankfurter Zeitung*, 7 July 1932

Brady, Philip, 'Symphony and Jungle-Noises', *Berlin: Literary Images of a City*, ed. Derek Glass *et al.* (Berlin: Erich Schmidt, 1989), pp. 83–106

Brecht, Bertolt, *Gesammelte Werke in acht Bänden* (Frankfurt am Main: Suhrkamp, 1967), vol. 1

Werke: Berliner und Frankfurter Ausgabe, ed. Werner Hecht *et al.*, 30 vols. (Frankfurt am Main: Suhrkamp, 1988–2000)

'Brecht führt Dialog-Regie', *Film-Kurier* 229 (30 September 1931)

Büchner, Georg, *Leonce und Lena, Werke und Briefe: Münchner Ausgabe*, ed. Karl Pörnbacher *et al.* (Munich: dtv, 1988)

Buck-Morss, Susan, *The Dialectics of Seeing: Walter Benjamin and the Arcades Project* (Cambridge, Mass.: MIT Press, 1989)

Bucovich, Mario von, *Berlin* (Berlin: Albertus, 1928)

Burgin, Victor, 'Paranoiac Space', *New Formations* 12 (Winter 1990), 61–75

'The City in Pieces', *New Formations* 20 (Summer 1993), 33–45

Butler, Judith, *Gender Trouble: Feminism and the Subversion of Identity* (New York/London: Routledge, 1990)

Bodies that Matter: On the Discursive Limits of 'Sex' (New York/London: Routledge, 1993)

Antigone's Claim: Kinship Between Life and Death (New York: Columbia University Press, 2000)

Canetti, Elias, *Die Fackel im Ohr* (Berlin: Volk und Welt, 1983)

Caruth, Cathy, *Unclaimed Experience: Trauma, Narrative, and History* (Baltimore/London: Johns Hopkins University Press, 1996)

Connerton, Paul, *How Societies Remember* (Cambridge: Cambridge University Press, 1989)

Cook, Roger F., 'Angels, Fiction, and History in Berlin: *Wings of Desire*', *The Cinema of Wim Wenders: Image, Narrative, and the Postmodern Condition*, ed. Roger F. Cook and Gerd Gemünden (Detroit: Wayne State University Press, 1997), pp. 163–90

de Certeau, Michel, *The Practice of Everyday Life*, trans. Steven Rendall (Berkeley: University of California Press, 1988)

de Man, Paul, *Allegories of Reading: Figural Language in Rousseau, Nietzsche, Rilke, and Proust* (New Haven/London: Yale University Press, 1979)

Deleuze, Gilles, 'What Children Say', *Essays: Critical and Clinical*, trans. Daniel W. Smith and Michael A. Greco (London/New York: Verso, 1998), pp. 61–7

Deleuze, Gilles, and Félix Guattari, *Kafka: Toward a Minor Literature*, trans. Dana Polan (Minneapolis: University of Minnesota Press, 1986)

Dimendberg, Edward, 'Transfiguring the Urban Gray: László Moholy-Nagy's Film Scenario "Dynamic of the Metropolis"', *Camera Obscura, Camera Lucida: Essays in Honour of Annette Michelson*, ed. Richard Allen and Malcolm Turvey (Amsterdam: Amsterdam University Press, 2003), pp. 109–26

Döblin, Alfred, *Die beiden Freundinnen und ihr Giftmord* (Berlin: Die Schmiede, 1924)

Briefe, ed. Walter Muschg (Olten: Walter, 1970)

Schriften zu Leben und Werk, ed. Erich Kleinschmidt (Olten: Walter, 1986)

Schriften zu Ästhetik, Poetik und Literatur, ed. Erich Kleinschmidt (Olten: Walter, 1989)

Kleine Schriften II, ed. Anthony Riley (Olten: Walter, 1990)

Karl und Rosa (November 1918, dritter Teil), ed. Werner Stauffacher (Olten: Walter, 1991)

Die Schicksalsreise: Bericht und Bekenntnis, ed. Anthony W. Riley (Solothurn: Walter, 1993)

Berlin Alexanderplatz: Die Geschichte vom Franz Biberkopf, ed. Werner Stauffacher (Zurich: Walter, 1996)

Berlin Alexanderplatz: Drehbuch von Alfred Döblin und Hans Wilhelm zu Phil Jutzis Film von 1931 (Munich: text+kritik, 1996)

Kleine Schriften III, ed. Anthony Riley (Zurich: Walter, 1999)

Dollenmayer, David B., 'An Urban Montage and Its Significance in *Döblin's Berlin Alexanderplatz*', *The German Quarterly*, 53.3 (May, 1980), 317–36

Downing, Taylor, *Olympia* (London: BFI, 1992)

Eberhardt, Joachim, *'Es gibt für mich keine Zitate': Intertextualität im dichterischen Werk Ingeborg Bachmanns* (Tübingen: Niemeyer, 2002)

Eichberg, Henning, 'Stadium, Pyramid, Labyrinth: Eye and Body on the Move', *The Stadium and the City*, ed. John Bale and Olof Moen (Keele: Keele University Press, 1995), pp. 323–47

'Ein Bert-Brecht-Film soll gedreht werden', *Film-Kurier* 157 (8 July 1931)

Elsaesser, Thomas, *Fassbinder's Germany: History Identity Subject* (Amsterdam: Amsterdam University Press, 1996), p. 233

Falcon, Richard, '*Run Lola Run/Lola rennt*', *Sight and Sound* 9.11 (November, 1999), 52

Fassbinder, Rainer Werner, *et al.*, *Berlin Alexanderplatz: Ein WDR-Film in 13 Teilen und einem Epilog* (ARD publicity brochure, 1980)

Fassbinder, Rainer Werner, and Harry Baer, *Der Film BERLIN Alexanderplatz: Ein Arbeitsjournal* (Frankfurt am Main: Zweitausendeins, 1980)

Feddersen, Anya, 'Kriegsfibel', *Brecht Handbuch*, ed. Jan Knopf, 5 vols. (Stuttgart: Metzler, 2001–3), vol. II, pp. 382–97

Fiebach, Joachim, 'Nach Brecht – von Brecht aus – von ihm fort?: Heiner Müllers Texte seit den siebziger Jahren', *Brecht 88: Anregungen zum Dialog über die Vernunft am Jahrtausendende*, ed. Wolfgang Heise (Berlin: Henschelverlag, 1987), pp. 171–88

'filmrhythmus, filmgestaltung', *bauhaus: vierteljahr-zeitschrift für gestaltung* 3.2 (April–June 1929), 5–11

Fischer, Robert (ed.), *Fassbinder über Fassbinder: Die ungekürzten Interviews* (Frankfurt am Main: Verlag der Autoren, 2004)

Fontane, Theodor, *Irrungen, Wirrungen, Werke, Schriften und Briefe*, ed. Walter Keitel and Helmuth Nürnberger, 20 vols. (Munich: Carl Hanser, 1962–97), part I, vol. II

Effi Briest, Werke, Schriften und Briefe, part I, vol. IV

Briefe: 1890–1898, Werke, Schriften und Briefe, part IV, vol. IV

Foucault, Michel, 'Of Other Spaces', *Diacritics* 16 (Spring 1986), 22–7

Freud, Sigmund, *Gesammelte Werke*, ed. Anna Freud *et al.*, 18 vols. (Frankfurt am Main: Fischer, 1999)

Fuechtner, Veronika, '"Arzt und Dichter": Döblin's Medical, Psychiatric, and Psychoanalytical Work', *A Companion to the Works of Alfred Döblin*, ed. Roland Dollinger *et al.* (Rochester: Camden House, 2004), pp. 111–39

Fuegi, John, *Brecht & Co.* (New York: Grove, 1994)

Fusco, Coco, 'Angels, History and Poetic Fantasy: An Interview with Wim Wenders', *Cineaste* 16.4 (1988), 14–17

Gersch, Wolfgang, and Werner Hecht, *Kuhle Wampe oder Wem gehört die Welt?* (Frankfurt am Main: Suhrkamp, 1969)

'Gespräch mit Alfred Döblin: Begegnungen mit Biberkopf', *LichtBildBühne*, 7 October 1931

Giersch, Ulrich, 'Berliner Sand … Materie, Medium und Metapher einer Stadt', *Mythos Berlin*, ed. Hickethier *et al.*, pp. 71–8

Giuriato, Davide, *Mikrographien: Zu einer Poetologie des Schreibens in Walter Benjamins Kindheitserinnerungen (1932–1939)* (Munich: Fink, 2006)

Gleber, Anke, 'The Woman and the Camera – Walking in Berlin: Observations on Walter Ruttmann, Verena Stefan, and Helke Sander', *Berlin in Focus: Cultural Transformations in Germany*, ed. Barbara Becker-Cantarino (Westport: Greenwood, 1996), pp. 105–24

Goebbels, Josef, 'Kampf um Berlin', *Der Angriff*, 9 December 1930

Goergen, Jeanpaul, *Walther Ruttmann: Eine Dokumentation* (Berlin: Freunde der Deutschen Kinemathek, 1989)

Goldhill, Simon, *The Poet's Voice: Essays on Poetics and Greek Literature* (Cambridge: Cambridge University Press, 1991)

Gombrowicz, Witold, *Berliner Notizen* (Pfullingen: Neske, 1965)

Götz, Susanne von, '"Ich habe der Arbeiterklasse ins Antlitz geschaut": Ein Gespräch mit Hermann Henselmann, Architekt der Stalinallee, über Brecht und den 17. Juni 1953', *Der Tagesspiegel*, 17 June 1993

Grass, Günter, *Die Gedichte: 1955–1986* (Darmstadt: Luchterhand, 1988)

Ein weites Feld (Göttingen: Steidl, 1995)

Grosch, Nils, '"Notiz" zum *Berliner Requiem*: Aspekte seiner Entstehung und Aufführung', *Kurt Weill-Studien* 1 (1996), 55–71

Grünbein, Durs, *Das erste Jahr: Berliner Aufzeichnungen* (Frankfurt am Main: Suhrkamp, 2001)

Hake, Sabine, 'Urban Spectacle in Walter Ruttmann's *Berlin, Symphony of the Big City*', *Dancing on the Volcano: Essays on the Culture of the Weimar Republic*, ed. Thomas W. Kniesche and Stephen Brockmann (Columbia: Camden House, 1994), pp. 127–42

'Urban Paranoia in Alfred Döblin's *Berlin Alexanderplatz*', *The German Quarterly* 67 (1994), 347–68

Harvey, David, *The Condition of Postmodernity* (Oxford: Blackwell, 1989)

Haußmann, Leander (ed.), *Sonnenallee: Das Buch zum Farbfilm* (Berlin: Quadriga, 1999)

Hecht, Werner, *Brecht Chronik: 1898–1956* (Frankfurt am Main: Suhrkamp, 1997)

Hegemann, Werner, *Das steinerne Berlin: Geschichte der größten Mietkasernenstadt der Welt* (Berlin: Gustav Kiepenheuer, 1930)

Heine, Heinrich, *Reise von München nach Genua*, in *Historisch-kritische Gesamtausgabe der Werke*, ed. Manfred Windfuhr, 16 vols. (Hamburg: Hoffmann und Campe, 1973–97), vol. VII.i

Henselmann, Hermann, 'Brecht und die Stadt', *Die Weltbühne*, 25 September 1973

Hickethier, Knut, *et al.* (eds.), *Mythos Berlin: Zur Wahrnehmungsgeschichte einer industriellen Metropole: Eine szenische Ausstellung auf dem Gelände des Anhalter Bahnhofs* (Berlin: Ästhetik und Kommunikation, 1987)

Hirschhorn, Thomas, *Ingeborg-Bachmann-Altar*, Neue Gesellschaft für bildende Kunst, www.ngbk.de/typo3/index.php?id=37&no_cache=1&sword_list[

Hoffmann, E. T. A., *Der Sandmann, Sämtliche Werke*, ed. Wulf Segebrecht *et al.*, 6 vols. (Frankfurt am Main: Deutscher Klassiker Verlag, 1985), vol. III

Des Vetters Eckfenster, Sämtliche Werke, vol. VI

Hoffmann, Hilmar, *Mythos Olympia: Autonomie und Unterwerfung von Sport und Kultur* (Berlin/Weimar: Aufbau, 1995)

Honold, Alexander, 'Der Krieg und die Großstadt: *Berlin Alexanderplatz* und ein Trauma der Moderne', *Internationales Alfred-Döblin-Kolloquium Berlin 2001*, ed. Hartmut Egge and Gabriele Prauß (Berne: Lang, 2003), pp. 191–211

Huyssen, Andreas, *Twilight Memories: Marking Time in a Culture of Amnesia* (New York/London: Routledge, 1995)

Present Pasts: Urban Palimpsests and the Politics of Memory (Stanford: Stanford University Press, 2003)

Ihering, Herbert, '*Berlin Alexanderplatz*', *Berliner Börsen-Courier*, 9 October 1931

Jacobs, Carol, 'Walter Benjamin: Topographically Speaking', *Walter Benjamin: Theoretical Questions*, ed. David S. Ferris (Stanford: Stanford University Press, 1996), pp. 94–117

Jameson, Fredric, *Brecht and Method* (London/New York: Verso, 1998)

Jelavich, Peter, *Berlin Alexanderplatz: Radio, Film, and the Death of Weimar Culture* (Berkeley: University of California Press, 2006)

Jirgl, Reinhard, *Abtrünnig: Roman aus der nervösen Zeit* (Munich/Vienna: Carl Hanser, 2005)

Jolles, Charlotte, '"Berlin wird Weltstadt": Theodor Fontane und der Berliner Roman seiner Zeit', *Berlin: Literary Images of a City*, ed. Derek Glass *et al.* (Berlin: Erich Schmidt, 1989), pp. 50–69

Kaemmerling, Ekkehard, 'Die filmische Schreibweise', *Materialien zu Alfred Döblin: 'Berlin Alexanderplatz'*, ed. Matthias Prangel (Frankfurt am Main: Suhrkamp, 1975), pp. 185–98

Kafka, Franz, *Briefe an Felice und andere Korrespondenz aus der Verlobungszeit*, ed. Erich Heller and Jürgen Born (Frankfurt am Main: Fischer, 1967)

Tagebücher, ed. Hans-Gerd Koch *et al.* (Frankfurt am Main: Fischer, 1990)

'Ein Landarzt', *Die Erzählungen und andere ausgewählte Prosa*, ed. Jürgen Born *et al.* (Frankfurt am Main: Fischer, 1996), pp. 253–60

Kiefer, Anselm, 'Der Mensch ist böse' (interview), *Die Zeit*, 3 March 2005

Kisch, Egon Erwin, 'Dies ist das Haus der Opfer', *Der rasende Reporter* (Berlin: Erich Reiss, 1925), pp. 258–61

Kittler, Friedrich, 'Die Stadt ist ein Medium', *Mythos Metropole*, ed. Gotthard Fuchs *et al.* (Frankfurt am Main: Suhrkamp, 1995), pp. 228–44

Klier, Michael, interview, *epd Film*, 8.8 (1991), 3–4

Knobloch, Heinz, *Der Berliner zweifelt immer: Feuilletons von damals* (Berlin: Der Morgen, 1977)

Herr Moses in Berlin: Auf den Spuren eines Menschenfreundes (Berlin: Der Morgen, 1979)

Kolker, Robert Phillip and Peter Beicken, *The Films of Wim Wenders: Cinema as Vision and Desire* (Cambridge: Cambridge University Press, 1993)

Kracauer, Siegfried, *Schriften*, vol. v, ed. Inka Mülder-Bach (Frankfurt am Main: Suhrkamp, 1990)

Kühl, Christiane, 'Endlich Schluß mit Grau! DDR in Farbe', *taz*, 7 October 1999

Kuzniar, Alice A., and Xavier Vila, 'Witnessing Narration in: Wings of Desire', *Film Criticism* 16.3 (1992), 355–67

Lacan, Jacques, *Le Séminaire IV: La relation d'objet* (Paris: Seuil, 1994)

Ladd, Brian, *The Ghosts of Berlin: Confronting German History in the Urban Landscape* (Chicago/London: University of Chicago Press, 1997)

Large, David Clay, *Berlin: A Modern History* (London: Allen Lane, 2001)

Lasker-Schüler, Else, *Werke und Briefe: Kritische Ausgabe*, ed. Norbert Oellers *et al.* (Frankfurt am Main: Jüdischer Verlag, 1996–), vol. IV.i

Mein Herz: Ein Liebesroman mit Bildern und wirklich lebenden Menschen, ed. Ricarda Dick (Frankfurt am Main: Jüdischer Verlag, 2003)

Lefebvre, Henri, *The Production of Space*, trans. Donald Nicholson-Smith (Oxford: Blackwell, 1991)

Libeskind, Daniel, *radix–matrix: Architecture and Writings* (Munich/New York: Prestel, 1997)

The Space of Encounter (London: Thames & Hudson, 2001)

Lissitzky-Küppers, Sophie, *El Lissitzky: Maler Architekt Typograf Fotograf* (Dresden: VEB Verlag der Kunst, 1967)

Loewenthal, Rudi, 'Der Alexanderplatz als Filmkulisse: Heinrich Georges fliegender Krawattenladen', *Die Filmwoche* 27 (1931), 848–50

Mattenklott, Gert, and Gundel Mattenklott, *Berlin Transit: Eine Stadt als Station* (Reinbek: Rowohlt, 1987)

Mendelsohn, Erich, *Amerika: Bilderbuch eines Architekten* (Berlin: Mosse, 1926)

Meyer, Jochen (ed.), *Alfred Döblin 1878·1978: Eine Austellung des Deutschen Literaturarchivs im Schiller-Nationalmuseum Marbach am Neckar* (Marbach: Deutsche Schillergesellschaft, 1978)

Miller, J. Hillis, *Topographies* (Stanford: Stanford University Press, 1995)

Mitchell, William J., *City of Bits: Space, Place, and the Infobahn* (Cambridge, Mass.: MIT Press, 1995)

Mitscherlich, Alexander, and Margarete Mitscherlich, *Die Unfähigkeit zu trauern: Grundlagen kollektiven Verhaltens*, 2nd edn (Munich: Piper, 1977)

Moholy-Nagy, László, *Malerei, Fotografie, Film* (Mainz/Berlin: Florian Kupferberg, 1967)

Moholy-Nagy, Sibyl, *László Moholy-Nagy, ein Totalexperiment* (Berlin: Mann, 1973)

Molderings, Herbert, *Umbo: Otto Umbehr 1902–1980* (Düsseldorf: Richter Verlag, 1995)

Morris, Pam (ed.), *The Bakhtin Reader: Selected Writings of Bakhtin, Medvedev and Voloshinov* (London: Edward Arnold, 1994)

Morshäuser, Bodo, *Liebeserklärung an eine häßliche Stadt: Berliner Gefühle* (Frankfurt am Main: Suhrkamp, 1998)

Müller, Heiner, *Werke*, ed. Frank Hörnigk, 9 vols. (Frankfurt am Main: Suhrkamp, 1998–2005)

Mulvey, Laura, 'Visual Pleasure and Narrative Cinema', *Visual and Other Pleasures* (Basingstoke: Macmillan, 1989), pp. 14–28

Münz-Koenen, Inge, 'Großstadtbilder im filmischen Gedächtnis: Vom *Rausch der Bewegung* (1927) zum *Gefühl des Augenblicks* (2002)', *Der Bilderatlas im Wechsel der Künste und Medien*, ed. Sabine Flach *et al.* (Munich: Fink, 2005), pp. 271–92

Neumüllers, Marie, 'Mahagonny, das ist kein Ort', *mahagonny.com: the brechtyearbook* 29 (2004), ed. Marc Silberman and Florian Vassen, 43–53

Nicodemus, Katja, 'Unsere kleine Traumfabrik', *Die Zeit*, 28 August 2003

Nooteboom, Cees, *Allerseelen* (Frankfurt am Main: Suhrkamp, 2000)

Nora, Pierre, 'Between Memory and History: Les Lieux de Mémoire', *Representations* 26 (1989), 7–25

Ören, Aras, 'Berlin'den Berlin'e Yolculuklar', *Forum* 1 (1985), 130–1

Pinthus, Kurt, '*Berlin Alexanderplatz*', *8 Uhr-Abendblatt*, 9 October 1931

Radisch, Iris, 'Die Schneekönigin', *Die Zeit* literatur, October 2004

Rathenau, Walther, *Die schönste Stadt der Welt* (Berlin/Vienna: Philo, 2002)

Reinig, Christa, 'Berlin', *Berlin am Meer: Eine Stadt in ihrem Element*, ed. Ulli Zelle (Berlin: Bostelmann & Siebenhaar, 2000), pp. 19–20

Richie, Alexandra, *Faust's Metropolis: A History of Berlin* (New York: Carroll and Graf, 1998)

Richter, Gerhard, 'Acts of Self-Portraiture: Benjamin's Confessional and Literary Writings', *The Cambridge Companion to Walter Benjamin*, ed. David S. Ferris (Cambridge: Cambridge University Press, 2004), pp. 221–37

Roehler, Oskar, *Die Unberührbare: Das Original-Drehbuch* (Cologne: Kiepenheuer & Witsch, 2002)

Rose, Gillian, *Mourning Becomes the Law: Philosophy and Representation* (Cambridge: Cambridge University Press, 1996)

Rühle, Alex, 'Hildegard Knef: Eine Frau wie Berlin', www.sueddeutsche.de/kultur/artikel/83/67016/

Rühle, Günther (ed.), *Materialien zum Leben und Schreiben der Marieluise Fleißer* (Frankfurt am Main: Suhrkamp, 1973)

Rutschky, Michael, and Juergen Teller, *Der verborgene Brecht: Ein Berliner Stadtrundgang*, ed. Inge Gellert and Klara Wallner (Zurich/Berlin/New York: Scalo, 1997)

Ruttmann, Walter, 'Der neue Film', *Illustrierter Film-Kurier*, 658 (1927)

interview, *Berliner Zeitung*, 20 September 1927

Sander, August, *Menschen des 20. Jahrhunderts: Portraitphotographien von 1892–1952*, ed. Gunther Sander (Munich: Schirmer/Mosel, 1980)

Santner, Eric, *On Creaturely Life: Rilke, Benjamin, Sebald* (Chicago: University of Chicago Press, 2006)

Schadt, Thomas, 'Das lädierte Gesicht von Berlin', interview with Ole Lasse Hempel, *Berliner Zeitung*, 31 May 2001

Berlin: Sinfonie einer Großstadt (Berlin: Nicolai, 2002)

Schadt, Thomas, *et al.*, *Berlin: Sinfonie einer Großstadt*, SWR brochure (2001)

Berlin: Sinfonie einer Großstadt, SWR *Programm* (2001)

Schärf, Christian, *Alfred Döblins 'Berlin Alexanderplatz': Roman und Film: Zu einer intermedialen Poetik der modernen Literatur* (Stuttgart: Steiner, 2001)

Scheffler, Karl, *Berlin – Ein Stadtschicksal* (Berlin: Fannei & Walz, 1989)

Scheunemann, Dietrich, *Romankrise: Die Entstehung der modernen Romanpoetik in Deutschland* (Heidelberg: Quelle & Meyer, 1978)

Schneider, Peter, *Der Mauerspringer* (Hamburg: Luchterhand, 1984)

Paarungen (Reinbek: Rowohlt, 1992)

Schobert, Walter, *The German Avant-Garde Film of the 1920s* (Munich: Goethe-Institut, 1989)

Schoeller, Wilfried F., *Nach Berlin!* (Frankfurt am Main: Schöffling & Co., 1999)

Schultze-Pfaelzer, Gerhard, 'Döblin sieht Gespenster', *Berlin am Mittag*, 22 November 1947

Scribner, Charity, *Requiem for Communism* (Cambridge, Mass.: MIT Press, 2003)

Sebald, Winfried Georg, *Der Mythus der Zerstörung im Werk Döblins* (Stuttgart: Klett, 1980)

Sieg, Katrin, 'Ethnic Drag and National Identity: Multicultural Crises, Crossings, and Interventions', *The Imperialist Imagination: German Colonialism and its*

Legacy, ed. Sara Friedrichsmeyer *et al.* (Ann Arbor: University of Michigan Press, 1998), pp. 259–319

Silberman, Marc, *German Cinema: Texts in Context* (Detroit: Wayne State University Press, 1995)

Silverman, Kaja, *Male Subjectivity at the Margins* (London/New York: Routledge, 1992)

Simmel, Georg, 'Berliner Gewerbe-Ausstellung', *Soziologische Ästhetik*, ed. Klaus Lichtblau (Bodenheim: Philo, 1998), pp. 71–5

Sontag, Susan, 'Fascinating Fascism', *Under the Sign of Saturn* (New York: Farrar, Straus and Giroux, 1980)

Sparschuh, Jens, 'Transitraum Berliner Zimmer', *Ich dachte, sie finden uns nicht: Zerstreute Prosa* (Cologne: Kiepenheuer & Witsch, 1997), pp. 11–19

Speirs, Ronald, 'Vom armen B. B.', *Brecht Handbuch*, ed. Jan Knopf, 5 vols. (Stuttgart: Metzler, 2001–3), vol. II, pp. 104–9

Stone, Sasha, *Berlin in Bildern* (Vienna/Leipzig: Epstein, 1929)

Taylor, Ronald, *Berlin and its Culture: A Historical Portrait* (New Haven/London: Yale University Press, 1997)

Tergit, Gabriele, *Käsebier erobert den Kurfürstendamm* (Frankfurt am Main: Fischer, 1978)

Theweleit, Klaus, *Männerphantasien*, 2 vols. (Reinbek: Rowohlt, 1980)

Till, Karen E., *The New Berlin: Memory, Politics, Place* (Minneapolis: University of Minnesota Press, 2005)

Töteberg, Michael (ed.), *Tom Tykwer: Lola rennt* (Reinbek: Rowohlt, 1998)

Tucholsky, Kurt (Ignaz Wrobel), 'Stahlhelm oder Filzhut?', *Die Weltbühne*, 17 May 1927

Tykwer, Tom, 'Werkstattgespräch' with Peter Kremski and Reinhard Wulf, *Filmbulletin* 229 (December, 2000), 33–40

'Wer in einer Menschenhaut wohnt', *Frankfurter Allgemeine Zeitung*, 8 February 2007

Tykwer, Tom, *et al.*, publicity brochure for *Lola rennt* (1998)

Vidler, Anthony, *The Architectural Uncanny: Essays in the Modern Uncanny* (Cambridge Mass.: MIT Press, 1992)

Warped Space: Art, Achitecture, and Anxiety in Modern Culture (Cambridge Mass.: MIT Press, 2000)

Virilio, Paul, *The Vision Machine*, trans. Julie Rose (Bloomington: Indiana University Press, 1994)

'Walter Ruttmanns Fahrkolonne', *Film-Kurier* 194 (20 August 1926)

Ward, Janet, *Weimar Surfaces: Urban Visual Culture in 1920s Germany* (Berkeley: University of California Press, 2001)

Webber, Andrew J., *The Doppelgänger: Double Visions in German Literature* (Oxford: Clarendon, 1996)

'The Manipulation of Fantasy and Trauma in *Orlacs Hände*', *Words, Texts, Images*, ed. K. Kohl and R. Robertson (Oxford: Lang, 2002), pp. 153–74

'Kafka, *Die Verwandlung*', *Landmarks in German Short Prose*, ed. Peter Hutchinson (Oxford: Lang, 2003), pp. 175–90

'Gender and the City: *Lola rennt*', *German as a Foreign Language* 1 (2003), 1–16 (www.gfl.journal.de/1-2003/webber.html)

'Unnatural Acts: Sexuality, Film, and the Law', *Sexuality Repositioned: Diversity and the Law*, ed. Belinda Brooks-Gordon *et al.* (Oxford: Hart, 2004), pp. 297–315

The European Avant-Garde, 1900–1940 (Cambridge: Polity, 2004)

'Büchner, *Leonce und Lena*', *Landmarks in German Comedy*, ed. Peter Hutchinson (Oxford: Lang, 2006), pp. 87–102

'Inside Out: Acts of Displacement in Else Lasker-Schüler', *The Germanic Review*, 81.2 (Spring 2006), 143–62

Weber, Samuel, 'Genealogy of Modernity: History, Myth and Allegory in Benjamin's *Origin of the German Mourning Play*', *Modern Language Notes* 106.3 (April 1991), 465–500

Mass Mediauras: Form, Technics, Media (Stanford: Stanford University Press, 1996)

Weigel, Sigrid, '"Die Städte sind weiblich und nur dem Sieger hold": Zur Funktion des Weiblichen in Gründungsmythen und Städtedarstellungen', *Triumph und Scheitern in der Metropole: Zur Rolle der Weiblichkeit in der Geschichte Berlins*, ed. Sigrun Anselm and Barbara Beck (Berlin: Dietrich Reimer, 1987), pp. 207–27

Body- and Image-Space: Re-reading Walter Benjamin, trans. Georgina Paul *et al.* (London/New York: Routledge, 1996)

Ingeborg Bachmann: Hinterlassenschaften unter Wahrung des Briefgeheimnisses (Vienna: Paul Zsolnay, 1999)

'Zum "topographical turn": Kartographie, Topographie und Raumkonzepte in den Kulturwissenschaften', *Kulturpoetik* 2.2 (2002), 151–65

Weill, Kurt, 'Marterl', *Song-Album* (Vienna and Leipzig: Universal-Edition, 1929), pp. 8–10

Weisenborn, Günther, 'Mit Brecht im Gestapo-Keller', *Sonntag*, 10 January 1965

Weiss, Peter, *Die Ästhetik des Widerstands*, 3 vols. (Frankfurt am Main: Suhrkamp), 1988

Wenders, Wim, *Die Logik der Bilder: Essays und Gespräche*, ed. Michael Töteberg (Frankfurt am Main: Verlag der Autoren, 1988)

The Act of Seeing: Texte und Gespräche (Frankfurt am Main: Verlag der Autoren, 1992)

Wenders, Wim, and Peter Handke, *Der Himmel über Berlin: Ein Filmbuch* (Frankfurt am Main: Suhrkamp, 1990)

Wilson, Emma, *Cinema's Missing Children* (London: Wallflower, 2002)

Witte, Bernd, *Walter Benjamin: An Intellectual Biography*, trans. James Rolleston (Detroit: Wayne State University Press, 1991)

Witte, Karsten, 'Fassbinders Serie "Berlin Alexanderplatz" an einem Stück: Die Gewalt des Ganzen', *Frankfurter Rundschau*, 18 October 1983

Wizisla, Erdmut, *22 Versuche, eine Arbeit zu beschreiben* (Berlin: Akademie der Künste, 1998)

Wolf, Christa, *Der geteilte Himmel* (Munich: dtv, 1973)

Unter den Linden: Drei unwahrscheinliche Geschichten (Berlin/Weimar: Aufbau, 1974)

Kindheitsmuster (Darmstadt: Luchterhand, 1979)

'Unter den Linden', *Gesammelte Erzählungen* (Frankfurt am Main: Luchterhand, 1988), pp. 54–96

Was bleibt (Hamburg: Luchterhand, 1993)

'Die zumutbare Wahrheit: Prosa der Ingeborg Bachmann', *Werke*, ed. Sonja Hilzinger, 12 vols. (Munich: Luchterhand, 1999), vol. IV, pp. 145–61

Leibhaftig (Munich: Luchterhand, 2002)

Wörner, Martin, *et al.* (eds.), *Architekturführer Berlin* (Berlin: Dietrich Reimer, 2001)

Young, James, 'The Counter-Monument: Memory against itself in Germany Today', *Art and the Public Sphere*, ed. W. J. T. Mitchell (Chicago/London: Chicago University Press, 1992), pp. 49–78

Zischler, Hanns, 'Brandmauern: Kleiner Nachruf auf eine grosse Sache', *Berlin: Metropole, Kursbuch* 137 (September 1999), 99–102

Index

Printed in Great Britain
by Amazon

46158660R00199